MONTH-BY-MONTH
GARDENING
in the
CAROLINAS

MONTH-BY-MONTH
GARDENING
in the
CAROLINAS

Bob Polomski

Dedication

To my mother and father who ignited my passion for reading, writing, and gardening.

Acknowledgements

I am grateful to Cool Springs Press for the opportunity to write this book and for
their support during the entire process.

Thanks to Ted Whitwell, Ph.D., Chair of the Department of Horticulture at
Clemson University, for endorsing this project.

Many thanks to the following gardeners and organizations who shared their time and expertise with
me—reviewing portions of the manuscript and offering helpful suggestions and advice:

Alison Arnold • American Rose Society • Bonnie Lee Appleton, Ph.D. • Robert G. Bellinger, Ph.D.
Richard E. Bir • Linda G. Blue •David W. Bradshaw, Ph.D. • Laura and Peter Brechbiel • Jeanne Briggs
Milt Brown • Linda Cobb • Beverly Colman • Tom Creagan • Erv Evans • Jenks Farmer • Bill Head
Robert M. Lippert, Ph.D. • Joe Maple • Linda T. McHam • Don and Cherrie McKinney • L. B. McCarty, Ph.D.
Bob Head • L. A. Jackson • The Netherlands Flower Bulb Information Center • Rekha Morris, Ph.D.
Albert J. Pertuit, Ph.D. • David M. Price • Peter J. Reynolds • Barbara Smith • Bill R. Smith, Ph.D.
W. Bryan Smith • Howard "The Rambling Rosarian" Walters • Sheree "The Rose" Wright • William B. Miller, Ph.D.
P. Diane Relf, Ph.D. • Roger B. Swain, Ph.D. • F. Clint Waltz • C. Bruce Williams • Jim Wilson

I am indebted to my horticultural editors Rekha Morris and Peter J. Reynolds (my father-in-law) for
skillfully pruning out wayward portions of the manuscript.

Finally, this book would never have been written without the love and unflagging support of
my spouse and soulmate Susan. Thank you for making me complete.

Polomski, Robert, 1960-
   Month-by-month gardening in the Carolinas / Robert Polomski
   p. cm.
   Includes bibliographical references (p.).
   ISBN 1-888608-23-4 (pbk.)
   1. Gardening -- NorthCarolina 2. Gardening South Carolina I. Title

SB453.2.N8 P65 2000
635'.09756--dc21   00-022577

Published by Cool Springs Press, a Division of Thomas Nelson, Inc.,
P.O. Box 141000, Nashville, Tennessee 37214.

First printing 2000

Printed in the United States of America
10 9 8 7 6

Visit the Thomas Nelson website at: www.ThomasNelson.com

Contents

Contents (CONTINUED)

The Benefits of a Gardening Plan

If you are new to gardening or new to gardening in the Carolinas, you will quickly discover that success depends on knowing how to do certain tasks and when to do them. Creating a flower bed that draws admiring looks from passersby; complementing the look and style of your home with well-placed trees, shrubs, and ground covers; and brightening your indoor living area with the colorful blooms and enchanting fragrances of indoor plants do not happen by chance. You can be assured that all of these are achieved with careful planning, know-how, and proper care.

Month-by-Month Gardening in the Carolinas helps you achieve such goals, guiding you throughout the year. Follow the calendar format throughout the year so you will be reminded when it's time for certain garden and landscape tasks.

Every season in the Carolinas presents a gardening opportunity. Start vegetables in the summer for a fall garden. Divide and replant fall-flowering perennials in the spring when their new growth emerges. Start or renovate a warm-season lawn in late spring and early summer. Just knowing how and when to catch the right month makes gardening easier and more fun, and greatly improves your chances of success.

Twelve categories of plants are described in this book. Each chapter takes you month-by-month through the year with reminders, "how to" items, and "helpful hints" that sharpen your gardening skills.

Folks smitten by the beauty and excitement of gardening in the Carolinas quickly discover that they need two additional gardening tools: pen and paper. Although you can write in the margins of this book, I strongly encourage you to start a gardening diary in a separate notebook. I use 100-page wide-ruled composition notebooks. I record observations on weather, especially first and last freezes; the names of vegetables, flowers, and shrubs that I've grown; and the bloom dates of choice flowering plants. I also make notes about fertilizer applications and pest problems. When I talk with and learn from other gardeners, I jot down interesting techniques or plants that I need to grow. All these handwritten comments have become my "gardening memory." My journal is a tool, just like my shovel and hoe.

Besides, a notebook also gives me the freedom to stuff old seed packets between the pages.

With the help of a number of seasoned gardeners from both North Carolina and South Carolina, I have attempted to place each activity into the appropriate month for both states. However, some fine-tuning will be necessary in your own garden and landscape. The seasons do not always arrive when they are expected, and most landscapes have microclimates within them—nooks and pockets in the landscape that have environmental conditions that are different from the other areas.

Gardening in the Carolinas

North and South Carolina share a 400-mile stretch of coastline. A band of sand, the Carolina Sandhills, runs through the midsection of both states, and in the west rise two mountain ranges—the Blue Ridge and the Great Smokies. These divide the Carolinas into three gardening areas with distinct prevailing climates and soil types: Coastal Plain, Piedmont, and Mountains. Use the map on p. 9 to locate your area. In this book I use these terms when special advice applies to them.

The Coastal Plain extends westward from the coast, gradually rising to the Piedmont. The soils of the Coastal Plain range from well-drained loamy sands near the coast to the coarse-textured sands of the Carolina Sandhills. They were once sand dunes comprising what was a prehistoric shoreline during the Ice Age, varying in width from five to thirty miles and extending from Rockingham and Pinehurst in North Carolina southward through Aiken and into Georgia. The mild winters across the Coastal Plain are offset by the suffocating heat and humidity of its long summers. However, summer's wrath is tempered along the coastal areas, which enjoy lower temperatures than inland areas due to welcome sea breezes. The climate along the coast north of Cape Hatteras is suitable for growing plants adapted to cool northern areas. By contrast, the coastal climate is subtropical from Bald Head Island, North Carolina, through South Carolina.

The Piedmont lies between the Coastal Plain and the Mountains. This plateau of rolling hills is comprised largely of heavy red clay soils that color a gardener's tools, clothing, and carpeting. These slowly draining soils can dry to near concrete hardness in midsummer and become wet and sloppy hog wallows in late winter. Fortunately, organic matter incorporated into these clay soils can convert them into a respectable growing medium. Summers in the Piedmont are also hot and humid, with correspondingly high nighttime temperatures. Winter is shorter than in the Mountains and seldom colder than 10 degrees Fahrenheit. Snowfall averages less than a foot a year across the Piedmont, often covering the ground for a short period of time before melting.

The Mountains are the coolest region of the Carolinas throughout the year. Winters are colder, but often interrupted by warm days, especially in the lower valleys. In the higher valleys of the North Carolina mountains and at elevations above 3,500 feet temperatures may drop, albeit infrequently, to 0 degrees F. In summer, hot, humid days give way to cool night temperatures that offer respite to plants and gardeners alike.

In the Mountains, the highest peaks, over 6,000 feet, are in North Carolina. Soils range from excellent loams in bottomland and coves to shallow rocky soil over bedrock at the higher elevations. Although the large differences in elevation here result in large variations in climate (meteorologists claim that North Carolina has the greatest variety of climate of any state east of the Rocky Mountains), cold-tolerant plants can be established here more successfully than elsewhere in the Carolinas.

Autumn is the driest season in the Carolinas, October and November the driest months. July and August are the wettest months. Almost every summer in the Carolinas, however, a certain amount of drought occurs, sometimes quite severe. Tropical storms and hurricanes pose a threat to the Carolinas, usually between August and

Carolina Regional Map

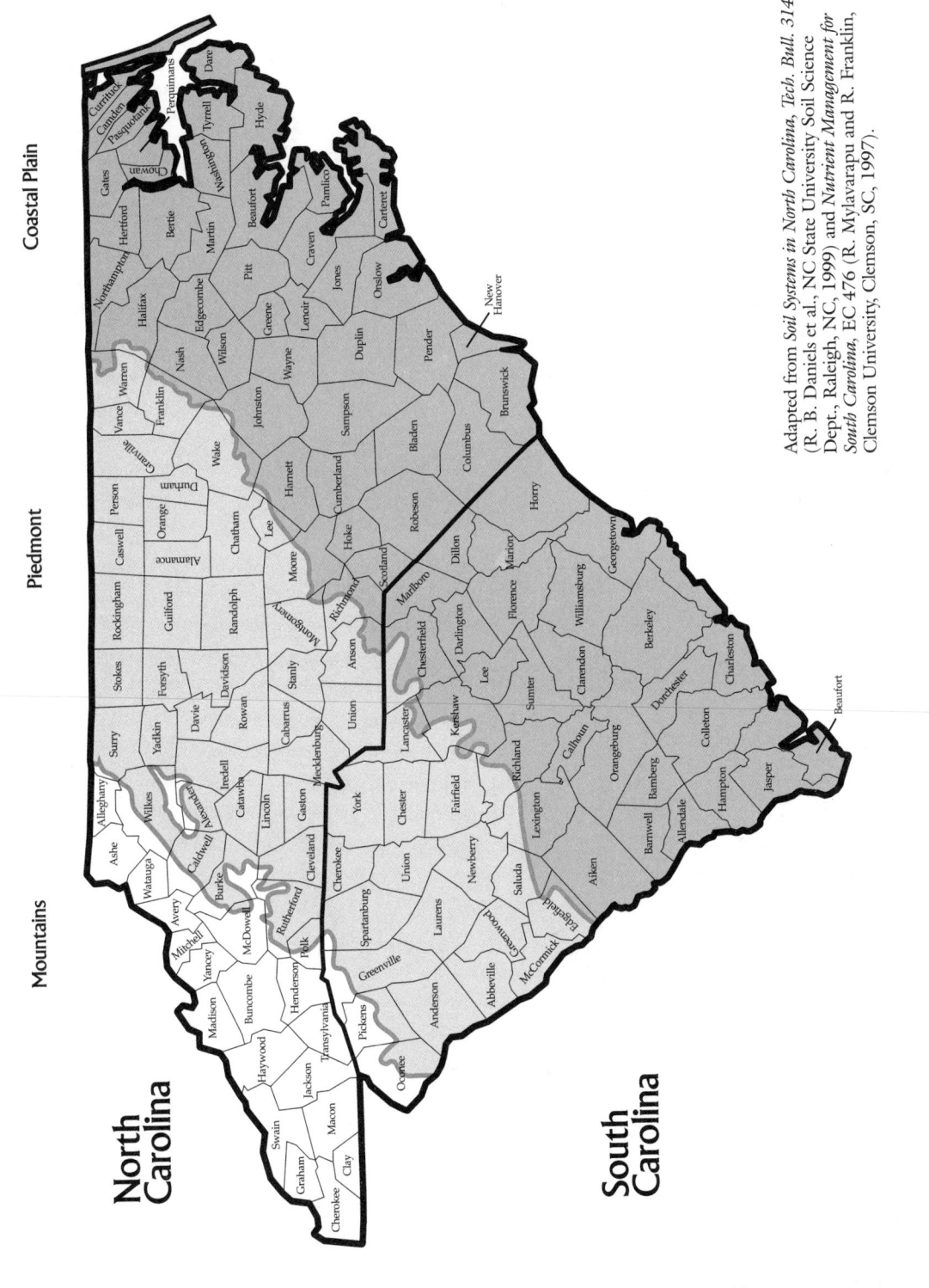

Adapted from *Soil Systems in North Carolina, Tech. Bull. 314* (R. B. Daniels et al., NC State University Soil Science Dept., Raleigh, NC, 1999) and *Nutrient Management for South Carolina,* EC 476 (R. Mylavarapu and R. Franklin, Clemson University, Clemson, SC, 1997).

October. For climate and weather information specific to your locality, contact your County Cooperative Extension Service office.

Planning the Garden

Whether you're creating a new landscape or renovating an existing one, plan the landscape on paper first. You will need a pencil, ruler, graph paper, and tracing paper. If you have house plans or a plat map on file, get them out.

1 *Create a base map.* This is simply a plan of your property drawn to scale on graph paper.

It shows the placement of your house on the property, its orientation to the sun, other structures on the site, and existing plants. A base map helps you to visualize your ideas and to plan for the kinds of plants and construction materials you need.

Using the graph paper, trace the outline of your house. Use the plat map, or simply measure the house and grounds. Measure at right angles from a house corner to the property lines, and from the corner to the road to establish where your house sits within your property. Measure from fixed points of the house to the driveway, deck, patio, and any walkways as well. Draw in any existing trees, shrubs, and flower beds.

Identify North on the plan. Plot all these measurements to scale on a large sheet of graph paper ($1/4$-inch grid allows for a scale of 1 in.=4 ft.)

2 *Analyze the land to familiarize yourself with the growing conditions of the property.* Lay a sheet of tracing paper over the base map and title it "Site Analysis." Make notes about sun and shade patterns (morning sun, afternoon sun, full sun), wind exposure, topography, and drainage. Coastal gardeners need to mark areas where salt spray can be a problem.

- Look for *microclimates*—areas with environmental conditions that differ from nearby areas. For example, you might have a south-facing spot between two large rocks which is warmer in winter than an open area facing the same direction. It will also be the hottest area in the summertime. A microclimate might also be an area that receives more water because there is drainage from the roof or there is a low spot where water collects.

- Examine drainage patterns and structural limitations like power lines and underground utilities.

Create a base map.

Gardening in the Carolinas

- Consider which plants you want to keep, and list factors that will affect the selection of new plants. Does your site require plants that tolerate cold, full sun, shade, drought, occasional flooding, or salt spray?

3 *Use another sheet of tracing paper over the base plan and site analysis to sketch out a landscape plan.* Draw in trees where you want them; add shrubs, ground covers, or flowering plants. Remember to keep plants about 4 feet from the foundation to allow for growth and to make house maintenance easier. Be aware of the ultimate height and spread of the plants in various areas. Note whether you want the plants that attract wildlife, birds, and butterflies. Group the plants based on their watering needs so you can water more efficiently.

Make some room in your landscape for a nursery if you can. Such a "halfway house," for rooted cuttings to grow up, is very handy. It also would be useful as a trial garden to evaluate plants before setting them into permanent locations in the garden. Use tracing paper overlays so you can arrange and rearrange the plants.

4 *If you're planning to irrigate, add the irrigation plan to your landscape design plan.* In-ground watering systems are not needed in every landscape, particularly if you choose drought-resistant plants. While plants are becoming established, however, it's very nice to have one. Do some research at this point on your probable watering needs, and you will be able to decide whether you need one, and which type.

5 *Now you're ready to select plants.* Be mindful of their maintenance requirements under the conditions at your site. Write the common name and scientific name (genus and species) on your plan. Common names are less specific than the scientific name and can be confusing when you're shopping for plants. For this step you should also consider other landscape materials that will be used for walkways, mulch, and borders.

6 *Do it.* Purchase high-quality plants and follow proper planting techniques to ensure their rapid establishment and long-term survival. If you were overly ambitious and planned for an incredible design, remember that you don't have to build it all in one weekend. Break the project into phases as your time and budget allow.

7 *Care for your plantings with proper watering, fertilizing, pruning, and mulching as described in chapters in this book.* By following the first six steps, you will avoid most later maintenance headaches and surprises.

8 *Enjoy.* Take photographs of your landscape to learn from your experiences and to share your knowledge with fellow gardeners.

Plants for the Carolinas

When you look at the hardiness zone ranges in the Planting Charts, keep in mind that they do not account for *microclimates*. Buildings, nearby structures, or trees that block the sun can create very cold winter conditions. Protected south-facing slopes can be warmer. Microclimates allow gardeners to overwinter plants listed as zone 8 in their zone 7 gardens. Respecting microclimates and heeding the hardiness information in selecting plants will keep you safe for an "average" winter, if there is such a thing in the Carolinas.

Gardening in the Carolinas

The climate of the Carolinas allows us to grow a wide variety of plants from the Coast to the Mountains. The limits of this book prevent me from including them all. Those included in the Planting Charts are available at local nurseries and garden centers as well as through mail-order catalogs.

Hardiness zones are listed in the Planting Charts. They are based on the U. S. Department of Agriculture Hardiness Zone Map. This map is often referred to in gardening magazines, books, and mail-order catalogs in describing plants. It divides North America into twenty zones based on average minimum winter temperatures. The Carolinas range from zone 6b in the North Carolina mountains to zone 8b along the South Carolina coast (see the map on p. 13). Plants labeled with a hardiness zone warmer than your zone must be protected to survive the winter in your area.

Those who garden with vegetables and annuals have no need for these hardiness zone maps. It's more important to know the dates of the first and last expected freezes. Refer to the maps on p. 14–15 that show the average dates of the first and last freezes.

Cold is not the only factor that limits the growth of plants. For perennials, shrubs, or trees to survive and grow year after the year, the plants must also be able to tolerate high summer temperatures. For this reason the American Horticultural Society published a Plant Heat-Zone Map in 1997. This map is used to characterize a plant's ability to tolerate high temperatures. I chose to use the USDA Cold Hardiness Zone map because many plants have already been categorized to its zones, and took into account the extreme heat tolerance range of the plants.

Look at the hardiness zones as guidelines and not guarantees of a plant's ability to survive in your landscape. In addition to heat and cold, a plant's destiny can be affected by elevation, soil pH, sun and wind exposure, and proximity to water. These elements create a variety of microclimates resulting in quite different growing conditions even within a small area.

Use the Planting Charts as a starting point. As you visit friends' gardens, botanical gardens, arboreta, and nurseries and garden centers throughout the Carolinas (refer to p. 368–69, for a list of Carolina botanical gardens and arboreta), jot them down in your gardening journal and start expanding your own Planting Chart.

Plant Names

The plants are identified by a common name and, in parentheses, a botanical name, which will help you purchase the correct plant. Every plant has a botanical name— a first and last name, if you will. The first name is the *genus* (always capitalized), and its second name is the *species,* in lower case (abbreviated as sp. or spp.). A plant may have a third name, its cultivar or variety. This is always capitalized and shown in single quotation marks.

A plant can have a number of common names, but it has only one scientific name. **Black mustard (*Brassica nigra*),** for example, has over forty common names worldwide. Common names differ even in the same state. For example, the common name **mockorange** is correctly applied to *Philadelphus* in the Piedmont of South Carolina, but in the Lowcountry it's applied to **cherrylaurel (*Prunus caroliniana*).**

USDA Cold Hardiness Zone Map

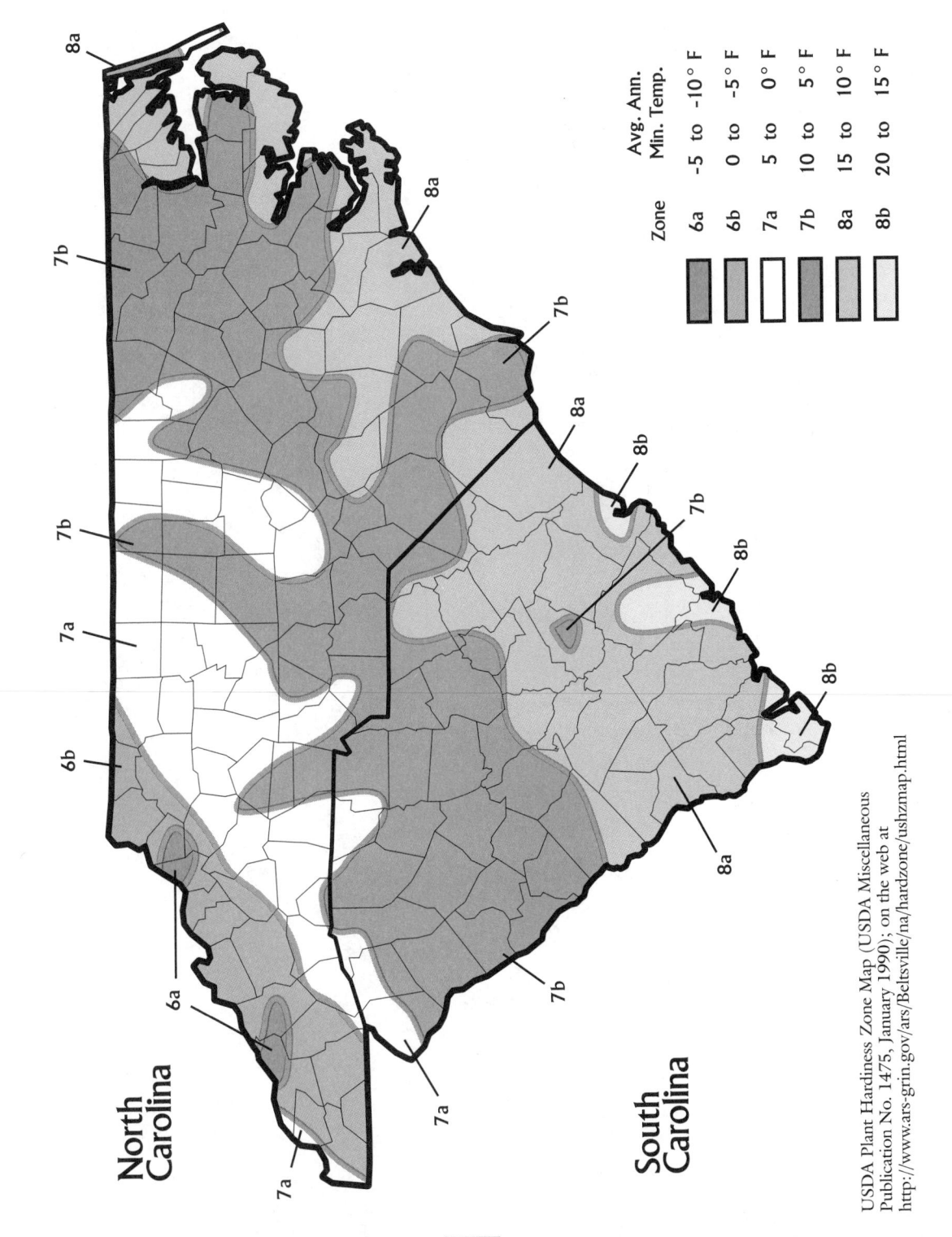

Zone	Avg. Ann. Min. Temp.
6a	-5 to -10° F
6b	0 to -5° F
7a	5 to 0° F
7b	10 to 5° F
8a	15 to 10° F
8b	20 to 15° F

North Carolina

South Carolina

USDA Plant Hardiness Zone Map (USDA Miscellaneous
Publication No. 1475, January 1990); on the web at
http://www.ars-grin.gov/ars/Beltsville/na/hardzone/ushzmap.html

Average Date of First Fall Freeze

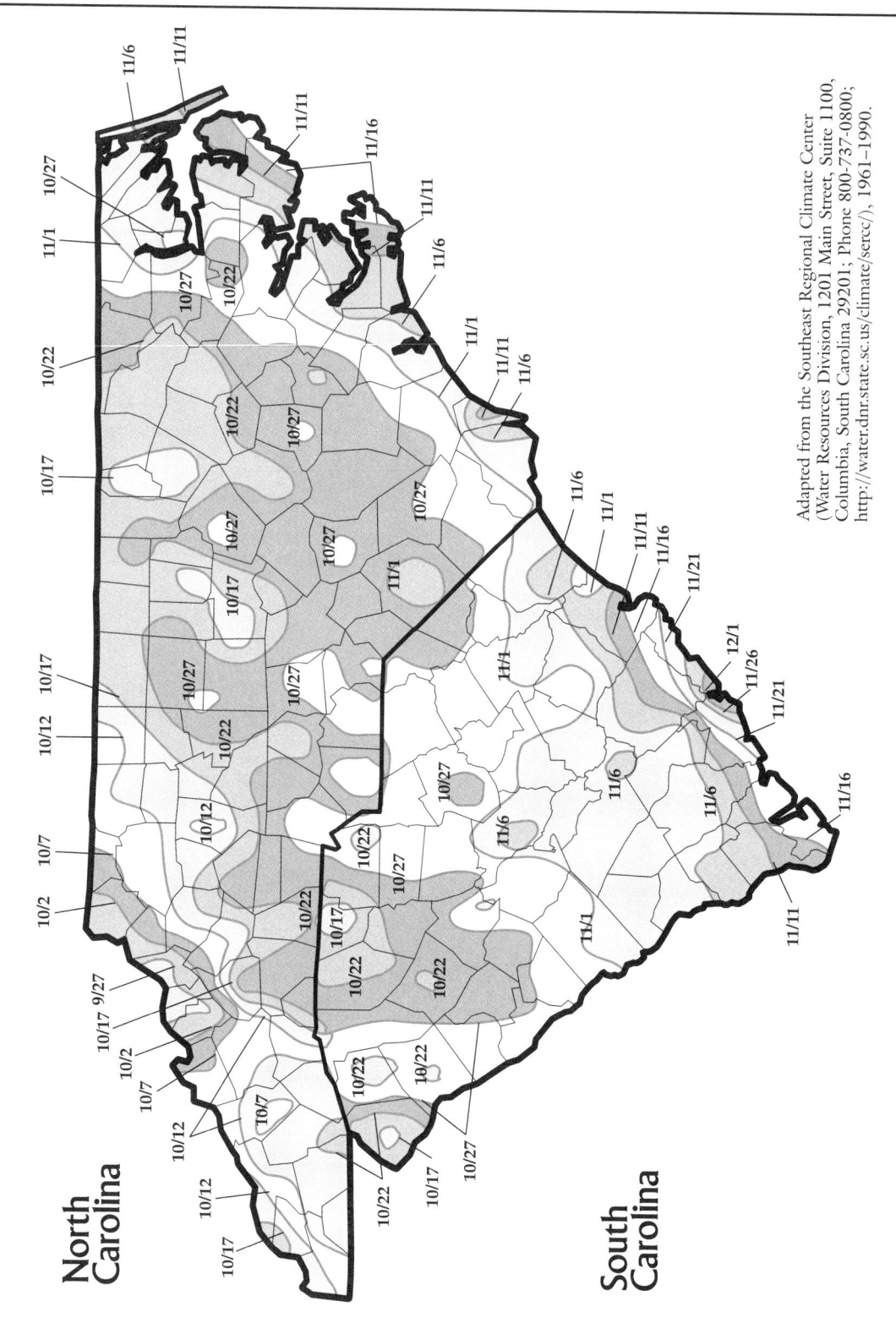

Adapted from the Southeast Regional Climate Center (Water Resources Division, 1201 Main Street, Suite 1100, Columbia, South Carolina 29201; Phone 800-737-0800; http://water.dnr.state.sc.us/climate/sercc/), 1961–1990.

North Carolina

South Carolina

Average Date of Last Spring Freeze

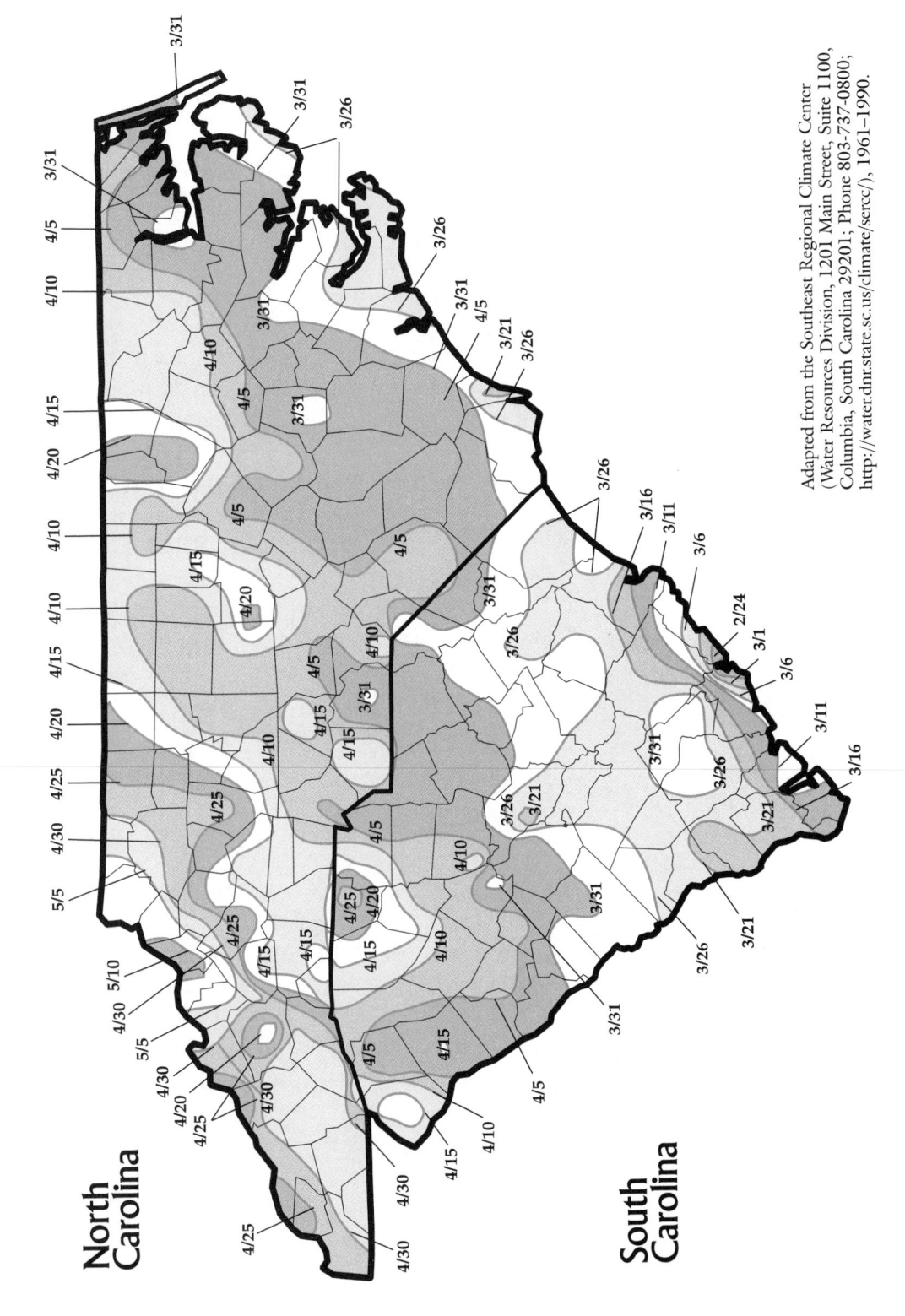

Adapted from the Southeast Regional Climate Center (Water Resources Division, 1201 Main Street, Suite 1100, Columbia, South Carolina 29201; Phone 803-737-0800; http://water.dnr.state.sc.us/climate/sercc/), 1961–1990.

North Carolina

South Carolina

General Gardening Practices

Building Healthy Soil

Gardeners often get caught up in the beauty of their plants without remembering that the foundation for any healthy garden, landscape, or lawn is the soil. A good soil allows air, water, and nutrients to be absorbed by plant roots and lets those roots roam freely.

How do you build healthy soil? Begin with a soil test through your local cooperative extension service center. The test will tell you the pH level of the soil and the level of nutrients available for plant growth. Stated in numbers, pH is a measurement of the acidity or alkalinity of the soil. On a scale of 0 to 14, a pH of 7 is neutral. Numbers below 7 indicate acid conditions and readings above 7 are basic or alkaline. Soil pH affects not only plant health, but also the availability of nutrients. If the soil is too acidic or too alkaline, minerals such as nitrogen, phosphorus, potassium, calcium, and magnesium can be "tied-up" and unavailable to your plants. Adding more fertilizer will not help. The soil pH will have to be corrected by mixing in the recommended amount of limestone to raise the pH or "sweeten" the soil.

Add sulfur if you need to lower the soil pH.

Maintaining the right soil pH is very important. It affects the uptake of nutrients by plants and creates an environment that supports helpful soil-dwelling organisms, including earthworms.

The results of your soil test will indicate the amount of limestone or sulfur required to bring the soil pH into an ideal range, between 5.8 and 6.5 for most vegetable and flower gardens, shrubs, trees, and lawns. Mix pulverized or pelletized limestone into the top 6 inches of soil to raise the pH; mix in sulfur to lower it.

The soil test also measures the levels of phosphorus, potassium, calcium, and magnesium. Since calcium and phosphorous move slowly in the soil, these minerals should be incorporated into the top 6 inches of soil.

Knowing which nutrients are already present will save you money. If your test shows your soil already has high levels of phosphorus and potassium, there's no need to add a fertilizer containing these two nutrients.

Good gardeners also add organic matter. It improves soil *tilth*—its physical condition or structure. When added to clay soil, organic matter holds the clay particles apart, improving air and water movement in the soil. This translates to deeper and more extensive root development from our plants.

The kind of organic matter you mix into your soil is your choice. My grandfather liked to use rabbit and chicken manure for his vegetable and flower beds. My mother liked using fish in her rose garden. As a child I buried fish heads, tails, and other inedible parts around her roses. If you are squeamish about using these organic materials, then add compost or shredded leaves. Cover crops or "green manure" such as crimson clover or annual rye are relatively inexpensive sources of organic matter. Sow these crops in the fall and then turn them under in the spring to enrich the soil.

Organic fertilizers derived from naturally occurring sources are a good alternative to synthetic plant foods. They include composted animal manure, cottonseed meal, and bloodmeal, among many others. Although they contain relatively low concentrations of actual

General Gardening Practices

nutrients compared to synthetic fertilizers, they increase the organic matter content in the soil and improve soil structure.

To avoid damaging soil structure, never dig or cultivate when the soil is too wet or too dry. Follow this simple test: if the soil sticks to your shovel—the soil is too wet. Postpone digging until the soil dries out.

Coarse-textured sandy soils have excellent drainage but hold little water. Add organic matter to them to increase fertility and water retention.

Sand has often been touted as the perfect fix for improving drainage in clay soils. Unless you add it at the rate of at least 6 inches of sand per 8 inches of soil, your soil will be better suited for making bricks than growing plants.

Planting

Plant properly. The health and long-term survival of plants that you set into their new home-indoors or out—is affected by how they're planted. Follow the step-by-step planting instructions in the introduction to each chapter to learn about proper planting. Your plant's survival depends on it.

Watering

Anyone can water; however, watering efficiently to meet the demands of the plant while conserving water requires some attention to detail. The chapters provide information on when and how often to water. The aim is to avoid the common mistakes of overwatering or underwatering—two practices that can injure or kill plants.

Water needs depend on the plant and the situation. Moisture-loving plants require more-frequent watering than plants adapted to dry conditions. Newly-set-out plants need to be watered after planting and during their establishment period. Once they become established, however, they may not require supplemental watering even during the hot, dry summer months. Some shrubs and trees are quite drought-tolerant and can withstand long periods without rain or irrigation.

Soil also affects watering. Plants growing in clay soils need to be watered less often than plants growing in sandy soils because sandy soils drain so rapidly.

Whether you water with a garden hose or an automatic below-ground irrigation system, water wisely. Refer to the Watering sections in the chapters for information on watering efficiently.

Fertilizing

Fertilizing could be the gardening practice most filled with confusion. Besides knowing when, how often, and how much to fertilize, the choices seem endless. Should you choose a fast- or slow-release nitrogen fertilizer? Would your plants prefer a diet of organic or inorganic nutrients? What do those numbers on the bag mean? Should you choose the 10-10-10 or the 16-4-8? Dry or liquid fertilizer? Before making an application, realize that fertilizing should be guided by soil-test results, the appearance of the plants, and the purpose of fertilizing.

Fertilizers are minerals added when the soil does not supply enough of those nutrients. The three most important—nitrogen, phosphorus, and potassium—are represented by three numbers on a fertilizer bag. For example, 16-4-8 give the percentage by weight of nitrogen (N), phosphate (P_2O_5), and potash (K_2O). In this case, nitrogen makes up 16 percent of the total weight, phosphate—which supplies phosphorus—accounts for 4 percent, and potash, a source of potassium, makes up 8 percent. The remaining weight (the total must add up to 100 percent) comprises a nutrient carrier.

General Gardening Practices

A fertilizer containing all three nutrients, such as a 16-4-8, is referred to as a "complete" fertilizer. If soil tests indicate high levels of phosphorus and potassium, then apply an "incomplete" fertilizer, one that supplies only nitrogen, such as 21-0-0.

In addition to the primary elements (N-P-K), the fertilizer may contain secondary plant nutrients including calcium, magnesium, and sulfur, or minor nutrients such as manganese, zinc, copper, iron, and molybdenum. Apply these nutrients if dictated by soil-test results.

You can choose dry or liquid fertilizers. Dry fertilizers are applied to the ground around your plants. They are available in fast- or slow-release nitrogen forms.

Fast- or quick-release nitrogen fertilizers dissolve readily in water and are almost immediately available to plants. They can also be quickly leached out of the root zone in fast-draining, sandy soils.

Liquid fertilizers can be absorbed through the leaves as well as the roots of plants. These have to be applied more frequently than granular types, usually every two to four weeks.

Slow-release fertilizers make nutrients available to the plant for an extended period up to several months. While more expensive than conventional fertilizers, they reduce the need for supplemental applications and the likelihood of fertilizer burn. Select a slow-release fertilizer that has at least one-half the total amount of nitrogen listed as "water insoluble nitrogen."

An alternative to synthetic slow-release fertilizers are organic fertilizers derived from naturally occurring sources such as composted animal manure, cottonseed meal, and bloodmeal, among many others. Although they contain relatively low concentrations of actual nutrients compared to synthetic fertilizers, they increase the organic matter content in the soil and improve soil structure.

A slow-release fertilizer is a good choice, especially for sandy soils, which tend to leach, or for heavy clay soils where runoff can be a problem. If the soil is properly prepared at the start, supplemental fertilization my not be necessary for several years after planting. When fertilizing your perennials, let their growth rate and leaf color guide you. Rely on soil-test results to help you make the right decision. If the bed is already highly fertile, the soil test will save you from the other, equally undesirable results of over-fertilizing, such as encouraging a lot of leafy growth at the expense of flowers.

Pruning

Pruning improves the health and appearance of plants. It can be as simple as nipping the dead heads of spent flowers from your zinnias (deadheading) or removing a large limb from your maple tree. In the following chapters, read the step-by-step instructions for pruning roses, shrubs, trees, and even houseplants.

You'll find that pruning will require you to have a purpose in mind. It can be to encourage more flowers on perennials, to reduce the height of plants, or to create a strong structure of trunk and limbs to support future growth in young trees.

Pest Control

You are bound to confront the three most common pests in your Carolina garden: insects, diseases, and weeds. (Deer, voles, and rabbits can also be considered pests and are addressed in the chapters.)

General Gardening Practices

Deal with them sensibly. In the Pest Control sections of this book I use the term *Integrated Pest Management* or *IPM.* IPM is a commonsense approach to managing pests that brings Mother Nature into the battle on the gardener's side. It combines smart plant selection with good planting and maintenance practices, and an understanding of pests and their habits. It starts with planning and proper planting to produce strong, healthy plants that, by themselves, can prosper with minimum help from you. As in nature, an acceptable level of pests is accommodated. Control is the goal, rather than elimination. Several techniques can be used in a home garden/landscape IPM approach.

IPM Cultural Practices

Proper soil management: Maintain the appropriate soil pH for your plants by testing your soil at least every three years. Add generous amounts of organic matter to build up soil fertility.

Plant selection: Match plants suited to the soil and climate of your area, and select species and cultivars resistant to pests. These plants are *resistant*—not immune—to damage. Expect them to exhibit less insect or disease injury than susceptible varieties growing in the same environment.

Watering: *Water late at night or early in the morning when dew has formed.* Avoid watering in early evening when leaves may remain wet for an extended period of time. This favors fungal infections.

Mulching: Apply a shallow layer of organic mulch such as compost, shredded leaves, or wood to conserve moisture, suppress weeds, and supply nutrients as they decompose.

Sanitation: Remove dead, damaged, diseased, or insect-infested leaves, shoots, or branches whenever you spot them.

IPM Mechanical Controls

Handpicking: Remove any insects by hand, or knock them off with a strong spray of water from the hose.

Exclusion: Physically block insects from attacking your plants. Aluminum foil collars can be placed around seedlings to prevent cutworms attacking plant stems. Plants can be covered with muslin or spun-bonded polyester to keep out insects.

IPM Biological Controls

Predators and parasites: Some bugs are on our side. Known as beneficial insects or natural enemies of damaging insects, they fall into two main categories: predators and parasites. Predators hunt and feed on other insects. They include spiders, praying mantids, lady beetles, and green lacewings. Parasites, such as braconid wasps and *Trichogramma* wasps, hatch from eggs inside or on another insect and they eat their host insect as they grow.

Releasing beneficial insects into your landscape or garden may offer some benefit, but it is better to conserve the beneficial insects already there. Learn to distinguish between pests and beneficial insects in your garden and landscape. Avoid applying broad-spectrum insecticides that will harm beneficial insects if it looks as if the harmful insects are already being kept to tolerable levels.

General Gardening Practices

Botanical pesticides and insecticidal soaps: Botanical pesticides or "botanicals" are naturally occurring pesticides derived from plants. Two common botanicals include pyrethrins, insecticidal chemicals extracted from the pyrethrum flower (*Tanacetum cinerariifolium*), and neem, a botanical insecticide and fungicide extracted from the tropical neem tree (*Azadirachta indica*) which contains the active ingredient azadirachtin. Insecticidal soaps have been formulated specifically for their ability to control insects. Soaps are effective only against those insects that come into direct contact with sprays before they dry.

These "natural" pesticides break down rapidly when exposed to sunlight, air, and moisture and are less likely to kill beneficial insects than insecticides that have a longer residual activity.

Microbial insecticides: These insecticides combat damaging insects with microscopic living organisms such as viruses, bacteria, fungi, protozoa, or nematodes. Although they may look like out-of-the-ordinary insecticides, they can be applied in ordinary ways—as sprays, dusts, or granules. The bacterium *Bacillus thuringiensis (BT)* is the most popular pathogen. Formulations from *Bacillus thuringiensis* var. *kurstaki* (BTK) are the most widely used to control caterpillars—the larvae of butterflies and moths.

Horticultural oils: When applied to plants, these highly refined oils smother insects, mites, and their eggs. Typically, horticultural oils such as Sunspray®, Scalecide®, and Volck® are derived from highly refined petroleum products that are specifically manufactured to control pests on plants. Studies have shown that horticultural oils derived from vegetable oils, such as cottonseed and soybean oil, also exhibit insecticidal properties.

Dormant applications generally control aphid eggs and the egg stages of mites, scale insects, and caterpillars like leafrollers and tent caterpillars. Summer applications control adelgids, aphids, mealybugs, scale insects, spider mites, and whiteflies.

Oils have limited effects on beneficial insects, especially when applied during the dormant season. Additionally, insects and mites have not been reported to develop resistance to petroleum or vegetable oils.

Traditional, synthetic pesticides: Synthetic pesticides, developed by people, should be your last resort when confronted by damaging pest levels. Use them sparingly to control the targeted pest. Specific names of synthetic pesticides are avoided in this book because products and their labels change rapidly along with the pesticide registration and use process. *When buying any pesticide, read the label and follow all directions and precautions before mixing and applying it, and before storing or disposing of it.*

Further Help

Clemson University or North Carolina State University each have an extension center or office in every county of the Carolinas. Many are staffed by Master Gardeners trained in horticulture. These volunteers are also available to answer your questions at many arboreta, botanical and other public gardens.

Help is available from the Garden Clubs of North Carolina and South Carolina and an array of societies devoted to specific plants, and from seminars and informative newsletters as well.

General Overview

The garden plants in this book are divided into twelve groups and arranged alphabetically to help you find the information you need for each month of the year.

Annuals are relied upon to deliver brilliant color and a long-lasting display of flowers all season long. In this chapter you will learn when to start them from seed indoors, when to transplant them outside, and how to care for them during the year so they look their best.

Bulbs, corms, rhizomes, and tubers are unique below-ground storage structures that encompass an exciting array of beautiful and durable plants. I refer to them collectively as bulbs for simplicity's sake. The chapter offers guidance on when to plant them and how and when to divide them.

Fresh **herbs and vegetables** can be grown and harvested year-round in most of the Carolinas. Knowing when to start seeds indoors and when to set transplants in the garden will help you keep your garden productive throughout the year. Refer to this chapter for monthly reminders. The pest control section highlights common pests and what to do about them.

Houseplants beautify and enrich our indoor living space. They also satisfy a gardener's need for cultivating plants when the weather outside forces us inside. This chapter offers tips and guidance on the care and feeding of indoor plants, along with help in matching the right plant to the conditions in your home.

Cool- and warm-season lawn grasses can be grown in the Carolinas. The timing of certain cultural practices differs for each type, so the chapters on lawns deal with each group of turfgrasses separately. Whichever thrives in your area, these chapters will show you some basic turf establishment and maintenance practices to keep your lawn healthy and attractive.

Perennials, technically "herbaceous" perennials, are so called to separate them from woody trees and shrubs. Over the years their popularity has grown, and with good reason. This group includes flowering plants, ferns, and ornamental grasses that can deliver unique colors and textures with flowers, seedheads, and leaves. Perennials have specific needs regarding pruning, deadheading, dividing, and transplanting. Treat them properly to get the most from this truly extraordinary collection of plants.

The rose, our national emblem, has been around since ancient times and continues to infatuate gardeners with its grace and beauty. This chapter focuses on "easy-care" roses that are suitable for gardeners who love them but aren't interested in intensive management. You'll learn in this chapter that selecting the right rose to fit your easy-going management style is only part of growing roses successfully.

General Overview

Shrubs come in a dizzying array of shapes, sizes, forms, and colors. Some have soft, naturally billowy forms, others sport showy, fragrant flowers or brightly colored berries, and still others deliver stunning fall color. Planting, pruning, fertilizing, and keeping an eye out for pests should be done at specific times of the year.

Trees are permanent landscape investments that grow in value with each passing year. Select them carefully, place them wisely, and plant them properly. They will need smart pruning and timely feeding to grow and look their best. Insects and diseases are a constant threat, but pest-resistant trees help. Refer to this chapter for advice and "how-to" help in caring for your trees.

Vines and ground covers are the workhorses of the landscape, combining functionality and beauty. Vines have traditionally been used to hide chain-link fences and unsightly views, and to provide some shade and privacy on the front porch. Ground covers are called upon to control soil erosion on steep slopes, to hide red clay in places where nothing else will grow, and to replace lawn grass in shady or wet areas where it just won't grow, even after several exasperating attempts. This chapter suggests how to use them to solve unyielding problems.

Water gardening offers a different set of challenges and experiences than does "terrestrial" gardening. Water and bog plants include a wide range of unique plants that like "wet feet." Select the right kinds of plants for your water garden and give them the proper care each month.

Now let's look at these plants in more detail.

Gardening . . . America's
Favorite Outdoor
Recreation Activity

Annuals and Biennials

Annuals are the workhorses of the garden. They can be relied on to deliver brilliant color and a long-lasting display of flowers all season long. Annuals do well in lead roles, planted *en masse* in sun or shade to produce a massive show of color. They can also do well as supporting cast members, serving as "fillers" to dress up open spaces that haven't yet been filled in by permanent plantings of perennials or shrubs. They work as screens, too. Use them to keep the garden looking well dressed by hiding the faded leaves of bulbs that have finished flowering and are going dormant.

Some annuals are especially attractive to hummingbirds and butterflies; some specialize in providing exquisite fragrance; some are unequaled in colorful bouquets. Still others adapt readily to containers and hanging baskets to provide a spot of color.

All of this from a group of plants whose entire life cycle lasts less than a year!

Biennials are often grouped with annuals. They usually complete their life cycle in two years. The first year they produce stems, leaves, and roots. In their second year, biennials flower, set seed, and die. Mild winters in parts of the Carolinas can trick some biennials into blooming in less than a year. Sowing the seeds of biennials in midsummer allows the plants to develop during the fall months. After exposure to winter cold, biennials will bloom the following season. In general, care for biennials like annuals. *Plant* most biennials in the fall to bloom the following spring.

Annuals differ in their ability to tolerate cold temperatures. They've been categorized as hardy, half-hardy, or tender. These are general guides to help you decide when to plant annuals. The two important dates to know in your area are the last expected freeze in spring and the first expected freeze in fall. Refer to the maps on p. 14–15 to determine the freeze dates in your location.

Hardy annuals are the most cold tolerant of the group, sometimes withstanding freezing temperatures. In many cases, the seeds can be planted outdoors a few weeks before the last freeze in spring or in fall after freezing temperatures have arrived but when the soil can still be worked. Hardy annuals include **calendula, larkspur, pansy,** and **stock.** Most hardy annuals are not heat tolerant and usually decline and die with the onset of hot summer temperatures.

Half-hardy annuals can tolerate cool, wet weather but will be damaged, set back, or killed by freezing temperatures. The seeds of most half-hardy annuals can be sown after the last anticipated freeze in spring. Although most do not require warm soil temperatures to germinate, some do. Refer to the seed packet for specific information about optimum temperature ranges for good germination. Many half-hardy annuals decline in the midsummer heat but may bloom again in late summer or fall.

Annuals and Biennials

Most tender annuals are native to tropical regions and cannot tolerate cold soils and air temperatures. They need warm soil temperatures to germinate and long warm summers to produce the best flower display. Typically, these seeds must be sown outdoors two to three weeks after the last spring freeze. But as we will discuss later, you can get a head start by starting the seeds indoors so that you can set out transplants when the time comes.

Planning the Annual Flower Garden

Annuals are high-impact plants that can change the look and feel of your landscape in a short time. When thinking about annuals, pay attention to their flower color and form, texture, and habit. Create a plan with the following guidelines in mind:

- **Season:** Annuals have certain seasons when they deliver the most impact with their flowers, leaves, or both. With the right selection of annuals, you can have a beautiful display during each of the four seasons.

- **Cultural needs:** Annuals vary considerably with respect to their environmental and cultural requirements. Some perform best in full sun while others do best in shade. Drought tolerance varies, and ideal planting times differ. Those that can tolerate drier conditions should be grouped together, making watering easier.

- **Spacing requirements:** Know the expected height and spread of the annuals to determine the number of plants needed for a bed. Plant annuals the right distance apart so they will grow into their allotted space as they mature. Avoid overcrowding at all costs. Leave enough space between plants to encourage air movement between the plants. Their leaves will dry off quickly to thwart the spread of fungal diseases that require moisture to grow and spread.

- **Color, form, and texture:** Serious gardeners spend time studying flower and leaf color, the form, or habit, of each plant (upright or spreading), and textures (from the fine needle-like leaves of **cosmos** to coarse **sunflower** leaves). Gardeners blend and contrast these features to create different impacts. There are some excellent reference books that offer a variety of designs and instructions on creating incredible impacts. When working with color, you may want to work with a color wheel to help you visualize complementary or contrasting shades. You can create solid beds of one color or mix them. Beds can be simple in all white, cool with blues, or hot with reds. There are design rules, but the bottom line is this: your garden is an expression of your tastes. Consider leaves when selecting plants. Some, like **coleus** and **dusty miller,** are cultivated just for their foliage. Group the plants in threes, fives, or sevens to create a natural, flowing look.

Make use of the planting chart (p. 28–29) as a starting point in making the right selections. Commercial catalogs are also good sources that provide detailed information on many varieties, colors, and sizes.

Annuals and Biennials

Starting Annuals and Biennials from Seed

Garden centers and feed'n seed stores offer only a limited variety of annuals and biennials. To widen your selection beyond those normally available in your area, start plants from seed. Before you run out and purchase dozens of seed packets, realize that it's most important that you can provide them with adequate light. Low light levels result in weak, spindly seedlings that "stretch," becoming long and lanky, and eventually flop over. To avoid relying on sunlight, buy or build an artificial light stand and grow your seedlings under lights. This portable light stand was designed by Joe Maple, a Spartanburg County (SC) Master Gardener. It can be taken apart and stored in a closet when the seed-starting season is over. This clever design is inexpensive and is easily constructed out of 1/2-inch PVC pipes. I've built light stands out of 1/2- and 3/4-inch PVC pipe and found that 3/4-inch pipe produces a sturdier stand.

See January Planting on p. 30 for step-by-step information on starting seeds indoors. To *direct-sow* seeds outdoors, see February Planting (p. 32).

Preparing the Soil

Annuals need a soil that is porous and drains well yet holds enough moisture and nutrients. Prepare your soil several weeks before planting by following these steps:

1   Dig the planting bed to a depth of 8 to 12 inches.

2   To improve drainage and fertility in clay soils, incorporate at least 2 inches of compost or composted pine bark (1/2 inch or less in diameter) into the top 8 inches of soil. Adding more than 4 inches of amendments may affect plant growth undesirably.

Inorganic materials can improve drainage in clay soils, especially when organic materials are also used. The inorganics include chicken grit, small (pea) gravel (3/8 inch or less), or stalite (marketed as Perma-till®, which has the appearance of pea gravel but weighs much less since each particle is filled with air). Apply a 2-inch layer to the

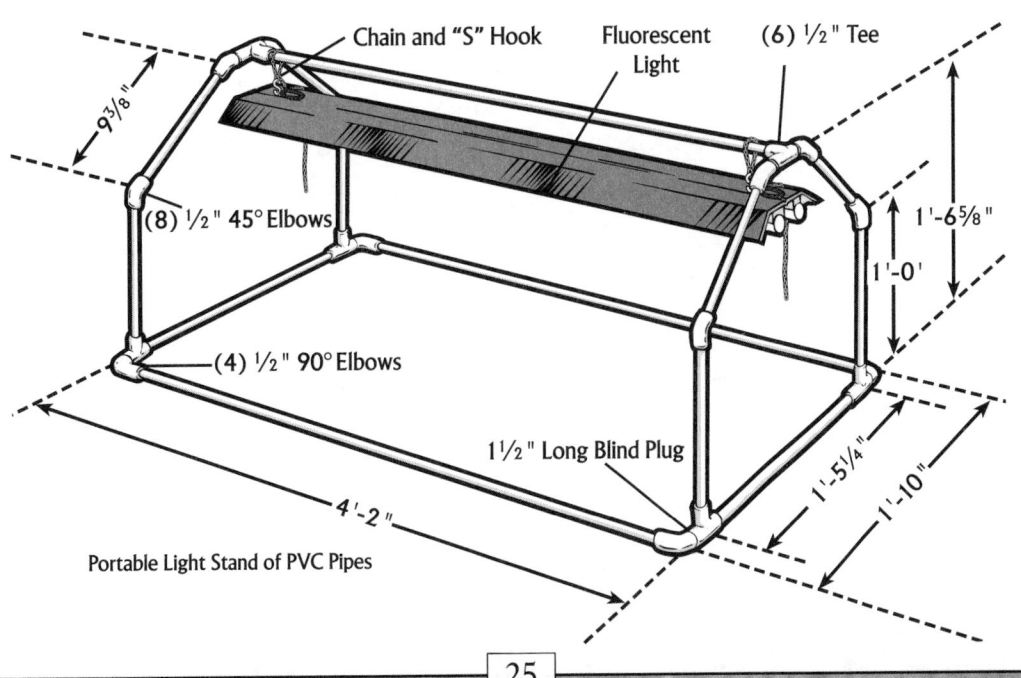

Chain and "S" Hook   Fluorescent Light   (6) 1/2" Tee

9 3/8"

(8) 1/2" 45° Elbows

(4) 1/2" 90° Elbows

1 1/2" Long Blind Plug

1'-6 5/8"

1'-0'

1'-5 1/4"

1'-10"

4'-2"

Portable Light Stand of PVC Pipes

surface of the bed and mix it in to a depth of 6 to 8 inches.

To improve the water-holding capacity of sandy soils, amend the soil with compost, composted pine bark, or peat moss. As with clay soils, at least 2 inches of material (but no more than half the digging depth) should receive amendments.

3 Have your soil tested through your local cooperative extension service. A pH of 5.5 to 6.5 is fine for most annuals.

If a soil test hasn't been taken for at least three or more years, apply 5 pounds of dolomitic limestone and 2 pounds of a fertilizer high in phosphorus and potassium with a 1-2-2 ratio, such as 2 pounds of 5-10-10 per 100 square feet. This is a fast-release fertilizer.

Instead of using a fast-release fertilizer such as 5-10-10, a slow-release fertilizer may be a good choice, especially in sandy soils prone to leaching. Apply the fertilizer using the manufacturer's label instructions.

4 *Mix* pulverized lime or sulfur and fertilizer as recommended by soil-test results into the top 6 inches of soil, paying special attention to phosphorus or calcium, both of which move very slowly in the soil.

5 Rake the bed smooth.

Transplanting Annuals

Plant annuals at the appropriate time. Use the first and last expected freezes in your area shown on p. 14–15 as a guide. See March Planting on p. 34 to learn how to plant them properly.

Caring for Your Annuals

You may have spent a lot of time raising or a fair amount of money purchasing healthy transplants, and you may have selected and prepared appropriate sites, but you can still meet with disappointment if you do not continue to give your flowering annuals the care they need.

Watering

Adequate water is necessary for annuals to grow vigorously and bloom continuously, especially during hot, dry summers. Some annuals require a continuous supply of water, while other, more drought-tolerant types can prosper with minimal regular watering.

Annuals and Biennials

Frequent watering, perhaps twice daily, is necessary when sowing seeds outdoors. Seedlings or newly planted annuals should be watered once a day. Once established, you can gradually begin to water them less frequently. *Water* deeply to encourage deep rooting. Established plants may need to be watered once a week in clay soils that hold more water than sandy soils. Sandy soils may need to be watered twice a week. Instead of following the calendar, water when the top 2 or 3 inches of soil feels dry.

There are several ways to water annual beds. Refer to Shrubs, May Planning, for several efficient approaches.

Fertilizing

Annuals need adequate nutrients to sustain them during the growing season. Before making any supplemental fertilizer applications, let their growth rate, leaf color, and a soil test be your guides. If the bed is already highly fertile, the soil test will save you from the undesirable results of overfertilizing. The rule of thumb for fertilizing is to apply a dry, granular, complete, fast-acting type of fertilizer such as 10-10-10, at a rate of one pound per 100 square feet monthly. That works out to 2 cups per 100 square feet, or 4 tablespoons per 10 square feet. Keep this up throughout the growing season; stretch the intervals between feedings up to six weeks, based on your observations.

Water-soluble fertilizers usually call for shorter intervals between applications. They are not only quickly available, but also quickly used up. Most should be mixed with water and applied every two weeks, following label directions. These fertilizers can be absorbed by both leaves and roots.

Slow-release or controlled-release fertilizers deliver small amounts of nutrients gradually over an extended period. Depending on soil moisture and temperature, release of the coated nutrients may extend over several weeks or months.

Typically, the first application is mixed into the bed just before planting. Some products will have to be applied a second time midway through the growing season. How much you apply and how often should be based on the manufacturer's instructions.

Controlling Pests

When controlling pests, practice Integrated Pest Management, or IPM. This is a commonsense approach focusing on establishing and maintaining healthy plants and understanding pests. See the introduction to Perennials, Pest Control, on p. 196 for more information.

Carolina Annuals

Common Name (Botanical Name)	Cold Hardiness	Bloom Season	Flower Color	Height (inches)	Light Exposure	Watering Needs
Ageratum (*Ageratum houstonianum*)	Half-hardy	Summer	Blue, pink, white	6 to 24	Sun to partial shade	Medium
Australian fan flower (*Scaevola aemula*)	Tender	Sring to fall	Bluish-purple, mauve, white	4 to 6	Sun to partial shade	Low
Black-eyed Susan, Gloriosa Daisy (*Rudbeckia hirta*)	Tender	Summer	Orange, red, yellow	24 to 30	Sun to partial shade	Low
Blue Daze (*Evolvulus glomeratus* 'Blue Daze')	Tender	Spring to fall	Blue	6 to 12	Sun	Low
Coleus (*Solenostemon scutellariodes*)	Tender	Late spring to early fall (leaves)	Not showy	8 to 20	Partial shade; sun for sun cultivars	High
Cosmos (*Cosmos bipinnatus*)	Tender	Spring to early fall	Lilac, pink, red, white, yellow	24 to 60	Sun	Low
Cosmos, Klondyke (*C. sulphureus*)	Tender	Spring to early fall	Gold, orange, red, yellow	12 to 36	Sun	Low
Dianthus, China Pinks (*Dianthus* hybrids)	Hardy	Spring to fall	Pink, purple, red, violet, white, and bicolors	6 to 18	Sun to partial shade	Medium
Flowering cabbage and kale (*Brassica oleracea*)	Hardy	Fall to spring (leaves)	Red to white, marbled leaves	8 to 14	Sun	High
Flowering tobacco, Nicotiana (*Nicotiana alata*)	Half-hardy	Summer to fall	Lime green, pink, red, white, yellow	12 to 48	Sun to partial shade	Medium
Foxglove (*Digitalis purpurea*)	Hardy Biennial	Late spring to summer	Pink, purple, white, yellow	24 to 84	Sun to partial shade	Medium
Gaillardia, Blanket flower (*Gaillardia pulchella*)	Tender	Summer to early fall	Orange, red, yellow	18 to 24	Sun	Low
Geranium (*Pelargonium × hortorum*)	Tender	Late spring to early fall	Bicolors, pink, red, salmon, white	12 to 24	Sun to partial shade	High
Globe amaranth (*Gomphrena globosa*)	Tender	Late spring to early fall	Lavender, orange, pink, purple, red, white	8 to 30	Sun to partial shade	Low
Gomphrena (*Gomphrena haageana*)	Tender	Late spring to fall	Orange, yellow	8 to 30	Sun	Low
Impatiens (*Impatiens wallerana*)		Late spring to fall	Orange, pink, purple, red, white	8 to 24	Partial shade to shade	High

Carolina Annuals

Common Name (Botanical Name)	Cold Hardiness	Bloom Season	Flower Color	Height (inches)	Light Exposure	Watering Needs
Johnny-jump-up (*Viola tricolor*)	Hardy	Fall, winter, spring	Blue, yellow, tricolored, lavender, violet	8	Sun to partial shade	Medium
Larkspur (*Consolida ambigua*)	Hardy	Spring	Blue, pink, purple, white	18 to 36	Sun to partial shade	Medium
Melampodium, Medallion flower (*Melampodium paludosum*)	Tender	Late spring to early fall	Yellow	18 to 24	Sun	Low to medium
Madagascar periwinkle, Annual vinca (*Catharanthus roseus*)	Tender	Spring to fall	Pink, purple, red, salmon, white	6 to 18	Sun to partial shade	Low to medium
Marigold, American, Aztec, or African (*Tagetes erecta*)	Tender	Late spring to fall	Gold, orange to reddish-brown, yellow	8 to 36	Sun	Medium
Marigold, French (*Tagetes patula*)	Tender	Late spring to fall	Gold, red, orange, bicolors	6 to 12	Sun	Medium
Mexican sunflower (*Tithonia rotundifolia*)	Tender	Summer to fall	Orange, yellow	36 to 60	Sun	Medium
Moss rose and Purslane (*Portulaca grandiflora* and *P. oleracea*)	Tender	Summer to early fall	Orange, pink, purple, red, yellow, white	4 to 8	Sun	Low
New Guinea impatiens (*Impatiens hawkeri*)		Spring to fall	Lavender, orange, purple pink, red, salmon, white	12 to 24	Sun to shade	High
Pansy (*Viola × wittrockiana*)	Hardy	Fall, winter, spring	Blue, purple, white, yellow	4 to 8	Sun to partial shade	Medium
Pentas or Egyptian star cluster (*Pentas lanceolata*)	Tender	Summer to fall	Lilac, pink, red, white	12 to 36	Sun	Low to medium
Petunia (*Petunia × hybrida*)	Half-hardy	Spring to summer	Purple, red, white, yellow	6 to 18	Sun	Medium
Sage, Mealy-cup (*Salvia farinacea*)	Half-hardy	Summer	Blue, white, bicolors	24 to 36	Sun	Low
Sage, Texas (*Salvia coccinea*)	Tender	Spring to fall	Red, white, bicolors	24 to 36	Sun	Low
Snapdragon (*Antirrhinum majus*)	Hardy	Spring to early summer, fall	Bicolored, bronze, pink, maroon, red, orange, white, yellow	6 to 36	Sun to part shade	Medium
Wax begonia (*Begonia* Semperflorens Cultorum Group)	Tender	Late spring to early fall	Pink, red, salmon, white, and bicolors	6 to 12	Sun to shade	Medium
Zinnia, Creeping (*Zinnia angustifolia*)	Tender	Late spring to early fall	Orange, yellow, white	6 to 12	Sun	Low

Planning

Plan to organize your seed packets this month to create a sowing schedule for your seeds. Look up the date of the last expected freeze in your area (see the map on p. 15). This is a guideline for planning, not a hard-and-fast rule to follow. Then check the instructions on the seed packets to find the number of weeks of growth required before each seedling can be transplanted to the garden outdoors. Count the weeks back from the last expected freeze to know when to sow your seeds, and make a record of it.

Make a growing chart, either on a spreadsheet on your computer or in your gardening journal. Record the name of the plant, the variety, and the day the seed should be sown. Write down the expected time of germination and when the plant can be expected to reach a size for outdoor planting.

Planting

Growing your own transplants from seed offers you a wider choice of varieties than is usually available at garden centers. It can also be a challenge. To grow stocky transplants indoors, expose them to plenty of light (see p. 25). Be sure to pay attention to timing. Avoid sowing seeds too early because they may be ready for transplanting before outdoor conditions permit. See Planning, above.

There are two ways of growing transplants from seed. In the one-step method, *sow* seeds directly into individual containers. *Transplant* them directly outdoors when they can be easily handled.

In the two-step method *sow* seeds in trays or flats until the "true leaves" emerge, then *transplant* them to pots for further growth before moving them to their permanent homes outdoors. Use aluminum foil pans if nursery flats are not available. Punch six or so holes in the bottom of the pans for drainage.

Here's how to sow seeds for either method:

1 *Moisten* a sterile, seed-starting mixture (soilless mixes are ideal), and fill the pots or trays to within $1/4$ inch of the top.

2 Sow very fine seeds with vermiculite or sharp sand. *Mix* the seeds with the vermiculite or sand, and pour the mix into the center of a folded sheet of paper. Tap it gently over the medium to sow the seeds.

If planting in individual pots, make a hole in the mix with a pencil point, chopstick, or other "dibbler." *Plant* the seeds no deeper than recommended on the label. A general rule is to cover seeds to a depth equal to twice their diameter. Drop one or two seeds in each hole.

When sowing medium to large seeds in the two-step method, use the end of a pencil to create furrows about 1 to 2 inches apart and about $1/8$ to $1/4$ inch deep across the surface of the growing medium with the end of a pencil. Sow the seeds in rows for easier labeling and transplanting.

3 Press extremely fine seeds such as **petunia, begonia,** and **snapdragon** lightly into the medium, or *water them in* with a fine mist spray. *Cover* the seed if light is not required for germination. A thin layer of vermiculite will do. Otherwise, leave the seed uncovered, exposed to light.

4 *Label* the pot or flat with the name of the crop and the date it was planted. Read the packet, and make note of the date the seed is expected to germinate so you will know when to expect sprouts to appear.

5 *Spray-mist* the seeds to water them in. If watering from the top may dislodge the seeds, place the entire container into a tub, sink, or bucket containing a few inches of water. After the potting mix is saturated, set it aside to drain.

6 *Cover* the pots or tray with plastic wrap, or put them in a plastic bag secured at the top to retain moisture. They won't have to be watered until the plastic wrap is removed.

7 Unless the seeds require cool temperatures, move them to a location between 65 and 75 degrees F. in bright but indirect sunlight. Germination can be hastened by providing warmth. Follow instructions on the seed packet; if there are no instructions, provide bottom heat of 75 to 85 degrees F. Use a bottom-heat mat or a waterproof insulated heating cable, or set the tray on top of the refrigerator.

When the seeds have sprouted, expose them to bright light to keep them short and stocky. *Remove* the plastic covering and put them under fluorescent lights. Two 40-watt cool white fluorescent lights are a cost-effective choice and provide the quality of light required by plants. Set the trays on your light stand and lower the lights so they're barely touching the topmost leaves. Keep the lights on for sixteen hours each day. An automatic timer will help. As the seedlings grow, raise the lights. Temperature can be 60 to 70 degrees F., 10 degrees lower at night. Tape aluminum foil to the back and sides of the light stand to concentrate light on plants.

When the soil can be worked, *direct-sow* **sweet alyssum; larkspur;** and **California, Iceland,** and **shirley poppies** later this month in the Coastal Plain. Although in the Piedmont and Coastal Plain they're better suited to fall sowing, you can sow them now. *Sprinkle* them on a roughly raked surface and *water in*.

Watering

Determine the need for watering by squeezing the top $1/2$ inch of medium between your thumb and forefinger. If water squeezes out easily, there's enough moisture. If the medium feels slightly moist but water is difficult to squeeze out, *add water*. Just remember to water the seed flats no more than necessary.

Fertilizing

Seedlings growing in soilless mixes need to be fertilized when the first true leaves appear. *Feed* at every other watering with a water-soluble fertilizer to promote faster growth until the plants are ready to plant outdoors. *Water* between feedings.

Pest Control

Diseases: Damping-off can be a problem on seedlings. This common fungal disease attacks the seedlings at ground level, rotting the stems and causing plants to topple over. Their stems look as if they have been pinched. See February Diseases, p. 33.

Planning

When planning your garden, think in splashes—not drops—of color. High-impact, car-stopping beds are achieved when annuals are planted *en masse*. Before you buy any plants or seeds, draw your garden plan on a sheet of graph paper. Draw it to scale and decide on the kinds of colors you want in that bed. As you look through catalogs, examine plant descriptions carefully. Take note of these features:

- Are they cool- or warm-season annuals?

- What is their expected height and spread at maturity? Will they require staking?

- Are they "self-cleaning"? The spent flowers of some of the modern varieties are shed by the plant and quickly disappear. Others have to be deadheaded to get rid of the old, faded flowers. This task is necessary for **cosmos, marigold, pansy,** and **pinks.** Deadheading not only prevents the formation of seeds, but also stimulates continued flowering.

Keep this information in a gardening journal, not only to help you plan your season, but also to evaluate the performance of these annuals in your landscape. Record your observations this year so that next year when you're at this point you can review your list and make the best choices.

Planting and Transplanting

Indoors: When seedlings produce their first set of true leaves, it's time to *transplant* them from the tray to individual containers.

1 You can fill the containers with the same soilless mix used for germinating the seeds. You'll get better results, however, if you mix one part perlite with two parts of the soilless mix. Perlite improves drainage and aeration.

2 *Firm* the moistened mix to within 1/2 inch of the top of the container.

3 *Loosen* the medium around the seedlings with a pencil and lift one out. Hold on to a cotyledon, or "seed leaf," a pair of first leaves that the seedling produces that are oval or round in shape. Avoid squeezing the stem.

4 Use your pencil to *poke* a hole in the medium that is large enough to accommodate the fragile roots, and *plant* the seedlings.

5 *Firm* the soil lightly around the plants, and *water* them in so the soil and roots are in good contact.

Don't leave the seedlings in the flat too long, or you'll be left with a tangled mess. Then you may have to sacrifice some seedlings by thinning them out. Don't pull them out. Simply *pinch off* their stems close to the surface of the medium.

Warm-weather annuals that require six to eight weeks from sowing to transplanting outdoors can be sown this month: **African daisy, ageratum, annual phlox, China aster, flowering tobacco,** and **Mexican sunflower.** Refer to the map on p. 15 to determine the last expected freeze date for your area.

Warm-season annuals that require four to six weeks can also be sown indoors now. Mountain gardeners can wait until next month. These annuals include **coleus, marigolds, salvia, snow-on-the-mountain, strawflowers,** and **zinnias.**

If your overwintered **coleus** has become leggy and gangly-looking, clip off the ends to take cuttings, and root them to produce short, stocky plants for planting this spring. Refer to the Care for Your Annuals section in August (p. 44) to learn how to propagate **coleus** from cuttings.

Outdoors: When the soil can be worked, continue sowing seeds of **larkspur** and **California, Iceland, and shirley poppies** in the Coastal Plain and Piedmont. Follow the recommended seeding date, depth, and spacing on the packet. Prepare the bed and pay close attention during germination and when they begin to grow. Most outdoor-grown seedlings should be thinned to the recommended spacing to allow remaining plants to have adequate light, water, nutrients, and space to develop fully above and below ground. *Water* them in after sowing.

Sow seeds of **sweet alyssum** four to six weeks before the last frost .

Plant transplants of **annual dianthus (pinks), calendulas, pansies, violas, snapdragon,** and **sweet william** as they become available in the garden centers in the Piedmont and Coastal Plain.

Care for Your Annuals

Indoors: Seedlings receiving inadequate light become spindly and floppy. Keep them in a south-facing window or place them under artificial lights for sixteen hours a day.

If you overwintered geraniums indoors, take stem cuttings and root them now or next month. See next month's Care for your Annuals on p. 34 for the step-by-step details.

Outdoors: *Pinch off* pansy flowers when transplanting to encourage branching and focus the plant's efforts on rooting and getting established.

Watering

See January, p.31.

Fertilizing

Feed indoor-grown transplants with a water-soluble fertilizer such as 20-20-20 at half strength every other week.

Coastal Plains gardeners can fertilize **pansies** when new growth resumes. A liquid fertilizer may have to be applied every two weeks.

Pest Control

Weeds: Control any winter annual weeds such as bittercress, common chickweed, and henbit by hand-pulling. *Suppress* them with a shallow layer of mulch.

Diseases: Damping-off is a serious disease that attacks and kills seeds and seedlings. It especially attacks weak seedlings when growing conditions are unfavorable. Overwatering, lack of drainage, poor ventilation, and crowding can foster an attack. With seedlings, the stem rots at or close to the soil surface. This is mainly caused by the fungi present in the seed-starting medium.

Damping-off is easier to prevent than cure. Use clean containers. If necessary, disinfect them with a 10 percent bleach solution (1 part bleach to 9 parts water). Use a sterile, well-drained medium. Provide good conditions for rapid seed germination and development. Avoid waterlogging the medium when watering. Damping-off can be reduced by cutting back the frequency of watering and increasing the amount of light. Several fungicides are available that may help. They are applied as a drench or heavy spray as soon as evidence of damping-off appears.

Planning

Before visiting the garden center, make a list of the kinds and quantity of annuals you need. Planning beforehand will help you avoid overindulging and purchase only what you need.

1 *Measure* the length and width of the flowerbed and calculate the area in square feet (area = length × width). If the bed is irregularly shaped—oval, round, or long and winding—make a rough estimate.

2 Jot down the kind of sun- or shade-loving annuals you would like to plant in the bed. Include their spacing requirements. Refer to the seed packet or catalog for the correct spacing.

3 Determine the number of plants you need by following April's Helpful Hint on p. 37.

Planting

Cool-season annuals to plant outside now in the Piedmont and Mountains include **alyssum, calendula, pansy, snapdragon,** and **viola.** Delay planting seeds of other annuals outside except for the hardy ones that like to sprout in cool weather. These include **alyssum,**

calliopsis or annual coreopsis, larkspur, poppies, and **sweet william.**

Plant this month in the Coastal Plains, next month in the Piedmont, and the month after that in the Mountains. Follow these steps to plant them properly:

1 *Moisten* the potting medium before taking the plant out of the container. This will keep the soil intact when you slide it out.

2 Hold your hand over the top of the pot with the plant stems between your fingers. Tip over the pot and gently *tap* the plant into your hand. Annuals growing in cell-packs can be pushed out from the bottom with your thumb. If they are reluctant, slit the walls of the container and peel it away. If there is a mat of tangled roots on the base, tease the bottom third of the rootball to loosen it up.

3 Dig a hole as wide as the rootball and the same depth. Plants growing in peat pots can be planted pot and all. *Moisten* the plants in the peat pot before planting.

4 After preparing the planting hole, plant the pot level with the soil surface. *Remove* any portion of the exposed pot.

(The exposed peat could act like a wick, drawing moisture away from the pot and soil, causing the plant to dry out quickly.)

5 *Pinch off* any open flowers to direct the plant's energy into building roots for speedy establishment.

6 Firm each plant in with your fingers, and *water it in.* Allow the plants the correct spacing. Refer to the seed packet for suggested spacing, and refer to the Helpful Hint in March.

Once you have finished planting, cover the bed with a 2- to 3-inch layer of mulch, tapering to a 1/2-inch layer near the crown but not covering it. During the next few weeks, keep the plants well watered to help them become established.

Care for Your Annuals

Any geraniums stored upside-down in the basement or crawl space over the winter should be brought out and rejuvenated at the beginning of this month.

1 *Prune back* any dead shoots.

2 *Repot* the geranium in fresh soil.

3 *Water,* and set in a warm place.

As growth begins, move the plants into a sunny window and begin regular watering and fertilizing.

Watering

Indoors, continue watering seedlings planted last month.

Pruning

Pinch out the growing tips of plants that have become rangy. They will branch from below the pinch and regain their bushy form.

Cut off dead blooms to encourage continued flowering in **pansies.**

Fertilizing

When the weather warms and growth resumes, fertilize your **pansies, violas,** and other winter annuals with a slow-release fertilizer, or give them a quick pick-me-up with a liquid such as 20-20-20, mixed according to label directions.

Helpful Hint

If you're toying with the idea of raising your own transplants, concentrate on annuals that require only a little attention. **Cosmos, marigolds,** and **zinnias** need only a month or two of daily care. Let nurseries grow the **geraniums, petunias,** and **dwarf snapdragons** that require three to four months to reach market size. Here's a table showing the time needed in weeks from seed to planting size for common bedding plants.

Cosmos	4–6	Verbena	8–10
Zinnias, Tall	4–6	Impatiens	9–10
Marigolds, Tall	5–6	Flowering tobacco	9–11
Zinnias, Dwarf	6–8	Salvia, Dwarf	10–12
Celosia	7–9	Ageratum	8–10
China aster	8–10	Petunia	11–15
Cleome	8–10	Dwarf snapdragon	12–14
Marigold, Dwarf	8–10	Portulaca	10–12
Salvia, Tall	8–10	Geranium	13–18
Snapdragon, Tall	8–10	Pansy	12–14

Pest Control

Insects: Spider mites can be a problem on indoor seedlings. See p. 362 for a description and controls.

Diseases: Damping-off can be triggered by waterlogged conditions in the growing medium. See February, p. 33, for more information.

Weeds: Pre-emergent herbicides are available for many of the more common bedding plants. These herbicides kill germinating weed seedlings before they appear. When selecting a pre-emergent herbicide, keep these pointers in mind:

- *Identify* the weed that you want to control.

- *Select* a herbicide that will control this weed but can be applied to the flowering annuals you're growing.

- *Read* the label carefully and *apply* only as recommended. For example, some pre-emergent herbicides are safe to use only on established bedding plants. If applied shortly after transplanting, injury may result.

Planning

In addition to using annuals to show off their flowers and leaves outdoors, make plans to cultivate a cutting garden to enjoy the flowers indoors. With careful planning, you can have flowers blooming from spring until fall. A cutting garden requires regular watering, the prompt removal of dead or dying leaves, and the continuous removal of spent flowers to encourage the production of more flowers. Try these flowers in the cutting garden: **celosia, China aster, gaillardia, globe amaranth, heliotrope, lisianthus, marigold, phlox, poppy, snapdragon, strawflower,** and **zinnia.**

Planting

Start hanging baskets early in April. **Impatiens** and **begonias** do well in shade. For sunny locations, try **dwarf marigold, petunias, scaevola, verbena,** and **annual vinca. Portulaca** is wonderful in baskets, as it tolerates hot sun and drought. For a bushier basket planting, keep the plant tips pinched. Start pots for your patio or porch.

Two weeks before the last frost, plant **cleome** seeds and **gloriosa daisy.**

Two to three weeks after the last freeze when the soil temperatures have warmed, **cosmos, gomphrena, marigold, portulaca, sunflower, zinnia,** and other warm-season annuals can be sown directly in the beds where they are to grow. Keep the seeded area moist until the seeds emerge. *Thin out* as soon as they are large enough to transplant. Any extras can be transplanted to other areas.

Care for Your Annuals

Tender annuals started indoors should gradually be *"hardened"* before planting them in the garden. Hardening is a procedure that prepares indoor-grown plants for the rigors of the outdoors. Reduce watering and set them outdoors during the day. Bring them inside at night. Continue this for three to four days. If the temperature drops below 50 degrees F, take the plants inside. After four days, allow the plants to be outside all day and night. After about a week or two, the plants should be hardened off and ready to be transplanted with a minimum of shock.

Some annuals will produce hundreds of seedlings from last year's flowers. Look for "volunteers" of **cosmos, cleome, impatiens, mel-**

ampodium, silk flower, vinca, and others. *Thin out* the seedlings or *transplant* them to other parts of your garden.

As you remove cool-loving **larkspurs,** shake the plant over the soil to scatter seeds. Alternatively, shake the seeds over a sheet of newspaper, collect them, and sow them next fall.

In the Coastal Plain and warmer parts of the Piedmont, other cool-season annuals can be removed to make room for warm-season annuals.

Watering

Keep transplants well watered and mulched to help them get settled in before summer's heat and humidity arrives.

Fertilizing

If you fertilized at planting with a slow-release fertilizer, you may not have to fertilize until mid-summer or later, depending on the fertilizer brand and formulation. Follow the label directions to learn the desired amount and frequency of application. Fast-release fertilizers can be applied every four to six weeks during the growing season. Plants can absorb liquid fertilizers through their leaves and roots, and they will have to be applied more frequently (typically, every two weeks).

Pruning

Prune or shear **alyssum** and **lobelia** after blooming—this will make them look neater and encourage them to produce more flowers. *Remove* spent flowers from **snap-**

dragons for another crop of flowers. The blooms will not be as large, but they will provide garden color.

Pest Control

Insects: Watch out for aphids and whiteflies on **China aster, impatiens,** and others. See the Pest Appendix on p. 363 and 365 for descriptions and controls.

Weeds: See p. 43 for controls.

Diseases: Damping-off can still be a problem on indoor seedlings. *Use sterile seed-starting medium and avoid overwatering.*

Gray mold is a fungus that commonly attacks **geraniums,** covering the flowers with a fuzzy grayish mold. It often infects dead or dying tissues first, and then spreads into living tissue such as leaves, stems, and flowers. Cool, damp weather favors the development and spread of this disease. *Remove spent flowers, dying leaves, and other dead tissues. Use fungicides according to label directions.*

Helpful Hint

If you want to plant your annuals on a square spacing, where each plant is spaced an equal distance from one another, refer to the square spacing chart on p. 321 in Vines and Ground Covers, March Helpful Hint. For more uniform beds, use a triangular spacing instead of a straight row or a rectangular grid. Triangular spacing requires more plants per square foot, but the resulting effect will be more attractive than plants placed in rows. To determine the number of plants needed for a given area, use the following formula: **Area of bed in square feet ×　Spacing Multiplier = Number of plants needed.** See the March Helpful Hint, Vines and Ground Covers, p. 321 for an example.

Square

Triangle

Triangular Spacing

In-row Spacing (inches)	Spacing Multiplier (# of plants needed per 1 sq. ft.)
4	10.4
6	4.6
8	2.6
10	1.7
12	1.2
14	0.8
16	0.7
18	0.5
24	0.3

Planning

Too busy to enjoy your garden during the daylight hours? Then plan to create an "evening garden" with annuals that look their best at twilight. Evening flowers open at night or release fragrance at night to attract night-flying pollinators such as moths. One of the more familiar night-blooming annuals is **flowering tobacco (*Nicotiana alata*).** Petunias open by day and release their scent at night. Try the varieties '**Celebrity White**', '**Ultra White**', or '**Apollo.**'

Other night-blooming annuals to consider are the **moonflower vine (*Ipomoea alba*),** angel's trumpet (*Datura inoxia*), **night phlox (*Zaluzianskya capensis*),** and **night-scented stock (*Matthiola longipetala*).** For a more comprehensive list, read *The Evening Garden: Flowers and Fragrance from Dusk till Dawn* by Asheville garden writer Peter Loewer (Macmillan, 1993).

Planting

Plant warm-season annuals for summer color. Set out those you started indoors. Continue to plant **zinnia** seed at intervals to have cut flowers until frost.

Overplant bulb beds with annuals using seeds or transplants. Take care to avoid injuring the bulbs when planting.

Although cool-season annuals such as **pansies** and **violas** may still be flowering, the heat will make them stretch and get leggy. *Pull them out* and replace them with heat-loving summer annuals such as **African daisy, ageratum, celosia, cockscomb, marigold, pentas, vinca or Madagascar periwinkle, petunia, portulaca, salvia,** and **zinnia** for sunny areas. **Geraniums** and **New Guinea impatiens** are excellent if you have afternoon shade. For shady areas, use **begonias, coleus,** and **impatiens.**

Grow your own dried flowers. Start seeds of **statice, globe amaranth, strawflowers,** and other everlastings to provide for this year's arrangements.

Care for Your Annuals

Thin out direct-seeded annuals to the correct spacing.

To make room for warm-season annuals, Mountain gardeners can remove cool-season annuals when they begin to decline.

Although plant breeders have developed compact, sturdy varieties that require no support, other tall-growing types need support for protection from buffeting winds and rain. See May, Care for Your Perennials, p. 208 for techniques.

Pruning

To promote bushy growth, *pinch back* annuals when 4 to 6 inches high:

- *Pinch out* the shoot tips of **marigolds, petunias, salvias,** and **zinnias.**

- *Pinch* the shoot tips of **cosmos** to encourage branching. If unpinched, the stems may require staking to keep them upright.

- *Shear* **alyssum** and **lobelia** after flowering.

- *Remove* the spent flowers of **sweet william.** It may flower for two or three years, although it will become progressively less vigorous with age.

- *Remove* the yellow flowers of **dusty miller** to keep the leaves looking good throughout the growing season. If the plant gets leggy, cut it back to about half its height to encourage branching and denser growth.

Fertilizing

Continue to make applications of a fast-release fertilizer every four to six weeks if necessary. Follow the label instructions. *Water* the fertilizer in to make it available to the plants.

When reworking flower beds, use a slow-release fertilizer, especially in sandy soils. The nutrients are released over an extended period, perhaps three or four months, depending on the product. Use as recommended on the label.

Watering

Newly set transplants should not be allowed to dry out. Keep the leaves dry: extended periods of wetness on the leaves promotes the growth and spread of diseases.

Pest Control

Insects and mites: Aphids, spider mites, whiteflies, snails, and slugs can be a problem. See p. 366 for descriptions and controls of snails and slugs.

Cutworms: Watch out for cutworms, which feed on plant stems near the soil surface. In their wake

Helpful Hint

Mountain gardeners in the higher elevations faced with a short growing season of fourteen or fifteen weeks (from late May to mid-September) can direct-seed annuals in the garden as an inexpensive way of obtaining a lot of plants; this approach sacrifices early flowering, however, so you'll have to be selective.

Start in early spring as soon as the soil is dry enough to work by sowing **ageratum, bachelor's buttons, shirley poppy, sweet alyssum,** and **sweet pea.** They will flower within eight to ten weeks of sowing.

Then there are annuals that are best sown only after the danger of frost is passed. These can be expected to flower in eight weeks or less: **cosmos, French marigolds, nasturtiums, nicotiana ('Domino' and 'Nikki' series), salvias (***S. coccinia*** and ***S. splendens***),** and **dwarf sunflowers.**

Finally, raise transplants indoors or purchase them from garden centers to double your season of bloom: you will be setting out plants that are already laden with flower buds. Let nurseries grow the **geraniums, petunias,** and **dwarf snapdragons** that require three to four months to reach market size. At home, concentrate on **cosmos, zinnias,** and **marigolds,** which need only a month or two of daily care.

they leave the fallen stems gnawed off at the base. They feed at night, so use your flashlight to inspect the seedlings at night. Handpick them when you see them. To control cutworms, till up the soil thoroughly before planting. Protect the transplants with a stiff paper collar made out of a paper cup with the bottom cut out and pushed 1 to 2 inches deep into the ground and about 1 to 2 inches high. Or create a collar with strips of cardboard 2 inches wide by 8 inches long and stapled into a band which is placed around the plants. Press the collar about an inch into the soil. *BT* (*Bacillus thuringiensis*), neem extract, and other insecticides will also control cutworms.

Diseases: Avoid leaf spot diseases by watering your annuals from below, keeping the leaves dry. Proper spacing with plenty of air movement will also reduce fungal infections.

Planning

This is a good month to visit public gardens to view the tremendous variety of annuals on display. Of special note are the All-America Selections (AAS) display gardens that exhibit the most recent All-America Selections Winners. See p. 368–69 for a list of AAS display gardens in the Carolinas.

Planting

It's not too late to plant annuals. If your needs are great or your budget small, consider sowing seeds directly into prepared garden beds. **Cosmos, cleome, marigold, Mexican sunflower, portulaca, sunflower,** and **zinnia** are good choices for direct-sowing. Just remember to keep the seedbed moist during the first few weeks after establishment.

Stagger the plantings of **sunflowers** a couple of weeks apart so you can enjoy fresh blooms longer.

Care for Your Annuals

Pull up and discard **pansies** as the heat causes them to look ratty. Replace them with transplants or seeds of warm-season annuals.

Look for a crop of self-sown seedlings or "volunteers" from last year's **impatiens, cleome, annual vinca,** and other annuals. Look around for them and *transplant* them as you like.

With the approach of midsummer, **geraniums** may go into a slump and start to decline: flowers are sparse and the plant begins to look ragged. This condition is most likely due to high nighttime temperatures. This is a common problem with plants that prefer cooler summers, such as **tulips, rhubarb,** and **horseradish.**

High nighttime temperatures cause the plants to consume more carbohydrates through respiration than can be produced by photosynthesis during the day. If you are determined to keep your **geraniums,** here are some tips for late summer:

- *Prune* them back one-half to three-quarters the length of the stems. Make your cuts above a node on the stem.

- *Fertilize* each plant to encourage root and stem growth. This should encourage your geraniums to bloom until they are killed by freezing weather.

- Try growing the humidity- and heat-tolerant cultivars **'Ringo Rose', 'Freckles',** and **'Hollywood Star.'**

Pruning

Some annuals need to be jump-started either now or next month. *Trim back* **petunias** toward the end of the month to keep them bushy and encourage the formation of new flowers. After watering and fertilizing, they'll soon be full and attractive again. *Remove* spent blossoms on annual flowering plants as often as possible. This encourages further flowering rather than seed production. Seed collectors and those who want the dried seedpods for arrangements might ignore this rule. In most cases, however, seed collectors should delay until the end of the blooming season. Then the last few blooms may be kept for seed. Seeds of hybrids will not reproduce true from the parent plant.

Cosmos reseeds readily. *Shear* the spent blooms, leaving some so they will germinate and grow during the warm summer weather.

JUNE

Watering

Leach containers occasionally to remove any mineral salt deposits that accumulate from fertilizer and hard water. A crusty surface on the walls of clay pots or over the potting medium indicates a salt problem. To leach the container, allow the water to run until it drains freely from the bottom holes. Wait a few minutes, then repeat.

When watering, apply sufficient moisture to soak the soil deeply to the root zone.

Fertilizing

Annual beds can use a boost, especially where the soil is sandy or the season has been rainy. Apply slow-release fertilizer for maximum benefit with minimum effort. For a quick but brief response, *water* plants with a liquid fertilizer such as 20-20-20.

Do not overfertilize **cosmos** or **nasturtiums,** or you will run the risk of having a lot of leaves and few, if any, flowers.

Helpful Hints

- Self-cleaning flowers save time and work in the garden by dropping dead blooms, thus requiring no trimming or deadheading. Among them are **ageratum, cleome, gomphrena, impatiens, New Guinea impatiens, pentas, wax begonia,** and **narrowleaf zinnia.**

- Weed seedlings and annual seedlings look similar when they're emerging. Make weeding easier by sowing annual seeds in patterns such as rows or circles. You will be able to readily identify and remove any weed seedlings that are out of formation early enough that they won't compete with the flowering annuals.

Pest Control

Insects and mites: Be on the lookout for aphids, spider mites, snails and slugs.

Allow beneficial insects such as lady beetles to reduce aphid numbers. Aphids can sometimes be washed from plants with a strong stream of water. Many insecticides are available, including insecticidal soaps, horticultural oils, or neem. Apply according to label directions.

Diseases: Avoid overhead watering, and remove spent flowers and dead or dying leaves. Keeping plants clean will reduce the chance of infection.

Look for signs of powdery mildew on your garden **zinnias.** Infected leaves have a whitish-gray powder on both sides. Heavy infestations can cause the leaves to become curled and eventually yellow and die. *Remove* any infected plants and discard them. *Thin out* the bed to improve air movement. Fungicides can be applied when the symptoms appear, until they're gone. In the future, select varieties that are resistant to powdery mildew.

Weeds: *Handpull* or hoe out any weeds to prevent them from stealing water and nutrients from your annuals. Suppress their emergence with a layer of mulch.

Animals: Rabbits and deer can be a problem. Commercially available mammal repellents can be applied to or near your flowers. To make your own repellent, see Shrubs, October Animals on p. 277.

Planning

If you're going on vacation this month and will be leaving your garden for a week or more, make plans to have someone take care of your plants while you're away. To make things easier for the caregiver, group plants in containers together near a water source and out of the afternoon sun. Grouping them will help plants conserve water; shade will help reduce the need for water. There may be some pots that need more attention than others: use tiny colorful flags used by utility companies to flag the pots that need attention, or tie a bright ribbon around a few of the plants to remind your caregiver that these pots or beds need to be inspected more often than the others. *Before you go, water everything thoroughly, weed, and deadhead any spent flowers.*

Planting

Indoors: Seeds of hardy annuals that will bloom in the fall and winter can be started this month. They include **alyssum, calendula,** and **ornamental cabbage** and **kale.** Biennials that can be planted for transplanting later include **foxglove, money plant,** and **sweet william.** Coastal gardeners can wait until next month to start these seeds.

Outdoors: Look for empty spaces in the landscape and fill them with warm-season annuals. If you're planting among bulbs or perennials that have gone dormant and disappeared, such as **bleeding hearts,** inspect the soil carefully to avoid damaging the perennial's crown.

Cleome, cosmos, marigolds, sunflowers, and **zinnias** can still be planted or sown for bloom until frost. When the seedlings are about 2 inches tall, thin them where they're too crowded, or *transplant* them to other parts of the garden. Some quick-growing and -flowering annuals that can be planted now from seed include **cosmos, gomphrena, Klondyke, marigolds, Mexican sunflowers, dwarf sunflowers,** and **zinnia.** For the price of a few seeds, they will make a spectacular late-summer show in five to six weeks.

Care for Your Annuals

See August, p. 44.

Watering

To learn how to water efficiently, refer to the July Helpful Hint in Roses on p. 241.

Fertilizing

If you use a slow-release fertilizer, now is the time to make your second application of the season (your first application should have been incorporated into the bed at planting time). Fast-release fertilizers should be applied every month or six weeks throughout the growing season. *Water* afterwards to make the nutrients available to your plants.

Pruning

Continue to *deadhead* spent flowers and cut back leggy annuals such as **salvias** and **garden zinnias.** In addition to encouraging bushiness, it also leads to the production of more flowers.

Low-growing **marigolds** tend to get leggy and produce fewer blooms in midsummer, especially in the Piedmont and Coastal Plains. *Shear* them down to within 6 inches.

Some classes of **petunia** tend to "stretch" during the summer months with the onset of higher temperatures. Their long, slender stems produce few flowers. Pinching them back—removing an inch or two from the ends of the stems—repeatedly during the growing season will encourage branching below the "pinch," keeping them stocky and well endowed with blooms. If you took a hands-off approach for the first half of summer, then you need to prune them back now to encourage branching and flowering. Cut back the shoots to half their length. This will force the plant to produce shoots or branches from below the cut. These branches will produce flower buds. Practice "staggered pruning." Stagger your pruning by cutting back one-third of a bed or container (every third plant) each week. By the third week, the first group of pruned plants will be blooming again, assuring some color during the entire pruning period.

Impatiens tend to grow leggy in the South in response to the high nighttime temperatures. They may grow a third taller than their labeled height. Cut them back by one-third, or grow impatiens that cope with the high temperatures by maintaining their short habit. The **'Impulse' series** and the **'Super Elfin' series** resist growing gangly.

Pinch the tips of **coleus** every month or so to keep them dense and compact. *Pinch off* any flower stalks as they appear.

Cleomes often grow vertically with few flowering stalks. Snip off a few inches from the tip before it blooms. Two flowering stalks will

Helpful Hint

Cutting flowers is best done with sharp shears or a knife to avoid injury to the growing plant. You can buy a special pair of cutting scissors that holds the cut-off stem, allowing the removal to be a one-handed operation. A slanting cut exposes a larger absorbing surface to water. It also prevents the base of the stem from resting on the bottom of the vase, interfering with its water intake. Instead of the familiar cutting basket, carry a bucket of water to the garden for collecting blooms.

replace one. If pinched two or three times, the plant will be covered with flowers.

Hanging baskets of **portulaca** should be cut back every month to keep them full in the center of the basket. *Snip away* old blooms to keep the plants blooming until the first frost.

Shear **annual coreopsis** to encourage another round of flowering in the fall. Save some flowers to produce seed for next year.

Pest Control

Insects and mites: Aphids, spider mites, and whiteflies continue to be on the prowl this month. They can be washed from plants with a strong stream of water. Insecticidal soap, insecticides, and miticides will keep their numbers in check.

Watch out for Japanese beetles this month. The adults eat flowers and foliage. Thankfully, there's only one generation a year. See p. 363 for controls.

Diseases: Watch out for powdery mildew on **zinnias.** Pull out and *discard* infected plants. Reseed the vacant areas. In the future, select **zinnias** that are resistant to powdery mildew.

Weeds: Start pulling weeds out of the flower beds. If they get a foothold, weeds will be tough to control. Pull them out by hand or lightly hoe them.

Planning

The heat and humidity of August can be a time to reflect on the past season and update your garden journal or notebook. Over a glass of iced tea, jot down the names of annual plants that didn't perform as well as you would like. List any that performed better than you expected. Make a note of any insect or disease problems.

As you collect your thoughts, begin making plans for next year's garden. Avoid those varieties that didn't do well. Focus on experimenting with varieties that performed well in your garden or that you've noticed doing well in display gardens.

Planting

If you have any leftover seed, go ahead and make a final planting of **marigolds, zinnias,** and other fast-growing annuals. You can do this during the first week of August in the Piedmont and early next month in the Coastal Plains.

Sow seeds of cool-season annuals that will be transplanted to the garden this fall. Plant **calendula, snapdragons,** and **stock** from seed. Use a sterile seed-starting mix and plant them as described on page 30–31. Sow seeds into sterile soilless mix in individual pots, and

transplant seedlings to individual containers before they become too crowded. *Water* as needed, give them plenty of sun, and fertilize weekly with a liquid fertilizer.

The seeds of **cabbage** and **kale** should be sown about eight weeks before the first freeze. Keep them cool after they sprout and move them outside when night temperatures begin to cool down in early fall.

Take cuttings of favorite annuals, or sow seeds in pots for winter flowering indoors. The following bedding plants root easily, allowing you to preserve your favorite varieties for next year: **coleus, geraniums, impatiens,** and **wax begonias.** Here's how to root **coleus:**

1 Select a terminal shoot that's at least 3 inches long and has two or three nodes or buds that will open into new leaves.

2 *Place* the cutting in a small pot filled with a soilless mix, such as three parts perlite to one part peat moss.

3 Place the potted cutting in a plastic bag twist-tied off at the top, and move it to a warm location between 70 and 75 degrees Fahrenheit. The warmer the temperature, the faster the cuttings will root.

Roots will sprout within 10 days and the plants should be ready to transplant within two or three weeks.

Keep the cuttings in a cool location, ideally between 40 and 50 degrees Fahrenheit, and under cool white fluorescent lights for up to twelve hours a day.

Care for Your Annuals

Do not disturb the soil in your flower beds during hot, dry August days. Loosening the soil through cultivation can damage surface roots and increase water loss from the soil. After you break up the soil around them, plants often look much worse.

Inspect the mulch in flower beds. If wind, rain, and natural decay have reduced its thickness to an inch or less, apply more mulch to raise the level to 2 to 3 inches. Apply a 2- to 3-inch layer of compost, pine straw, pine bark, or shredded wood between the plants, but only about 1/2 inch around the bases of the plants.

If the cutting garden looks bedraggled, clear out the annuals that have finished blooming or are overgrown.

Many plants in the flower border will make excellent houseplants this winter. Refer to the August Planting (p. 130) in the Houseplants chapter to see how to bring them indoors so they can continue flowering during the fall months and into early winter.

Watering

Check the soil in flower beds to determine if you need to water. *Water* deeply to wet the entire root zone of the plants.

Container-grown flowers can dry out quickly, especially when located in full sun. Feel the soil in containers at least once a day to check for moisture. When water is necessary, apply it long enough so that it runs out of the drainage holes. Keep in mind that clay pots, which allow water to be lost to evaporation, will need to be watered more often than plastic pots. Also, small pots will dry out faster than large planters.

Check on the water needs of hanging baskets daily in the summer. Wind and sun dry them much more quickly than plants in other kinds of containers.

Fertilizing

If they haven't been fertilized in over six weeks, leggy plants that were cut back will benefit from a light feeding with a fast-release fertilizer. Fertilize container-grown annuals with a water-soluble fertilizer such as 20-20-20, following label directions. *Water* the soil first, then apply the fertilizer.

Pruning

Early this month, pinch back fall-planted **snapdragons** to produce bushier plants. *Deadhead* any faded flowers or seedpods from **snapdragons** that survived the summer; this will encourage another round of flowers this fall.

Pest Control

Insects and other pests: Be on the lookout for aphids and spider mites. Plants infested by spider mites have faded, stippled leaves. *Remove* these pests with a strong spray of water. Resort to a pesticide if their numbers are high and damage is great. If these plants are going to be removed and replaced by cool-season annuals, spraying with a pesticide may be unnecessary.

Helpful Hint

When selecting flowers for dried arrangements, be mindful that bright-yellow, orange, pink, and blue flowers preserve their colors best. Red and purple petals become darker and less attractive, while white flowers usually fade to a buff or tan color.

Nematodes may threaten your plants as well. See July Pest Control in the Roses chapter (p. 240) for more information.

Diseases: Fungal leaf spots, powdery mildew, and other diseases could be afflicting your warm-season annuals. Evaluate the extent of damage to determine if a fungicide application is necessary. Heavily infested plants should be removed and discarded. Avoid wetting the leaves when watering.

Weeds: Control weeds by hand-pulling and maintaining a shallow layer of mulch. Prevent weeds from going to seed by removing the flowers. Keeping the beds weed-free will also remove overwintering sites for spider mites.

Planning

Plan to obtain seeds or transplants early this month for fall planting. Let your journal be your guide. It should document the annuals that performed well in your garden, or those that you've admired during your travels. Try your hand at annuals mentioned in conversation with friends and acquaintances.

Be adventurous: experiment with something new. For example, Jenks Farmer, Curator of Botanical Gardens at Riverbanks Zoological Park and Botanical Gardens in Columbia, South Carolina, has added to the palette of winter annuals with the following colorful vegetables: **purple mustard** (*Brassica juncea rugosa* 'Miike Giant' and 'Red Giant'), **mizuna** (*Brassica rapa nipposinica*), **Japanese mustard-spinach** (*Brassica rapa peviridis*), **tatsoi** or **flat pak choi** (*Brassica rapa* var. *rosularis*), and **arugula** or **roquette** (*Eruca sativa*). These minimum-care greens can be terrific fall and winter bedding plants that make a great foil for **pansies** and **calendulas.**

Planting

Plant seeds of **California, Iceland,** and **shirley poppies:**

1 Use a small jar with two or three small nail holes in the lid.

2 *Shake* seeds out where you want them.

3 Create a shallow V-shaped trench and *sow* seeds in the trench.

4 *Cover* the seed very lightly with soil.

Mountain gardeners can set out **calendulas, pansies,** and **violas** when they become available at local nurseries. Start setting out **ornamental kale** and **cabbage** for winter color. You will have to pull out some robust-looking annuals now or early next month to make room for them. In the warmer areas of zone 8, **petunias,** especially the **species petunia** (*P. integrifolia*) and the "supertunias" in the **Wave series,** can generally be left in place. They usually bounce back unperturbed after a hard freeze, and continue flowering.

Sowing seeds of hardy annuals (such as **calendula, calliopsis, sweet alyssum, larkspur,** and **pinks**) now will give the seedlings time to get established and develop good root systems before the coldest part of winter. This gives them a head start on growth and flowering next spring.

Care for Your Annuals

Start taking cuttings of your annual plants to bring indoors to carry through the winter. **Coleus, geranium, impatiens, wax begonia,** and others do best when stem cuttings are rooted and kept in pots indoors during cold weather. Be sure to place pots where they receive plenty of light and cool temperatures. *Root* some cuttings of **bedding geraniums** by following these steps:

1 Use a sharp knife or razor blade to take 3- to 4-inch cuttings of terminal growth. Make an angled cut just below a node (the point where the leaf joins the stem). *Remove* the lowest leaf or two.

2 *Dip* the cut end into rooting hormone suited for herbaceous plants (0.1 percent indolebutyric acid or IBA).

3 *Fill* a small pot with equal parts peat moss and perlite.

4 Use a pencil to poke a hole in the potting medium before inserting the cutting. This will prevent the rooting powder from being scraped off.

5 When you have stuck in all the cuttings, *water* them well and place the pots in a plastic bags that are closed at the top with a twist-tie.

Set the pots in a bright location, but not direct sunlight. Rooting should occur in two to three weeks. When the cuttings have rooted, remove the pots from the bag and move them into direct sunlight in a cool room between 55 and 65 degrees Fahrenheit. You will end up with bushier, more floriferous geraniums if you pinch each of these young plants back at least once.

Helpful Hint

This is the ideal time for taking soil samples to be tested by your cooperative extension service office. Pick up soil boxes and forms at the office, garden centers, or "feed'n seed" stores. Follow directions carefully. Identify each sample by what is to be grown in that area so the lab can offer you specific recommendations for the particular grass, flower, or shrub. Results should be available in time for you to take any corrective measures this fall and early winter.

Fertilizing

Apply a slow-release fertilizer when planting cool-season annuals.

Pruning

Trim back leggy annuals and continue removing faded flowers to encourage more blooms.

Watering

Fall is the driest season in the Carolinas. Keep newly-set-out transplants well watered to help them establish quickly.

Pest Control

Diseases: Discouraged by powdery mildew on your **zinnias?** This late in the season, fungicides may not be warranted. **Zinnias** will soon be removed to make way for cool-season annuals. Make a note in your gardening journal to select mildew-resistant zinnias next year.

Insects: Check for evidence of snails and slugs. Set out baits or traps for them as the weather turns cooler and wetter.

Weeds: Do not turn your back on the weeds in your flower beds. Summer annual weeds like crabgrass and goosegrass have matured and are going to seed. Winter annual weeds like annual bluegrass, chickweed, and Carolina geranium are germinating. Hoe them out or *handpull* them now.

Planning

With the onset of cooler temperatures, begin planning new beds or converting the beds to new plantings of perennials or shrubs. Refer to your journal to guide your decisions to expand your beds, reduce them, or add different kinds of plants. Start making lists of the plants you will need for these beds. You will be ready when catalogs begin to arrive in the next couple of months.

To help you design new beds, use a garden hose to outline the shape. Enrich the soil with organic matter. Take a soil sample and send it in for testing.

Planting

In the Piedmont and Coastal Plains, sow seeds of **calliopsis, foxglove, Johnny-jump-ups, larkspur, money plant, stock,** and **shirley, Iceland,** and **California poppies** directly into well-prepared garden soil before the first expected freeze. These plants need cool temperatures to germinate. Fall sowing tends to produce stronger plants than seeds sown in early spring. Leave the soil surface bare, or use a very light mulch.

When garden centers and nurseries have these plants available, plant ornamental **cabbage** and **kale, pansies,** and **violas** to help them get established quickly before cold weather sets in. Allow at least six weeks before the first expected freeze. Mulch **pansies** in the Mountains after the ground freezes. Now is also a good time to set out **calendula, dianthus, sweet william, snapdragons, stock,** and **sweet alyssum** before the night temperatures drop consistently below 40 degrees F.

Care for Your Annuals

Pentas, or **Egyptian star cluster,** long grown as a houseplant in zone 10, has become popular as a heat- and drought-tolerant outdoor annual. Pentas grows 2 to 3 feet high and produces 4-inch flat-topped clusters of small, star-shaped flowers in white, pink, lilac, or red all summer long. Because plants will be killed by freezing temperatures, make cuttings in the fall by taking 3- to 4-inch stem cuttings of non-flowering shoots just below a leaf. Follow the same rooting procedure that was described for geraniums on p. 46 (September Planting). When rooting occurs—usually after one month—uncover the new plant and grow it indoors as a houseplant. Next year, plant it outside after the last freeze in spring.

Pot up and bring some **geraniums** (*Pelargonium × hortorum*) indoors for the winter before the first frost. In February you will be able to take cuttings to produce a bevy of new plants for next year's garden. If you decide to do this, cut back the plant now so it will have produced a number of new shoots for cutting by January.

You can also shake the soil off the geraniums' roots and hang them upside-down with twine, or in a paper bag in a cool, dry location such as a crawl space or basement. This old-fashioned method of storing **geraniums** is possible because their thick, fleshy stems allow them to survive during periods of drought. The location must remain above freezing yet be cool and moist enough to avoid excessive dehydration of the bare roots. Periodic moistening of the roots may be necessary. Light is neither necessary nor desirable, provided the temperature is cool enough.

Despite this drastic treatment, the **geraniums** can be repotted in the spring, their tops cut back by half or two-thirds, and returned to bright light and regular watering. New roots will emerge from the green stems below the soil surface, new shoots above. The ready availability each spring of new **geranium** plants at nurseries and garden centers has made this practice much less common than it once was.

Care for Your Annuals

Piedmont and Coastal Plain gardeners can pull up frost-tender plants like **marigolds, impatiens,** and **zinnias** toward the end of the month before the first expected freeze. Although it may be disconcerting to lift up completely healthy plants, you need the space to plant cool-season annuals, like **pansies,** in their place. The cool-season annuals will need the time to get settled in before temperatures begin to cool down.

Fertilizing

Use a slow-release fertilizer at planting time to lightly fertilize hardy annuals such as **calendulas, pansies,** and **sweet alyssums.** This will encourage establishment and flowering.

Pruning

Deadhead spent flowers from **pansies** planted last month.

Watering

Keep an eye on the watering needs of your annuals, especially emerging seedlings and newly-set-out transplants. *Check* the soil for moisture; don't wait until the plants begin to wilt. Rake up fallen pine needles and use them for mulch.

Pest Control

Insects and mites: Inspect the annuals you brought inside for the winter. Whiteflies and spider mites could have hitchhiked their way inside. Keep the plants quarantined, and control pests before you introduce them to your other indoor plants. Insecticidal soap applied to the upper and lower leaf surfaces will control these pests. If the plant is not listed on the label, you may have to test a small area on your plant for injury. It may take seven to ten days to see if any damage occurs. If your plant shows sensitivity, rinse the soap off once the whiteflies and spider mites are killed.

Helpful Hints

Collect seeds of annuals such as **cleome, cosmos, flowering tobacco, sunflower,** and **zinnias** for next year. Keep the seeds in an envelope and put them in a jar or film canister in the refrigerator during the winter months. Hybrid varieties probably won't come back true-to-type. Other open-pollinated types, however, will reproduce faithfully. The offspring may come in different heights and colors from the original parents. Who knows? You may get some interesting surprises!

Diseases: Leaf spots may be a problem on **zinnias** and other warm-season annuals. Since they're going to be removed, or killed by impending cold temperatures, a fungicide may not be necessary. Any heavily infected plants can be pulled out immediately.

Weeds: See September, p. 47.

Planning

Garden tools can add up to a large investment. Make plans this month to clean them off and repair or replace any broken ones. As soon as seed flats and pots are emptied of fall transplants, wash and sterilize them with a 10-percent bleach solution (1 part bleach to 9 parts water) before storing them so they'll be ready in the spring.

This is also a good month to think about building a cold frame, which is sort of like a halfway house for seedlings as they make their way from the windowsill or light table to the outdoors. The cold frame is basically a bottomless box, made of wood, stone, or brick, with a transparent or translucent cover. It's like a miniature unheated greenhouse outdoors.

Cold frames are typically rectangular in shape, 3 by 6 feet or so. The back of the cold frame should face north, and should be 18 to 30 inches high. The front should be slightly lower, between 12 and 24 inches to allow enough headroom for the plants inside. *Tilt* the cover to the south by sloping the sides about 1 inch per foot. More adventurous gardeners can even add an automatic opener to the cover. These devices lift the cover automatically as the temperature rises during the day, and gradually close it with the falling evening temperatures.

Planting

Set out **forget-me-nots, pansies, pinks, snapdragons, sweet william, violas,** and other hardy plants for flowers and leaves in winter and early spring.

If you didn't sow them last month, Piedmont and Coastal Plains gardeners can go ahead and sow the seeds of **calliopsis, foxglove, johnny-jump-ups, larkspur, money plant, stock,** and **shirley, Iceland,** and **California poppies.**

Care for Your Annuals

Clean up the garden. Chop up the plants and compost them. Add organic matter to beds. Either shred leaves and use them as mulch, or compost them to improve soil. *Cover* the garden with mulch to prevent soil loss.

Move containers holding live plants to a protected spot, if possible. Protect the roots by covering the soil and the container with a thick layer of straw or leaves. *Check* the moisture level of the pots every few weeks, and *water* if needed. Annuals overwintered indoors should be kept in a cool location in bright light.

Watering

If the month is dry, *water* newly planted transplants.

Fertilizing

If you didn't incorporate a slow-release fertilizer last month at planting, lightly fertilize with a liquid fertilizer such as 20-20-20 now.

Pest Control

Weeds: See September.

Planning

There's not much to be done with annuals this month, and you must not expect much from them—they expect little from you. If you've kept up with the autumn chores outdoors and your green thumb still itches, swing your focus to your houseplants. Review your journal and draw some conclusions. Could you have grouped your annuals better? Remember the rule of threes: three plants, each set at the point of a triangle, grow together to multiply their impact. Could you have streamlined the care process? Plants with similar growing needs (sun, water, feeding, etc.) thrive better and are easier to care for if grouped together. Incorporate these principles in your design for next year's beds. Have a plan ready before the seed catalog bombardment starts. Steel yourself to resist the tugging and pulling of the seed merchants that take you out of your plan. And if you find a way to do this, please tell me!

Planting

Hardy cool-season annual transplants may still be set out in the Coastal Plain, particularly near the coast.

Care for Your Annuals

Pansies and other winter annuals can be pushed out of the ground in the winter in the colder Mountains and Piedmont. This "frost-heaving" (when the freezing and thawing of the soil lifts plants out of the ground and damages roots) can be reduced by mulching. Cut up your Christmas tree and lay some of the branches over flower beds to insulate the soil.

Watering

Water cool-season annuals after fertilizing. Newly planted transplants should be watered more often to speed up establishment.

Fertilizing

Lightly *fertilize* winter annuals such as **pansies** and **ornamental cabbage** and **kale** between bouts of cold weather. If you didn't fertilize last month and the weather is mild, apply a complete fertilizer such as 10-10-10 in the absence of a soil test.

Helpful Hint

A small envelope of seeds collected from your garden makes a thoughtful gift to enclose in your holiday cards. **Label** the envelope with the collection date and the name of the flower.

Bulbs, Corms, Rhizomes and Tubers

This group deserves a place in your garden. When you think of easy-care, no-fuss-no-muss plantings, think of bulbs. Their wide range of sizes and colors allows them to fit in any corner of the garden.

Technically, they're geophytes—literally "earth plants." Geophytes contain in their subterranean storage structures everything needed to sprout and flower. Their leaves produce food that recharges the bulb for the next cycle.

They can be divided into six types: true bulbs, corms, rhizomes, tubers, tuberous roots, and enlarged hypocotyls. Collectively, they're called bulbs. Knowing something about the different types helps with planting and propagating them.

Bulbs are also traditionally classed by blooming period: *Spring/ early-summer-flowering bulbs,* the so-called Dutch bulbs, are planted in the fall. Most are completely hardy in the Carolinas. *Summer/fall-flowering bulbs* include both hardy and tender bulbs that are planted in the spring, summer, or fall.

Some bulbs bloom through late fall and winter in the Carolinas. Depending on your location, you can select some bulbs to provide a colorful outdoor display the year round. But if winter temperatures won't let you, consider "forcing" bulbs into bloom indoors.

Planning and Preparing the Bulb Garden

Location is the key to successful bulb culture. Plan with the following two factors in mind.

Soil: Good drainage is a must. Test the drainage before planting. Fill a foot-deep hole with water. Next day, fill it again. If that refill drains away in less than ten hours, most bulbs will thrive there. If drainage is a problem, consider creating a raised bed—or add organic matter such as composted yard trimmings or composted pine bark to improve drainage. In sandy soils that lose water too fast, add organic matter. Mix no less than 2 inches to a depth of 8 to 12 inches. If you want, you can add organic matter until it makes up half the soil volume. Some bulbs thrive in waterlogged soil (sometimes known as "hog wallows"), but choices are limited. Try moisture-loving bulbs such as **canna, summer snowflake** (*Leucojum aestivum*), **Dutch iris** (*I. × hollandica*), **rain lily** (*Zephyranthes*), **crinum** (*Crinum*), and **spider lily** (*Hymenocallis*).

Light: Most spring-flowering bulbs prefer light shade to full sunshine. Pick a location that offers at least six hours of direct sunlight a day. It doesn't have to be full sun year-round. A spot near deciduous trees that gets sunlight before the trees leaf out is perfect for spring bulbs. A few bulbs that tolerate partial shade are **crocus, daffodils, squill, and wood hyacinths.** Summer-flowering bulbs are not so fastidious about light. Be mindful that inadequate light usually results in poor flowering. Too much light during the summer months, however, can bleach the flowers and leaves of some bulbs.

Planting

Plant spring- and early-summer-flowering bulbs in the fall to satisfy their cold requirement and to develop a good root system by bloom time. That cold requirement ranges from six to sixteen weeks, depending on the species or cultivar. Delay planting until the soil temperature at planting depth is below

Bulbs, Corms, Rhizomes and Tubers

True bulbs include **common onions, tulips, daffodils, Dutch iris, hyacinths,** and others. On the bottom of the egg-shaped bulb is a basal plate which gives rise to roots. The bulb itself is comprised of scales—fleshy modified leaves which store food and enclose the flower bud. Some bulbs, like **tulips,** have tightly packed scales protected by a dry papery "skin" or tunic. Others, such as **crown imperial (*Fritillaria*)** and **lily (*Lilium*),** lack a protective covering. They're easily damaged or dried out when they're out of the ground. **Plant** true bulbs with the broader, root-forming end facing down. Lift them, when necessary, after their leaves turn brown and die back. While they are out of the ground, look for the new bulblets attached to the basal plate. Some types, such as **lilies,** produce bulblets underground and small above-ground bulbils in the joints of their leaves. **Replant** them immediately in the garden, or pot them for nurturing in a cold frame.

True Bulb

Corms are like bulbs, but they're more flattened and have "eyes" from which the topgrowth emerges. Each year a new corm forms atop the old one. Tiny corms known as cormels form around the base of the parent corm, as with **crocus, freesia,** or **gladiolus,** or in long chains as with **crocosmia. Plant** corms with the wide side facing down and the "eyes," or buds, looking up.

Tubers. The best-known tuber is the **potato.** In flower beds, **caladiums** are a good example of tubers. Growth buds, or "eyes," scattered over the surface give rise to both roots and shoots. **Plant** them with the eyes up.

Tuberous roots. Dahlias and **sweet potatoes** grow from tuberous roots, as do **anemone** and **ranunculus.** Buds form only on the crowns, and roots grow from the opposite end. Lay them horizontally when planting. **Rhizomes** grow horizontally, usually below the soil surface. Roots grow from the underside and shoots develop from buds on the top and sides, usually near the tip. **Calla lily, canna,** certain species of **iris,** and **lily-of-the-valley** are examples.

Hypocotyls. Cyclamen and **tuberous begonias** store food in thickened stems that grow larger every year. It is a bit difficult to discern which end is up. On **tuberous begonias,** look for crater-like markings where the stem once sprouted—that's the top. The bottom should show traces of spiny roots. **Cyclamen** has a concave side that should be planted facing up.

Bulbs, Corms, Rhizomes and Tubers

60 degrees Fahrenheit. This usually occurs around the time of the first expected freeze, or when trees begin to lose their leaves. In the Carolinas, October is the preferred planting time in zone 6, November through early December in zones 7 and 8a, and mid- to late December for South Carolina Coastal gardeners in zone 8b.

Summer- and fall-flowering bulbs except for **autumn crocus** or **meadow saffron** (*Colchicum autumnale*) and **fall-blooming crocuses** (*Crocus niveus, C. speciosus*, and others) should be planted in the spring after the last expected freeze. Refer to the Planting Chart (p. 57) for specific planting times for bulbs that don't follow the rule.

Here's how to plant the bulbs: *Arrange* the bulbs on the surface of the bed before you plant them individually. Set them at the right depth. In general, plant small bulbs (1 inch in height) in holes 3 inches deep, and larger bulbs in holes 6 inches deep. *Space* small bulbs 1 to 2 inches apart, medium-sized bulbs about 3 inches apart, and large bulbs 4 to 6 inches. The Planting Chart (p. 56–57) has more specific information. When in doubt, follow this simple rule of thumb: *Plant at a depth two times the bulb height, measured from the base to the "nose" or top of the bulb.*

For large beds, an easy method is to excavate the bed to the right depth and set the bulbs at the right spacing. Then just fill in with soil. For smaller areas among other plants or with fewer bulbs, cultivate as large an area as possible, then *dig* each hole with a trowel or bulb planter. To finish up, press the soil firmly around the bulbs. *Water* thoroughly to settle the soil and *cover* with 2 or 3 inches of mulch. For large beds, an easy method is to excavate the bed to the right depth and set the bulbs at the right spacing. Then just fill in with soil. For smaller areas among other plants or with fewer bulbs, cultivate as large an area as possible, then *dig* each hole with a trowel or bulb planter. Finish up by pressing the soil firmly around the bulbs. *Water* thoroughly to settle the soil, and *cover* with 2 or 3 inches of mulch.

Care for Your Bulbs

Nearly all bulbs eventually become overcrowded. Clumps must be divided and bulbs replanted. Some large producers of bulblets require division every two or three years. Others can remain in place for years. At the end of their growth cycle when their leaves turn brown and wither, gently *lift* the bulbs without damaging them and pull them apart. Corms can also be divided this way.

Cut rhizomes and tubers into sections, either at the end of their growing season or just as it begins. Make sure each division contains at least one eye. Replanted, each will produce a new plant. Tuberous roots such as **dahlia** can be split apart. Each division should have a small piece of crown tissue attached. After dividing, either *replant* them right away or store them for planting later in the season.

Cut rhizomes and tubers into sections, either at the end of their growing season or just as it begins. Make sure each division contains at least one eye to produce a new plant.

Watering

Spring-flowering bulbs usually receive enough moisture from natural rainfall, so watering is usually unnecessary. Summer-flowering bulbs, however, may have to be watered weekly during dry spells while they're actively growing. *Water deeply* to soak the ground thoroughly.

Covering with a 2- to 3-inch layer of mulch will conserve moisture. Compost, bark, pine needles, and many other materials are suitable.

Bulbs, Corms, Rhizomes and Tubers

Fertilizing

If the plants look robust and are growing in a well-prepared, fertile site, fertilizing may be unnecessary.

You can, however, encourage spring-flowering bulbs to bloom resplendently in subsequent years with a shot of a complete fertilizer in the fall. Use a slow-release nitrogen fertilizer to reduce the likelihood of fertilizer burn. Follow the manufacturer's recommendations. Fast-release plant food works, too, but you'll need to apply again in the spring when 1 or 2 inches of the shoots show.

Do not fertilize spring-flowering bulbs when they're blooming or immediately after they flower. At these times the nitrogen in the fertilizer can encourage the development of the fungal disease Fusarium. You can recognize it by the sour smell it gives to rotting bulbs.

Feed summer-flowering bulbs with a slow-release fertilizer when the shoots appear in the spring. Depending on the formulation, a second application may be needed in mid- to late summer. Follow the manufacturer's directions.

Water-in the fertilizer so that it becomes available to the plant.

Pest Control

Diseases: Good gardening practices will thwart many diseases. Prepare a well-drained, fertile bed, and plant healthy bulbs, discarding any diseased or damaged ones. Bulb rot, gray mold or botrytis, and powdery mildew are a few of the common diseases that may afflict bulbs. *Remove* any heavily infected leaves or dig out the bulbs.

Insects and mites: Aphids, thrips, and spider mites are the most common bulb pests. Watch for them and learn to identify them. As you visit your garden, take a moment to examine the leaves and flowers. Try to accept less-than-perfect-looking leaves and flowers.

When trouble strikes, turn to non-chemical controls first. Insects such as aphids can be hosed off with a strong spray of water. Sometimes it is necessary to resort to more potent measures such as insecticidal soap and neem (a botanical insecticide extracted from the tropical neem tree) to control soft-bodied insects such as aphids and spider mites.

You may have to occasionally resort to the more toxic pesticides, especially when you feel the damage is more than you or your bulbs can tolerate. Consider spot-treating heavily infested plants instead of making a blanket application that can destroy beneficial insects such as ladybugs, predatory mites, and green lacewings. Use recommended pesticides and apply according to label directions.

Animals: Voles, rabbits, and deer relish many kinds of flower bulbs such as **crocuses** and **tulips.** To protect bulbs from voles, *cover* the bulbs with heavy wire mesh screening that allows the shoots to grow through. Dig down about 10 to 12 inches and spread the 1/2-inch mesh across the bottom, up the sides, and over the top. A simpler technique that offers less protection is to spread a handful of sharp crushed pea-sized gravel around the bulbs at planting.

Carolina Bulbs

Winter/Spring-Flowering

Common Name (Botanical Name)	Type of Bulb	Hardiness Zones	Light Needs	Planting Season	Planting Depth to Top of Bulb (inches)	Spacing Between Bulbs (inches)
Amaryllis (*Hippeastrum* spp.)	Bulb	7 to 10	Sun to partial shade	Fall/Spring	1	12 to 15
Crocus (*Crocus* spp. and hybrids)	Corm	4 to 8	Sun to partial shade	Fall	4	2 to 6
Daffodil (*Narcissus* spp. and hybrids)	Bulb	5 to 9 (depends on classification and cultivar)	Sun to full shade	Fall	6 (large bulbs) 4 (small bulbs)	6 to 8 4 to 6
Glory-of-the-snow (*Chionodoxa luciliae*)	Bulb	4 to 7	Sun to partial shade	Fall	4	1 to 3
Grape hyacinth (*Muscari botryoides*)	Bulb	4 to 8	Sun to partial shade	Fall	2	2 to 4
Hyacinth (*Hyacinthus orientalis*)	Bulb	3 to 6	Sun to partial shade	Fall	6	4 to 6
Iris (*Iris reticulata*)	Bulb	4 to 8	Sun to partial shade	Fall	4	4 to 6
Ornamental onion (*Allium* spp.)	Bulb	4 to 8	Sun to partial shade	Fall	6 (large bulbs) 4 (small bulbs)	12 to 18 (large) 4 to 6 (small)
Snowdrop (*Galanthus nivalis*)	Bulb	4 to 7	Sun to partial shade	Fall	4	2 to 4
Spring snowflake (*Leucojum vernum*)	Bulb	3 to 9	Sun to shade	Fall	3	4
Tulip (*Tulipa* spp. and hybrids)	Bulb	3 to 8	Sun to partial shade	Fall	5 to 8	4 to 6

Carolina Bulbs

Summer/Fall Interest (Flowers and/or Foliage)

Common Name (Botanical Name)	Type of Bulb	Hardiness Zones	Light Needs	Planting Season	Planting Depth to Top of Bulb (inches)	Spacing Between Bulbs (inches)
Autumn crocus (*Crocus* spp.)	Corm	5 to 9 (depends on species)	Sun	Late summer	4	2 to 6
Autumn crocus or Meadow saffron (*Colchicum autumnale*)	Corm	4 to 7	Sun to partial shade	Summer or early fall	4	6 to 9
Caladium (*Caladium bicolor*)	Tuber	10 to 11	Partial shade	Spring	1	12 to 18
Canna (*Canna × generalis* and other species)	Rhizome	7 to 10	Sun	Spring	Just covered with soil	15 to 18
Crocosmia or Montbretia (*Crocosmia × crocosmiiflora*)	Corm	6 to 10	Sun	Spring	3	6 to 8
Dahlia (*Dahlia* hybrids)	Tuberous root	7b to 10	Sun	Spring	2 to 3	15 to 30
Gladiolus (*Gladiolus × gandavensis*)	Corm	7 to 10	Sun	Spring	4 to 6	4 to 6
Lily (*Lilum* spp. and hybrids)	Bulb	4 to 9	Sun to partial shade	Fall or spring	4 to 6	9 to 18
Madonna lily (*L. candidum*)					1	9 to 12
Magic lily (*Lycoris squamigera*)	Bulb	5 to 7b	Sun	Summer	Neck even with soil surface	6
Milk-and-wine lily (*Crinum* spp.)	Bulb	7 to 10	Sun	Fall or spring	"Neck" above ground	12 to 18
Rain lily (*Zephyranthes* spp. and hybrids)	Bulb	7 to 10	Sun	Fall/Spring	1	3
Red spider lily (*Lycoris radiata*)	Bulb	8 to 10	Sun	Summer	Neck even with soil surface	6
Society garlic (*Tulbaghia violacea*)	Bulb	8 to 10	Sun to partial shade	Spring	1	6 to 12
Tuberose (*Polianthes tuberosa*)	Bulb	8 to 10	Sun	Spring	2	6 to 8

Planning

As garden catalogs arrive each day, plan for some spare moments to gaze at the spectacular pictures and mouth-watering descriptions of summer- and fall-flowering bulbs. Keep your gardening journal handy so you can take notes of bulbs worth cultivating in your landscape. While reading the descriptions of the bulbs, pay attention to bloom time, color, height, and hardiness. As you admire the bulbs that you are forcing over the next few months (see October Planting on p. 76 for details), take a moment to record some observations in your gardening journal. This journal can be as simple as a spiral-bound notebook, or as high-tech as a spreadsheet program on your computer. Whatever you use, make records of your activities so you can improve your technique and learn from experience. Some of the information worth recording in your journal:

- Name of variety

- Where the bulbs were cooled (for example, in a cold frame outdoors, crawl space, or garage)

- Length of chilling period (weeks or months)

- Observations about rooting and flowering (write down the cultivars that performed best and those that didn't do very well)

- Records of techniques that have to be fine-tuned next fall when you force another crop of bulbs to flower outside their normal season

Planting

Coastal gardeners in zone 8b can plant **tulips** and **daffodils** that have been precooled or refrigerated for at least six to eight weeks. Refer to October Planting, p. 76, for details. If you're going to be preparing a new border for bulbs, now is a good time to mix compost, lime, or other amendments into the bed. If the soil is wet and sticks to your shovel, wait a few days or you could do more harm than good. When the soil crumbles easily in your hand, it's a good time to dig.

Care for Your Bulbs

If a few mild days of winter have encouraged shoots to emerge, don't fret about the health of your bulbs. The leaves are quite cold hardy and will not require any special protection. If they are damaged, expect new leaves to emerge.

Maintain a blanket of mulch at the feet of your bulbs, especially in the Mountains where freezing and thawing can lift the bulbs out of the ground, leaving them to dry out or be harmed by cold. An insulative layer of mulch will break the cycle of freezing and thawing.

Bring out one or two pots of bulbs each week so you will have a steady stream of flowers in your home. Start them out in the coolest spot in your home, which will allow the flowers to last longer in bright, but indirect, light. When the leaves turn green and begin to grow, place in a sunny window and flowers should open up shortly.

As blossoms fade, either *compost* the bulbs or put the pots in a sunny place where the leaves can recharge the bulbs so they can be planted outdoors.

Watering

Check the potting mix in pots that will be forced indoors. The mixture should be evenly moist without standing water. The easiest way to determine moisture is to *lift* the pots. A dry pot will be lighter than a wet one.

Helpful Hint

There are more than 4,000 **tulip** cultivars that represent virtually all colors, but many are not notably persistent in the South and usually decline after the first year. This decline is typically the result of the high night temperatures which sap the storage reserves in the bulbs, and the warm summer soils which encourage attacks from insects and diseases. There are some things you can do to help. August De Hertogh, professor of horticulture at North Carolina State University and one of the nation's leading authorities on bulb culture, offers a few suggestions that will encourage **tulips** to perennialize:

Provide good drainage as described in the introduction to this chapter on p. 52. **Tulips** grow best in a partially shaded or full-sun location with a soil pH between 6 and 7. (Have the soil tested by your local cooperative extension service to determine its pH and fertility levels.)

1 **Tulip** bulbs require a cool moist winter and a warm summer, but the bulbs should not be exposed to temperatures above 70 degrees Fahrenheit. De Hertogh recommends planting the bulbs a full 8 inches deep measured from the bottom of the bulb to the soil surface. He also recommends planting annuals or perennials over the bulbs so the shade of their leaves will keep the soil and the bulbs cool. **Fertilize** in the fall with a slow-release fertilizer such as **9-9-6**.

2 After the bulbs have bloomed and the flowers begin to fade, **clip off** the flower stalks. This prevents seed development and encourages the plants to focus their energy on the bulbs. Allow the foliage to die back naturally. You can hide or draw attention away from the dying **tulip** leaves by interplanting or bordering the bed with summer-flowering annuals or perennials.

Allow the **tulip** leaves to "ripen" and turn brown to replenish the bulbs.

3 Choose varieties that will perennialize. You can expect encore performances most often from perennializing **tulips** that come from cultivars of **Triumph tulips ('Don Quichotte', 'Kees Nelis', and 'Oscar'), Darwin Hybrids ('Golden Parade,' 'Parade', and 'Oxford'), Single Late tulips ('Demeter', 'Ile de France', and 'Make Up'), and species tulips** such as *T. fosteriana, T. greigii, T. bakeri* **'Lilac Wonder', Lady or candy tulip (** *T. clusiana*), **Waterlily tulip (** *T. kaufmanniana*), and others.

Pest Control

Diseases: *Check* the condition of your stored bulbs such as **caladiums, dahlias,** and **tuberous begonias.** *Discard* any bulbs that show signs of rot, which attacks improperly stored tubers in warm, humid conditions. *Discard* all diseased tubers. Avoid damaging tubers when digging them up, and store them in a cool, dry, dark place.

Planning

Make plans now to order summer-flowering bulbs for new beds or as complements to existing plantings. Give some thought to trying new varieties of tried-and-true standbys, such as **lilies,** which offer newer colors and long-lasting color in midsummer. Experiment with some of the "little" bulbs with long flowering periods between summer and fall, such as the **summer scillas** (*Scilla autumnalis* and *S. scilliodes*), **alliums** (*Allium globosum* and *A. senescens*), **hardy cyclamens** (*C. graecum* and *C. hederifolium*), and the **zephyr lilies** (*Zephyranthes candida*). Though small in stature, they're ideal for adding sparkle to containers and small cozy spots in the garden.

Planting

Gardeners in the Mountains and cooler areas of the Piedmont who want to have **tuberous begonias** for summer-long flowering in pots, beds, or hanging baskets outside should start the tubers indoors late this month or early next month. To sprout the tubers:

Use a mix of equal parts perlite, sphagnum peat moss, and vermiculite. This should be kept damp (not soggy) in a shady window with a temperature in the lower 60s Fahrenheit.

Place the tubers, hollow side up, fairly close together in shallow, well-drained pans.

Transplant the tubers to pots when growth starts, normally within three weeks.

Place them outside only after all threat of freezing temperatures has passed.

Care for Your Bulbs

It's not unusual for some spring-flowering bulbs to send up a few leaves in the late fall or early winter. The bulbs will remain safe over the winter and will still produce flowers next spring. It's not too late to send soil samples to your local county extension office for testing. Since some additives, like limestone, take time before increasing the soil pH (ideally between 6 and 7), the sooner you submit a sample, the better. *Continue to take out potted bulbs for forcing indoors.*

Watering

As the bulbs are being forced, keep the potting mix moist. Do not, however, keep the medium waterlogged.

Fertilizing

The best fertilizer for bulbs is a soil that's rich in organic matter. Adding nutrients periodically to replace nutrients absorbed by the growing plants, however, will help them bloom in top form. Spring bulbs whose shoots have emerged should be fertilized with a complete fertilizer such as 10-10-10. Apply 1 rounded teaspoon per square foot. Brush off any fertilizer from the leaves. *If you fertilized with a slow-release fertilizer last fall, it is not necessary to fertilize now.*

Pest Control

Insects: Watch out for aphids on forced bulbs. These soft-bodied insects suck plant sap with their piercing-sucking mouth parts, causing the leaves to curl and become malformed. Aphids can be controlled with insecticidal soap and other insecticides.

Helpful Hints

- Not all bulbs need a cold period in order to bloom reliably. Coastal Plain gardeners who have to precool bulbs prior to planting may consider some magnificent tropical flowering bulbs that require no cold whatsoever. **Amaryllis (*Hippeastrum* cultivars)** and **cannas** are the most famous of the lot. Others you should seek out include **gloriosa lily (*Gloriosa superba*), aztec lily (*Sprekelia formosissima*), spider lily (*Hymenocallis caroliniana*), Peruvian daffodil (*Hymenocallis narcissiflora*), pineapple lily (*Eucomis* species), hurricane lily (*Lycoris aurea*), society garlic (*Tulbaghia violacea*),** and **zephyr lily (*Zephyranthes* species).** Outside the Coastal Plain, these bulbs may be safely overwintered outdoors with a hefty mulch layer; in the Piedmont, they may be lifted and stored.

- **Daffodils** make nice tabletop bouquets; they differ from other cut flowers, however, when it comes to conditioning. To get the longest vase life, a week or more, here's what you should do:

  Harvest the daffodils very early in the morning. To avoid any skin irritation from the sap, use a gloved hand to remove the flower stem or scape at its base. Gently pull it to one side and twist it off. Pick single-flowered daffodils when the neck is bent roughly at a 90-degree angle to the stem; this is called the "gooseneck" stage. The flower bud should just barely be open to reveal its color. Multiflowered stems with several flowers should be picked when at least one from the bunch is fully open.

  To prevent any stem-clogging air bubbles from interfering with water uptake, **cut** the white, pith-filled bottom end of the scape at an angle underwater with a clean sharp knife or razor blade. Put the stems in warm water that has a little household bleach added ($1/2$ teaspoon per quart). Keep the flowers in a cool, dark area for twelve hours or, ideally, overnight.

  Since daffodil sap can harm other cut flowers, notably **carnations, freesias, irises, roses,** and **tulips,** condition them separately. They should be placed in water for twenty-four hours, then rinsed before combining them with other flowers.

Diseases: A number of fungal diseases attack both growing plants and stored bulbs. Fungi invade planted bulbs through wounds, causing them to rot in the ground and not come up. The plants may look stunted, their leaves become yellow, and the plant dies. Bulbs attacked by these rots include **daffodil, dahlia, gladiolus,** and **tulip.** Stored bulbs may become infected through wounds or nicks in the tissue. Bulbs feel spongy and are discolored.

Fungicides can be used to treat healthy bulbs dug from infected beds prior to replanting in another part of the garden. The infected area can be treated with an appropriate fungicide at least six months before replanting.

Depending on the disease and the course of action, the diseased bed may have to be avoided for several years. In the future, purchase and plant healthy bulbs. Since cultivars vary in their resistance to diseases, cultivate the more resistant types. Use care when digging up bulbs to avoid damaging them.

Planning

As your spring-flowering garden begins to go into glory this spring, take photographs so you can refer to them later in the year. The photos will come in handy when you're making plans to spruce up your garden or extend your beds with spring-flowering plants this fall. In addition to taking photographs, sketch a planting map in your gardening journal to show where the bulbs are located. With an accurate plot plan, you will know where to plant spring-flowering bulbs this fall. You'll also be able to plan for continuous flowering by sowing or transplanting annual or perennial flowers among the bulbs after their display has ended.

Planting

If you've forced **paper-white narcissus (***Narcissus tazetta***)** bulbs indoors (see December Helpful Hint, p. 80), plant them directly in the garden after the last spring freeze in your area. **Paper-whites** will thrive outdoors in zones 7 to 9. They should flower next spring if you forced them in a medium that has available nutrients, such as a soil-based mixture or a soilless peat-based mix with added nutrients. If you forced them in water, you may have to wait a couple of seasons before they bloom. Choose a well-drained location in full sun or filtered shade, and *plant* them at a depth that's twice the height of the bulb. Encourage your **paper-whites** to perennialize by applying a complete slow-release fertilizer once a year in the fall. Potassium is most important for **daffodils,** so apply a 5-10-12 or 5-10-20 fertilizer according to label directions.

If you received an **amaryllis (***Hippeastrum*** hybrids)** over the holidays, you can move it to a permanent location outdoors in the garden if you live in zone 7 or warmer, and if you keep it mulched during the winter months. After the last spring frost, *plant* your **amaryllis** in a well-drained fertile site in full sun to partial shade. The neck of the bulb where the leaves emerge should be 2 to 4 inches below the soil surface. *Mulch* with a 2- to 3-inch layer of compost to conserve moisture and suppress weed growth. Make a single application of a slow-release complete fertilizer after planting and then in subsequent springs when the shoots appear. Expect your **amaryllis** to bloom every year in early summer.

Care for Your Bulbs

After flowering, the leaves of your spring-flowering bulbs will turn an unsightly yellow. Temper your urge to remove the leaves, or braid them into attractive ponytails. The bulbs need the leaves to harvest energy that's channeled to the bulb for next year's flowers. Bulbs that were forced indoors can be fertilized while in bloom, then planted in your garden to allow the leaves to mature and replenish the bulb. Expect the bulbs to flower again next year.

Watering

Outdoor-growing bulbs seldom need watering this time of year. When plants are a few inches tall, begin watering to keep them evenly moist throughout the period of growth and bloom. Bulb roots grow deeply, so *water thoroughly* without just sprinkling the surface. How much water you add depends on the weather and the rate of growth. Bulbs need a lot of water when they are actively growing. Continue to water them after the blooms fade and until the leaves start to turn yellow.

Fertilizing

When the leaves of spring-flowering bulbs emerge, apply a complete fertilizer to ensure quality blooms next year. *Do not fertilize* them after they've bloomed; these bulbs are going dormant.

Pruning

Snip off the spent blooms of spring-flowering bulbs to prevent seedpods from forming. If you expect them to repeat their show next spring, allow leaves to mature and die down naturally before removing. Unless the leaves have an opportunity to store a good supply of carbohydrates and nutrients in the underground bulb, the plants won't flower next year.

Pest Control

Diseases: Gray mold, or botrytis blight, is a springtime disease that is most active during cool and wet weather. It attacks dead or dying leaves and flowers and can quickly spread to healthy tissues. Bulbs and corms may also be infected, leading

Helpful Hint

Occasionally the flower buds of **daffodils** fail to open, and when you cut them open, they are brown and dry inside. This disorder is called "bud blast" and commonly affects late-blooming **daffodils** and double-flowering cultivars. It's been speculated that drastic temperature changes, inadequate moisture, and wet autumns are responsible. Studies involving irrigation, mulching, and shading treatments, however, have not prevented bud blast from occurring. Late-blooming cultivars that may perform better in your landscape include **'Baby Moon', 'Grace Note', 'Geranium',** and most of the *poeticus* hybrids.

to rot. A wide range of plants are infected, including **amaryllis, bulbous iris, dahlia, hyacinth,** and **tulip.** Warm, humid, rainy conditions foster this fungal disease which produces yellow, orange, brown, or reddish-brown spots on the leaves and flowers. The spots on the leaves and flowers grow together, causing them to collapse and become slimy. Eventually they're covered with a telltale gray fuzzy mold.

To control botrytis, collect and discard faded flowers. Fungicides can be applied at the first sign of disease. Provide good air movement by not overcrowding the plants. Use wide spacings to allow leaves and flowers to dry off quickly. Avoid overhead watering; this fungus spreads

through splashing water and wind. Most important, keep the plants healthy. Examine your stored bulbs and discard any that show signs of rot.

Weeds: If weeds occur in bulb beds, do not remove them by cultivation. Pull them by hand so the bulbs and roots will not be disturbed.

Planning

Evaluate your plantings of spring-flowering bulbs and make notes in your gardening journal. Note which bulbs and cultivars met or exceeded your expectations. If any looked disappointing, make plans to replace them or give them another year or two to settle in.

Combine your bulb evaluation notes with remarks about the growing environment and their culture. Was the winter and spring unseasonably warm or mild? Was there an unexpected spurt of freezing temperatures? Did you fertilize the bulbs last fall with a slow- or fast-release fertilizer? When was the last time you tested the soil for pH and fertility levels? It is ideal to have soil tested by your cooperative extension service every three years to determine if any minerals need to be added to the soil.

Planting

Summer-flowering bulbs such as **crocosmia, dahlia,** and **lily** can be planted after the threat of freezing temperatures has passed. Refer to the Planting Chart (p. 57) for other bulbs. Mountain gardeners can wait until next month to plant.

In the warmer parts of the Carolinas, *dig, divide, and replant* **cannas** and **dahlias.** The best time to do it is after the eyes have sprouted but before they have grown more than an inch. Each tuber should have a short piece of old stem attached. *Discard* those that show signs of growth. *Dust* the newly cut surfaces with a fungicide before putting them in the ground.

Stake **dahlia** tubers soon after planting so you can insert the stake without skewering the tuber.

Plant **gladiolus** corms every two weeks until July to create a continuous succession of flowers. Plant the corms at least 4 inches deep to stabilize them as they produce their long flower stalks. You can also mound soil around the base to avoid having to stake them.

Avoid planting **caladium** tubers too early in the spring, because they can rot. The soil temperature must be above 70 degrees Fahrenheit. *Plant* the tuber shallowly, only an inch or two deep. Since roots and shoots emerge from the top, place it knobby side up.

Bulbs forced indoors and have finished flowering can be moved outdoors. *Cut off* the faded flowers and *transplant* bulbs into the garden.

Wait until the last freeze before transplanting **Easter lilies** (*Lilium longiflorum* var. *eximium*) outdoors (they are hardy to zone 6) in a well-drained location. *Space* the plants 12 to 18 inches apart. Since **lilies** like their "feet in the shade and their heads in the sun," *mulch* with a 2-inch layer of compost, pine straw, or shredded leaves. As the leaves and stems of the original shoots die back, prune them off. New growth will soon emerge, sometimes producing a second round of flowers. **Easter lilies,** which were forced to flower under controlled greenhouse conditions in March or April, will flower naturally in May or June. In addition, you will get a taller plant, one that grows to a height of 3 feet or more.

Find a gardener who's willing to share his or her **red spider lilies** (*Lycoris radiata*) and **magic lilies** or **naked lilies** (*Lycoris squamigera*) with you. When the bulbs go dormant as signaled by the yellowing, dying leaves, *dig up* these bulbs and *transplant* them immediately. Excessively deep planting can cause either species to fail to flower.

Plant them shallow with their "necks"—the point where the leaves emerge and the tunic ends—just sticking out of the ground. Planting too shallow is better than planting too deep since the bulbs possess contractile roots that will pull the bulb down into the soil until it is the right depth. When planted too deep, *Lycoris* will spend a few nonflowering years producing a completely new bulb.

Pruning

When the flowers fade on your spring-flowering bulbs, *cut them off* to prevent seeds from developing. Don't cut or remove the leaves, which should be allowed to die naturally. Overcome the urge to braid the leaves or tie them into neat bundles.

Watering

Spring is usually a wet time of year, so supplying supplemental water may not be necessary. If you have to water, keep leaves and flowers dry.

Fertilizing

Fertilize summer bulbs when new leaves emerge, using a single application of a slow-release nitrogen fertilizer. Instead of a slow-release fertilizer, you may use a balanced fast-release nitrogen fertilizer such as 8-8-8 or 10-10-10. An application every month or two during the growing season may be necessary to satisfy the needs of **dahlias, gladiolus,** and **lilies.** Avoid overfertilization, which can encourage the production of leaves at the expense of flowers. Let the appearance of the plant guide you. If plants look robust and are growing in a well-prepared, fertile bed, fertilizing may be unnecessary.

Pest Control

Insects and mites: Inspect the leaves of your bulbs for aphids and spider mites. Dislodge them with a strong spray of water in early morning, giving leaves plenty of time to dry before evening.

When iris leaves appear thin and limp, watch out for iris borers. These grublike insects can ruin an entire planting if not detected and eradicated early. Eggs overwinter in old, dried iris leaves and other debris. They hatch in mid- to late spring when the tiny larvae crawl up the young iris leaves and feed, producing telltale notches. Then they enter the leaves, producing pinpoint holes. As they slowly mine their way down toward the rhizomes, the borers leave a ragged, water-soaked tunnel in their wake. When you spot such a tunnel, squash the borer inside by pressing the leaf between your thumb and forefinger. Alternatively, spray your plants with an insecticide when the leaves are 5 to 6 inches tall.

Diseases: See March, p. 63.

Weeds: *Handpull* winter annuals such as common chickweed, henbit, and Carolina geranium to prevent them from reseeding. A shallow layer of mulch will suppress them.

Planning

As spring-flowering bulbs begin to fade, make plans to fill their voids with flowering annuals that are either direct-sown as seed, or planted from transplants. Refer to the Annuals chapter (p. 28–29) for suggestions. Avoid injuring bulbs when overplanting them.

Summer- and fall-flowering bulbs also make good fillers for a continuous floral display. Piedmont and Coastal gardeners can continue to plant summer bulbs; Mountain gardeners need to wait until the last expected freeze this month. When selecting bulbs for the summer and fall landscape, use your list of recommended types and cultivars. Pay particular attention to height and spread, bloom time, flower color, and fragrance. Finally, determine how many bulbs you'll need so you won't come home shorthanded.

Planting

After the last freeze, *plant* tender summer bulbs such as **cannas, dahlias, ginger lilies,** and **tuberoses** that have been stored over the winter or purchased from mail-order companies or garden centers. In the Mountains, *plant* **tuberous begonias,** but don't set the pots out until after the last expected freeze. *Plant* **caladium** bulbs when soil temperature goes above 70 degrees Fahrenheit. Caladiums prefer shade to partial shade; recently introduced cultivars called the **Florida series** (which includes **Florida Pride, Florida Queen,** and **Florida Sweetheart**), however, tolerate sun and have a dense growth habit.

Care for Your Bulbs

After blooming, *cut off* spent flowers and stalks from **bearded irises.** *Stake* **lilies** and **dahlias** early in their growth when it's still clear where the bulb ends and the soil begins.

Watering

Water newly planted bulbs to settle them in. Apply a shallow 2- to 3-inch layer of mulch to conserve moisture, suppress weeds, and keep the soil cool.

Fertilizing

Lightly fertilize summer bulbs when their shoots emerge, using a slow-release fertilizer. Follow the manufacturer's instructions regarding the amount and frequency. *Water-in* thoroughly afterwards.

There is no benefit to fertilizing spring-flowering bulbs during or after bloom. In fact, as the soil warms up after flowering, nitrogen in the fertilizer can encourage the development of the fungal disease Fusarium. Rotting bulbs infected with Fusarium have a sour smell.

Pruning

Cut flower stalks back to the ground on **daffodils** and other spring-flowering bulbs as flowers fade. Do not cut the leaves until they die naturally. (Leaves are necessary for producing strong bulbs capable of reflowering.) If you have to hide the dying leaves, consider these tips:

- *Interplant* with perennials that will grow above and hide the bulb leaves.

- *Plant* taller flower bulbs behind lower-growing shrubs.

- *Intersperse* clump-forming plants such as **ornamental grasses, liriopes,** and **daylilies.**

- *Underplant* with low-growing, sprawling ground covers like **junipers** and some **cotoneasters,** which allow you to tuck the leaves beneath the branches.

Pest Control

Insects and mites: There are several insect pests that afflict bulbs. Watch out for aphids and spider mites. See April Pest Control, p. 65, for controls.

Japanese beetles skeletonize the leaves of **canna, dahlia,** and others. *They can be handpicked and discarded in a jar of soapy water.*

Flower thrips are tiny ($1/16$ inch long) yellowish-brown-to-amber-colored insects that damage the flowers of **dahlia, gladiolus, lily,** and others by rasping the tissues and then sucking up oozing sap. Their feeding causes buds to become streaked with brown. Often the buds fail to open or the flowers look distorted. To check for thrips, *open up* a suspected flower over a sheet of white paper and search for what look like tiny scurrying slivers of wood. *Thrips are difficult*

to control. Fortunately, they're preyed upon by minute pirate bugs, ladybugs, lacewings, and big-eyed bugs. Remove and discard any infested flowers. Apply recommended insecticides.

Narcissus bulb flies are specific pests of **daffodils.** The life cycle of the narcissus bulb fly begins with the adult, which looks like a small bumblebee. The adult fly lays eggs on leaves near the soil's surface, or on the crowns. When eggs hatch, the plump, grayish-white-to-yellow larvae tunnel into the bulbs, where they feed on the soft tissue. The larvae overwinter in the bulbs, then move into the surrounding soil to pupate and begin their life cycle all over again. A bulb that has been attacked is soft and spongy. It usually has a telltale entry hole through the basal plate and is difficult to save. *Most often, just dispose of an infested bulb promptly. You can attempt to kill the maggot by stabbing it with a needle inserted through the hole in the basal plate. There is always a chance of not hitting the maggot and simply adding damage to the plant tissue. The best strategy is to keep your daffodils healthy by maintaining a shallow mulch layer and fertilizing your bulbs in the fall. When you divide your daffodils, discard any bulbs that show signs of infestation.*

Helpful Hint

In the spring, put colorful plastic golf tees in a circle around your bulbs so you know where they're growing when the foliage dies down. It is also helpful to know where to fertilize them in the fall. If golf tees look too tacky, try the natural approach by planting **grape hyacinths (*Muscari* species)** around plantings of **daffodils.** Their foliage emerges in the fall, which is a good time to find the **daffodils** for fertilizing.

Diseases: Several leaf spots will affect the leaves of summer bulbs. Depending on the level of infection, fungicides may not be necessary. *Remove any heavily infested leaves and discard them.*

Weeds: *Handpull* or hoe weeds in beds. Pre-emergent herbicides will control weeds before they emerge; make sure that the bulbs are listed on the label.

Planning

As part of your summer vacation, visit public gardens throughout the Carolinas to witness the splendor of summer-flowering bulbs. Refer to the Appendix (p. 368–71) for a list of gardens and their addresses. Bring along your camera and gardening journal to take pictures and notes of some favorite high-performing bulbs that deserve a place in your own garden. Don't forget to make some time for updating your gardening journal by recording the past performance of spring-flowering bulbs in your own garden. Were there any outstanding **daffodil** cultivars? Are there areas of your garden that need to be replanted or beds that need to be renovated this fall? Don't fret about spelling or punctuation when you write these thoughts in your journal. The information will help you order the bulbs you need for this fall and will help you spruce up your landscape with winning bulbs. So start making your list of favorite spring-bloomers now.

Planting

Bearded irises can be planted now while in bloom. Wait until late summer or early fall to divide or transplant existing clumps. **Bearded irises** form the beginnings of next year's flowers in the six or eight weeks after blooming. Disturbing the plants too early risks next year's flowers.

Plant autumn crocuses (*Colchicum autumnale*) now. Plant the corms as soon as you purchase them. These unusual bulbs flower on bare stems in fall and produce leaves the following spring. Use golf tees to mark their position so you can plant something in the void when leaves die down next summer.

Dahlia tubers may still be planted for fall bloom. Place them 6 to 8 inches deep and 3 to 4 feet apart.

Since the leaves of most spring bulbs have finished maturing by now or have died back, they can be cut back to ground level. *Dig up* any crowded bulbs that have declined and produced few, if any, flowers. *Replant* larger bulbs and *discard* smaller ones, unless you are willing to see them grow to blooming size, which may take two years or more. The spaces vacated by spring-flowering bulbs can be seeded or planted with annual transplants to provide summer and fall color.

Divide overcrowded **daffodil** bulbs after the foliage has ripened and died down. Use a flat-tined garden fork to unearth the bulbs.

Carefully pry out a clump of bulbs. Handle them gently to avoid bruising them. **Brush off** the excess soil with your fingers, and separate the bulbs as you remove the soil.

Carefully break apart the bulbs that are loosely connected to one another, but leave the offsets or small bulbs that are firmly attached to the mother bulb. Any damaged, soft, or rotten bulbs should be discarded.

Plant the bulbs immediately, or *store* them for planting in the fall. If you choose to store them, let the bulbs cure by putting them on an old window screen in a well-ventilated shade spot. After a few days of curing, put the bulbs into paper bags and store them in a cool, dark, well-ventilated place.

Replant the bulbs, saving the largest ones for planting where you want the showiest display. The smaller offsets will not flower for the first few years, so you can use them in a naturalized area where a few bulbs that haven't flowered won't be obvious. Select a well-drained location that receives full sun or part shade. Loosen the soil 8 to 12 inches deep and mix in several inches of compost. After watering, *cover* the bulbs with an inch or two of mulch such as shredded leaves or compost to conserve moisture and suppress weeds.

Care for Your Bulbs

Loosely tie **gladioli** to stakes, or mound soil around the base of the plants to prevent them from toppling over.

Watering

Be prepared to *water* summer bulbs if little rain occurs this month. Keep water off the leaves.

Fertilizing

If summer-flowering bulbs weren't fertilized when their shoots emerged, it may be necessary to fertilize them now. Follow the manufacturer's instructions regarding the rate and frequency of application. Avoid overfertilization, which can encourage the production of leaves at the expense of flowers. Let the appearance of the plant guide you. If the **dahlias, gladioli,** and **lilies** look robust and are growing in a well-prepared, fertile bed, fertilization may be unnecessary.

Pruning

Remove spent **tuberous begonia** blooms. They may be infected by the fungus disease gray mold. *Clip off* **amaryllis** and **iris** blooms after they've faded.

Pest Control

Insects and mites: Pests to watch for include aphids, spider mites, thrips, and Japanese beetles. *Handpick* Japanese beetles and *discard* them into a jar of soapy water. Neem can be applied to the leaves to reduce feeding by the adults. Use other insecticides for heavy infestations. If the rhizomes of your **bearded irises** are riddled with holes, they could be infested with iris borers. See April Insects (p. 65) for a description and controls.

Diseases: Watch out for fungal leaf spot diseases during wet spring and summer seasons. To control leaf spot diseases, remove blighted leaves during the season. *Remove* and *discard* any infected foliage in the fall. Fungicides can be applied to control certain leaf spot diseases.

Powdery mildew may be a problem on **dahlias.** This fungal disease commonly occurs during the spring and fall seasons, when the days are warm and humid and the nights are cool. This fungus is more severe on plants that are shaded or crowded. Powdery mildew gets its name from the grayish-white powder that occurs on the young leaves, shoots, and flower buds. Its spores are spread by the wind to susceptible plants. *To reduce the chance of infection, improve air movement by siting them in an open location and by selectively pruning out interior growth to eliminate congestion. Pick off and destroy infected leaves.*

Weeds: *Handpull* weeds when they are young and easier to remove. Suppress them with a shallow layer of compost. *Another way of handling weeds is to plant companion plants among your bulbs whose leaves will shade the soil and deprive the young weeds of sunlight.*

Planning

Your summer bulbs can be enjoyed outdoors in your flower borders, or indoors as cut flowers. Plan on creating a cutting garden to relieve you of any concern about color combinations and other design features. A cutting garden is a working person's garden: it produces lots of flowers for adorning tables, bringing to picnics, or sharing with friends. The U. S. Netherlands Flower Bulb Information Center (www.bulb.com) recommends the following list of cut flowers for indoor arrangements. They have sturdy stems, interesting flowers with color that doesn't fade, and gobs of fragrant blossoms:

African corn lily (*Ixia*), lush petals in red, cream, orange, pink, or yellow, atop wiry stalks.

Calla lily (*Zantedeschia*), sheath-shaped flower of flawless beauty in white and pastel shades.

Crinum lily, majestic white-and-rosy-red-flecked blossoms.

Fragrant gladiolus (*Acidanthera*), delicate swanlike cousin of the **gladiolus** which has creamy white flowers, delicate scent.

Gladiolus, a flower made for cutting, tall stately stalks covered with huge florets, in every color imaginable

Pineapple plant (*Eucomis*), creamy-white flowers blooming from the base of a pineapple-like flower head.

Liatris, tall, spiky wand of orchid florets, long-lasting.

Asiatic Lily, generally early summer bloomers.

Oriental Lily, the most flamboyantly flowered of the lilies, blooming in mid- to late summer.

Summer hyacinth (*Galtonia*), bell-shaped flowers atop 2- to 3-foot stems; they bloom when **gladioli** do, so use them together in arrangements.

Tuberose (*Polianthes*), tall, exceedingly sweet, waxy white blossoms.

Planting

Plant reblooming **irises.** Those that have performed well in the South Carolina Botanical Garden in the Piedmont include **'Autumn Tryst', 'Clarence', 'Harvest of Memories', 'Raven's Return', 'Violet Music',** and several others. They require a little more attention to fertilizing and watering, but their two seasons of flowering in late spring and early fall are well worth the effort.

Lift and divide overgrown clumps of **bearded irises** after they've bloomed in the Mountains. See next month's Planting (p. 72) for step-by step instructions. Gardeners in the Piedmont and Coastal Plain can wait until the next month or early fall when the temperatures get cooler.

Care for Your Bulbs

Support any leaning **dahlias, glads,** and **lilies** to prevent them from toppling over.

Watering

Water regularly and adequately. Water early in the day to keep leaves dry. Spring-flowering bulbs do not require water while they're dormant.

Fertilizing

Evaluate the growth rate and appearance of your summer-flowering bulbs prior to fertilizing them with a fast-release fertilizer. If they look robust, fertilizer won't be necessary. To enrich the soil, top-dress the beds lightly with composted manure. Mountain gardeners can lightly fertilize **bearded irises, Louisiana irises,** and **Siberian irises** with a low-nitrogen fertilizer such as 5-10-10. Avoid contacting the rhizome with fertilizer. *Water-in* the fertilizer afterwards so the nutrients can be absorbed by the roots.

Pruning

As flowers fade from your summer bulbs, clip them off. This will prevent them from producing seeds, allowing them to replenish themselves for next season. Removing old flowers from **tuberous begonias** will control gray mold, which can infect the leaves. Deadheading spent flowers and developing seedpods tidies them up and encourages continuous flowering.

Pest Control

Insects and mites: Look for the telltale signs of pests. Japanese beetles skeletonize leaves and feed on buds and flowers. Aphids occur in clusters near the tips of shoots and their feeding causes leaves to become wrinkled, sticky, and sometimes coasted with a black sooty mold. Spider mites cause yellow or bronze stippling on the leaf surface. Thrips damage flower buds, creating streaks or spots on the open blooms and brown edges on flower buds that fail to bloom.

Watch out for the lesser canna leaf roller. It attacks young growth, causing leaves to become frayed, tattered, and shot full of holes. Some will appear to be sealed together with webbing. The adult brown moths with 1-inch wing spans emerge in March and April, and the females lay yellowish white eggs in small patches on the emerging foliage. When the tiny caterpillars hatch, they tunnel into the canna leaves, as many as six invading a single rolled leaf. The larvae, which eventually grow to nearly an inch in length, have cream to greenish bodies and yellow heads. The caterpillars typically feed only on the upper surface of the leaf, but will sometimes bore through the furled leaf, creating a series of holes when the leaf unfurls. To shelter themselves, however, the caterpillars often fasten the edges of leaves with silk to prevent them from unrolling, and older larvae can reroll older leaves and hold them closed with silk. When fully grown, the caterpillars pupate inside a filmy cocoon. There are usually two generations per year. *The easiest way to control the lesser canna leaf roller is with early applications of* **Bacillus thuringiensis (BT).** *Direct the spray into the center of furled leaves, where the caterpillars are feeding. Cleaning up and discarding above-ground portions of cannas after the first freeze will also remove overwintering caterpillars.*

Nematodes: Nematodes are microscopic, soil-inhabiting, eel-like worms that damage the roots of **dahlias** and other bulbs. No chemicals are available for homeowners to combat these troublesome pests. If nematodes are a threat, the best defense is a healthy plant. See p. 240 for more information. In the future, plant in sites free of nematodes.

Helpful Hint

To cut flowers for indoor arrangements, use sharp shears or a knife to avoid injury to the growing plant. A special pair of cutting scissors may be bought that holds the cut-off stem, allowing the removal to be a one-handed operation. A slanting cut will expose a larger absorbing surface to water and will prevent the base of the stem from being sealed off by resting upon the bottom of the vase. It is best to carry a bucket of water to the garden for collecting blooms, instead of the familiar cutting basket.

Planning

As your summer bulbs approach the end of their season while the fall-flowering bulbs start theirs, make plans to lift and divide the overcrowded, poorly flowering clumps of bulbs and corms. Periodic dividing will improve their performance as well as giving you a lot of extra plants. The best time to divide most of these summer-flowering plants is at the beginning of their dormant period when the leaves start to turn brown and die.

After lifting the bulbs or corms, detach the offsets carefully. Bulbs such as **ornamental onions (*Allium*), magic lilies (*Lycoris*),** and **spider lilies (*Hymenocallis*)** produce daughter bulbs or offsets, which are always attached to the basal plate where the roots are attached. ***Replant*** hardy bulbs and ***store*** tender ones.

Tiny corms called cormels can be planted right after you lift your **gladioli** or **crocosmias.** Tender corms can be stored indoors along with their offspring.

When you lift and divide **lily** clumps, be careful not to bruise or break the fragile scales. ***Plant*** them immediately. Bulbils—tiny bulbs in the leaf axils (the nook where the leaf joins the stem)—can also be planted or potted up and overwintered in a cold frame outdoors.

Planting

Plant or ***move*** summer-flowering bulbs that have already bloomed, such as **amaryllis, crocosmia, iris,** and **lily.**

Divide bearded irises so the plants will have plenty of time to become established before cooler weather arrives. Gardeners in the warmer parts of the Carolinas can wait until September, which will allow the divisions to settle in after the heat of summer has passed.

1 ***Loosen*** the soil around the rhizomes (horizontally creeping underground stems) with a spading fork. Watering the bed the day before will make digging easier.

2 ***Dig up*** the clumps and ***separate*** the rhizomes. ***Divide*** each rhizome into sections with a sharp knife, making sure that each section has at least one bud or fan of leaves. The young rhizomes will be growing from the sides of the older, spongy rhizomes.

3 ***Cut*** the young rhizomes away from the older sections with a sharp knife. ***Discard*** the older pieces and any sections that are undersized or diseased. (Don't think twice about throwing away the old rhizomes. They bloom only once and then become a flowerless food reservoir). The rhizomes may be infested with borers. ***Discard*** heavily infested rhizomes. Salvage others by digging out the pinkish larvae with a pocketknife and trimming away any damaged tissue. Because the larvae's feeding creates opportunities for bacterial soft rot, soak the damaged rhizomes for half an hour in a 10 percent solution of household bleach and water. Then ***dust*** them with powdered sulfur and allow the cut surfaces to air-dry in a shady place for several hours before replanting. Before you replant the irises in their original location, comb the soil carefully for signs of brown pupal cases. Collect and destroy them to prevent the dusky brown adult moths from emerging in the fall and laying eggs on or near your plants.

4 ***Trim*** leaves to about one-third to one-half their height to reduce moisture loss. Make sure that each division consists of a firm rhizome with a fan of healthy leaves.

5 To help prevent infection, ***dust*** the cut ends with powdered sulfur. Lay the trimmed plants in a shady spot for a few hours to allow the cut ends to dry and heal.

6 *Replant* the **bearded irises** in a sunny, well-drained location. *Dig* the hole 8 to 12 inches deep, then *form* a cone of soil in the center, making it high enough so the rhizome will be planted just above ground level on heavy clay soils. For lighter sandy soils, the top of the rhizome may be 1/2 inch or less below ground level. Spread the roots around the top of the cone, then press them firmly into the soil. *Space* the divisions about 12 to 18 inches apart. Plant them in groups of three to form a natural-looking clump.

7 *Cover* the freshly planted rhizome lightly with soil. Use about 1/2 inch of soil—less for very small rhizomes.

8 *Water* the young plants to settle soil around the roots. *Mulch* in the Mountains to prevent freezing and thawing of the soil, which can heave the plants out of the ground. *Remove* the mulch in early spring, or too much moisture may remain around the rhizomes.

Care for Your Bulbs

The leaves of your summer-flowering bulbs may look tattered and unattractive, but don't remove them until the foliage and shoots turn yellow. Cut them off a few inches above the ground.

Watering

Water regularly and thoroughly. During hot, dry, August days, avoid deep cultivation in your flower beds. Loosening the soil under these conditions reduces water uptake by increasing loss of soil water and damaging surface roots.

Fertilizing

Piedmont and Coastal Plain gardeners can lightly fertilize **bearded irises, Louisiana irises,** and **Siberian irises** early this month with a low-nitrogen fertilizer such as 5-10-10. Water the fertilizer in afterwards so the nutrients can be absorbed by the roots.

Pruning

Remove spent flowers as they fade. If the weather is hot and the flowers are in afternoon sun, blooms will not last very long. Cut the flowers and use them in arrangements inside your home.

Pest Control

Insects and mites: Spider mites are especially troublesome during the hot, dry weather of this month. See April Pest Control, p. 65 for controls.

Disease: Watch out for powdery mildew. Warm, humid days and cool night temperatures in the milder areas of the Carolinas favor the growth of this grayish-white foliar disease.

Weeds: *Handpull* any weeds and suppress their growth with a layer of mulch. Watch out for particularly aggressive weeds such as ground ivy and Indian mockstrawberry, which can escape from flower beds and invade lawns.

Planning

As you make plans to visit a garden center to purchase spring-flowering bulbs, begin with a shopping list. Rely on your gardening journal, newspaper and magazine articles, and catalogs. Look at colors, bloom period, and height. If you can't find a particular cultivar, find another one with closely matching characteristics.

Check the merchandise carefully. Remember that "bigger is better" when it comes to bulbs. Bigger bulbs produce bigger blossoms. Stay away from soft, mushy, moldy, or heavily bruised bulbs. It doesn't matter if the tunic (the dry, papery, onion-skinlike covering) is loose or torn, but it should not harbor any insects or diseases.

Do not dismiss bargain bulbs that are smaller in size and less expensive than the larger ones. They may not give you the big impact you are looking for next year, but they will bring some color to large areas of the landscape (along the backyard fence, along the driveway, etc.) for the right price. In a few seasons, they will bulk-up sufficiently so no one will know they were bargain bulbs.

Finally, plan to try something new. It may be a bulb that produces screaming pink flowers, or one that has a botanical name that's difficult to pronounce, but produces extraordinary blooms. Record your purchases in your journal so you can document their performance next year.

Planting

Plant fall-blooming bulbs, such as **autumn crocus (*Colchicum*), autumn daffodil (*Sternbergia lutea*), fall-blooming crocus (*Crocus speciosus*),** and **nerine lily,** as soon as you receive them.

Plant the summer-flowering **madonna lily (*Lilium candidum*)** now or in early spring with no more than 1 inch of soil covering the "nose" of the bulb.

Plant **lily** bulbs soon after you receive them because they do not have a truly dormant period.

Prepare beds for spring-flowering bulbs as soon as possible. Cultivate the soil and add generous amounts of organic matter to improve water drainage. *Bulbs will rot without proper drainage.*

Care for Your Bulbs

If you cannot plant bulbs right away, *store* them in a cool (60 to 65 degrees Fahrenheit) location to prevent them from drying out before planting. Temperatures higher than 70 degrees Fahrenheit can damage the flower inside spring-flowering bulbs. The bulbs can be stored in ventilated bags but not in paper or plastic bags unless specified. Since rhizomes, tubers, and tuberous roots dry out faster than bulbs and corms, *store* them in peat, perlite, or vermiculite.

Bulbs can be stored for several weeks in a cool place (35 to 55 degrees Fahrenheit) such as a refrigerator. Vegetable crisper drawers can be used, but avoid storing bulbs in the same drawer as ripening fruit or vegetables, which give off ethylene, a gas that can cause problems with flowering. Since some bulbs are poisonous, this storage method is not recommended for households with young children.

Mountain gardeners should dig and store **caladium** bulbs before the frost. Here's how:

Lift the tubers from the ground before frost. Shake the soil from the tubers and leave them in a sunny location to dry for seven to ten days. If rain or frost is forecast, *move* the tubers indoors temporarily.

After this drying period, pluck off the withered leaves from the tuber and brush off any remaining soil.

Store the tubers over the winter in a box or basket filled with dried vermiculite or perlite. Place the container where the temperature will not drop below 60 degrees Fahrenheit. Next spring, *plant* the tubers in the garden when the soil temperature rises to 70 degrees.

Watering

September and October tend to be dry months. Continue watering regularly.

Fertilizing

It's not necessary to fertilize newly planted spring-flowering bulbs if they're going to be treated like annuals for one season of bloom. The bulbs can grow and bloom without any additional nutrients.

If you want your bulbs to naturalize or perennialize, *fertilize* newly planted spring-flowering bulbs with a slow-release fertilizer. Instead of making one annual application of a controlled-release fertilizer, apply a fast-release fertilizer at planting and a second application the following spring when the new shoots emerge. *Water* after fertilizing to make nutrients available to the bulbs.

Winter-blooming bulbs such as **cyclamen** and **crocus** do not have to be fertilized in most well-prepared garden soils. A light top-dressing, however, with a balanced fertilizer such as 10-10-10 will encourage abundant blooms and keep corms healthy.

Pest Control

Insects and mites: Aphids and spider mites may still be active. Evaluate the extent of injury and decide if pest control measures are warranted. Use a water wand on a weekly basis, preferably early in the morning, to wash mites from plants.

Diseases: Clean up dead, fallen leaves. They can harbor disease and insect pests over the winter if allowed to remain on the ground.

Weeds: *Handpull* any young winter annuals, or *cover* them with a shallow layer of compost. Weeding is never fun, but the cooler temperatures can make it more bearable.

Animals: Voles, rabbits, and deer relish many kinds of flower bulbs, such as **crocuses** and **tulips.** To learn how to protect bulbs from voles, refer to the Animals section in the introduction on p. 55.

Helpful Hint

For naturalizing large areas with **daffodils,** consider purchasing smaller, less expensive bulbs. **Daffodils** multiply and grow larger each year, so if you can be patient and wait a year or two, these bulbs will enlarge and produce bigger flowers.

Planning

Learn about some of the "minor" or "specialty" bulbs this month, and plan to grow them in your landscape. These "minor" bulbs are not as famous as the "major" bulbs like **daffodils, hyacinths,** and **tulips.** But minor spring-flowering bulbs such as **crocus, cyclamen, Dutch iris, snowdrops,** and **winter aconite** are quite easy to grow and can be used in a variety of landscape situations:

- Plant them beneath the rising stems of **tulips** and **daffodils** to highlight the color and forms of their taller brethren.

- Interplant early-spring-flowering **crocuses** with groundcovers such as **vinca.**

- Plant **grape hyacinths, anemones,** or **crocus** *en masse* in borders.

- Plant them as a focal point for a perennial border or mixed planting with shrubs. Eyecatchers include **giant onion (***Allium giganteum***),** with its towering purple globe-shaped flower head, and **crown imperial (***Fritillaria imperialis***),** with pendulous flowers topped by a pineapple-shaped crown.

Planting

Spring-flowering bulbs require an extended cold period to bloom reliably. When bulbs do not receive sufficient weeks of cold treatment (usually in the warm coastal areas of zone 8b), they produce flowers close to the ground on shortened stalks, which are often hidden by the leaves. Coastal gardeners can purchase precooled **tulips** and other spring-flowering bulbs. Alternatively, chill them yourself by storing them in an old refrigerator for a minimum of ten weeks (and up to sixteen weeks) prior to planting in December or January. After chilling, *plant* the cooled bulbs immediately.

Forcing bulbs: Making bulbs flower outside their normal season is a wonderful way of ushering spring into your home. With careful planning, you can produce a parade of color throughout the winter and spring months. Bulbs that can be easily forced at home include **daffodils, hyacinths (***Hyacinthus***),** and **tulips.** Minor bulbs that can easily be forced include **crocus, glory-of-the-snow (***Chionodoxa* **spp.), grape hyacinth (***Muscari* **spp.), netted iris (***Iris reticulata***),** Siberian squill (*Scilla siberica*), **spring snowflake (***Leucojum vernum***), snowdrop (***Galanthus nivalis***), winter aconite (***Eranthis*** spp.),** and **wood hyacinths (***Hyacinthoides non-scripta***).** Follow these steps to force bulbs:

Buy bulb cultivars that are recommended for forcing. Pot up the bulbs anytime from mid-September to December in a well-drained potting medium. Use commercial potting soil or make your own mix composed of equal parts of potting soil, sphagnum peat moss, and perlite. Since the bulbs already contain enough food for the developing flowers and roots, fertilizing is unnecessary. Select a shallow pot or bulb pan pot that is at least twice the height of the bulbs. Fill it three-quarters full of mix and set the bulbs in place. Leave at least 1 to 2 inches of soil beneath large bulbs. **Tulips** and **daffodils** can be left with their tips showing; completely *cover* smaller bulbs such as **crocus, snowdrop,** and **grape hyacinth.** When planting **tulips,** position the flat side of the bulb toward the outside of the pot; when the first and lowest leaf emerges, it will gracefully arch over the rim to give a balanced look.

Fill the pot with soil to within $1/4$ to $1/2$ inch of the rim. Add water until it seeps through the drainage hole in the bottom of the pot. *Label* each pot, marking the name of the cultivar, the planting date, and the date to be brought indoors for forcing.

Cool the bulbs by exposing them to temperatures between 35 and 50 degrees F for twelve to sixteen weeks. *Store* them in an old refrigerator, unheated basement, cold frame, or in the ground buried up to their rims. *Protect* the potted bulbs from freezing outdoors by covering them with sawdust, straw, leaves, or peat moss. After twelve weeks of chilling, *check* the pots. When you wiggle the bulb in the pot and it stays in place and roots can be seen through the drainage holes, bring the pot indoors for forcing. Gradually expose the pots to light and warm temperatures. Start with a cool, 60- to 65-degree room in indirect sunlight. When the shoots turn green, expose the pots to warmer temperatures and more light to stimulate flowering. Rotate the pots regularly so that all the leaves receive an equal amount of light. After a week, *move* the pot to warmer temperatures and more light to encourage flowering. Keep the soil moist. The flowers will last longer if you move the pots to a cool room at night.

If you wait until after the last freeze, most forced bulbs can be planted into the garden. During their time indoors, keep them in bright sunlight and *fertilize* them with a water-soluble houseplant fertilizer. Plant hardy bulbs that have been forced into bloom in the garden once spring arrives, or allow them to go dormant in their pots and then plant them in the fall. **Daffodils, crocus, squills,** and other hardy bulbs can be transplanted into the garden in the spring, and will flower normally the following year. Other bulbs, such as **tulips** and **hyacinths,** are best discarded after forcing.

store **caladium** bulbs before the frost in the Piedmont and Coastal Plain. See September's Care for Your Bulbs section, p. 74.

Watering

If fall is dry, provide sufficient water to newly planted spring-flowering bulbs. *Check* bulbs being forced in beds or cold frames and water them to keep the potting medium moist (but not sopping wet).

Fertilizing

See September, p. 75.

Care for Your Bulbs

In the fall, cut back **lily** stalks to soil level after they have turned yellow. When they are completely dry, the stalks can be pulled out easily. Mountain gardeners should lift **cannas, dahlias, gladioli,** and **tuberous begonias** after their foliage is killed by frost. Because they won't survive the winter outdoors, they need to be cleansed of soil and stored indoors in a cool but frost-free location. Dig and

Pest Control

Diseases: Watch out for storage diseases, including Fusarium bulb rot and botrytis. Avoid damaging bulbs and tubers when lifting them out to be stored.

Weeds: Weeds, especially weedy grasses, may be in beds. *Handpull* or hoe out the clumps.

Planning

While bulbs are commonly planted in formal beds, borders, and even containers, many lend themselves to naturalized plantings where they bloom and spread in ever-widening drifts. Plan to create some naturalized areas in your landscape in the following ways:

1. Randomly scatter **crocuses, daffodils, grape hyacinths, snowdrops,** and **snowflakes,** and plant them where they fall. They look better when planted in clumps or drifts, so you may have to move them around. These bulbs will root and establish themselves by spring.

2. Plant spring-flowering bulbs along the edges of woodland areas or beneath the canopies of deciduous trees. They should receive plenty of sunlight and finish blooming by the time the trees leaf out.

3. Insert bulbs such as **crocuses** in your warm-season lawn. The **crocuses** will brighten up the lawn before it awakens from its winter dormancy in the spring. By the time the crocuses finish replenishing themselves, it will be time to mow the grass and remove the spent crocus leaves.

Keep in mind that naturalized bulbs need to be fertilized on an annual basis to encourage perennialization. Failure to fertilize them often results in a gradual reduction in their numbers.

Planting

Freesias can be grown indoors this winter; keep in mind that they've got exacting requirements. The delicate spikes of tubular, often fragrant, flowers in a range of colors from white to lavender, purple, blue, yellow, orange, pink, and red are well worth the effort.

1. *Plant* dormant corms in well-drained sterile potting soil with a neutral pH, such as Pro-Mix BX. If you are blending your own mix, it should contain no more than one-third perlite because **freesias** are susceptible to the fluoride that the perlite contains. Leaf scorch is a symptom of fluoride toxicity.

2. *Fill* the pots to within 2 inches of the rim and place the corms, pointed ends up, 2 to 3 inches apart in each pot.

3. *Cover* the corms with an inch of mix and *water thoroughly.*

4. For the most compact growth, precool these pots for 45 days in a location where the temperature is 55 degrees Fahrenheit. Until the leaves appear, light is unnecessary; an unheated garage or basement will work fine. After this precooling period, green leaf tips should be visible.

5. Move the pots to a well-lit location that averages 65 degrees—higher temperatures delay flowering and increase bud drop. A combination of coolness and brightness will yield the best plants. Keep soil moist and *fertilize* every two weeks with a complete fertilizer such as 20-20-20.

6. *Stake* the straplike leaves to prevent them from falling over. You can use ready-made ring stakes or connect bamboo stakes with lengths of twine. Depending on conditions and the cultivars you choose, blossoms should appear two to four months after planting and continue for a month.

Now is a good time to plant spring-blooming beauties such as **anemones, crocus, daffodils, scillas,** and **snowdrops.** Use a time-release bulb fertilizer at planting time. Follow the suggested planting depth in the Planting Chart on p. 56. When in doubt, follow this general rule: *Plant bulbs at a depth equal to three times the height of the bulb.*

Summer bulbs which could be killed by winter freezes should be lifted, dried, and stored (if you did not already do so last month). *Divide* and *replant* crowded **dahlias** after a freeze kills their top growth. Where they won't survive the winter outdoors in zones colder than 7b, they will have to be lifted and overwintered indoors in a cool (35 to 50 degrees Fahrenheit), dry place. Here's how:

Cut the tops back to 6 inches, *lift out* the clumps with a spading fork, *brush off* the soil, and turn them upside-down to dry. Inspect each clump and pare away any damaged parts. *Remove* infested or dead tubers at the neck. *Dust* the tubers with sulfur to prevent rot in storage, making sure all the surfaces are coated. *Store* them in a ventilated crate or basket filled with peat moss. Place each tuber upside-down, stacking them no more than two deep. Inspect them monthly and *discard* any rotting tubers.

Care for Your Bulbs

Mulch plantings with compost, pine straw, or salt hay to protect

tender and semihardy bulbs from the winter cold.

Clean up and *remove* old, dried **iris** leaves, stems, and other debris in the fall to help eliminate overwintering eggs or iris borers.

Watering

Check potted bulbs that will be forced during the winter months. Bulbs stored outdoors in cold frames or in the ground may need to be watered. *Water* newly planted bulbs to encourage rooting before cooler temperatures arrive.

Fertilizing

Fertilize new and established beds with a slow-release nitrogen fertilizer. Don't wait until spring, because the bulbs are producing roots and foraging for nutrients now.

Pest Control

Diseases: Examine stored bulbs for signs of rot and *discard* any diseased ones. In the future, avoid damaging tubers when digging them up, and *store* them in a cool, dry, dark place.

Planning

Despite the holiday rush this month, make plans to spend some quiet time updating your gardening journal. What bulbs stopped you in your tracks when you first noticed them in bloom? Were any bulbs troubled by insects or diseases? Did any "minor" bulbs stand out among the rest?

During the year you may have saved newspaper and magazine clippings of articles from garden writers who touted certain bulbs. Perhaps you wrote down the names of bulbs or growing techniques suggested by friends, staff at public gardens, or speakers at gardening symposia. Now's the time to compile these notes to act upon them next year.

Planning

Buy commercially prepared **lily-of-the-valley** pips from your florist or garden center. Plant as many as possible in pots to secure an abundance of fragrant blooms. One bonus of these bulbs is that they tolerate more heat than other commonly forced bulbs. Spring bulbs, which are late bloomers, can still be planted, though bulbs that bloom in February (**crocuses, snowdrops,** etc.) may not flower if planted now. Try to get them in the ground before midmonth.

Helpful Hint

There are some bulbs that can be forced without cooling. **Paper-white daffodils (*Narcissus tazetta*)** are winter-blooming tender bulbs that can be forced without having to expose them to cool temperatures. Here's how to force them in a soilless mixture: 1) Set them in an undrained decorative bowl or dish that is at least 2 to 3 inches deep, with enough pebbles, pea gravel, or coarse sand to reach about 1 inch below the top. 2) **Add** water until it's barely below the surface of the gravel. 3) Set the bulbs on top and hold them in place with enough gravel to **cover** the bottom quarter of each bulb. Carefully **maintain** the water level. 4) **Move** them to a cool 50- to 60-degree-Fahrenheit location in low light until they are well-rooted and the shoots appear—usually in about two to three weeks. **Bring them gradually into direct sunlight and warmer temperatures.**

Care for Your Bulbs

Have soil samples taken from your beds if not done in the past two or three years. Since lime can take up to six months to react and increase the soil pH, the sooner you have your soil tested, the sooner you can apply lime to your beds if necessary.

Watering

See November, p. 79.

Fertilizing

See September, p. 75.

Pest Control

Diseases: *Discard* any bulbs that show signs of rot, which attacks improperly stored tubers in warm, humid conditions.

Weeds: *Handpull* any young winter annuals, or *cover* them with a shallow layer of compost. Weeding is never fun, but cooler temperatures can make it more bearable.

Animals: Mice may get into outdoor bulb beds or cold frames. Use hardware cloth to keep them out. Voles, also called meadow or field mice, can feed on a wide variety of plants, including your bulbs. Two kinds of voles, pine voles and meadow voles, reside in the Carolinas. See p. 55 for controls.

Herbs and Vegetables

We are lucky in the Carolinas where fresh herbs and vegetables can be grown and harvested year-round. Compact varieties can be tucked in almost anywhere in the landscape. With the right conditions, the vacant spots among your shrubs and flowers can accommodate herbs and vegetables that look as good as they taste. Of course, you can take the traditional approach and allot some space in the landscape to these edibles.

Before you plant, make a plan.

Planning the Herb and Vegetable Garden

Before you get swept up with thoughts of harvesting vine-ripened tomatoes or sprigs of home-grown oregano, spend some time planning your garden. Follow these steps to find the right location and make the right selection of herbs and vegetables:

1 Locate a fertile, well-drained spot that gets six to eight hours of sun. That is the amount of light that fruit-producing vegetables, such as **peppers** and **tomatoes,** need. Leafy vegetables such as **beets, cabbage, lettuce,** and the like do all right in partial shade. So do herbs like **angelica, parsley,** and **sweet cicely.**

2 List your favorite vegetables—think about taste, cost, nutrition, and appearance—and note their planting dates (see the Planting Chart on p. 85–87).

Cost. Many people grow the expensive, unique, and flavorful vegetables and buy the others. High-value vegetables for home growing include **orange sweet peppers, gourmet lettuces, tomatoes,** and some **squash.**

Nutrition. Some vegetables pack more vitamins and minerals than others. Nutrient-dense vegetables include **sweet potatoes, carrots, spinach, collard greens, red pepper,** and **kale.**

Beauty. The flowers, leaves and fruits of some herbs and vegetables add beauty to the landscape.

3 Decide on the quantities you will need. Then it's a simple step to allocate the garden space you'll need to devote to each crop.

4 Start planning your garden on paper. Graph paper where $1/4$ inch represents a foot works well. A 12-by-16-foot space is enough to grow a good selection of greens, some herbs, and a supply of tomatoes, peppers, beans, and cucumbers

Orient the rows east to west. Allow room to walk between rows to take care of the garden. Put the tallest and trellised plants on the north so they won't shade the shorter ones. Place perennials like **asparagus** and **horseradish** to the side where they will not be disturbed. For a four-season garden, use a different sheet for each season.

Herbs and Vegetables

Soil Preparation

With your plan in hand, stake out your garden and prepare the soil.

1. *Check the pH and nutrient levels of your soil.* Have the soil tested through your local cooperative extension service at least every third year. A pH of 5.5 to 7.0 is fine for most vegetables.

2. *Add organic matter.* Compost, old manure, or decaying leaves and weeds release nutrients and improve soil structure. Water and nutrients move less quickly out of the root zone in sandy soils amended with organic matter. In heavy soils, organic matter improves drainage.

3. *Cultivate the soil.* Dig to at least 8 inches, mixing in nutrients and any lime or sulfur recommended by a soil test.

Planting the Herb and Vegetable Garden

The best time to plant vegetables outdoors depends on the cold hardiness of the species or variety. Vegetables can be divided into two classes based on temperature requirements: cool-season and warm-season crops.

Cool-season vegetables originated in temperate climates and grow best in cool weather. They often continue to produce well past the early fall freezes, but they should be started in time to mature before hard freezes begin.

Warm-season crops came primarily from subtropical and tropical regions. Thus they need warm weather for seed germination and growth. Freezes injure or kill them and they need to be protected from spring frosts. They are planted in the summer to mature in the fall; get them in early enough so they can be harvested before fall's killing freezes arrive.

The Planting Chart on p. 85–87 will help you time your plantings. Knowing the number of days required to reach maturity and the average dates of the first and last freezes in your area (see the maps on p. 14–15) will help you avoid disappointment.

Starting Herbs and Vegetables from Seed

Growing vegetables and herbs from seed gives you access to a wider range of varieties than are offered in stores. It also produces transplants fairly inexpensively. Follow the step-by-step instructions for starting seeds indoors on p. 30 in the Annuals chapter.

Select varieties that are well adapted in your area, with resistance to local insects and diseases. Contact your county cooperative extension service for recommended varieties.

Fertilizing

Your soil-test report has told you what nutrients you need. Apply the fertilizer by broadcasting it over the garden, or by individually feeding each plant. Use a cyclone or drop spreader to broadcast, applying half the total in one direction and the other half at right angles to the first (refer to Warm-Season Lawns, February Planning, p. 174, to learn how to calibrate your spreader to apply the correct amount of fertilizer). Till it at least 3 inches into the soil.

Herbs and Vegetables

Better yet, incorporate half the plant food deeply into the soil with a spade or rototiller. Then sprinkle the other half on top and rake it in lightly. This distributes fertilizer throughout the root zone.

A more efficient way of using fertilizer is to drop some 2 or 3 inches from the side and at least 3 inches below the seeds. Placing fertilizer closer to the seeds may injure or kill emerging plants.

Apply plant food sparingly to leafy, fast-growing herbs. Heavy applications of fertilizer, especially those high in nitrogen, can reduce the concentration of desirable essential oils that make herbs flavorful.

Watering

Since vegetables are made up of 80 to 90 percent water, yield, fruit size, and quality can be affected by a lack of water. Water prevents disorders such as toughness, off-flavor, poor filling of pods or tips, cracking, blossom end rot, and misshapen fruit. There is no ironclad schedule of how much and how often to water. Correct watering requires common sense and observation. Follow these "ground rules" for proper watering:

- Water often enough to keep the soil from drying out around newly planted vegetables. Gradually reduce the frequency but continue to water deeply to encourage development of a deep, extensive root system.

- Water vegetables in porous sandy soils more frequently than vegetables in dense clay soils.

- Water more frequently when temperatures are high.

- Water deeply, wetting as much of the root zone area as possible.

- Keep the leaves dry by applying water to the soil surface. Fungal leaf diseases rely on moisture to infect and spread.

- To reduce evaporation and suppress water-stealing weeds, mulch your herbs and vegetables with a 2- or 3-inch layer of compost.

Pest Control

When growing vegetables and herbs you are bound to confront insects, diseases, and weeds. Do not be discouraged. *Learn about pests and try to outsmart them.*

It may mean planting **squash** early to avoid squash vine borers. Or you might hold off spraying the Mexican bean beetles on your **snap beans** because the assassin bugs are keeping the pests at levels that can be tolerated by your plants. To thwart any emerging weeds, plant your vegetables close together so they will shade the soil.

All these strategies are summed up in an approach called Integrated Pest Management: using a mix of mechanical, biological, cultural, and chemical techniques to control rather than eradicate pests. Some keys to IPM:

- Practice good soil management to grow healthy plants that can resist pests and diseases.

- Select plant varieties that are suited to your area and resistant to local pests.

- Rotate crops. Do not grow related vegetables in the same place year after year. Rotate species within the garden or relocate the entire garden (See the March Helpful Hint on p. 93).

- Time your planting. Select planting dates that are favorable for the crop and unfavorable for the pest.

Herbs and Vegetables

- **Interplant.** Plant different kinds of vegetables together in your garden since many insect pests attack plants of a certain family and avoid unrelated ones. Plants not preferred by pests can act as a buffer to slow the spread of harmful insects to pest-preferred plants.

- **Thin out** young plants to avoid overcrowding and weak growth that invites problems.

- Keep the leaves dry when watering to thwart the spread of fungal diseases that require moisture to grow and spread.

- **Stake or cage** plants to keep fruits off the ground and reduce sun scald. Slip boards under melons to prevent rot.

- Avoid injuring plants. Cuts, bruises, cracks, and insect damage invite infection. Cut, rather than pull off, fruit that is difficult to pick, such as cucumbers and watermelons. Avoid cutting into the plant roots when you cultivate.

- **Mulch** to suppress weeds and reduce water stress and soil splashing.

- **Pull weeds** as they appear. They often harbor pests and compete for nutrients and water.

- Keep your garden clean. **Remove** infected leaves or plants as you see them. Clean up debris after harvest to destroy overwintering eggs and pests.

- **Handpick** egg clusters, bean beetles, caterpillars, and other insects as often as possible. Drop them into soapy water.

- **Use biological controls.** Rely on natural predators and parasites to control harmful insects. Learn to recognize the eggs and larvae of lacewings, ladybugs, and praying mantids.

A microbial insecticide is a living, insect pathogen that is safe to use on beneficial insects. The bacterium **Bacillus thuringiensis (BT)** *is the most popular pathogen. Formulations from* **Bacillus thuringiensis** *var.* **kurstaki** *are the most widely used. BTK (sold as Dipel®, Thuricide®, and others) controls most caterpillars, which are the larvae of butterflies and moths, such as cabbage looper, imported cabbageworm, and tomato fruitworm. When caterpillars ingest the bacteria, they stop feeding and die shortly thereafter. BTK works best when caterpillars are very small, and it remains effective for only a day or two after application because it is broken down by sunlight. Expect to get the best results when you spray BTK as soon as you see the first tiny caterpillars, and repeat applications as additional eggs are laid.*

- Use botanical pesticides and insecticidal soaps. Refer to IPM Biological Controls in the Introduction to this book on p. 20 for more information about these "natural" pesticides.

- As a last resort, turn to synthetic pesticides. Apply them sparingly, according to need and not season, and in strict accordance with manufacturer's instructions. They may kill a broad spectrum of insects and require a waiting time between application and harvest.

Before using any pesticide, read and follow the label directions.

Carolina Vegetables

Growing Season by Region

	SPRING			FALL		
	M	**P**	**CP**	**M**	**P**	**CP**
Asparagus crowns	Feb. to Mar.	Feb. to Mar.	Jan. to Feb.			
Bean, bush (snap)	May to June	mid-Apr. to mid-May	mid-Mar. to mid-April	early to mid-July	mid-July to mid-Aug.	Aug.
Bean, bush (pole)	May to July	Apr.	mid-Mar. to mid-Apr.	–	July	late July to early Aug.
Bean, bush lima	mid-May to June	May to early June	early to mid-Apr.	June to mid-July	early to mid-July	mid-July to early Aug.
Bean, pole lima	May to early July	mid-April to mid-June	mid-Mar. to mid-June	early to mid-July	mid-July to early Aug.	early to mid-Aug.
Beets	early Apr. to early June	mid-Mar to mid-Apr.	mid-Feb. to early Apr.	mid-July to mid- Aug.	early to mid-Aug.	mid-Aug. to mid-Sept.
Broccoli*	early Apr. to early May	mid-Mar. to mid-Apr.	mid-Feb. to early Apr.	mid-July to mid-Aug.	mid-July to early Sept.	early Aug. to mid-Sept.
Brussels sprouts*	–	–	–	early to mid-July	mid-July to mid-Aug.	early Aug. to early Sept.
Cabbage*	early Apr. to early May	early Feb. to mid-Mar.	mid-Jan to early Mar.	early July to early Aug.	early to mid-Aug.	early to mid-Aug.
Chinese cabbage	Apr.	Mar. to early Apr.	Feb. to Mar.	Aug.	late July to mid-Sept.	mid-Aug. to late Sept.
Muskmelon	early to mid-May	mid-Apr. to early June	early Apr. to early June	–	–	–
Carrot	early Mar. to mid-Apr.	mid-Feb to early Mar.	early Jan. to early Feb.	early to mid-July	mid-July to Aug.	early Aug. to mid-Sept.
Cauliflower*	early Apr. to early May	mid-Mar. to early Apr.	Feb. to Mar.	mid-July to mid-Aug.	mid-July to late Aug.	early Aug. to early Sept.
Collards	–	–	–	early July to mid-Aug.	mid-July to mid-Aug.	early Aug. to early Sept.
Corn, sweet	mid-May to mid-June	mid-Apr. to early June	mid-Feb. to early Apr.	–	–	–
Cucumber	mid-May to early July	mid-Apr. to mid-May	mid-Mar. to mid-Apr.	early to mid-July	early to mid-Aug.	early to mid-Aug.
Eggplant*	mid-May to mid-June 15	May	early Apr. to early June	–	early to mid-July	mid-July to early Aug.
Kale	mid-Mar. to early May	early Mar. to early Apr.	mid-Feb. to mid-Mar.	early Aug. to early Sept.	mid-Aug. to mid-Sept.	mid-Aug. to mid-Sept.
Lettuce, leaf and head*	mid-Mar. to May	late Feb to Mar.	mid-Jan to mid-Feb.	mid-July to mid-Aug.	early Aug. to early Sept.	mid-Aug. to mid-Sept.
Mustard greens	mid-Mar. to Apr.	early Feb. to mid-Mar.	mid-Jan to early Mar.	Aug. to early Sept.	mid-Aug. to mid-Sept.	mid-Aug. to early Oct.

M = Mountains   **P** = Piedmont   **CP** = Coastal Plain   *transplants

Carolina Vegetables

Growing Season by Region

	SPRING			FALL		
	M	**P**	**CP**	**M**	**P**	**CP**
Okra	mid-May to mid-June	early May to early June	mid-Apr. to early June	–	–	–
Onion, plant or sets	mid-Feb. to mid-Apr.	Mar.	Jan. to Feb.	Sept. to Oct.	Sept. to Oct.	Oct. to Nov.
Onion, seeds	mid-Feb. to early Apr.	early Feb. to early Apr.	Jan. to Feb.	early Aug. to early Sept.	mid-Sept. to early Oct.	early Oct. to early Nov.
Peas, garden (English)	Mar. to Apr.	Feb.	mid-Jan. to early Feb.	mid-July to early Aug.	Aug. to early Sept.	Sept.
Peas, southern	mid-May to mid-June	early May to early July	early to mid-Apr.	–	–	early July to early Aug.
Pepper*	mid-May to mid-June	early May to early June	early Apr. to early May	–	mid-July to early Aug.	mid-July to early Aug.
Potato, Irish	mid-Mar. to mid-Apr.	mid-Feb. to mid-Mar.	early Feb. to early Mar.	June to July	mid-July to early Aug.	late July to Aug.
Potato, sweet*	early June to early July	mid-May to mid-June	mid-Apr. to early July	–	–	–
Pumpkin	May 15 to June 15	Apr. 15 to June 15	Apr. 1 to July 1	–	–	–
Radishes	early Mar. to early Apr.	mid-Feb. to mid-Mar.	mid-Jan. to early Mar.	Aug. to early Sept.	mid-Aug. to early Oct.	early Sept. to early Nov.
Rutabaga	early Mar. to mid-Apr.	early Feb. to early Apr.	early Feb. (mid-Jan. in SC) to early Mar.	mid-July to mid-Aug.	early to mid-Aug.	mid-Aug. to Sept.
Spinach	early Mar. to mid-Apr.	mid-Feb. to mid-Mar.	mid-Jan. to mid-Feb.	early to mid-Aug.	mid-Aug. to mid-Sept.	early Oct. to early Nov.
Squash, summer	mid-Apr. to mid-June	mid-Apr. to mid-May	early to mid-Apr.	mid-July to early Aug.	mid-July to mid-Aug.	early Aug. to early Sept.
Squash, winter	May 15 to June 15	Apr. 15 to June 15	Apr. 1 to July 1	–	–	–
Swiss chard	early Apr. to early June	mid-Mar. to mid-Apr.	mid-Feb. to early Apr.	early July to mid-Aug.	early to mid-Aug.	mid-Aug. to mid-Sept.
Tomato*	mid-May to mid-June	mid-Apr. to mid-May	early Apr. to early May	–	mid-July to mid-Aug.	mid-July to early Aug.
Turnips	early Mar. to early May	mid-Feb. to mid-Mar.	mid-Jan. to early Mar.	mid-July to late Aug.	early Aug. to early Sept.	early Sept. to early Oct.
Watermelon	mid-May to mid-June	mid-Apr. to early June	early Apr. to early June	–	–	–

M = Mountains **P** = Piedmont **CP** = Coastal Plain

*transplants

Carolina Herbs

Annual and Biennial Herbs

Common Name (Botanical Name)	Hardiness Zones	Exposure	Height (inches)	Spacing (inches)	Propagation
Summer savory (*Satureja hortensis*)	Annual	Sun	18	18	Sow seed in early spring
Sweet basil (*Ocimum basilicum*)	Annual	Sun	20 to 24	6 to 12	Seed; start indoors as transplants for early season
Mexican marigold (*Tagetes lucida*)	Annual	Sun	18 to 24	12 to 18	Seed or stem cuttings
Coriander, cilantro (*Coriandrum sativum*)	Cool-season annual	Sun, partial shade	24	12 to 18	Biennial grown from seed
Dill (*Anethum graveolens*)	Cool-season annual	Sun, partial shade	3 to 5 ft.	3 to 12	Seed
Parsley (*Petroselinum crispum*)	Biennial	Sun	6	6	Biennial; sow seed in early spring

Perennial Herbs

Common Name (Botanical Name)	Hardiness Zones	Exposure	Height (inches)	Spacing (inches)	Propagation
Sweet bay (*Laurus nobilis*)	8b to 9	Partial shade	4 to 12 ft.	NA - one plant	Stem cuttings
Florence, fennel (*Foeniculum vulgare* var. *dulce*)	6 to 9	Sun	4 to 5 ft.	4 to 12	Seed; divide established plants
Sweet marjoram (*Origanum marjoram*)	7 to 9	Sun	18	12	Seed, crown division, or stem cuttings
Chives (*Allium schoenoprasum*)	3 to 9	Sun, partial shade	12	12	Seed or division
Lavender (*Lavandula angustifolia*)	6 to 9	Sun	24	18	Seed or stem cuttings
Oregano (*Origanum vulgare*), Greek oregano (*O. vulgare* subsp. *hirtum*)	5 to 9	Sun	24	8 to 12	Stem cuttings or division
Parsley (*Petroselinum crispum*)	Biennial	Sun	6	6	Biennial; sow seed in early spring
Arp rosemary (*Rosmarinus officinalis* 'Arp')	7 to 10	Sun	3 to 6 ft.	2 to 3 ft.	Seeds slow to germinate; stem cuttings, layering, or crown division
Sage (*S. officinalis*)	5 to 8	Sun	18	12	Grows slowly from seed; stem cuttings, crown division, or layering
Sweet marjoram (*Origanum majorana*)	7 to 9	Sun	8	12	Grow from seed, crown division, or cuttings
French tarragon (*Artemisia dracunculus* var. *sativa*)	3 to 7	Sun	24	12 to 18	Crown divisions or root cuttings
Thyme (*Thymus vulgaris*)	4 to 9	Sun	4 to 8	6 to 12	Cuttings, seed, or crown divisions

Planning

Intensive gardening can be accomplished in a number of ways to increase production from a limited space. You can shift the garden layout from rows to raised beds, which uses most of the ground formerly used for pathways. Make these permanent rectangular beds as long as you like and 3 to 4 feet wide so they can be worked from either side. Plant intensively in these beds. Consider "square-foot gardening," where the bed is divided into square blocks. Each plant or seed is planted in the center of each square.

Another intensive gardening approach is vertical gardening, which exploits the air space above the bed. Vining and sprawling plants such as **cucumbers, melons,** indeterminate **tomatoes,** and **pole beans** can be supported with trellises, nets, strings, or poles. Since they occupy little garden space, the remaining space can be planted with low-growing vegetables.

Planting and Transplanting

Some gardeners grow their seedlings indoors in the bright direct light of a south-facing window, greenhouse, or sunporch. Others prefer the outdoors, using a cold frame (see November Planning, p. 108). In the milder areas of the Piedmont and Coastal Plain, gardeners can move their seedlings outdoors during the day to expose them to full sunlight. Be aware that you will have to contend with some cloudy, overcast days. Instead of relying on sunlight, you can buy or build an artificial light stand and grow your seedlings under lights (see p. 25).

See January Annuals on p. 30 to find out how to organize your seed packets to create a sowing schedule for your seeds, and for step-by-step information on producing transplants from seed indoors to get a jump on the growing season.

Coastal Plain gardeners can sow **basil, chives, parsley, sage, summer savory,** and **sweet marjoram** indoors. To encourage **parsley** seeds to sprout more rapidly, soften the seeds by soaking them overnight in warm water. Coastal Plain and Piedmont gardeners can sow seeds of **broccoli, cabbage,** and **cauliflower** indoors for trans-

planting within six to eight weeks. **Head** and **leaf lettuce** can be set out four to six weeks after sowing. Piedmont gardeners can wait until next month before starting these vegetables.

Outdoors, gardeners in the warmer coastal areas can sow **beets, carrots, garden peas (English peas** and **edible pea pods), lettuce, mustard, radishes, spinach,** and **turnips.** Wait until later this month and early next month in the more inland areas of the Coastal Plain. Coastal Plain gardeners can plant **asparagus** crowns (see next month's Planting for the step-by-step procedure); wait until the next month or two in the Piedmont and Mountains.

Watering

See January Annuals on p. 31.

Fertilizing

Fertilize seedlings growing in soilless mixes when the first true leaves appear. (January Annuals, p. 31.)

Helpful Hint

Sowing seeds into pots and then waiting for the seedlings to emerge can be an act of faith. To avoid those feelings of helplessness and anxiety when sowing vegetable seeds, try my father-in-law's sealed-lid seed-starting technique. I have used it for germinating large-seeded vegetables like **tomatoes, peppers, cucumbers, squash,** and **melons.** The materials for the sealed-lid method include a small plastic container that has a clear or translucent plastic lid such as a leftover margarine or whipped-cream container, and a piece of paper towel about 6 inches square.

1 Cut the paper towel into postage stamp–sized squares and place them on the inside of the lid.

2 Wet each square towel with a few drops of water. Then place one seed in the center of each square.

3 For small seeds, picking them up may be a challenge. Break a toothpick, wet the jagged end, and touch the seed with it. The seed readily sticks to the end and can be easily deposited on the paper.

4 Once you have placed the seeds on the lid, close the container, using the lid as the floor and the container as a makeshift greenhouse. Put the container on top of the refrigerator or some other warm, out-of-the-way place.

5 Depending on the seed, germination may take place in a few days or it may take a week or more. Inspect the seeds every now and then by looking through the underside of the lid for signs of the "seedling root" or radicle peeking through.

6 Once you see the radicle or seedling root, a welcome sign that germination has occurred, remove the container from the lid. Gently pluck the germinated seeds off the lid with tweezers and plant them in small pots filled with potting mix. Use the eraser end of a pencil to dibble a shallow planting hole. After placing the seed in the pot, run the pointed end of the pencil alongside the hole to cover the seed.

I have found the sealed-lid method to be highly efficient and economical. For example, instead of sowing a whole packet of tomato seeds, germinate only the number you want to eventually transplant in the garden. If you want six tomato plants, germinate six seeds (I like to add two extra seeds for insurance).

Care for Your Herbs and Vegetables

Continue harvesting **carrots, radishes,** and **turnips. Lettuce** and spinach growing in a cold frame or under the protection of a fabric row cover (spun-bonded polypropylene) or plastic tunnel can also be picked.

Pest Control

Diseases: Damping off is a serious disease that attacks and kills seeds and seedlings. See February Annuals on p. 33 for a description and controls.

Planning

To keep your garden in continuous production, plan to use any of three intensive approaches.

1 **Interplanting** or intercropping involves growing different kinds of vegetables together at the same time. The basic approach is to combine a slow-growing or early-maturing crop with a fast-growing or late-maturing crop. The quick-growing vegetable will mature and be harvested before the slow-growing crop needs the space; thus two crops can grow in the same area without crowding each other.

2 **Succession planting** is another intensive approach in which a crop is grown, harvested, and removed and another is planted in its place. Just avoid planting vegetables in the same family in the same place right after one another. For example, try following **peas** with **okra,** or plant **cucumbers** after **spinach.** Planting a spring, summer, and fall garden is another form of succession planting. Cool-season crops (**broccoli, lettuce, peas**) are followed by warm-season crops (**beans, peppers, tomatoes**), and these may be followed by more cool-season plants or even a winter cover crop.

3 **Relaying** consists of staggering the planting times of one type of crop to extend the harvest season over a long period of time instead of having one big harvest all at once. One approach is to plant one variety several times, at about two-week intervals (more time between early plantings in colder soil, but only ten days between the last plantings). For instance, **sweet corn** may be planted at two-week intervals for a continuous harvest. Another relaying approach is to make one planting of two or more varieties that differ in maturity time, for example, try fifty-day with sixty-day **beans** or early-, mid-, and late-season varieties of **sweet corn.**

Planting

In the Coastal Plain, sow warm-season vegetables indoors in flats or trays—try plants like **eggplant, pepper,** and **tomato. Cucumber, muskmelon, summer squash,** and **watermelon** should be sown in individual pots or peat pellets because their growth may be hindered if their roots are disturbed.

Piedmont gardeners can sow **basil, chives, parsley, sage, summer savory,** and **sweet marjoram** indoors. To encourage parsley seeds to sprout more rapidly, soften the seeds by soaking them overnight in warm water.

Coastal Plain gardeners can set out (outdoors) hardened-off vegetable transplants of **broccoli, cabbage,** and **lettuce.** Set out small tubers or "seed pieces"—a piece of a large tuber containing at least one "eye" or bud—of **white** or **Irish potatoes.** The soil temperature should be above 50 degrees Fahrenheit. Wait until next month in the Piedmont.

Coastal Plain and Piedmont gardeners can sow **mustard, garden peas, radishes, spinach,** and **turnips.** Wait until next month in the Mountains.

Plant dormant **asparagus** crowns without any green shoots showing into a bed enriched with organic matter such as compost, manure, or shredded leaves. Here's how:

1 Place the crown into the bottom of an 8-inch-deep furrow and cover with about 2 inches of soil (in heavier clay soils set them 6 inches deep). Set the crowns 12 inches apart in the trench.

2 As the new shoots emerge and grow, add another 2-inch layer of soil—do this every two to three weeks until the trench is filled.

3 *Mulch* with a 2-inch layer of compost to conserve water and control weeds.

4 Begin harvesting **asparagus** spears in the third year. (If you must, harvest lightly in the second year, for no more than two weeks. Harvesting too much and too early results in weak plants).

Plant "short-day" onion transplants for **bulbing onions** in the Coastal Plain.

Helpful Hint

Wood ashes are a good source of potassium for plants, and they will also increase soil pH. Before applying wood ashes to a garden, have your soil tested through your county extension center. If the soil is already in the 5.8 to 6.5 range and no lime is recommended, do not apply ashes–they are likely to make the soil too alkaline, tying up micro-nutrients such as zinc and manganese that are needed for good plant growth. If lime is recommended, you can spread an equivalent amount of wood ashes over the soil surface and work it into the soil instead. Wood ashes are low in calcium compared to limestone, and some supplemental gypsum (a source of calcium) will be needed if the calcium level, as indicated on the soil-test report, is medium or low.

Store the wood ashes in a closed container to prevent rainwater from leaching the nutrients away. Because fresh ashes can be caustic, do not spread them directly over the roots of plants or on young seedlings.

Care for Your Herbs and Vegetables

When the soil can be worked, turn under the cover crops planted last fall. Till the soil to a depth of 8 to 12 inches. Never work the soil when it is wet—working wet soils, especially silty or clay types, destroys the structure and makes the soil hard, compacted, and unproductive. There are two indicators of wet soil: (1) soil sticks to the shovel and (2) a handful of soil sticks together in a ball and does not crumble when squeezed.

Watering

Do not overwater seedlings or transplants. Water them when the surface of the medium feels dry.

Fertilizing

Fertilize indoor-grown transplants with a water-soluble fertilizer such as 20-20-20 at half-strength every other week. Outdoors, fertilize the newly emerging growth of established **asparagus** beds with a nitrogen-containing fertilizer. Gardeners on the coast can sidedress **beets, carrots,** and **English peas.** See March Fertilizing on p. 92.

Pest Control

Diseases: Damping-off can be a problem on seedlings. Refer to p. 33 for control recommendations.

Weeds: Control any winter annual weeds such as bittercress, common chickweed, and henbit by hand-pulling. *Suppress* them with a shallow layer of mulch.

Planning

If you are serious about growing herbs and vegetables, plan to start a journal this month. It will document your observations, thoughts, and plans for the future. In your journal list the herbs and vegetables you planted in the garden. Include the names of seed companies, plant name, variety, planting date, and harvest date.

Planting

Indoors in the Mountains, sow **basil, chives, parsley, summer savory,** and **sweet marjoram.** To encourage parsley seeds to sprout more rapidly, soften the seeds by soaking them overnight in warm water. Indoors Mountain gardeners can also sow seeds of **broccoli, cabbage,** and **cauliflower** for transplanting within six to eight weeks.

Piedmont gardeners can sow warm-season vegetables in flats or trays—try **eggplant, New Zealand spinach** (a heat-tolerant substitute for spinach), **pepper,** and **tomato.** Vegetables that resent any root disturbance, such as **cucumber, muskmelon, summer squash,** and **watermelon,** should be sown in individual pots or peat pellets. Avoid sowing seeds too early or they may be ready for transplanting before outdoor conditions permit.

Sweet potatoes are started from "slips"—shoots that sprouted from last year's crop. Purchase them as transplants or start your own by placing a sweet potato in a glass half-filled with water. Place it in bright light. Detach the plants from the mother root when they are 6 to 8 inches long, pot them up, and then plant them in the garden about three weeks after the last freeze.

In the Coastal Plain, plant perennial herbs such as **chives, oregano,** and **thyme** when they become available in garden centers. Coastal Plain and Piedmont gardeners can sow **parsley** and **dill.** Sow **beets** and **Swiss chard** in the Coastal Plain and Piedmont. Since each "seed" is actually a dried fruit containing up to six seeds, expect a cluster of seedlings to emerge. When their first "true leaves" appear, thin out the bunches by pinching off the extra seedlings near ground level.

In coastal areas after the last freeze, set out **eggplant, onion, pepper,** and **tomato.** Sow seeds of **butter beans (lima beans), pole beans, snap beans, sweet corn, summer squash,** and **watermelon.**

Piedmont gardeners can buy seed potatoes and cut them into egg-sized pieces containing one or two eyes. Allow the cuts to dry and callous for a day or two before planting. Plant them when the soil temperature remains above 50 degrees F.

In the Piedmont and Mountains, plant **asparagus** crowns before new growth emerges from the buds. *Set out* transplants of **broccoli, cabbage,** and **cauliflower** as well, up to four weeks before the last spring freeze. Sow seeds of **carrots, lettuce (leaf and head), garden peas, mustard, radishes, rutabaga,** and **spinach.**

Mountain gardeners can sow **mustard, garden peas, radishes, spinach,** and **turnips.**

Care for Your Herbs and Vegetables

Before moving home-grown or store-bought transplants into the garden, harden them (see Care for Your Annuals, April, on p. 36).

Watering

Continue watering trays or pots of seedlings indoors.

Fertilizing

Some vegetables have heavier demands for nitrogen than

others and need extra nitrogen during the growing season. These heavy-feeders benefit from an application of primarily a nitrogen-containing fertilizer applied along one side of the row about 4 to 6 inches from the plants. The application of fertilizer to growing plants is called sidedressing. Use a nitrogen fertilizer such as calcium nitrate, bloodmeal, or cotton seed meal.

Sidedress **beets** and **carrots** four to six weeks after planting. **Broccoli, cabbage,** and **cauliflower** benefit from an application two to three weeks after planting and again four to six weeks later. *Sidedress* **lettuce** soon after the seedlings emerge and grow; a second application is optional and should be based on the appearance and growth rate of the lettuce crop. *Fertilize* **English peas** when they are 4 to 6 inches tall.

Pest Control

Insects: Look for imported cabbage worm caterpillars on **cabbage, cauliflower,** and to a lesser extent, other members of the family including **broccoli, kale, mustard,** and **lettuce.** Prevent the butterflies from laying eggs in the spring by covering the young plants with a layer of spun-bonded row cover. Handpicking the larvae is another way to control them, but their

<table>
<tr><td colspan="2">

Helpful Hint

Rotate your vegetables by not planting the same vegetable or related vegetable in the same location year after year. Rotate at least once every three years. If you have to, and if space permits, rotate the entire garden to another part of the garden the following year and allow the original garden to remain fallow. By rotating vegetables from different families you can prevent the buildup of insect and disease problems. Refer to the following list of vegetable families when rotating your garden.

- **Carrot family:** carrot, chervil, celery, coriander, dill, Florence fennel, parsley, and parsnip
- **Goosefoot family:** beet, spinach, and Swiss chard
- **Gourd family:** cucumber, gourd, cantaloupe, watermelon, pumpkin and squash
- **Grass family:** popcorn and sweet corn
- **Lily family:** asparagus
- **Mallow family:** okra
- **Mustard family:** bok choi, broccoli, Brussels sprouts, cabbage, Chinese cabbage, cauliflower, collards, cress, kale, horseradish, kohlrabi, mustard greens, radish, rutabaga, and turnip
- **Nightshade family:** eggplant, pepper, Irish potato, and tomato
- **Onion family:** chive, garlic, leek, onion, and shallot
- **Pea family:** beans and peas
- **Sunflower family:** endive, chicory, globe artichoke, Jerusalem artichoke, lettuce, salsify, and sunflower
</td></tr>
</table>

camouflage makes them difficult to locate. Use a biological control, *Bacillus thuringiensis* var. *kurstaki* (BTK), sold as Dipel®, Thuricide®, and others. *Spray* BTK as soon as you see the first tiny larvae, and repeat applications as additional eggs are laid. Other less specific (and highly toxic) insecticides are

available. They may kill a broad spectrum of insects and require a waiting time between application and harvest.

Diseases: See January.

Weeds: See February.

Planning

Summer is around the corner—plan to water your herbs and vegetables efficiently when hot weather arrives. Take a look at the irrigation methods described in Shrubs, May Planning on p. 266, and select an appropriate one for your garden.

Planting

After the last expected freeze, *set out* the transplants of herbs you started indoors. Mountain gardeners can divide **chives, thyme, mint,** and **tarragon** when new growth emerges. A simple way of propagating rosemary and thyme is by layering. See Shrubs, March on p. 262 for details.

In the Coastal Plain and Piedmont after the last freeze sow **beans, corn, cucumbers,** and **southern peas.** Avoid planting **okra** seeds too early. The soil temperature should be above 75 degrees Fahrenheit; soak **okra** seed overnight before planting in the garden.

Set out transplants of **eggplant, muskmelon, peppers, summer squash, watermelon, New Zealand spinach,** and **zucchini** after the last expected freeze when the nights are continuously above 50 degrees F.

Avoid purchasing **tomato** or **pepper** transplants that are already in bloom. Once the plant starts flowering, it is forced into the dual responsibility of maintaining flowers and trying to produce roots. If a plant is blooming when transplanted, it will concentrate on fruiting rather than growing. The end result will be a small plant that bears little fruit. You are always better off planting one that's not in bloom.

Plant determinate bush-type **tomatoes** for canning or preserving so the fruit will ripen all at once, all within a week or two of each other. For vine-ripened tomatoes, plant indeterminate **tomatoes** that have an extended fruiting period; they vine, flower, and fruit all the way up to the first frost.

Without protection plant **tomatoes** one to two weeks after the last expected freeze. Plant transplants either on their side in a shallow trench with only the topmost leaves showing, or dig a deep hole with a shovel or posthole digger to set the transplants straight down.

In the Piedmont and Mountains, make another planting of **beets, broccoli, cabbage, carrots, potatoes,** and **radishes.**

Care for Your Herbs and Vegetables

To keep the **cauliflower** curds pure white, loosely tie the long outside leaf onto the flat, open head when it is 1 to 2 inches across. Hold the leaves together with a rubber band until the head is ready for harvesting.

Continue to harvest **asparagus** in the Mountains until the spears become thinner than a pencil.

Root crops must be thinned, no matter how ruthless this practice seems. *Thin* **beets, carrots, onions, Swiss chard,** and **turnips** so you can get three fingers between individual plants.

You should be enjoying the harvests of your late winter/early spring labor: home-grown **beets, carrots, lettuce, onions, peas,** and **turnips.**

Watering

The first few weeks after planting and transplanting and during the development of fruit or storage organs are times when plants may be adversely affected by shortages of water. Be sure they are watered well.

Fertilizing

Fertilize asparagus with a nitrogen-containing fertilizer to encourage the production of large ferny growth. Research has shown that the bigger the topgrowth, the better the yield. *Sidedress* young garlic plants when the new growth is 6 inches high. *Sidedress* Irish potatoes when the sprouts begin to break ground.

Pruning

Both lavender (*Lavandula augustifolia*) and sage (*Salvia officinalis*) can be cut back in the spring as new growth begins. In both cases, do not cut below the point of new buds. With lavender this is usually 6 or 8 inches above the ground. Sage can be cut back lower still, provided you leave at least one pair of healthy green leaves on each stem from whose bases the new shoots will appear. Shearing lavender after the blossoms fade will also help keep the plants compact.

Pest Control

Insects: Mexican bean beetles—both adults and larvae—feed on bush, pole, and lima beans by skeletonizing the leaves from below. *Handpick* and destroy beetles and larvae on the leaves, or deposit them in a jar of soapy water. Parasitic wasps help control the beetles. Insecticides are available.

Look for flea beetles on eggplant. They are about $1^{1}/_{2}$ inches long, shiny black in color, and chew tiny holes in leaves. Control with the appropriate insecticides.

Cutworms damage seedlings and transplants by cutting stems a few inches below or just above ground level. They feed mainly at night. See May Annuals, Cutworms, p. 39 for a description and controls.

Leaffooted bugs feed mostly on tomato, potato, bean, cowpea, and okra. Both nymphs and adults suck sap from pods, buds, blossoms, fruit, and seeds, causing distorted leaves and distorted or deformed fruit. Their life cycle lasts about forty days, with many generations per year. Plant early to avoid the first generation. Handpicking and destroying the eggs are time-consuming but effective measures. Insecticides are available.

Weeds: Control weed seedlings when they are young since they grow rapidly and can be more difficult to remove later. A sharpened hoe is a good friend in the garden.

Planning

If you lack the space for an herb and vegetable garden or if you prefer to have them within easy reach on a balcony, patio or porch, then consider growing them in containers. Keep these points when container-gardening:

1 Choose white or light-colored containers which absorb less heat than dark-colored ones in full sun.

2 The container should be large enough to provide enough root-growing space. A 1-gallon container is suitable for **beets, carrots, lettuces, onions,** and **radishes.** A 2-gallon pot is fine for **bush beans, mustard,** and **turnips.** A minimum of 5 gallons would be necessary for **bush squash, cabbage** and other cole crops, **cucumbers, melons,** and **tomato.**

3 Use a soilless potting mix for small containers. Since the expense of prepackaged or soilless mixes can be high for large-container gardens, prepare your own soil by mixing equal parts of peat moss, potting soil, and clean coarse builder's sand or perlite.

4 Container-grown vegetables and herbs have the same requirements for light, moisture, and nutrients as garden-grown plants. Being confined to containers, however, means they require more-frequent watering, which leaches out nutrients quickly. They also require more-frequent fertilizing; use a slow-release fertilizer to make fewer applications.

Planting

Sow warm-weather vegetables such as **beans, cucumber, okra,** and **southern peas.** Extend your **sweet corn** harvest by planting successive crops when the previous crop has three to four leaves, or plant early, mid-, and late-maturing varieties all at the same time. Set out herb transplants. Continue setting out transplants of warm-weather vegetables such as **eggplant, muskmelon, New Zealand spinach, peppers, summer squash, sweet potato slips, tomatoes,** and **watermelon. French tarragon** doesn't like the heat and wet weather in the warmer areas of the Coastal Plain. A heat-tolerant substitute is **Mexican mint marigold** (*Tagetes lucida*), which is a beautiful, yellow-flowered, fall-blooming herb that tastes like tarragon.

Care for Your Herbs and Vegetables

Harvest **broccoli** when the florets are still tight and green. After harvesting the main head, broccoli will put out smaller-size heads from the side shoots. Pick **cauliflower** before the curds or flower parts begin to separate, and **cabbage** before it bolts. Pick **green, sugar snap,** and **snow peas** every couple of days to keep more coming. Stop harvesting **asparagus** spears when they get close to pencil size; overharvesting is one of the greatest killers of **asparagus.** Fasten indeterminate **tomatoes** to a stake and train them to two or three branches to grow right up the stake. This will keep their fruit off the ground to avoid disease problems. Determinate **tomatoes,** which branch more and ripen their fruit pretty much all at once, are best enclosed in a reinforced wire tomato cage. Wind their branches around the inside of the cage as they grow.

Watering

Water deeply, keeping the leaves of your vegetables dry. Invest in soaker hoses or drip irrigation.

"Seep-irrigate" with plastic milk jugs. Punch holes in the sides of a jug with a large nail, spacing them about 2 inches. Bury the jug, leaving the neck above the soil. Fill the jug with water (solutions of liquid fertilizer may be used to water and fertilize at the same time) and screw the cap on firmly. The water will gradually seep out, providing a slow, deep irrigation for nearby plants.

Fertilizing

Sidedress **sweet corn** when it is 8 to 12 inches high and again when the tassel is just beginning to show. Use a nitrogen fertilizer such as calcium nitrate, bloodmeal, or cottonseed meal.

Pruning

Pinch out the "suckers" of staked indeterminate **tomatoes** to harvest larger tomatoes. Suckers are shoots that develop in the "U" between the main stem and a branch. If left in place, they will eventually become larger branches with their own flowers, fruits, and even suckers. Your plant will produce smaller tomatoes, but lots of them. *Remove* the suckers with your fingers.

Pest Control

Insects: Look for curled or puckered leaves on your vegetables caused by aphids. Slugs and snails produce large, ragged holes on leafy crops, especially **lettuce** and **cabbage.** See Pest Appendix on p. 367 for descriptions and controls. Watch out for leaffooted bugs. See April's Insects on p. 95 for controls. Green-striped cucumber beetles attack the leaves, stems, and fruit of **beans, corn, cucumber, melon, pumpkin,** and **squash.** They transmit bacterial wilt disease. Expect two or more generations per year. Handpicking is time-consuming but effective. Fabric row covers such as spun-bonded polyester provide an effective barrier between the insect and young plants. *Remove* the covers during flowering to ensure pollination. Insecticides are available.

Diseases: Early blight is an early-season disease of **tomatoes.** Look for small, sunken, dark-brown spots with yellow haloes on the lower leaves and stem. Eventually the spots enlarge to form a "bulls-eye" pattern. *Mulch* to keep the soil-borne fungal spores from splashing onto the leaves, and avoid wetting the leaves when watering. If necessary, apply a fungicide. Squash fruit rot is a fungal disease that attacks **summer squash** blossoms and fruit. Avoid wetting fruit when watering and avoid overcrowding of plants. Powdery mildew infects

Helpful Hint

When planting **squash** or **cucumbers** in a circle or hill, place a stick upright in the middle of the circle and leave it there. Later, when the main roots are hidden by vines, use the stick to show you where to water them.

beans, cantaloupe, cucumbers, okra, peas, and **squash.** Leaves are covered with patches of whitish to grayish powdery growth. They eventually turn yellow, then brown, then dry up. Plant resistant varieties and avoid crowding. If necessary, use fungicides. Verticillium wilt is a cool-season disease that attacks **tomatoes, potatoes, eggplants,** and **peppers.** It does not occur in South Carolina. Fusarium wilt is a warm-season disease that only attacks **tomatoes.** The best defense against both of these is genetic resistance. Select varieties that have "VF" after their name in the catalog, signifying that they are resistant to both of these diseases. **'Big Beef', 'Celebrity', 'OG 50', 'Pilgrim',** and **'Quick Pick'** are a few possibilities.

Weeds: Prevent weed seed germination, destroy weeds that sprout before they bear seed, and do not use mulches or compost contaminated with weed seeds.

Planning

If you've planted more than you can use, you can always plan on sharing your bounty with friends and neighbors. What about your community? Make plans to share your vegetables and herbs with your community soup kitchen or food bank. Herbs are especially welcome because they provide nutrients as well as flavor. Get the address of the nearest food pantry or soup kitchen that needs fresh produce—you can get it from a church organization that helps the needy or from the Social Services department at your town hall.

Planting

Sow another batch of **sweet basil** seeds for late summer. Mountain gardeners can sow seeds of summer crops such as **beans, cucumbers, okra, pumpkins, southern peas, and squash,** and a last planting of **sweet corn.** Also, *set out* transplants of **pepper** and **tomatoes** and **sweet potato** slips.

Care for Your Herbs and Vegetables

The best time to harvest most herbs is just before flowering when the leaves contain the maximum essential oils.

Harvest **beans, cucumbers, okra,** and **squash** daily to keep the plants producing. Pick **cucumbers** when the fruits are small and before they turn yellow.

Harvest **okra** pods when they are 2 to 4 inches long. Wait much longer and the pods become tough and fibrous and the plant stops producing—an exception is **'Burgundy'**, whose pods can stay tender even when 6 to 8 inches long. Pick **yellow squash** when the fruit is 4 to 6 inches long, **zucchini** when it is 6 to 8 inches long, and **pattypan** when it is 3 to 5 inches wide.

Pick **eggplant** after the fruit reaches 3 to 5 inches in length. The skin should be glossy and fully colored. Dull skin indicates overripeness.

Dig **onions** when about half the tops begin to turn yellow and fall over. Brush the soil off and cure them in a dark, warm (80 to 85 degrees F.) well-ventilated space for two to three weeks. Store them in a mesh bag in a dry, dark, cool place.

Harvest **Irish potatoes** when the vines have died back about halfway. Save some of the small potatoes, refrigerate them, and plant them whole in the fall.

Watch out for blossom end rot, a disorder that causes **tomatoes** to turn black on the blossom-end. It occurs when there are extremes in soil moisture, which result in a calcium deficiency in the fruit. When rain or irrigation follows a dry spell, the roots cannot take up calcium fast enough to keep up with the rapid fruit growth. Blossom end rot also occurs if the delicate feeder roots are damaged during transplanting or by deep-cultivation near the plants. Here's how to fight it:

- Keep moisture levels fairly uniform by regular watering and by maintaining a mulch layer around the base of the plants.

- Maintain a pH between 6 and 6.5 and an adequate calcium level by liming or applying gypsum.

- Finally, avoid overfertilizing, which inhibits calcium uptake.

- *Remove* the flowers and fruits from late-season tomato transplants before setting them out.

Watering

Corn needs water at two crucial times: when the tassels at the top are beginning to show, and when the silk is beginning to show on the ear. If rainfall is scarce at these times, *water.*

Fertilizing

Stop cutting **asparagus** when the spears become thin. *Fertilize* the bed and allow the "ferns" to grow during the summer to store food in the roots for next year's crop. After they have set their first fruit, *sidedress* **eggplants, peppers,** and **tomatoes** with a nitrogen fertilizer such as blood-meal, calcium nitrate, or cottonseed meal; *sidedress* **sweet potatoes** six weeks after planting.

Pest Control

Insects and mites: Corn earworm caterpillars chew on **corn** ears, gaining entry through the cornsilks. Avoid this pest by planting corn earlier in the season, or apply mineral oil on the cornsilks five days after they emerge from the husk. Insecticides are also available.

Watch out for leaffooted bugs. See April's Insects on p. 95.

Mites feed on nearly all vegetable crops, but are commonly a problem on **beans, tomato,** and **eggplant.** Whiteflies are tiny insects that attack **tomato, pepper, bean, cucumber, squash, melon,** and **okra.** See the Pest Appendix on p. 367 for descriptions and controls.

Pickleworms mostly attack **cantaloupe, cucumber,** and **squash.** The young larvae usually feed on leaves and flowers. The older larvae bore into the sides of the fruit and continue to feed. *Grow resistant varieties and plant early to harvest before the insects arrive.*

Squash vine borers are the larvae of a wasplike clearwing moth which lays oval, flat brown eggs on the stems and leaf stalks of **squash** and **gourd.** Upon hatching they bore into the stem, causing the vine to wilt and die. *Squash vine borers are difficult to control with pesticides. Once inside the stem, they cannot be reached. The best control is prevention:*

- Cover seedlings or transplants with a layer of spun-bonded row cover to keep the adult moths at bay. This will have to be removed to allow for pollination.

- To find stems attacked by borers, look for an entry hole near the base and some fine, brown sawdust-like frass (insect feces). Carefully split the stem lengthwise with a penknife and remove the borers or kill them with a long pin or needle.

Diseases: Pinch or prune out any diseased leaves or stems on herbs. Watch out for bacterial wilt on **tomatoes.** See July's Diseases for information about this disease.

Weeds: In most gardens, annual weeds can be controlled by mulching and handweeding. Using a herbicide in a herb and vegetable garden is difficult, because there are few herbicides that can be safely applied to the wide range of plant species grown in the garden.

Planning

Start planning your fall garden. Choose early-maturing vegetables when you can. Sow **beans, cucumbers,** or even short-season **corn.** They will replace those early vegetables you harvested this month and will be ready to pick before freezing weather comes. Sketch out a plan, list the crops, and mark their locations. Note the dates to remind you when to plant them—allow adequate time to mature before the first expected freeze.

Planting

Sow another round of **basil, cucumbers, squash,** and **southern peas.** Consider varieties that offer disease resistance, earlier yields, or better flavor.

Sow **pumpkins** for Halloween.

Mountain and Piedmont gardeners can start seeds of **Brussels sprouts, cabbage,** and **cauliflower** for the fall garden. Also sow seeds of **eggplant, pepper,** and **tomato** for planting out in July for a fall crop. Sow seed indoors or in a partly shaded area outdoors.

Make a first planting of some fall crops including **broccoli, Brussels sprouts, cabbage, carrots, collards,** and **cauliflower.** Attention to watering will be needed to get these up and growing. Wait until next month in the Coastal Plain.

Care for Your Herbs and Vegetables

Continue to cut and dry herbs for winter use. Keep picking **beans, cucumbers, okra, peppers,** and **squash** so they will remain productive. If going away for a few days, invite neighbors to help themselves.

You can tell **cantaloupe** is ripening when green skin begins to lighten. Pick them when they slip easily from the stem and are fragrant.

A **watermelon** is ready when the underside turns from whitish to creamy yellow and the stem starts to wither. Dig **Irish potatoes** when half their tops have die down. Pick **sweet corn** just before cooking. It's ready when the silks turn brown and the pierced kernel releases a milky juice. Most varieties maintain peak sweetness for one or two days. Super-sweet types stay sweet four or five days after picking.

Watering

A vegetable garden thrives on an inch of water each week of summer. When rain is sparse, water deeply once a week on clay soils and every three days on sandy soils to encourage deep rooting.

Fertilizing

Restore soil fertility before planting your fall crops by working in fertilizer or manure. ***Do not fertilize*** drought-stressed plants. Wait until after watering or rainfall and the plant has dried.

Pruning

Cut back **basil, mint,** and **oregano** to keep them compact and to keep these herbs from going to seed.

Pest Control

Insects and other pests: Squash bugs feed on pumpkin and squash plants. Early planting for an early harvest can usually beat them. Capture them with a shingle. Bugs will gather under it during the heat of the day and can be destroyed.

If your vegetables looked stunted, poorly colored, and wilted, check the roots for signs of a nematode infestation. These microscopic roundworms are commonly found in coarse-textured sandy soils and feed on plant roots. The root knot nematode produces knots or galls in the roots. Have the soil analyzed through your county extension center. If the findings reveal damaging levels of nematodes, the course of action includes rotating vegetables away from this site, and planting nematode-resistant vegetables such as **Carolina Wonder** and **Charleston Belle bell peppers, Colossus southern pea, Better Boy, Celebrity,** or **OG 50 tomatoes,** and **Jewel sweet potato.** Soil solarization as described at right will also reduce their numbers.

See June's Insects, p. 99, for help in controlling leaffooted bugs, pickleworms, and spider mites.

Diseases: Bacterial wilt attacks **tomatoes, Irish potatoes, eggplants,** and **peppers.** It causes an entire fruiting plant suddenly to wither and die. To control this disease: *Remove and dispose of infected plants, roots and all. Rotate susceptible vegetables to different locations in your garden every year.* Currently, no chemicals or totally resistant tomato plants available. Two cultivars show promise, and you may want to try **Tropic Boy** or **Neptune tomatoes.**

Helpful Hints

- To make a produce cleaning station, replace the bottom of a wooden box with half-inch hardware cloth or chicken wire. Place fresh-picked vegetables in the box and rinse them off in the garden so the soil remains there. Only final cleaning will be necessary indoors.

- To suppress soil pest problems such as nematodes, bacteria, fungi, weeds, and insects, solarize the soil. Solarizing uses clear plastic or polyethylene to intensify sunlight, which raises soil temperatures and kills soilborne pests. The best time to solarize the soil is during the hottest part of summer. Follow these steps:

1 Cultivate the soil to a depth of 6 to 8 inches. Level the soil. **Remove** weeds, plants, and crop debris, and break up large clods of soil so the plastic will come in close contact with the soil.

2 Moisten the soil to conduct heat more deeply into it.

3 Dig a shallow trench around the plot to hold the edges of the plastic.

4 Stretch a clear plastic sheet that is 1 to 4 mils thick over the bed. A plastic that contains ultraviolet inhibitors will prevent it from deteriorating too quickly. Tuck it into the trench and bury the edges with soil to secure it in place.

5 Leave the plastic in place for four to six weeks in full summer sun.

Soil Solarization

Planning

As you update your garden journal, note the vegetables and herbs that didn't live up to expectations, and those that exceeded them. Make a note of insect and disease problems. In your plans for next year's garden, focus on varieties that performed well for you or that you have noticed did well in other gardens.

Consider heirloom vegetables. They are prized for flavor and tenderness and are saved year after year for generations. Select heirloom vegetables adapted to your area's soil, climate, and pests.

Beans and **tomatoes** are popular heirloom vegetables partly because they are easily maintained true-to-type—their seed produces fairly similar plants from one generation to the next. Heirlooms often have unique names like 'Mortgage Lifter' **tomato** and 'Turkey Gizzard' **bean.**

Planting

Set out cloves of **garlic** for a harvest early next summer. In the Piedmont and Coastal Plain sow **beans, beets, Brussels sprouts, cabbage,** carrots, broccoli, cauliflower, lettuce, rutabaga,** and **squash.** Plant greens, such as **kale, mustard,** and **turnips,** in intervals now and next month to lengthen the harvest season. In the Mountains, plant the last fall garden vegetables. For hardy crops like **cabbage, cauliflower,** and **collards,** count back from your average first frost date the number of days the particular variety requires to mature; plant at the appropriate time. For half-hardy crops like **beets** and **carrots,** allow an additional week. **Lettuce, radishes, beets, spinach, mustard, turnip,** and **peas** can be started from seed. *Set out* transplants of **kale, lettuce, broccoli, cabbage, cauliflower,** and **collards.**

Care for Your Herbs and Vegetables

Dry herbs. Gather bundles of each type of herb and spread on cheesecloth or hang upside-down in a warm, dark, dry place. Harvest **garlic** when the leaves turn yellow. Lift the entire plant and dry it in a well-ventilated, covered space. Save some for replanting and eat the rest. To protect **pumpkins** from rot, slip a shingle under ripening fruits to lift them off the soil. **Winter** squash is ready to harvest when the rind is hard and cannot be punctured with your thumbnail. Pull out plants that have stopped producing, including **bush beans,** early **cucumbers,** and **summer squash.** High temperatures slow **tomato** production. There is nothing to do but wait for the weather to cool. Then they will start producing again. The same goes for **bell peppers.** Too much fertilizer can cause **pepper** blossoms to fall off. **Peppers** are moderate feeders, needing only a little fertilizer at planting and a light sidedressing after the first fruits have set.

Watering

Watering properly is critical in the heat of summer. Slow, deep soakings are best done with trickle irrigation or soaker hoses.

Fertilizing

Feed **basil** with a liquid fertilizer to keep it productive into fall. Trim off seedheads so the plants will spend their energy on flavorful foliage.

Pest Control

Pests reach record numbers in the fall months. ***Remove*** old plants that have stopped producing to eliminate shelters for insects and disease organisms. Nematodes can be a problem with vegetables. ***Remove*** and discard infected plants. Watch for signs of leaffooted bugs and spider mites. See April Insects on p. 95.

Diseases: Gummy stem blight is a fungal disease that mostly infects **cantaloupes, cucumbers,** and **watermelons** in the Coastal Plain. Look for brown lesions on leaves and stems. If the stem is infected, the vine beyond the lesion will wither and die. Pull out and destroy infected vines. ***Remove*** and discard crop debris at the end of the growing season. Rotate with other vegetables other than vine crops or melons for two years. Avoid wetting the leaves when watering. Fungicides are available.

Helpful Hints

- Here's an old-time trick for starting seeds in midsummer: Plant and water them well, then set a board over the row. When the sprouts just reach the soil surface, remove the board.

- Before storing root crops like **carrots** and **beets,** cut off the green tops. They pull moisture from the roots, reducing quality.

- Leave 3 inches of stem when you harvest **winter squash** and **pumpkins;** they'll keep longer.

- Herbs make attractive, fragrant wreaths, especially when combined with boxwood or ornamental grasses. Green herbs are easier to work with, but wreaths must be hung to dry when completed.

- **Sunflower** seeds gain flavor if flower heads are left on until their backs turn brown. Then you can rub two heads together to knock off the seeds. Dry them for a few days, pack in airtight jars and refrigerate to retain that flavor. Eat them raw, or toast for 15 minutes at 300 degrees F. They are high in minerals, vitamins, protein, and oil.

Planning

Whether you garden year-round or hang up your hoe at summer's end, start tidying up the garden and take steps to build up the soil for next spring. Certain insects and diseases overwinter in plant debris. Time spent now burying plant stalks, debris, and mulch will eliminate winter havens for pests.

Consider the steps you will take to build the soil for next season. Planting a cover crop or "green manure" this fall that you will turn under in the spring is a great way to improve soil fertility and structure, hold valuable topsoil in place, improve water and nutrient retention in sandy soils, facilitate water and air movement in clay soils, attract earthworms and other beneficial critters, and suppress winter weeds. The most useful cover crop for home gardeners is one of these legumes: **crimson clover, Austrian winter pea, rough pea,** or common, smooth and hairy **vetch.** They can be planted at least a month before the first killing frost, add nitrogen as well as organic matter to the soil, and are relatively inexpensive. Non-legume cover corps provide less nitrogen but more organic matter. Mainly grasses like **oats, buckwheat, rye,** and **barley,** they are planted in late summer. *In the spring, turn under your cover crop three weeks before planting your garden.*

Planting

Pot up **chives, parsley,** and other herbs, and bring them into the house to extend the growing season.

Take cuttings or buy small plants of **rosemary, oregano, sage,** and other herbs. Grow them in 6-inch containers in a sunny window. Keep well watered; if possible, set them in a shallow tray of pebbles and water to increase humidity. Opening the window on mild days can help.

In the mild winter areas of the Piedmont and Coastal Plain, plant **cilantro,** a winter annual whose seeds are called **coriander**.

Plant **beets, carrots, kale, lettuce, spinach, turnip,** and **radish.** Soak seed furrows well before sowing seed, and mulch lightly. Water daily to promote germination and growth.

All sorts of fall vegetables can go in right away, including transplants of **leaf lettuce, Swiss chard, broccoli, Brussels sprouts, cauliflower,** and **cabbage.** Plant **onion** sets any time this month.

Mountain gardeners can plant **onion** sets—small bulbs stored from last year's onion crop—any time this month. Gardeners in the Piedmont and Coastal Plain should wait until the next month or two when cooler weather prevails. Choose small, firm sets that are less than $3/4$ inch in diameter for bulb onions. Larger sets can be used for **green onions**, since they tend to "bolt" and produce a seedstalk instead of a bulb.

Sow **onion** seeds or set out transplants. Use short-day **onions** in South Carolina and intermediate and long-day types in North Carolina. Contact your county extension center for recommended varieties.

Plant **parsley** and perennial herbs such as **sage, thyme,** and **rosemary,** and annuals like **dill** and **coriander.**

Care for Your Herbs and Vegetables

Harvest herbs to dry for winter use. Freeze **chives.** Take cuttings for a windowsill garden.

Start drying herbs such as **basil, oregano, sage, summer savory,** and **tarragon.**

Dig **sweet potatoes** before frost, being careful to avoid bruises and scrapes. Cure them for two or three weeks in the warmest room in the house to toughen the skin. Then store them where it is cool and dark.

Every two weeks, cull out any showing signs of decay.

Harvest **luffa gourds** when they begin to turn brown, feel light and dry, and rattle when shaken. Let any that remain after the first killing freeze dry on the vine. To make useful, biodegradable scrubbers for you and for your pots and pans:

- Soak in warm water until the sponge can be slipped out.

- Whiten sponges by dipping them into a 10 percent solution of household bleach.

- After thorough drying, store them in mesh bags.

- Discard worn-out sponges in your compost pile.

Harvest **winter squash** and **pumpkins** when fully mature but before they are damaged by frost. Cut the fruits from the vine, leaving a short piece of stem. They will keep for several months in a cool, dry basement.

Harvest **garlic** when the tops die. Cure the bulbs for six weeks in a warm, dry, shady, airy place, then move them to a cool, dry, airy spot.

Helpful Hints

- **Tomatoes** won't ripen when average daily temperatures fall below 65 degrees Fahrenheit. Then is the time to nip off all blossoms so plant nutrients flow to tomatoes already set. Not all green tomatoes ripen off the vine to an acceptable taste. Rescue from frost for later ripening only those showing a white or yellow star or a pink tinge at the blossom end. Delay ripening by storing at 50 to 60 degrees. Light is not needed, so put them where you can keep an eye on them.

- Use your microwave oven to dry herbs. Heat them between paper towels for one minute or until leaves are crisp. They'll keep their color and flavor stored in the dark in jars.

After mid-month, pinch new blossoms off **tomatoes, peppers,** and **eggplants** to help smaller fruits mature before cold weather.

Fertilizing

Apply fertilizer to vegetables as needed.

Watering

Keep watering. Many crops, such as **corn, pepper, squash,** and **tomato,** won't mature nicely if stressed due to lack of water.

Pest Control

Insects: Cucumber beetles, squash bugs, Colorado potato beetles, and European corn borers pass the winter in garden debris. Compost or plow under dead plants. This will limit your pest population next year to insects that migrate into the garden.

Planning

Envision a winter herb garden. Most herbs do very well on a south-facing windowsill. **Sweet basil, lemon verbena, summer savory,** and **tarragon** are the exceptions. They either go dormant or shed their leaves excessively.

Oregano, thyme, parsley, and **sage** can all be grown in small pots and trimmed as needed for the kitchen. Pots of **rosemary** and **sweet bay** (*Laurus nobilis*) are equally valuable, though they need more space.

In the onion family, windowsill candidates include **chives, onion** sets, and **garlic** cloves. The **onions** and **garlic** can be started in pots.

If you have only an east- or west-facing windowsill, try mints such as **peppermint, spearmint,** or **lemon balm.** Provided they are sheared regularly, these, too, make excellent houseplants.

If you find you have insect pests, it's best to discard infested plants rather than use pesticides.

Indoor herbs grow best in a mixture of two parts potting soil to one part coarse sand or perlite. Setting the pots in trays lined with gravel will keep them from getting wet feet should you overwater. Cool temperatures (60 degrees F.), especially at night, will keep herbs at their best.

Planting

Chives, coriander (cilantro), dill, and **parsley** can be direct-sown in the fall in the milder areas of the Piedmont and Coastal Plain so it will grow during the fall and winter months.

Piedmont and Coastal Plain gardeners can divide **chives, thyme, mint,** and **tarragon** when new growth emerges.

Plant **garlic** now for harvest in late summer. It likes a sunny, well-drained spot. Set bulb tips 2 inches beneath the surface.

Most herbs have lost their best flavor by now; discontinue drying for winter use. **Chives** and **parsley,** however, taste better than ever in cool weather; use them lavishly (French cooks mince fresh **chives** and **parsley** together and let diners spoon desired amounts onto fresh vegetables or baked potatoes. The flavors complement each other and parsley cuts the oniony aftertaste of chives).

Extend the gardening season well into the winter. **Lettuce, radish,** and **spinach** can all be grown in cold frames. Piedmont and Mountain gardeners might consider buying transplants for quicker results. In cooler weather, insulate the outsides of the frame with banked soil or sawdust. Cover the top with sacks stuffed with straw or other insulation during cold nights.

Plant **onion** sets and **garlic** cloves now to mid-November in the Coastal Plain. Plant **spinach** in October to do well this fall and winter.

Care for Your Herbs and Vegetables

Listen for frost warnings and be prepared to cover **tomatoes, eggplants, peppers,** and other tender vegetables. The weather often warms up again after the first frost, so this protection can prolong the harvest for weeks.

When there is a threat of frost, harvest your **cucumbers, eggplant, okra, pepper,** and **summer squash** before the fruits are frost-damaged.

Bring in **tomatoes** for ripening when daytime temperatures are consistently below 65 degrees F. Pick only those fruits that have begun to change color.

Harvest **sweet potatoes** before frost as well as **gourds, pumpkins,** and **winter squash.** To store **pumpkins:** *Pick only solid, mature pumpkins of a deep orange color. Try not to injure the rind; decay-*

causing fungi attack through wounds. Dip them in a chlorine solution of 4 teaspoons bleach per gallon of water. Allow fruit to dry, but do not rinse until ready to use. Cure them at room temperature for a week to harden the rind, then store in a cool place. They will keep about two months.

When you can no longer protect your plants, pull them and add them to the compost heap. Till or spade the soil in cleared areas to expose insects that are planning to overwinter. Then plant a hardy cover crop or mulch with shredded leaves, fresh manure, or spoiled hay to minimize winter erosion and provide nutrients for next year. Mountain gardeners can plant a cover crop of clover or winter grain as described in September Planning on p. 104.

For bigger and better **Brussels sprouts,** *pinch out* the top of the plant when sprouts at the bottom are fully grown. The smaller, upper sprouts will grow larger than they would otherwise.

Helpful Hints

You can store **Hubbard squash** up to six months, **butternut** about three, and **acorn** up to two. Here's how:

- Pick when they've developed a deep color, an indication of maturity. Leave about one inch of stem.

- Handle the fruit gently. Damaged rinds shorten storage life.

- Cure the rind in full sun for 10 days. If frost is expected, cover the squash.

- Pack in single layers in a crate, with crumpled newspapers between the layers.

- Store them between 50 to 60 degrees Fahrenheit. Squash are injured by temperatures below this range.

Thin **turnip** and **radish** plantings to give each root enough room to develop.

Watering

Cool-season vegetables perk up in the milder areas and grow vigorously. Water during dry spells and feed as necessary.

Pest Control

Clean up the garden. *Remove* any diseased or insect-infested plant debris. That's where pests spend the winter. Cabbage loopers and cabbageworms are the bane of the fall garden. If your **cabbage** leaves look like lace, *spray* with BTK (sold as Dipel® or Thuricide®). This microbial insecticide will not harm humans but will put a stop to hungry caterpillars. Control aphids with insecticidal soap.

NOVEMBER

Planning

Map out a plan of action to cut back or close down gardening operations for the winter. Do not forget to:

- Bring in your rain gauge to avoid freeze damage.

- Drain and store water hoses to extend their lives.

- Protect your investment in garden tools. Clean them up. Repair or replace broken ones.

Plan for the spring. As soon as seed flats and pots are emptied of fall transplants, wash and sterilize them. Use a 10 percent solution of household bleach and dry them thoroughly before storing them.

This is also a time to consider building a cold frame. Think of it as a sort of halfway house for seedlings as they make their way from the windowsill or light table to the outdoors. Make the cold frame, which is basically a bottomless box, of wood, stone, or brick with a transparent or translucent cover. It's like a miniature unheated greenhouse outdoors.

Typically cold frames are rectangular in shape, 3 by 6 feet or so. The back of the cold frame should face north and should be 18 to 30 inches high. The front should be slightly lower, between 12 and 24 inches to allow enough headroom for the plants inside. Tilt the cover to the south by sloping the sides about 1 inch per foot. More adventurous gardeners can even add an automatic opener to the cover. These devices lift the cover automatically as the temperature rises during the day and gradually close it as the evening temperatures fall.

Planting

Plant **lettuce** and hardy vegetables such as **beets, cabbage,** and **spinach** in cold frames for winter or early spring crops. Grow leafy vegetables such as **lettuce, Chinese cabbage,** and **spinach** in a cold frame or beneath a row cover for harvesting all winter long.

Continue enjoying fresh-picked cool-weather crops as they mature.

Harvest **kale** by picking just a few leaves from each plant; this will encourage continued production of new leaves.

Care for Your Herbs and Vegetables

A light mulch of shredded leaves or straw on **carrots, turnips,** and other root vegetables will help protect against freezing. Pick **tomatoes** when frost is predicted and store in a single layer in a cool location. Harvest **broccoli** while the heads are still compact. Tie the leaves around **cauliflower** heads to blanche the curds.

Pruning

Remove **asparagus** ferns after frost kills them.

Helpful Hint

Cultivating the soil this month can leave it exposed throughout fall and winter and can result in problems with soil erosion. Since it's too late to plant a cover crop to hold the soil, apply a blanket of mulch such as shredded leaves or compost to keep the soil in place. To learn more about making compost, refer to Trees, September Planning, p. 302. You will find information about recycling leaves and other yard trimmings.

Planning

Take inventory of your seed collection. Decide what to save, trade, or toss out. To decide what stays and what goes, ask yourself:

- How old is the seed? Seeds have a limited shelf life and remain viable (capable of germinating) for a certain period of time. Here are the ballpark ages of several vegetable seeds that when stored under cool, dry conditions should be expected to produce a good stand of healthy seedlings.

  1 year or less: **onions, parsley, parsnips,** and **salsify**

  2 years: **corn, okra,** and **peppers**

  3 years: **beans, southern peas (cowpeas),** and **peas**

  4 years: **beets, fennel, mustard, pumpkins, rutabagas, squash, Swiss chard, tomatoes, turnips,** and **watermelons**

  5 years: **Brussels sprouts, cabbage, cauliflower, collards, eggplant, muskmelons, radishes,** and **spinach**

- Is the seed viable? Perform a simple germination test. Take two or three layers of moistened paper towel and lay ten to twenty seeds on the surface. Gently roll up the towels enclosing the seeds and put the roll inside a plastic bag. Label with the variety and date of sowing and place the bag in a location where the temperature is between 70 and 80 degrees F. After two or three days, unroll the paper towels and examine the seeds, and do so daily thereafter. At the end of three weeks, total up the number of seeds that have germinated. If ten of the twenty have sprouted, expect a 50 percent germination rate when you sow the remainder.

- Is the seed the actual variety you wanted to save? If the vegetables are self-pollinated like **beans, peas,** and nonhybrid **tomatoes,** expect to grow true-to-type varieties. Expect surprises, however, when planting the seeds from insect- or wind-pollinated varieties. Cross-pollination will occur between different varieties of insect-pollinated vegetables such as **cucumber, melon, squash,** or **pumpkin.** The same goes for wind-pollinated **beets, sweet corn, spinach,** and **Swiss chard.** You may want to discard these seeds.

- Was the seed collected from a hybrid? Hybrid or F1 hybrid seed is the offspring of a cross made between two parent varieties. If you want the original hybrid, discard these seeds. The offspring from an F1 hybrid will be a mixture of traits, most of which will be inferior to the original parent.

- Do you have any seeds or varieties that a fellow gardener would be willing to swap for? In the eyes of some gardeners, a "Mickey Mantle" or "Joe DiMaggio" could take the form of a Sweet Baby Blue corn or a Super Italian Paste tomato. Perhaps you can save these seeds and trade them for something else.

Planting

Piedmont: Sow **onion** seeds. Piedmont and Coastal Plain gardeners can sow **lettuce** and other greens in cold frames for winter use.

Care for Your Herbs and Vegetables

Continue to harvest **chives, cilantro,** and **parsley.** In the Piedmont and Mountains, protect winter greens with a fabric row cover or with plastic tunnels—plastic stretched over metal hoops for protection from hard freezes. **Brussels sprouts, broccoli, mustard, cabbage, turnips,** and most **lettuces** will be damaged by a hard freeze (more than six hours below 26 degrees Fahrenheit).

Houseplants

Growing plants indoors relieves an itchy green thumb when the weather keeps us inside. A wonderful variety of shapes, colors, sizes, textures, and fragrances can beautify and enrich our indoor living space.

The trees, vines, ferns, and flowering plants in this chapter make good houseguests. They enrich our indoor atmosphere, exchanging carbon dioxide for oxygen. Certain plants can even reduce indoor levels of air pollutants like formaldehyde and benzene. Whether you cultivate them for their beauty or for your health, it's fun, and easy, to succeed as an indoor gardener.

Planning an Indoor Garden

The plants grown as houseplants originate in temperate, subtropical, and tropical regions, and they flourish in a wide range of growing conditions. In nature, some plants are exposed to direct sunlight while others grow beneath taller trees and receive only filtered tropical sun. Still others thrive in the deep shade on the forest floor.

To successfully grow plants indoors, find some suited to the growing conditions in your home. And become familiar with light, water, temperature, humidity, fertilization, and potting medium, as well as the effects of all of these on your houseplants.

Plants need light. In most cases, light is the limiting factor in growing plants indoors. When given the light intensity, or brightness of light, that closely matches their needs, plants develop well-colored leaves, are well-branched, and have a full-looking appearance; flowering plants will initiate flower buds and bloom.

For simplicity, houseplants can be categorized by their light requirements:

- **High Light:** Plants must be within 3 feet of a south-, east-, or west-facing window that receives direct sunlight for most or part of the day.

- **Medium Light:** Plants must be in a well-lit position 3 to 5 feet inside a south-, east- or west-facing window or one that receives bright indirect or filtered sunlight (the light may be filtered through a translucent curtain or screened by tree limbs).

- **Low Light:** Plants can be 5 to 6 feet away from a high-light window or near a well-lit north-facing window. If placed farther than 6 feet away from a sunny window source of sunlight, some plants may maintain their appearance for a period of time before declining. Then they will have to be moved to a brighter location.

These are only general light categories. The amount of light entering a room depends on a number of factors such as the size and position of the windows, the season, the weather, and trees or nearby buildings that may block incoming light.

Air Layering

Winter is a good time to propagate houseplants by a fairly foolproof method called **air-layering.** Suitable candidates include tall tropical and subtropical plants, such as **dieffenbachia, dracaena, fatsia,** and **rubber plant,** whose leaves are clustered at the top of naked, "leggy" stems. Air-layering results in two plants by inducing one to form roots along its stem while it's still attached to the mother plant. After the rooted top is removed, the mother plant will produce leaves below the cut. Here's how to air-layer:

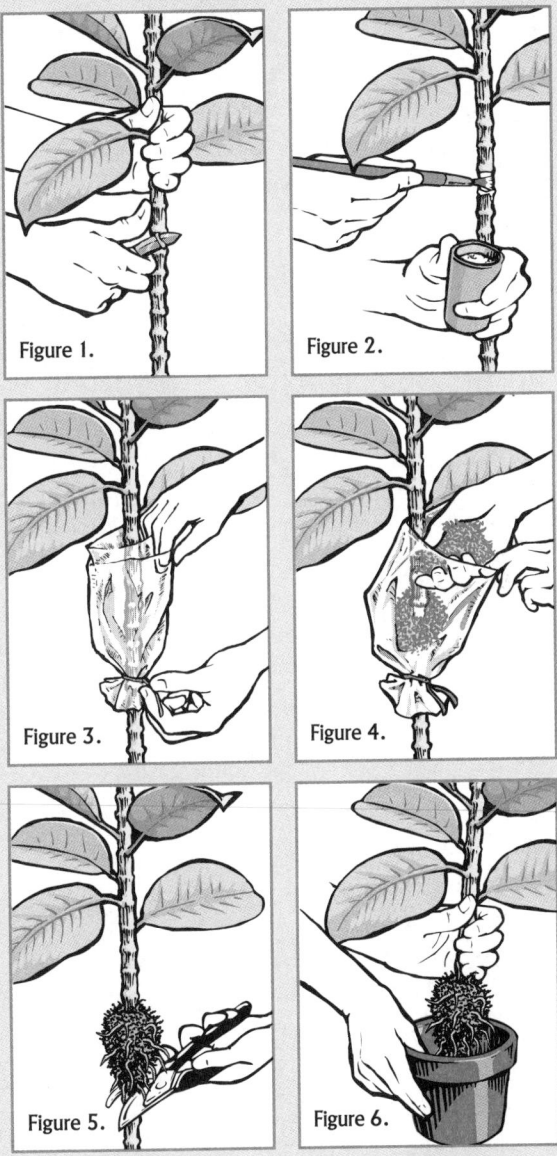

Figure 1.

Figure 2.

Figure 3.

Figure 4.

Figure 5.

Figure 6.

1 Select a healthy, vigorously growing main stem or lateral branch from last season's growth. Make a slanting upward cut 1 to 2 inches long on one side of the stem, cutting halfway through the stem. (Figure 1.)

2 **Insert** a toothpick between the two cut surfaces to keep them apart, and **dust** the cut surfaces with a rooting hormone. (Figure 2.)

3 Arrange a plastic bag around the stem, securing it below the cut with masking tape. (Figure 3.)

4 Soak a handful or two of long-fibered sphagnum moss in water, squeeze out the excess, and pack the wet moss around the cut and into the plastic bag, holding it in place with the plastic bag so it will fit around the stem. (Figure 4.) A good substitute for the moss is a peat pellet that has been soaked in water and formed a pot. Slice it vertically on one side and open it up so it will fit neatly over the plant's stem.

5 Secure the bag above the cut with masking tape to keep the moss inside damp. Add water if you see the moss beginning to dry out.

Once you see a healthy ball of white roots beneath the plastic, **sever** the new plant just below the moss ball, remove the wrapping (being careful not to damage the roots), and pot it up in a suitable mixture. (Figures 5 and 6.)

Houseplants

Watering

Become familiar with the particular water needs of your plants, which may vary with the seasons. When the plants are resting during the winter months, water sparingly. The planting chart on p. 115 includes some comments about the watering requirements of certain kinds of plants. Other houseplant reference books will have information about the watering needs of specific indoor plants.

Humidity

Maintaining enough moisture in the air is the greatest challenge. During the winter months, relative humidity drops to 10 or 15 percent indoors. That's fine for cactuses and succulents like **snake plant** *(Sansevieria)*, **cast-iron plant** *(Aspidistra)*, and various **dracenas**. Most others need a relative humidity of 40 to 60 percent. At lower humidity levels, the leaves of most plants lose water faster than their roots can absorb it. As a result, the leaves curl and their tips turn brown; flowering plants may drop their flower buds or their flowers may wither up prematurely.

During the winter months, move your plants to cooler locations or to rooms that tend to be more humid than others like the bathroom, the kitchen (away from the oven), or a well-lit basement.

You can also boost local humidity levels in the following ways.

- **Clustering:** water lost by leaves and potting mix raises moistens the air of its neighbors.

- **Using a room humidifier or cool-mist vaporizer:** track humidity levels with a digital hygrometer so you can increase to the levels that will match your comfort, too. The ideal moisture level for people is between 30 and 50 percent relative humidity.

- **Setting pans of water on radiators or wood stoves.**

- **Placing high-humidity lovers on a pebble-filled tray of water inside an aquarium tank with an adjustable opening at the top:** a small fan will improve air circulation, and a heating cable under the tray will speed up evaporation.

Temperature

In general, houseplants thrive at day temperatures of 70 to 80 degrees Fahrenheit, with a 10-degree drop at night. Blooming houseplants prefer the lower ranges. *But houseplants are resilient.* They can tolerate slightly higher or lower temperatures for part of the time. Don't make yourself uncomfortable to accommodate them.

Fertilizing

Plants make their own food as long as they have adequate light, minerals, and water. Minerals are present in soil-based potting mixtures, while soilless, peat-based mixtures have to be supplemented with fertilizers to supply minerals. *Fertilize* plants to correct deficiencies brought about by a lack of nutrients. Look for these signs: little growth, pale leaves, weak stems, absent or poorly colored flowers, and early drop of lower leaves. Make sure that these symptoms are not the result of insects, diseases, improper watering, or inadequate light.

Houseplants

You can also fertilize plants to maintain growth; be careful, however, that you don't fertilize too often, which can result in the production of rampant, vigorous growth that can easily overgrow the space.

Fertilize plants when they're actively growing in spring and summer. During the short days of winter, many indoor plants that receive little or no artificial light will rest. Don't fertilize resting plants—excessive fertilizer can injure or kill them. Always take care to follow the instructions on the fertilizer label.

Repotting

Plants like **African violets, clivia,** and **cactuses** flower better when slightly potbound. But as roots fill the pot, the soil loses its ability to absorb and hold water. Then it's time to repot. Repotting is best done in early spring when new growth occurs.

1 Choose a clean pot that is one size larger or no more than 2 inches larger than the original. *Cover* its drainage hole with a coffee filter. Don't put a layer of gravel or stones at the bottom—save that space for the roots. *Research has shown that such a layer can decrease drainage and keep the potting mix waterlogged.*

2 If the plant is small enough, upend the pot, holding your hand over the soil with the stems between your fingers. Gently tap the pot's lip on a table to *loosen the rootball.*

Loosen the rootball.

3 If the plant is potbound, the container will be filled with roots. Some may even be spiraling around the outside of the rootball. *Cut* them with a sharp knife, making shallow cuts on opposite sides of the rootball and along the bottom to free the congested roots.

4 *Cover* the bottom of the new pot with a layer of moist potting mix. Aim to center the plant in the new pot with the top of the rootball an inch below the rim. Set it on a cushion of potting mix. Adjust the height by adding or removing mix.

Adjust the height.

5 Fill in around the sides, firming the soil with your fingers or by tapping the pot on the tabletop.

6 *Water* thoroughly to settle the soil. Do not feed the plant for the next month or so.

Care for Your Houseplants

At least weekly, tidy up your plants:

- *Remove* dying, dead, or damaged leaves and stems and any spent flowers.

- Peek under the leaves and along the stems for pests.

Houseplants

- ***Pinch out*** and remove an inch or less of new stem and leaf growth from long, unbranched stems to stimulate growth behind the pinch.

- Snip off the brown leaf tips with sharp scissors.

Pruning

Houseplants need regular pruning so as to:

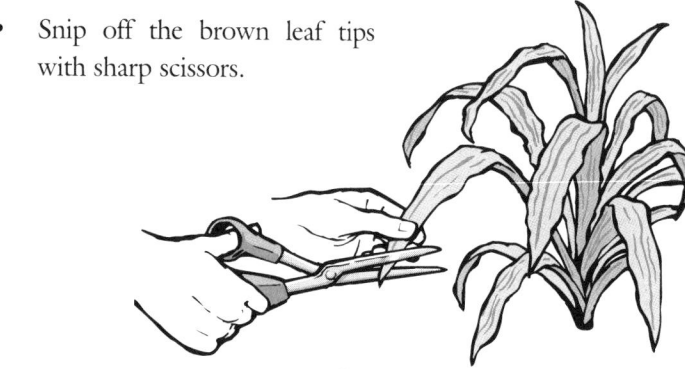
Snip off brown leaf tips.

- Keep the leaves clean. Use a soft cosmetic brush on plants with hairy leaves such as **African violets, gloxinias,** and **rex begonias.** Clean smooth leaves with a damp sponge or cloth.

- Give your plants a turn to expose all sides to sunlight.

- remove broken, diseased-or insect-infested shoots.

- train them to a desired shape.

- keep them in bounds.

- improve sunlight penetration and air movement by removing tangled, messy growth.

- create bushy, dense growth.

Spring is the best time for pruning most plants, right before new growth begins. Broken, dead, or insect-or disease-ridden limbs, however, can be removed whenever you spot them. Houseplants that have produced an abundance of growth outdoors during the summer can be pruned back before they're brought indoors in the fall.

Pest Control

The best line of defense against pests is a healthy, well-maintained plant. Inspect your plants regularly by turning over the leaves and looking in the nooks and crannies of the stems. It's best if you can catch infestations early before they explode into full-blown assaults that will leave you and your plants in misery. Refer to the monthly "Pest Control" sections for common houseplant pests and their controls.

Keep the leaves clean.

Planting Chart

Foliage Houseplants

Common Name (Botanical Name)	Propagation	Light*	Comments
Cast-iron plant (*Aspidistra elatior*)	Divide clumps in spring	Medium to Low	"Hercules" of houseplants; 'Variegata' combines strength with beauty
Chinese evergreen (*Aglaonema modestum*)	Division, cuttings, or air-layering	Medium to Low	Easy-to-grow bushy plant with bold-looking leaves; remove overgrown shoots to maintain a compact, dense growth
Golden pothos (*Epipremnum aureum*)	Stem cuttings in spring or summer	High to Low	Extremely durable vines that can tolerate occasional forgotten waterings
Ivy, grape (*Cissus rhombifolia*)	Stem cuttings	High to Medium	Tough, fast-growing vine that tolerates some neglect
Palm, parlor (*Chamaedorea erumpens*)	Seed	Medium	Tolerates dry air but prefers high humidity
Peperomia, watermelon (*Peperomia argyreia*), Emerald Ripple (*P. caperata*), Pepper Face (*Peperomia obtusifolia*)	Stem cuttings in spring and summer	Medium	Often overwatered which leads to wilting and root rot; otherwise, very dependable and easy-going houseplant

Flowering Houseplants

Common Name (Botanical Name)	Propagation	Light*	Comments
African violet (*Saintpaulia* spp. hybrids and cultivars)	Seeds or leaf cuttings in spring	High to Medium	High humidity; will flower year-round with adequate light
Clivia or Kaffir lily (*Clivia miniata*)	Divide clumps, pot up offsets, or sow seed	High	Blooms better when potbound
Hibiscus, Chinese (*Hibiscus rosa-sinensis*)	Stem cuttings in spring or summer	High	Flowers are borne on new shoots, so shorten stem in spring before growth begins
Orchids Cattleyas or Corsage orchid (*Cattleya* hybrids) Moth orchid (*Phalaenopsis*) Venus' Slipper (*Paphiopedilum*)	Division	High	Magnificent blooms over an extended time period; select these and other hybrids that are well-suited for growing indoors; Moth and Venus' Slipper require cool temperatures to produce flower buds; Cattleyas require bright light
Peace lily (*Spathiphyllum* spp.)	Division or seed	High to medium	Keep moist when growing
Wax plant (*Hoya carnosa*)	Layering or stem cuttings	High	Evening-blooming flowers have an enchanting fragrance; remove the faded flowers without damaging the woody spurs

*See introduction, p. 110, Planning an Indoor Garden.

Planning

With the holiday season behind you, make plans to spend some of your time on improving the lighting conditions for your indoor plants. During the winter months the sun is lower and farther to the south; your plants will receive fewer hours of light, and the light they do receive will be less intense. Plants located close to an unshaded south window, however, may receive more direct sunlight in the winter because of the low sun angle.

You may need to make some adjustments to the location of your plants. Houseplants that thrive in low light on the north side of the house can be moved to east windows at this time. Plants on the east windows can receive more sun if moved to a south window. Plants that are usually placed on plant stands away from direct sunlight can be located closer to a less-exposed window to give them more light. Consider rotating the plants every week or so if the room is dimly lit.

If you choose not to corral your plants near windows, plan on giving them artificial light. Give them as much natural sunlight as possible and then supplement with an additional five or six hours of cool-white fluorescent light in the evening. A nice bonus: Lighted plants lend dramatic effects to a decorating scheme.

Care for Your Houseplants

When extremely cold nights are expected, move your tender plants away from the windows. Keeping a curtain or windowshade between the plant and the window will reduce the chances of cold injury.

Keep your flowering holiday gift plants looking their best by moving them to a spot that's 10 degrees cooler at night.

Plants growing under fluorescent lights need to rest at night. Rely on an automatic timer to keep the lights on for about twelve to sixteen—but no more than eighteen—hours per day before shutting them off automatically during darkness.

Encourage your **amaryllis** to bloom next year. Remove the withered flowers and give it plenty of sunlight and nutrients to produce carbohydrates, which, in turn, produce flower buds. Once the flower withers, remove it and place the amaryllis in bright, indirect sunlight. Fertilize twice a month with a liquid houseplant fertilizer to promote healthy leaves. A bulb will generally produce a flowering scape after producing three or four leaves; the more leaves it produces, the more flower scapes you can expect next season.

Wipe the dust off the smooth hairless leaves of your **Chinese evergreen, dieffenbachia, philodendron, rubber plant, schefflera,** and the like with a damp cloth. A soft paint or cosmetic brush works well to clean the hairy leaves of **African violets** and **gloxinias.**

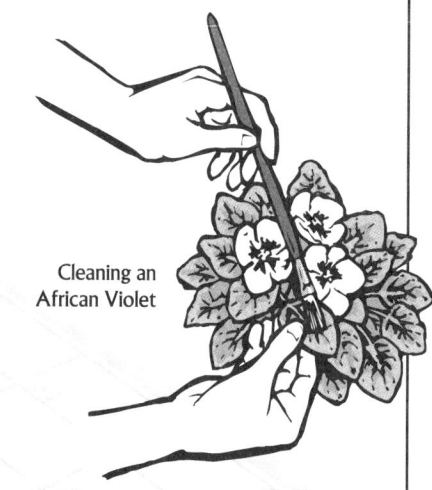

Cleaning an African Violet

Protect store-bought or traded houseplants before transporting them outdoors. Use paper bags, paper or plastic sleeves from the store, or three or four layers of newspaper wrapped and stapled shut. In your car, keep the plant in the front seat and turn on the heater. Don't put the plant in the trunk where it can be damaged or killed by the cold. Many foliage plants will be damaged if the air temperature drops much below 50 degrees Fahrenheit, so keep them as warm as possible.

Watering

Overwatering encourages root rot. *Water* according to the needs of the plant. Plants that are resting now should be watered sparingly. Flowering plants such as **amaryllis, clivia, cyclamen, holiday cactus,** and **poinsettia** can be kept moderately moist and watered when the surface of the medium feels dry.

Fertilizing

Avoid fertilizing resting houseplants this month. *Fertilize* your plants only when they're actively growing.

Pruning

Clip off any dead leaves and spent flowers to clean up the plant and reduce the chances of diseases from occurring.

Pest Control

Insects and mites: Check all houseplants for insects and spider mites. Look carefully because some of them can hide very well and may not be seen until damage is quite severe.

Quarantine gift plants for a few days until you determine that they aren't harboring any pests.

Watch out for mealybugs and soft-scale insects. Both of these sucking insects excrete honeydew when they feed on plant sap. Mealybugs are easier to see because their bodies are surrounded by white cottony tufts of wax. Look for mealybugs on the undersides and axils of the leaves, on the shoot tips, and in the crevices of stems or branches.

Mealybugs can be removed with a toothpick or tweezers. Spot-treating them with a cotton-tipped swab dipped in rubbing alcohol or using an insecticidal soap is also effective.

Soft-scale insects tend to be more difficult to see, especially those species that take on the color and appearance of the stem or trunk. Adult scales often noticeably protrude from the leaf or twig.

Use a magnifying glass to inspect both sides of the leaves, stems, and limbs closely. Try to dislodge any strange-looking bumps with a pin or sharp pencil point. A shiny spot of honeydew may remain where the scale was attached.

Soft-scales are difficult to control. The adults can be picked off by hand or with a pair of tweezers. Small populations can be killed using the cotton swab and rubbing alcohol treatment described for mealybugs.

Before using an insecticidal soap, check the label to see if your plant is listed. You may have to test a small area on your plant with the soap and check for signs of injury. It may take seven to ten days for damage to appear. If your plant shows sensitivity, rinse the soap off once the insects are killed.

Diseases: If you've clustered plants together to improve moisture conditions around them, watch out for diseases, particularly gray mold (a fuzzy gray fungus that thrives on dead plant tissues such as spent flowers and fallen leaves).

Snip away any diseased tissues with a sharp scissors. Improve air movement around the plants.

Helpful Hint

Now is a good time to propagate houseplants by a fairly foolproof method called air-layering (see p. 111).

Planning

This is a good time to organize your work area and supplies in preparation for work later this month and the following month. If some of your plants need to be repotted, start looking at some new containers, or wash old containers and reuse them. If you're planning on propagating plants, get your flats and potting medium ready. Sharpen your scissors, knives, or pruning shears.

Take a look at the fluorescent lights in your light table to see if you need new ones. Have the ends begun to darken? Fluorescent lights should generally be replaced each year because they become less efficient as they age. Instead of discarding the tubes that still work, put them in other fixtures or in light fixtures over plants that have lower light requirements. Replace one tube at a time because increased light intensity can injure plants. Wait about a month before replacing additional tubes. Mark the date with a grease pencil as a reminder of when the tubes have to be replaced. Dust off the tubes and the reflective surfaces on a monthly basis.

Planting

Now is a good time to repot plants, especially those whose roots may be escaping through the drainage holes. See Repotting in the introduction to this chapter on p. 113.

When repotting **cactuses,** grasp spiny plants with kitchen tongs or wrap a folded newspaper or paper towel around its waist. With this handle, gently tease it out of its container. Be gentle so that you don't crush the spines.

This is a good time to root softwood stem cuttings of many houseplants, including **philodendrons, peperomias,** and **devil's ivy.**

1 Take 4- to 6-inch-long cuttings with a sharp knife or razor blade. *Cut* below a leaf joint or node. *Remove* any leaves from the bottom of the stem.

2 Remove the bottom from a clear plastic 2-liter soda bottle. Cut the bottom of the bottle so it can be fitted over the base. *Fill* the base with a well-drained, moistened medium such as equal parts of peat and perlite. Make a hole with a pencil and *insert* the cutting so the node is below the surface of the medium. *Firm* around the base with a pencil. A rooting hormone is unnecessary with many houseplants; using a rooting hormone for softwood cuttings, however, will improve the density and uniformity of roots.

3 *Water* the cuttings and then secure the bottle inside the base. Move the bottle to a spot that receives indirect sunlight.

4 If there's too much condensation inside the bottle, take off the cap to let in some air. *Test* the cuttings each week by giving them a few tugs. When the cuttings have developed vigorous roots evenly distributed around the base in about three to four weeks, take the pot out of the bag and move it into brighter light. *Transplant* the rooted cuttings into a pot with your favorite potting mixture.

Layer the "babies" from plants that produce stolons or runners such as **spider plant, piggyback plant,** and **strawberry-begonia** while they're still attached to their "mother." Pin down a plantlet in a pot next to its "mother." When new growth occurs, sever the rooted offspring. Another way to propagate is to sever the plantlets and pot them up; they may need to be treated like a division, however, and placed in a plastic "mini-greenhouse" to encourage rooting.

Care for Your Houseplants

Turn houseplants regularly so that all sides are exposed to incoming sunlight.

Clean the dust and grime from large, smooth-leaved houseplants with a damp sponge or cloth. Small plants can be moved to the shower or laundry sink for rinsing.

Watering

Houseplants can be watered more frequently now and will have to be checked often with the onset of new growth.

Fertilizing

When houseplants begin to show signs of growth, they can be fertilized. *Apply* the fertilizer according to manufacturer's instructions, making sure that the soil is moistened beforehand.

Pruning

Always remove insect-damaged, diseased, or broken limbs and shoots first. Use sharp tools for pruning your plants—shears for woody plants, a razor blade or knife for soft-stemmed plants. Then focus on pruning and training your plant into the shape you want by directing growth in a particular direction or cutting back to encourage compact, bushy growth.

Hanging baskets of **philodendrons, piggyback plants,** or **pothos** may have leaves clustered at the ends of their stems. Cut them all the way back to the rim of the pot. During the next few months the new growth will trail over the sides of the pot to hide it once again. Instead of composting the trimmings, root them as stem cuttings (see "Planting" for details).

Pest Control

Insects and mites: Inspect your plants carefully for signs of aphids, scale insects, and mites.

Aphids or "plant lice" are soft-bodied insects that suck plant sap and cause new growth to turn yellow, curl, and become distorted. They are usually green but may be pink, brown, black, or yellow. They are often found on new growth, clustered at the tips of new shoots. Even if you can't see them, you may see telltale signs of their presence: skins cast off as they molt and a sugary substance, called honeydew, that they exude on leaves and stems, making them feel sticky.

Remove the plant from the area and take measures to control the pests. Light infestations can be controlled by handpicking, showering them with water, or using insecticidal soaps. If you prefer to use an insecticide or miticide, follow label directions and make sure that your plant is listed on the label.

Diseases: Remove any diseased leaves or trim away any infected spots with sharp scissors.

To thwart infections, keep the leaves dry when watering.

Planning

All winter long your houseplants have been inside, toughing out the low light levels and the cool temperatures of winter. Now as spring comes marching in with longer and warmer days, you need to prepare your houseplants for the next several months of growth and plan on taking them outdoors. Look for shady locations in the garden where they can rest in containers or where they can be tucked into the ground in flower borders. Make notes in your journal so you can coordinate the placement of your houseplants with the placement of your annuals, perennials, and shrubs.

Planting

Continue repotting any potbound plants. For plants that have reached their maximum pot size, consider *topdressing* as a short-term alternative to repotting:

1 Gently tease away the top inch or two of potting mixture with a kitchen fork, making sure to avoid causing too much injury to the roots.

2 *Refill* the pot with fresh potting mixture to the original level.

A better approach, albeit more risky, is to root-prune:

1 Ease the plant out of its container.

2 Using a sharp knife, *trim* away a shallow slice from the sides and bottom of the rootball.

3 *Repot* the plant in the same container, providing it's clean and free of salts, then add fresh potting mix.

Root-pruning is a drastic measure that can induce "transplanting shock." Give a root-pruned plant the best growing conditions to help it regenerate new roots. Sometimes for insurance, especially for invaluable old specimens, it's a good idea to propagate the plant from cuttings before undertaking this procedure.

Pot-up the cuttings that you rooted last month.

In the spring, move flowering annuals that were overwintered as houseplants outdoors. Either move the entire plant, or propagate a number of stem cuttings for transplanting outside.

Care for Your Houseplants

Move your houseplants outside on mild days, out of direct sun that can scorch the leaves. If the temperature is expected to go below 50 degrees Fahrenheit, bring them inside.

Watering

Water newly potted houseplants, thoroughly wetting the soil.

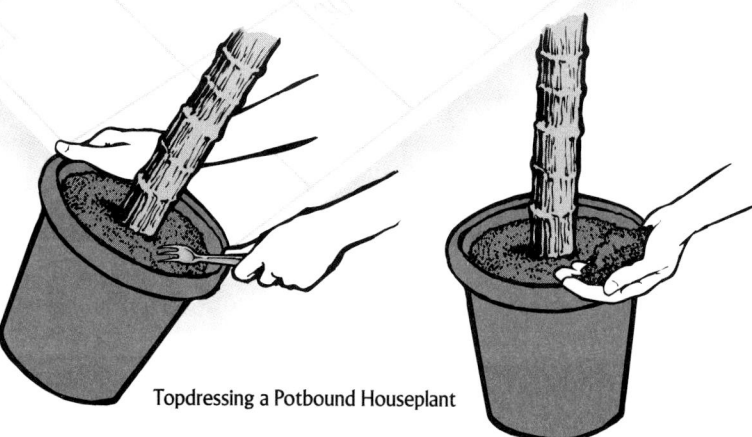

Topdressing a Potbound Houseplant

Fertilizing

With longer days, most houseplants begin growing vigorously and can be fertilized. Newly potted plants can be fertilized a month after being repotted. Follow the fertilizer label instructions.

Pruning

Pinch out the growing tips of **fuchsia**, **grape ivy**, and **kangaroo vine** to encourage branching and fullness.

When tall single-stemmed plants such as **Chinese evergreen** (*Aglaonema*), **dieffenbachia**, and **dracaena** get top-heavy with clusters of leaves at the top and long, leafless leggy stems below, *prune* them: cut back the top—no lower than 6 to 8 inches from the pot—to force new leaves to emerge. Eventually the plant will look as good as new.

Pest Control

Insects and mites: As the days get warmer, expect pests to become more active, which means that you'll have to be more vigilant to spot infestations and to control them. Keep an eye on those plants that you've brought outside and returned inside in the evening. Look for aphids, mealybugs, scales, and spider mites.

Aphids can be found clustered at the tips of new shoots.

1   *Pinch out* the infested tips and discard them.

2   Small plants can be turned upside down and dipped in a bucket of water to dislodge the aphids.

3   Use a cotton-tipped swab dipped in alcohol. Don't over-apply because alcohol may burn the leaves.

Apply an insecticidal soap labeled for your plant. For severe pest infestations, you may have to rely on chemical controls.

Spider mites feed on the undersides of the leaves, sucking plant sap with their needlelike mouth parts. Their feeding causes tiny specks to appear on the surface of the leaves. Heavily infested plants are covered with fine webbing. When left unchecked, leaves turn bronze or yellow, and the plant may die.

Check for mites—shake a leaf over a piece of white paper and look for moving specks the size of the period at the end of this sentence.

Remove them by showering the plants with warm water. Follow up with a spray of insecticidal soap, being sure to contact the undersides of the leaves. If mites are still present after two weeks, treat again with insecticidal soap.

Diseases: *Clip off* any dead or dying foliage and discard it.

Planning

If you plan on moving your houseplants outdoors, wait until the night temperatures stay above 60 degrees Fahrenheit. Plants can be chilled by low temperatures and sunburned by high-light levels. "Harden-off" your indoor plants (gradually expose them to their outdoor environment to toughen them up) so they can escape injury. Move them outside during the day for a few hours and then gradually increase their time outside for up to two weeks or more. Keep them in shaded locations and gradually *expose* them to brighter light. Some plants such as **begonias, ferns, ficus trees,** and **philodendrons** can stay in full to partial shade beneath trees or on shaded decks. Mountain gardeners should be cautious this month, since chilly temperatures can cause tender plants to drop their leaves.

Planting

To learn the basics of starting houseplants from seed, refer to Annuals, p. 30.

Repot your **orchids** if they've outgrown their pots or if the potting medium has broken down and no longer drains freely. The best time to repot depends on the orchid. If it's one that produces pseudobulbs

(bulblike, swollen stems that store food and water) such as **Cattelya,** *repot* it when new growth begins but before the new roots have begun to elongate. Orchids that have succulent leaves and lack pseudobulbs such as **moth orchid *(Phalaenopsis)*** or **Venus' slipper orchid *(Paphiopedilum*)** can be repotted at any time, although it's best to do it when the plants are not in flower.

1 Gently remove the orchid from the pot. Pry apart the roots and shake off as much of the old potting mixture as possible.

2 *Clip off* any dead or damaged roots with a sharp knife or shears.

3 Add a commercially prepared fir bark–based mixture for orchids to a clean pot. The mixture comes in either fine or medium-sized chunks, usually with some admixture of coarse peat, redwood fiber, charcoal, perlite, or tree-fern fiber. The medium should offer excellent drainage.

4 Tamp the pot on a table to help settle the smaller particles around the larger ones.

If you haven't repotted potbound plants, *repot* them this month.

Divide plants that have grown too large for their containers. Take good care of the divisions to help them avoid transplant "shock."

Bromeliads can be propagated by dividing the offsets, the small plants that emerge at the base of the mother plant. These offsets replace the mother rosette that flowers only once in a bromeliad and then gradually dies. You can leave the offsets in the pot (since the withered old rosette can eventually be removed), or you can detach the offsets.

1 *Sever* the offsets or plantlets with a sharp knife when they are one-third the size of the mother and have at least five well-developed leaves.

2 *Pot* them in containers filled with equal parts of peat moss and perlite.

3 Loosely enclose the container in a clear plastic bag to keep humidity levels high until the roots have formed.

4 When the offsets have rooted, *transfer* them to a 4-inch pot filled with a commercial bromeliad mix, or make your own of equal parts ground conifer bark, peat moss, and perlite.

5 Locate your bromeliad in bright, indirect sunlight with a room temperature between 60 and 85 degrees Fahrenheit.

6 *Fertilize* monthly with a diluted houseplant fertilizer mixed at half the recommended rate. Apply the fertilizer to the "cup" of the bromeliad's rosette and over the potting medium after it has been moistened. Empty the plant's "cup" every now and then to prevent the water from stagnating.

7 Expect the offsets to bloom one or two years later.

Watering

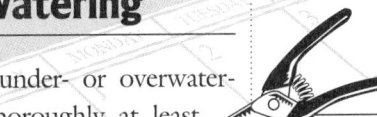

Avoid under- or overwatering. *Water* thoroughly at least once a month, more often if needed, so that water runs out of the bottom of the pot. This will dissolve any salts and flush them out to reduce their buildup. Empty the drip saucer so your plant doesn't sit in a pool of water.

Do not use softened water in which calcium and magnesium have been replaced with sodium. Sodium accumulates in the soil and can injure or kill plants.

Fertilizing

Evaluate the growth and appearance of your plants to decide whether or not to fertilize them. Plants growing in low light need less fertilizer than plants growing in brighter light. For the gradual release of nutrients over an extended period of time, consider slow-release fertilizers that act like time-release capsules. They can be applied less frequently than fast-release fertilizers. Follow the manufacturer's label instructions for the proper amounts.

Pruning

Deadhead (remove the faded flowers of) houseplants that have bloomed. *Pinch out* the tips of vining plants to encourage the production of leaves behind the cuts.

Pest Control

Check your plants for signs of pests whenever you water them. Early infestations can often be eliminated by handpicking or by washing the plants with an insecticidal soap solution. Since pests may be hidden or in the egg stage, it often takes more than one treatment to eliminate them.

Planning

If you shuffled your house-plants around indoors in January, you may want to plan a weekend to move them back to their favorite summer homes. As the days get longer, the sun's path takes it higher above the horizon, resulting in more intense light. Plants that prefer low-light conditions can be returned to a north-facing window. Some plants may have to be shaded from the intense sunlight, while others will have to be moved closer to the window to give them more direct sunlight. Wherever you move your plants, keep them away from air conditioners and registers. The cool air can damage the leaves.

Planting

The best time to repot palms is in spring and early summer. Single-stemmed or monopodial palm species such as parlor palm (*Chamaedorea elegans*) cannot be divided. Palms that produce a clump of stems or sympodial growth can be easily divided. Clump-forming palms include **bamboo palm (*Chamaedorea erumpens*), pygmy date palm (*Phoenix roebelinii*),** and **lady palm (*Rhapis excelsa* and *R. humilis*).** Pot up the younger shoots and discard or compost the older stems.

1 Unpot the palm and separate the divisions with as much rootball as possible. Avoid cutting or damaging too many roots.

2 Repot each division (at the same level it was originally planted) in a mix consisting of 6 parts peat, 3 parts pine bark, and 1 part sand.

3 Water the divisions well and keep them in indirect light until they show signs of renewed growth. Then move them to their favorite location.

Divide and *repot* houseplants that have formed many new stems from crowns such as **ferns (asparagus, Boston,** and **Dallas),** miniature plantlets such as **African violets** and **snake plants,** or offsets ("pups") such as **clivia.**

1 Select a clean pot that is the same size or an inch or two smaller.

2 Remove the plant to be divided and carefully tease apart the roots. Try to keep a good chunk of roots with each clump of leaves. Some plants such as Boston ferns will have to be cut with a knife.

3 Put a screen or coffee filter over the drainage hole to prevent potting mixture from seeping out and add a shallow layer of mix.

4 *Repot* the division so it's at the same level it was in the original container.

5 Water each potted division thoroughly. Add any additional mix if necessary.

6 Move the division to a shaded location for a week or two to help it recover. Then move it back to brighter light. Start fertilizing when new growth occurs.

When placing your indoor plants outdoors in your flower borders during the summer, clay pots can be set directly in the ground so the soil is 1 to 2 inches below the pot rim, allowing moisture to go through the porous clay. If your plants are in plastic or glazed containers, *repot* them to clay containers or check frequently for water—moisture will not move through the plastic.

Care for Your Houseplants

Move your houseplants outdoors when the night temperatures stay above 60 degrees Fahrenheit. Avoid sunburning the leaves by moving the plants gradually from the relative darkness of the house to their bright summer location. Start by putting them in a well-shaded location and progressing to increasingly lighted areas little by little.

Remember to double-pot plants to be placed outdoors in attractive containers or planters that don't have drainage holes. Lay an inch or two of gravel in the bottom of the decorative container. Place the potted plant (in a pot that has drainage holes) on top of the gravel layer. Apply enough gravel so the pot will rest comfortably inside and won't be seen.

- Large-leaved plants or those with very thin leaves usually require more frequent attention to watering.

- If the plant is in a clay pot rather than a plastic one, expect more evaporation from the sides of the pot.

- Pay close attention to the watering needs of flowering plants and vigorously growing plants which tend to dry out quickly.

Fertilizing

Before fertilizing, evaluate the growth of the plant and the need for fertilizer. Never fertilize wilted plants. *Water* houseplants prior to fertilizing to avoid injury to the roots.

Watering

Water your plants when they need to be watered and not according to the calendar. Some other pointers with regard to watering:

- Plants growing in warm sunny locations need more-frequent watering.

Pruning

Continue to *deadhead* and *pinch* plants when necessary. *Prune out* broken or damaged branches.

Pest Control

Insects and mites: If you spot pest problems indoors, *quarantine* the infested plant to prevent the pests from attacking other plants.

Move the infested plant to a separate room free of houseplants. With a severe infestation, it may be best to compost the plant along with its soil. If the plant is valuable, a pesticide may be necessary. After identifying the pest, select an appropriate insecticide or miticide that lists the plant and pest on the label. Read all label directions and precautions prior to using the pesticide and follow them carefully. You may want to treat your plant outdoors and bring it inside after treatment.

Diseases: Root rot may be a problem on plants indoors.

Use a well-drained potting mixture and water based on need.

Planning

If you haven't repotted your houseplants before taking them outside, make plans this month to do so. They are capable of making a lot of growth during the summer months, especially when the outdoor conditions are similar to their native tropical and subtropical habitats. They shouldn't be confined in a pot that could cause them to suffer from a lack of moisture or poor fertility. If some of these plants are simply too large to repot, *root* some cuttings so you won't have to lose the plant. Share some of the cuttings with your friends.

Planting

Transplant your **poinsettia** into a pot about 2 to 4 inches bigger than the original inner pot. Use a soil mix that incorporates a considerable amount of organic matter such as peat moss, compost, or leaf mold. For a bushier plant, *pinch back* the shoot tips or *prune back* branches now or next month.

African violets can be transplanted at any time, whether or not they are flowering. Select a shallow pot that is at least one-third the diameter of the African violet to be moved. To reduce transplant shock, separate your African violets when the medium is on the dry side.

Plants can still be divided. Avoid doing this during the end of the growing season when the plant won't be able to recover.

Care for Your Houseplants

If you keep your houseplants indoors all summer, keep them out of the draft of the air conditioner or register vents.

"Why doesn't my **bougainvillea** bloom?" is a question asked by many gardeners. The answer lies in meeting the growing conditions: bougainvillea prefers full sun. Its best flowering period is during the short days of early spring and early fall. Cool night temperatures of 60 degrees Fahrenheit or less also promote flowering. Flowering will still occur during the longer days of summer, but often more leaves will be produced before flowers are initiated. During the growing season, follow these steps:

1. *Trim away* weak, spindly growth in the spring, and cut back long shoots to short spurs with two or three buds. Keeping your bougainvillea potbound will encourage flowering.

2. Before taking your bougainvillea outside after frost danger has passed, gradually *expose* it to increasing levels of light. Eventually move it to a full-sun location.

3. Keep your bougainvillea on the "dry side" during the growing season by allowing it to wilt slightly between waterings. When the soil is moist, *fertilize* monthly with a liquid water-soluble fertilizer such as 20-20-20.

4. During the growing season, *trim away* unwanted growth and *pinch* the plant occasionally to keep it bushy and attractive.

5. In the fall before the first freeze, *move* your bougainvillea to a cool, dark location, and *water* it sparingly during the winter months.

Watering

Leach container soils occasionally to remove any mineral salts accumulated from fertilizer and hard water. Brown leaf edges and crusting on the sides of clay pots are two indicators of a salt problem. To leach large containers, *water* until the soil is soaked, then allow water to run slowly from your hose into the pot for about 20 minutes. For small pots, *water* each container until it drains freely from the bottom holes. Wait a few minutes, then repeat. Drain the saucer so the plant doesn't stand in water.

One thorough, deep watering just before leaving for a short vacation will usually be sufficient. (A thoughtful neighbor can literally kill your plants with kindness by overwatering them.)

Hanging baskets exposed to sun should be checked daily and watered if needed, and outdoor hanging containers should be sheltered from high winds. Indoor plants won't dry out as quickly during the growing season as plants outdoors.

Fertilizing

Houseplants that are outside require regular watering and fertilizing. Avoid excessive fertilization—it can make flowering plants produce a lot of leaves but few flowers. Be mindful that encouraging a lot of growth through fertilization may force heavy pruning in the fall so you can bring them inside.

Pruning

Clip off insect-damaged, broken, and pest-damaged leaves and shoots.

Pest Control

Insects and mites: Keep inspecting your houseplants inside and out for signs of pests. Take appropriate measures to prevent light infestations from becoming full-blown problems that may spread to other plants. Severely infested plants may have to be composted.

Diseases: Stem or root diseases are common problems on houseplants, often caused by over- watering or poorly drained potting mixture. Plants growing outside and exposed to heat and humidity should be checked often for diseases. Keep the leaves dry when watering, and *clip off* any diseased leaves when they appear. Fungicides can be used on plants. Identify the disease prior to treating it with a fungicide, and make sure the plant is listed on the fungicide label.

Helpful Hints

To prevent slugs and similar pests from entering the drainage holes of potted plants that have been set into the ground during summer, slip the pot into the toe of an old nylon stocking. This allows water to get through, but keeps out pests.

To avoid soaking the soil when washing off the leaves of potted plants, use a shield. Slit an aluminum foil pie plate from the rim to the center. Turn under the cut edges and slip it around the plant stem so it covers the soil and allows the water to run off.

Planning

When you make plans for your vacation this month, be sure to include your houseplants. If a friend or neighbor will be taking care of them, offer instructions on how to water and feed them.

Make plans to visit the conservatories at Carolina botanical gardens. Learn about the tropical and subtropical habitats of your houseplants.

Planting

It's not too late to transplant potbound plants or to divide them. *Transplant* into a pot the same size as the one in which the plant is growing, or an inch or two wider, using either a commercially prepared potting mix or a peat-perlite mix.

Some plants can be propagated by their leaves. The thick leaves of **snake plant** (*Sansevieria*) can be cut into 3- to 4-inch-long segments. Cut the bottom at a slant or create a v-shaped notch in the bottom so you can tell which end is down. Insert each leaf section vertically into a potting mixture. A new plant will form at the base of the leaf piece.

Care for Your Houseplants

Move plants to calmer spots if leaves are being wind-damaged. If pots dry out rapidly, move plants into a place that has some protection from wind or shade, or **repot** if needed.

Be sure houseplants are kept away from cold drafts caused by air-conditioning vents.

When transporting houseplants during the summer months, **shade** them from the direct sun while they are in the car. Avoid leaving plants in the car with the doors and windows closed in the summer—the heat can kill or damage them.

In summer, **protect** indoor plants from strong sunlight that can scorch the leaves. Closing sheer curtains or partially shutting blinds will shield the tender leaves.

Watering

Continue regular watering. Allow water to drain through the drainage holes in pots of plants growing indoors and out. This will prevent the buildup of salts in the medium. To determine the need for watering, try one of these two techniques:

- Touch the potting mix. Stick your finger into the mix up to the first joint; if it is dry at your fingertip, you need to water.

- Weigh the pot in your hand. With a little practice, you can get a pretty good feel for the level of moisture in the pot by knowing how heavy it is when it's been thoroughly wetted compared to when it has dried out to the point of needing water.

Don't chill tropical houseplants by watering them with cold tap water. Let the water stand until it reaches room temperature so that delicate root hairs won't be harmed, or even killed, by low temperatures.

Fertilizing

Fertilize only if necessary—overdoing it will result in a lot of soft succulent growth that will be susceptible to diseases. Besides, the plant may outgrow its container, requiring repotting, and it may not be able to assume its original place in your home without being drastically cut back.

Pest Control

Insects: Monitor houseplants that are spending the warm months outside. Make sure pest problems don't get out of hand. Whiteflies may be on the prowl on your houseplants growing outside. The tiny mothlike adult whiteflies usually lay eggs on the undersides of the leaves. Whiteflies feed by sucking plant sap from the leaves. Lightly infested leaves develop a mottled appearance while higher populations cause leaves to yellow, shrivel, and die prematurely. Heavy infestations result in sticky leaves covered with a thin black film of sooty mold, a fungus which feeds on the honeydew excreted by the whiteflies. Insecticidal soaps can be used to suppress whitefly populations. Care must be taken to thoroughly cover the undersides of the leaves with the soap solution. The insecticidal soaps cause soft-bodied insects to dehydrate, but they will not work if they do not come into direct contact with the insect.

Diseases: Keep the leaves dry when watering your plants in order to reduce the chances of infections. Allow plenty of space between your plants to allow air movement that will dry the leaves and thwart moisture-requiring diseases. If you spot leaf infections, use a pair of sharp scissors to remove the infected part. Fungicides can be used to control diseases; however, it's best to identify the disease first, evaluate the extent of injury to see if trimming away the infected parts would help, and then compare the cost of treatment with the cost of replacing the plant.

Helpful Hints

If you're going to leave your houseplants behind when you vacation, especially for an extended period, ask a friend or neighbor to care for them. If that's not possible, try these three simple techniques to keep your plants moist:

Create a miniature greenhouse for your plants. **Water** each plant well and enclose it in a clear plastic bag. Large plants can be enclosed in dry-cleaner bags. Insert some tall stakes into the medium to prevent the bag from collapsing on the plant. The plants will be in a warm, humid environment, and any water that condenses can be absorbed by the plants through the drainage hole (this technique may be a problem for hairy-leaved plants).

Try double-potting. Pot up the plant in a clay pot and insert it in a larger plastic pot. Fill the gap between the two pots with moistened sphagnum peat moss. **Water** the peat moss. Water from the peat will be absorbed through the porous walls of the clay container.

A capillary mat is best used on plants in plastic containers. Arrange the end of a length of thick felt or felt rubber mat over the dish-draining area of your sink and let the rest of the mat hang into the sink, which is filled with water. Place the potted plants on the mat on the dish-draining area. Water will be carried from the sink through the capillary mat to the bottom of the plants. The soil will be moistened through capillary action.

AUGUST

Planning

Take advantage of the cool temperatures inside to catch up on writing in your garden journal and reading about houseplants. If you haven't kept up with regular journal entries, plan some time this month to sit down and record your observations of the performance of your plants, any pest problems, control measures, and thoughts about what needs to be done as summer closes and gives way to fall. Note any plants that need to be composted or given away.

Find some good books about houseplants, and learn more about improving their growth both indoors and out. Spend some time on chapters that will help you "read" symptoms of poor growth that can be the result of environment, culture, or pests. Sometimes it's like playing detective when you read the clues and draw conclusions about "who or what dunnit." Knowledge and lots of practice will make you a better plant detective.

Don't forget about those mail-order houseplant catalogs that you received earlier this year. In addition to the luscious photographs, you may find some helpful information and tips that you can apply to your own indoor garden. You may even find a few houseplants that you just have to add to your collection.

Planting

To turn summer annuals into winter houseplants that can be transplanted outdoors next spring, either *move* entire plants indoors or take cuttings and *root* them now.

When moving plants indoors, follow these steps:

1 Six to eight weeks before the first freeze, severely *cut back* the top of the plant to a height of about 4 to 6 inches.

2 *Dig up* the rootball and place it into a suitably sized container. By removing a large part of the top, you should compensate for any roots that were lost while digging up the plant. Any houseplant potting soil is fine, as long as it allows good drainage and is heavy enough to support the plant.

3 Allow the plant to recover before moving it indoors.

If you choose to take cuttings:

1 Make your cut just below a node (the point where the leaf joins the stem) with a sharp knife or razor blade. Cuttings should be 4 to 6 inches long, of new growth with at least three sets of leaves (they can be taken from the annuals you transplanted into containers).

2 *Pinch off* any flowers or flower buds.

3 Before sticking the cuttings in a propagation medium, dip the cut end in a rooting hormone to speed up rooting (many annuals will root without it). Any commercially prepared rooting medium will be fine. Most contain various combinations of perlite, vermiculite, coarse sand, and sphagnum peat moss. You can even create your own medium with these ingredients, making sure that the result is porous enough to admit water and air.

4 Wet the soil and then *enclose* the container in a plastic bag tied off at the top with a twist-tie. The plants can be brought indoors into a brightly lit area or left outside out of direct sunlight to avoid overheating while inside the plastic bag. Within this humid "greenhouse," the cuttings should root in a week or two for some annuals, such as **marigolds,** and a month or longer for bush-type **geraniums** and others.

5 When the roots are about $1/2$ to 1 inch long, transplant them to a container filled with houseplant potting soil. For the first few days, protect the plants from direct sunlight. After that time, place them in a bright

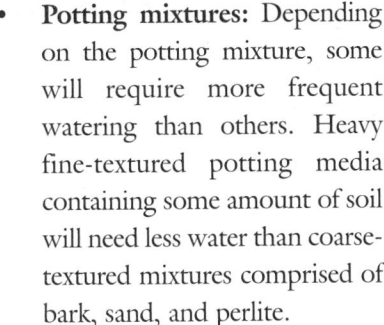

south-facing window. To produce a bushier plant with more flowering branches, *pinch off* the tips of the main stems.

Here are a number of common annuals that can be overwintered indoors. Some may flower all winter long and others may bloom until January before the dry indoor conditions and short days make them decline: **Flossflower** (*Ageratum houstonianum*), **Madagascar periwinkle**, **wax-leaf begonia**, **impatiens**, **geranium**, **petunia**, **portulaca**, **wishbone flower** (*Torenia fournieri*), and **dwarf marigold**.

Watering

Check your houseplants both indoors and out to make sure they're not suffering from a lack of water. Keep these pointers in mind:

- **Plant size:** A large plant growing in a small pot will need to be watered more often than a small plant that hasn't completely filled a large pot. Also, plants with a lot of leaves will need more-frequent watering than plants with few leaves.

- **Potting mixtures:** Depending on the potting mixture, some will require more frequent watering than others. Heavy fine-textured potting media containing some amount of soil will need less water than coarse-textured mixtures comprised of bark, sand, and perlite.

- **Pot:** More water will be lost through the walls of untreated clay pots than through plastic or nonporous glazed clay walls.

Fertilizing

Fertilize plants only if necessary. Growth will begin to slow down towards the fall.

Pruning

Plants that will be brought indoors can be clipped back now. Thin out any straggling or wispy branches.

Pest Control

Insects and mites: Watch out for aphids, mealybugs, spider mites, and scale insects. Inspect your houseplants for signs of insect damage. Pest control is much easier and safer while the plants are outside for the summer than it will be after you bring them in this fall.

Diseases: Plants may have leaf spots. Clip off the dead and diseased tissue and discard it.

Helpful Hint

If you went on vacation last month and didn't heed the advice in that month's Helpful Hint, your plants may have wilted. To revive a plant, follow these steps:

1 Use a fork to lightly break up the dry surface. Peat-based mixtures and the rootball shrink away from the pot sides, so any water will be shed and run off.

2 Immerse the pot in a bucket of warm water. Wait until the mixture becomes completely wet and the bubbles stop appearing.

Allow any excess water to drain away and then put the plant into a cool, well-lit location. If you caught the plant in time, it should recover in a few hours.

SEPTEMBER

Planning

Make plans to bring your plants indoors. Just as you acclimatized your plants to the outdoors, you can reduce "shock" by moving them now when the outdoor temperatures are about the same as those inside (in the Mountains, move them later in the month; in the Piedmont and on the Coastal Plain, move them next month). If you plan on moving plants to rooms that have reduced light levels, get your plants accustomed to the new location now by moving them to a more-shaded environment outdoors. A stepped approach (such as a covered porch or carport for a few weeks, inside to a bright window for a spell, and then eventually to its winter resting place) will reduce the chances of yellowing leaves and leaf drop. Some plants can be left outside for the present. They are those that require shorter days and cool temperatures to encourage flowering, such as **holiday cacti, jade plants,** and **moth** and **Venus' slipper orchids.** Don't forget to check the plants for insects before you bring them inside. It's easier to treat plants while they're still outside.

Planting

Pot up any cuttings and get them ready for their winter's rest. The air-layered shoot on your rubber tree should have lots of roots by now. *Cut* the rooted plant just below the moss ball, remove the wrapping (being careful not to damage the roots), and pot it up in a suitable mixture. *Trim* the mother plant, making a cut just above a node.

Pot up the stem sections of your **dracaena** and **dieffenbachia.**

Care for Your Houseplants

Stop fertilizing and watering your **amaryllis.** This forces it to go dormant. Just leave it in its pot and put it in a cool location (55 to 60 degrees Fahrenheit) where it can remain dry for about eight to ten weeks.

Don't wait for frost warnings to move your houseplants indoors. Temperatures of 60 degrees Fahrenheit or lower can damage many tropical plants.

Holiday cactus will produce flower buds naturally when the days become shorter and the night temperatures go below 65 degrees Fahrenheit. Being pot-bound also helps. After flowering in November to December, allow the top half-inch of soil to dry out before watering this forest-dwelling cactus again. When new stem growth begins in the spring, resume regular watering and fertilizing. For best growth, your cactus should receive bright, but not direct, sunlight.

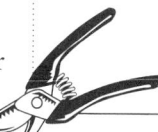

Pruning

Houseplants that grew vigorously this summer outdoors on the porch or in the landscape may need to be pruned. An exception is **poinsettia:** do not *pinch* it back after September 1.

Watering

As the days shorten and plants enter their winter rest period, reduce the frequency of watering. (In the lower Piedmont and Coastal Plain, watering can be gradually tapered off next month.)

Fertilizing

It is not necessary to encourage growth with fertilizer unless the plants are really showing signs of hunger.

SEPTEMBER

Pruning

When you prepare the plants for the indoors, remove any dead or broken stems first. Use sharp pruning shears or knife and make clean cuts.

Pest Control

Insects and mites: As you bring your houseplants back inside, make sure they're not carrying any hitchhiking pests. It's easier to treat the plants outside than indoors. If you had buried your pots in the garden and hadn't blocked the drainage hole, check to see if any insects may have crawled inside. Knock the plant out of the pot and remove any pests before bringing it inside.

Diseases: Trim any diseased leaves from the plants.

Helpful Hints

As an **African violet (*Saintpaulia* species)** ages, it tends to develop a "neck": beautiful leaves and flowers perched high above a bare, leafless stem. A neck forms when the oldest leaves turn yellow and are removed from the stem. Here's how to improve the appearance of a short-necked African violet:

1 Scrape the rough stem above the soil line with a sharp knife to expose the green tissue beneath the bark.

2 Slip the plant out of the pot and cut away the bottom third of the rootball.

3 **Repot** the African violet up to the first set of leaves into a container of fresh medium. New roots will emerge and grow from the main stem.

The second method is suitable for long-necked plants with 3 inches or more of bare stem:

1 Using a sharp knife, remove the rosette with 1 or 2 inches of stem and root it in a potting mixture of equal parts sphagnum peat moss, perlite, and vermiculite. Add 1 part sterilized potting soil if you want the pot to be a permanent home.

2 **Water** the African violet before placing it in a plastic bag tied off at the top with a twist-tie to maintain high humidity levels.

3 Move it to a location receiving bright filtered light.

4 After roots have formed, usually in about four to six weeks, take it out of the bag. An African violet rooted in soilless propagation medium should be repotted into a mixture containing potting soil.

Don't toss out the original plant. Trim the stump to about an inch high and keep the soil moist. After a few weeks, new leaves will emerge from the sides of the stem.

Planning

This is a good month to shop for houseplants to replace any you may have lost this summer or to add more variety to your collection. But before you do, evaluate your home environment, keeping in mind the six requirements for houseplants: *light, water, temperature, humidity, nutrients,* and *potting medium.* Refer to your gardening journal to review any experiences that you have recorded over the past few months and notes about any houseplants that you may have desired. Check your "gotta have" list with houseplant reference books so you can match up the right plants with your home environment, your ability, and the amount of time you wish to devote to its care. Like outdoor plants, houseplants are an investment that requires careful consideration.

Planting

It's time to pot up your cuttings. If your **rubber plants** have plenty of roots, pot them up in 6-inch pots with a commercial potting mixture, or make your own out of equal parts of potting soil, peat moss, and sand or vermiculite. Pot up the cane cuttings of **dracaena** and **dieffenbachia.** Make sure the pot isn't too large, or watering will be a problem.

Take leaf-petiole cuttings of plants with fleshy or hairy leaves such as **African violets, peperomia, gloxinia,** and **hoya:**

1 Snip a leaf from the parent plant with at most $1/2$ inch of the leaf stalk or petiole.

2 Poke a hole in the moistened potting medium (the medium may be equal parts peat moss and perlite). Insert the leaf stalk into the hole at a 45-degree angle.

3 Enclose the pot in a plastic bag twist-tied at the top to create a makeshift greenhouse to increase humidity levels.

4 Roots and then plantlets will develop from the base of the leaf stalk or petiole. When they are one-third the size of the parent leaf, lift them out of the medium. Carefully cut apart the plantlets with a razor blade to avoid damaging the roots.

5 Pot them up in your favorite mix.

Care for Your Houseplants

Houseplants need to come indoors before they are damaged by the cold (below 60 degrees Fahrenheit). First be sure to check them for pests. Rinse the plants' leaves to dislodge any pests.

If you saved your **poinsettia** (*Euphorbia pulcherrima*) from last Christmas because you couldn't bear to compost it, now is the time to encourage it to set flower buds so by the time Christmas arrives it'll be decked with bright red bracts. A poinsettia is a short-day plant that will set buds and produce flowers as nights become longer.

1 For an 8- to 10-week period starting on October 1, keep the plant in complete darkness for fourteen continuous hours each night at a room temperature between 60 and 70 degrees Fahrenheit. Keep the poinsettia in darkness by moving it to a closet or by covering it with a large box.

2 Every day, *expose* the plant to six to eight hours of bright sunlight. *Water* the plant when the surface of the potting medium feels dry. A typical regimen would be putting the plant in darkness at 6 o'clock in the evening and then exposing it to light at 8 in the morning.

3 Be aware that if the night temperature climbs too high or drops too low, flower bud setting may be delayed or halted.

Any stray light, such as that from a streetlight or flash-light, shining near the plant during this critical dark period of fourteen hours may delay or disrupt the blooming process. Continue this regimen for about eight to ten weeks when the small yellow flowers called cyathia in the center of the colorful bracts (modified leaves) start to open.

Fertilizing

Fertilizers at this time of year do little good. Houseplant growth slows as the days get shorter and light intensity is reduced. This means that they will need less-frequent watering and fertilizing until next spring. Too much of either in the winter months can cause weak growth.

Watering

Be careful when watering **desert cactuses** and **succulents** during the winter months. Give them bright light, but keep them on the dry side. Keep them in a cool location and *water* to prevent them from shriveling.

If you use plastic pots instead of clay ones for your houseplants, you won't have to water as much or as often. Clay absorbs soil moisture, minimizing the dangers of overwatering, but it does require that you be more attentive to watering. To reduce water loss from clay pots, place them in decorative glazed or plastic planters.

Pruning

With little growth, pruning may not be necessary. If you are bringing plants in and you live in the Piedmont or Coastal Plain, cut them back now. Take care with winter-blooming houseplants so you don't prune away the flower buds.

Diseases: Most disease problems are caused by waterlogged potting mixtures. Be careful when watering, knowing that plants going into a winter rest period have reduced water requirements.

Pest Control

Insects and mites: Watch out for mealybugs, scale insects, and mites as you bring your plants inside. If they need to be treated with a pesticide, the days should be mild enough to make the application outside during the day. If you use an insecticidal soap, coat the upper and lower leaf surfaces.

Planning

If you're going to give someone a houseplant for a gift plant, now's the time to plan to get the right one. If you're planning on giving someone a plant that won't have to be composted shortly after it flowers, then take the time to research the needs of that plant. When you give the plant, include a "care card" that will let the caregiver know where it should be located in the home or apartment, its light exposure, favorite temperatures during the winter and summer months, watering, and feeding requirements. Take time to research the needs of the plant and also the environment in which it will reside. It's well worth the effort.

Planting

Now is the time to force your **amaryllis** into flower. Remove the top inch of potting mixture and replace it with fresh medium. Trim away any withered leaves and resume watering. *Move* your amaryllis to a south-facing window. As the flower stalk begins to lengthen, it will lean toward the light. Rotate the plant every few days to keep it more vertical. Amaryllis bulbs may not bloom if they are in a pot that is too large. There should be no more than 1 inch of space on each side of the bulb. At least a third of the bulb should be above the soil line.

Care for Your Houseplants

Encourage **African violets** to bloom by giving them plenty of light. They can be in a south window during dark, winter months. Plants grown entirely under fluorescent lights should be placed 6 to 12 inches below two 40-watt tubes for fifteen to eighteen hours per day.

Once your potted annuals stop flowering, keep them alive in a cool spot in the home or in a cold frame outdoors if the winter is mild enough.

Clivia must be exposed to a winter rest period where the temperature is between 45 and 50 degrees Fahrenheit. The soil should be kept nearly dry but never allowed to dry out completely. Too much warmth or too much water during this period will inhibit flower development. After 6 to 8 weeks of this treatment, or when flower stalks appear, begin increasing the amount and frequency of watering. *Move* the plant to a warmer location, around 65 degrees during the day and between 50 and 55 degrees at night. Clivias require bright indirect light and cool temperatures. When the buds appear, you can begin fertilizing with a complete liquid type of fertilizer on a monthly basis until the plant's winter rest. After the flowers fade, remove the flower stalk to prevent seed set. This will encourage the plant to bloom next year. When it blooms on short stalks with the flowers nearly hidden by the base of the leaves, it could be for one of two reasons: the clivia was not properly rested or the room was too warm.

Purchase **amaryllis** bulbs and pot them up yourself. Be sure the pot has at least one or more drainage holes. Since amaryllis like to be pot-bound, choose a pot that is no more than an inch or two wider than the diameter of the bulb. Clay pots are better than plastic because their added weight will support the amaryllis, which tends to get top-heavy when in bloom. The top third of the bulb should extend above the soil.

Watering

Water houseplants carefully at this time. It's easy to overwater and kill them; water too little, and they'll dry out. Soil pulled away from the pot rim means inadequate watering and resulting root problems. It is difficult to add sufficient water overhead to rewet soil in this condition. Soak the pot in a sink full of water, then drain it thoroughly (see August's Helpful Hint, p. 131).

Most plants should not be watered until the soil feels dry. *Water* thoroughly, let the water soak in, then water again until water drains into the saucer. Empty the saucer so the plant won't be standing in water.

If you use plastic pots instead of clay pots for your potted plants, you won't have to water as often. Be careful not to overwater. Clay pots absorb excess soil moisture, minimizing the danger of overwatering.

During the cooler temperatures and shorter days of the winter months, the growth rate of most houseplants slows. Unless plants are grown under an artificial light source for sixteen hours per day, new growth will be minimal until spring. Reduce fertilization and water until late April or May when new growth resumes.

under fluorescent lights can be fertilized to bolster flowering and growth. **Cyclamen** and other winter-growing plants can be watered and fed, if necessary, during the winter months.

To produce more flowers from the flowering annuals that you brought indoors, such as **marigold, snapdragons,** and **geraniums,** *deadhead*, or remove the spent flowers which do not naturally fall from the plant.

Pruning

Remove yellow leaves and overgrown stems. *Trim off* the browned leaf tips with a sharp pair of scissors.

Pest Control

Insects and mites: Watch out for whiteflies on **poinsettias.** Check them daily.

Diseases: Clip off and discard any infected leaves.

Fertilizing

Do not fertilize houseplants that aren't growing. Plants growing

Planning

Is there Christmas flowering color "beyond poinsettias"? If you're looking for something besides the traditional Christmas **poinsettia** to decorate your home for the holidays, look for **kalanchoe, florist's gloxinia, amaryllis** hybrids, and **florist's cyclamen.**

Planting

Take cuttings from **pothos** or **philodendron** and root them in water to feed your urge for planting. Pot up more **amaryllis** bulbs.

Care for Your Houseplants

Cluster plants to help them cope with the low humidity levels in your home.

Remove or punch holes in decorative foil around holiday plants and place them on saucers. Allowing water to collect inside the foil can cause root rot to occur. Alternatively, take the plant out of the foil and water it at the sink. Allow it to drain before returning it to its plastic cover.

Rotate houseplants in dim locations to sunny spots to keep them all in prime condition.

The colorful bracts of **poinsettia** (*Euphorbia pulcherrima*) may stay bright for months if you provide the proper care. Here are some tips for helping a poinsettia thrive in the home during the holiday season:

- Make sure it receives at least six hours of bright, indirect sunlight every day. Putting it in direct sunlight may fade the color of the bracts. The bracts are modified leaves, not flowers. The flowers are the small yellow blossoms, called cyathia, in the center of the colorful bracts.

- To prolong the bright color of the bracts, daytime temperatures should not exceed 70 degrees Fahrenheit. Don't put a poinsettia near drafts, excessive heat, or dry air from appliances, fireplaces, or ventilating ducts.

- Poinsettias are sensitive to cold. If the temperature drops below 50 degrees Fahrenheit, chilling injury and premature leaf drop will occur.

- *Water* your poinsettia thoroughly when the surface of the potting mix feels dry to the touch.

- Don't fertilize when the plant is in bloom.

Watering

Growing plants, especially those with newly unfolding leaves or flower buds poised to open, need more water than do plants that are resting in the winter. Plants in a warm, dry, sunny location need more-frequent watering than they would in cool, low-light situations.

Overwatering is the biggest cause of houseplant death in December; check carefully before watering.

Fertilizing

Many gift plants may not need to be fertilized until spring.

Pest Control

Insects and mites: When receiving holiday gift plants, inspect them carefully. While such close inspection may not be appreciated by the gift-giver, pests like whiteflies and spider mites can wreak havoc on your other houseplants. Isolate new plants from your other ones for a few weeks so if there is an infestation, you can control it before it spreads.

Diseases: Diseases are not a problem at this time.

Cool-Season Lawns

A landscape architect sees a lawn as a green canvas upon which the rest of the landscape is painted. I see it as a place to picnic, play football and volleyball, and tussle with my children. You can have both!

And you can achieve a lawn that looks good and is functional and still have your weekends free. You just have to understand its needs and then try to meet them.

Keep in mind that each maintenance practice influences another. Fertilizer affects how often you mow. Your mowing height affects how often you need to water and how many weeds you will have. Become familiar with some basic turf establishment and maintenance practices and you can have a lawn you will enjoy.

In the Carolinas we can grow either cool-season, cool-climate grasses or warm-season, warm-climate grasses. Cool-season grasses (**Kentucky bluegrass, perennial ryegrass, tall fescue,** and **creeping red fescue**) grow well during the cool months (60 to 75 degrees Fahrenheit). They are adapted to the Piedmont and the Mountains. **Tall fescue** can be grown in the uppermost reaches of the Coastal Plain in North Carolina, but expect only a marginal performance.

Warm-season grasses (**bahiagrass, bermudagrass, carpetgrass, centipedegrass, St. Augustine or "Charleston grass",** and **zoysiagrass**) thrive in hot weather, looking their best when the temperatures are 80 to 95 degrees F. They go dormant and turn brown when the weather cools. They can be grown in the Piedmont and the Coastal Plain. See the Warm-Season Lawns chapter, p. 165, for information about growing warm-season lawns.

Kentucky bluegrass (*Poa pratensis*) is a beautiful turfgrass that's often the standard by which other grasses are judged. It has green to dark-green shiny leaves with a distinct boat-shaped tip. **Kentucky bluegrass** forms a very thick lawn because it spreads by tillers and underground stems called rhizomes. It's often used on athletic fields for its ability to stand up to foot traffic and recover rapidly from injury. **Kentucky bluegrass** tolerates full sun or half-day sun, and it does best at the higher elevations in the Mountains because of its need for cool summer temperatures. The price for its beauty is lots of water, fertilizer, and time.

Tall fescue (*Festuca arundinacea*) can also be grown in the Mountains and Piedmont of the Carolinas. It doesn't spread by rhizomes like **Kentucky bluegrass.** Instead, it forms a clump. **Kentucky 31** is one of the pasture-type tall fescues that's being replaced by new and more attractive cultivars referred to as **"turf-type" tall fescues.** These refined turf-types have a slightly finer leaf blade, as fine as **Kentucky bluegrass.** They're darker green in color, thicker, and tolerate shade better than **Kentucky 31.** Established **tall fescue** lawns tend to thin out and become "clumpy" after summer dry spells and may need periodic reseeding in the fall.

These two turfgrasses are often mixed together to take advantage of the best attributes of both. **Kentucky bluegrass** contributes wear tolerance and rapid recovery from wear and tear, while **tall fescue** contributes drought tolerance.

Fine fescues are often combined with **Kentucky bluegrass** or in a three-way mixture that includes **tall**

Cool-Season Lawns

fescue (because of its exceptional shade tolerance.)

Perennial ryegrass (*Lolium perenne*) and **annual ryegrass (*Lolium multiflorum*)** are used to overseed dormant warm-season lawns. These grasses will provide a green cover during the time when the warm-season grasses turn brown. **Perennial ryegrass** is unreliable as a permanent lawn because of its susceptibility to diseases in hot weather.

Refer to the Planting Chart, p. 143, to help you select the right turfgrass for your lawn.

Starting a Lawn

Cool-season grasses can be established using seed or sod. Whatever method you choose, follow these steps prior to planting:

1 Choose a turfgrass that fits your management style. For an updated list of recommended turfgrass varieties in your area, contact your county extension office. Use a blend of three or more varieties to take advantage of the varying levels of disease resistance in each one.

2 Take a soil sample of the area and have it tested for soil pH and fertility levels through your cooperative extension service office. The soil-test report will indicate how much fertilizer or lime needs to be applied.

Prepare the site by controlling perennial weeds with a nonselective herbicide. If your major weed problems are crabgrasses and other summer annuals, you can turn them under into the bed where they'll decompose. Perennial grassy weeds such as bermudagrass and dallisgrass should be handpulled or sprayed with a nonselective herbicide containing glyphosate (Roundup Pro® or others).

3 If you have heavy clay or very sandy soils, *spread* a 1- to 2-inch layer of organic matter such as compost over the soil.

4 *Till* the soil to a depth of 6 to 8 inches and thoroughly work in the organic materials.

5 If lime is recommended by the soil test, mix it into the top 3 to 5 inches of soil.

6 Right before planting, *broadcast* the fertilizer and lightly *rake* it in.

The best time for seeding is August in the Mountains, to mid-October in the Piedmont. Here's how:

1 Apply the seed with a drop-type or rotary spreader to get uniform distribution. Sow the required amount in two directions at right angles (half in each direction) to help ensure good coverage.

2 Lightly *rake* the seeds into the top 1/4 inch of soil. Then roll the seedbed with a light or empty lawn roller (water-ballast roller) to ensure good seed-to-soil contact.

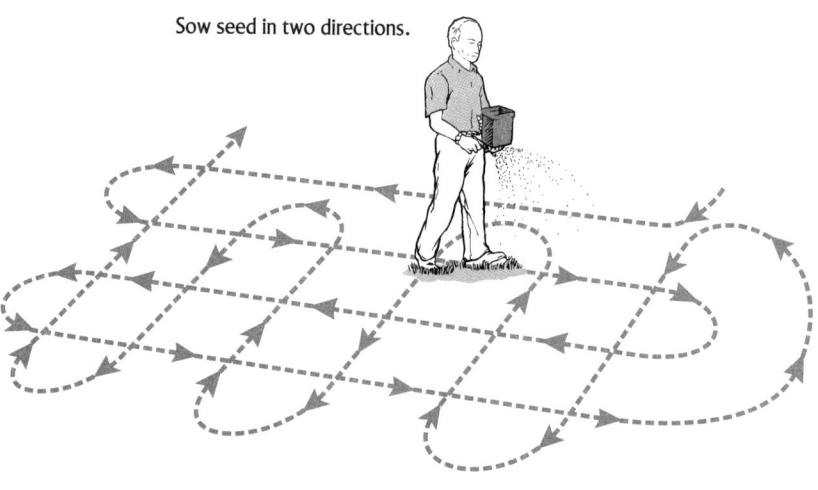

Sow seed in two directions.

3 *Mulch* the seedbed to prevent soil erosion, retain moisture, and prevent crusting of the soil surface. The most commonly used mulch is straw—it is important to use **weed-free** straw. Use enough weed-free straw so that one-half to three-quarters of the bare ground is covered. If it's not spread too thickly, straw can be left to decompose.

4 *Water* the lawn after seeding. Water lightly and frequently so the seeds don't dry out. The goal is to water often enough to keep the seedbed moist but not waterlogged until the plants can develop a sufficient root system to take advantage of deeper and less-frequent watering. This may mean watering a few times a day for several weeks until the seedlings emerge and become established. As the seedlings mature and the root system develops, water more deeply and less frequently.

5 *Mow* the lawn when the grass is one-third higher than the desired height. For example, if you want to maintain your **tall fescue** lawn at 3 inches, mow the grass when it reaches a height of 4 inches.

When compared to seeding, sodding gives you an instant lawn in the shortest time. Sod of cool-season grasses can be installed anytime during the year when the soil isn't frozen. Sodding in the summer, however, will require adequate irrigation and plenty of attention to help it cope with the stressful hot, humid weather. To avoid placing the turf roots in contact with the excessively dry and hot soil, it helps to dampen the soil just before laying the sod. If you want to sod a lawn, refer to March Planting, p. 146, for the step-by-step approach.

Watering

New lawns should be watered frequently to keep the top half-inch of soil moist. Keep the soil moist until the seedlings or sprigs become established. Gradually cut back on the frequency of watering, but water longer to encourage deep rooting. A lawn is considered established when it's been mowed three times.

Established lawns should be watered to a depth of 6 to 8 inches to encourage deep rooting. This can be accomplished by applying 1 inch of water per week to clay soils. (It takes 640 gallons of water to apply 1 inch of water to 1,000 square feet of lawn.) Since clay soils absorb water slowly, you may have to start and stop watering to allow the water to soak in without running off. Wait a half-hour and then water again until you've applied the full inch. On fast-draining sandy soils, apply $1/2$ inch of water at a time, every three days. Refer to June Watering, p. 152, to learn how to calibrate your sprinkler to apply the right amount of water.

Fertilizing

Before you fertilize your lawn, know its area. Refer to the base map described in the Introduction to this book, p. 10, to calculate the area (length ¥ width) occupied by your lawn. If you have several smaller areas, simply add them up to get your total lawn area. Record this number in your garden journal for future reference.

The kind and amount of fertilizer you apply should be based on soil-test results. Although lawns require nitrogen, phosphorus, and potassium in the greatest quantities, the fertilizer recommendation is based on nitrogen, a nutrient that's most likely to be deficient in the soil.

Depending on the level of maintenance and overall lawn quality, apply either $1/2$ or 1 pound of nitrogen per thousand square feet of lawn area. *This is not fertilizer I am talking about, but actual nitrogen.*

Cool-Season Lawns

To determine how much *fertilizer* to apply to deliver 1 pound of nitrogen, use this equation:

100/ percent Nitrogen = number of pounds of fertilizer required per 1,000 square feet in order to apply 1 pound of nitrogen.

So, if you have a 16-4-8 fertilizer, using the formula:

100/16 = 6 (This means 6 pounds [12 cups] of 16-4-8 fertilizer should be applied per 1,000 square feet.)

To apply 1/2 pound of nitrogen per 1,000 square feet, use this equation:

50/ percent Nitrogen = number of pounds of fertilizer required per 1,000 square feet in order to apply 1/2 pound of nitrogen.

See the chart on page 143 for common fertilizers and their application rate.

Depending on your spreader and type of fertilizer, you may have to calibrate your spreader to apply the correct amount. Applying too much can be hazardous to your lawn and to the environment. See Warm-Season Lawns, February Planning on p. 174 to learn how to calibrate your fertilizer spreader.

Apply the fertilizer uniformly with a drop-type or rotary spreader. Apply half of the total amount in one direction and the other half at right angles to the first to apply it uniformly. *Keep a record of the total amount of fertilizer applied over the year.*

General Fertilizer Guidelines for Cool-Season Lawns

For high-maintenance **Kentucky bluegrass, fine fescue,** and **tall fescue** lawns, apply 1 pound of nitrogen per 1,000 square feet; 1/2 pound of nitrogen per 1,000 square feet is fine for low-maintenance lawns. Suitable months for applying fertilizer are March, September, and November (according to soil-test results). The total yearly amount may be 1 to 3 pounds of nitrogen per 1,000 square feet—the higher rates are suited for lawn owners interested in higher quality and maintenance.

Suggested Mowing Heights

Newly established lawns should be mowed when the grass is one-third higher than the desired height. For example, if you want to maintain your **tall fescue** lawn at 3 inches, mow the grass when it reaches a height of 4 inches. Suggested mowing heights are given in the chart on p. 143. *Measure the height of the mower on a level surface and adjust it to the proper height.*

Pest Control

The secret to thwarting pests is to work with nature. Create conditions for the grass to thrive and resist invasion from weeds and attacks from insects and diseases. As they say: "An ounce of prevention is worth a pound of cure." If problems occur, identify the problem before taking action. If you need help, contact your cooperative extension service.

Carolina Cool-Season Lawns

Turfgrass Planting Chart

Lawn Grass	Fine Fescue	Kentucky Bluegrass	Tall Fescue
Area Best Adapted	Mountains and Piedmont	Mountains	Mountains and Piedmont
Planting Time	Late summer and early fall	Late summer	Late summer and early fall
Method of Establishment	Seed or sod	Seed or sod	Seed or sod
Tolerance to Drought	G	F to G	G
Shade	VG	G	G
Traffic	F to G	G	G

VG = Very good   G = Good   F = Fair

Common Fertilizers

Fertilizer Analysis (Numbers on bag)	Fertilizer Ratio (N-P_2O_5-K_2O)	Amount (lbs.) needed to supply 1 pound of nitrogen per 1,000 sq. ft.
12-4-8	3-1-2	10
12-3-6	4-1-2	8
16-4-8	4-1-2	6
20-5-10	4-1-2	5

Suggested Mowing Heights

Lawn Grass	Mowing Height (inches)
Kentucky bluegrass	Winter: 1.5 to 2.5 Summer: 2.5 to 3
Fine fescue	Winter: 1.5 to 2.5 Summer: 2.5 to 3
Tall fescue	Winter: 2 to 3 Summer: 2.5 to 3.5
Ryegrass (Overseeded)	Winter: 1 to 2.5

Planning

If you're planning on hiring a lawn-care service company to maintain your lawn, decide on the level of quality you want. Can you tolerate a few weeds, or do you expect a completely weed-free lawn? Would you be willing to allow it to go dormant summer dry spells, or would you prefer that it stays watered and green? Be realistic when you decide on the kind of quality you expect from your lawn and from the company. Here are a few pointers to help you select the right lawn-service company:

1 Know what lawn or landscape services you want. Once you decide on the services you want, get several cost estimates from companies that offer those services. Ask neighbors and friends for recommendations.

2 Obtain a written service agreement. Find out if the service is automatically renewed each year. If so, request an annual written confirmation. Ask if there are any penalties should you decide to cancel your service agreement.

3 Ask if the company is licensed and insured. Don't be afraid to ask for proof.

4 Ask if the company is a member of a state or national trade association, such as the Professional Lawn Care Association of America. Trade associations help keep their members informed of the latest technical information in the industry, as well as keeping members educated in the safe use of pesticides.

5 Pesticides and other lawn-care chemicals should be used only as needed. Ask the company to tell you what lawn-care chemicals it plans to use and why.

6 A company should always provide advance notice of chemical applications so that lawn furniture and toys can be removed from the area before treatment.

7 Check out the company. Check with the Better Business Bureau to see if there have been any complaints lodged against the company. Ask the company for references from local customers.

Planting

Sod can be installed anytime the soil isn't frozen.

Watering

See February.

Fertilizing

Do not fertilize this month.

Mowing

If mowing is necessary, remove no more than one-third of the grass height with a sharp mower blade.

Pest Control

Weeds: *Handpull* winter annuals such as common chickweed and henbit.

Helpful Hint

To reduce winter damage, avoid walking on a frozen lawn.

Planning

Plan to service your lawn mower yourself or take it to a lawn repair shop some time this month. A few of the items that should be looked at include:

- Air filter—clean or replaced it if it's damaged.

- Spark plug—clean it or replace it if it's cracked.

- Oil—check to see that it's filled to the right level. Change the oil as recommended by the manufacturer.

- Mower blade—replace it if it's chipped, cracked, or bent. Maintain a sharp mower blade to cut the grass cleanly, which improves its look and also ensures rapid healing and regrowth. A dull mower blade tears the grass, leaving a rough appearance. If the blades on your reel-type mower require special equipment to sharpen them (refer to your mower's instruction manual), consider leaving this task in the hands of a professional.

- Tires—examine the tires for wear and replace them if necessary to give you better traction and maneuverability.

- Check for loose screws and bolts on the handle controls and the motor now and throughout the season.

If you do-it-yourself, be safe. Disconnect the wire from the spark plug for safety and keep the manual within reach.

Planting

Sod can be installed whenever the soil is not frozen. Sodding gives you an instant lawn in the shortest time compared to seeding. See March Planting.

Watering

Newly sodded areas should be moistened for the sod to "knit" into the soil. *Water* immediately after sodding to wet the soil to a depth of 3 or 4 inches. Don't let the soil dry out until the sod has "knitted" or rooted into the soil. Observe established lawns for signs of drought stress and apply an inch of water per week (in the absence of precipitation).

Fertilizing

Do not fertilize at this time.

Mowing

Maintain **Kentucky bluegrass** between $1^1/2$ and $2^1/2$ inches in height. *Mow* **tall fescue** between 2 and 3 inches high.

Pest Control

Weeds: If your lawn has a history of weed invasions, determine why the weeds invaded and correct the problem. Weeds are often found in lawns with a thin or weak stand of grass. The most common causes of a poor lawn are using a grass that's not adapted to your region and improper mowing, watering, and fertilizing. Other factors that affect the condition of the lawn include insects, diseases, compacted soil, and thatch.

Helpful Hint

Spend some time learning more about establishing and maintaining your lawn. Visit your local cooperative extension service for publications regarding recommended turfgrass varieties and techniques for starting, managing, and repairing lawns. They often offer short courses on lawn care.

Planning

The first bagging mowers made their debut on American lawns in the early 1950s. Somehow, collecting and removing grass clippings and putting them into garbage bags with the trash caught on. But you should really plan to recycle your grass clippings as you mow. Returning your grass clippings to the lawn saves time, energy, and money—and look at recycling grass clippings as a way of fertilizing your lawn. Grass clippings contain about 4 percent nitrogen, $1/2$ to 1 percent phosphorus, 2 to 3 percent potassium, and smaller amounts of other essential plants nutrients. This is basically a 4-1-3 fertilizer.

Planting

If you didn't seed thin or bare patches last fall, which is the best time to seed **Kentucky bluegrass** and **tall fescue,** you can attempt to seed now; however, be prepared to accept some losses. Cool-season grasses prefer cool temperatures, especially for seed germination, and the longer you delay seeding, the less time the seedlings will have to become established before the arrival of summer's heat. And be mindful that what you do for your lawn grass seedlings will also benefit emerging weeds. Even if you get

a fairly good stand, you'll have a long road ahead of you to keep the young lawn alive during the summer months.

If you can justify the expense, install **tall fescue** or **Kentucky bluegrass** sod; you'll have to have plenty of water available to help make it through the summer.

If you can delay seeding until the fall . . . then wait.

To sod a lawn, follow these steps:

1 Measure the area to be sodded and calculate the amount of sod you'll need. (You may need to refer to your base map—see the Introduction to this book, p. 10—to help you identify the area to be planted in turf).

2 Schedule delivery only after you prepared the bed and are ready to install. Insist on prompt delivery after the sod is harvested.

3 Keep the sod in a shady place to prevent it from drying out. Lay it as soon as possible.

4 Start sodding from the longest straight edge such as a driveway, curb, or sidewalk. Stagger the blocks or strips as if laying bricks. Butt the sod firmly and stretch each piece so it lies flat against the soil. In dry, hot weather, lightly wet the surface before laying and water each small area well immediately (within one hour) after laying. Use a knife, spade, or sharpened concrete trowel to trim the pieces.

5 On steep slopes, lay the sod across the angle of the slope; it may be necessary to peg the sod to the soil with home-made wooden stakes to keep it from sliding.

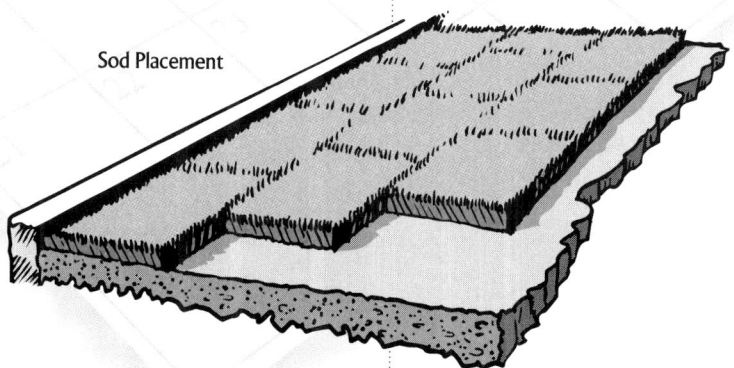

Sod Placement

6 Immediately after laying the sod, tamp down the sod or roll the lawn perpendicular to the direction the sod was laid with a lawn roller (water-ballast roller). This eliminates any air spaces between the soil and the sod and ensures good sod-to-soil contact.

7 *Water* immediately afterwards to wet the soil below to a depth of 3 or 4 inches. Don't let the soil dry out until the sod has "knitted" or rooted into the soil. More thorough watering can then be done as the roots begin to penetrate the soil.

8 Start mowing when the sod is firmly rooted and securely in place.

Care for Your Lawn

Wait until fall to aerify compacted soil (see September, p. 158).

Fertilizing

Kentucky bluegrass or **tall fescue** can be fertilized this month according to the results of a soil test. See the Fertilizer Chart on p. 143. If the lawn has good color and vigor, however, postpone any fertilizer applications until the fall to avoid making hay this spring.

Watering

Do not allow newly sodded areas to dry out. When the sod has "knitted" or rooted into the soil, reduce the frequency of irrigation and water deeply as the roots begin to penetrate the soil.

Mowing

Two kinds of mowers are used for mowing turfgrasses: rotary mowers and reel mowers. Rotary mowers have a whirling blade that cuts the grass at high speeds. It can be used to mow lawns down to an inch. Reel mowers have a series of blades that cut the grass like scissors. The blades press against a bar at the bottom to slice the grass, giving the lawn a highly finished look. With either type of mower, follow the "proper mowing" described in the basic rules of the Warm-Season Lawns introduction, p. 170.

Pest Control

Weeds: Later this month in the Piedmont, and early next month in the Mountains, you can apply a "crabgrass preventer" or pre-emergent herbicide to control summer annuals such as crabgrass and goosegrass. Apply the herbicide when they germinate but before they emerge. A pre-emergent herbicide forms a barrier at or just below the soil surface and kills the emerging seedlings when it comes into contact with it. Crabgrass seed germinates when the day temperatures reach 65 to 70 degrees Fahrenheit for four or five days; it coincides with the time when **forsythia** and **crabapples** are in bloom. Goosegrass germinates about three or four weeks after crabgrass.

Prevent winter annuals such as common chickweed and henbit from going to seed by handpulling, mowing off the flowers, or spot-treating with a broadleaf herbicide.

Helpful Hint

To take some of the strain out of mowing, eliminate hard-to-mow spaces and sharp angles in beds and borders. Combine single trees or shrubs into a large planting connected with mulch or ground covers.

Planning

Serious about growing a healthy, attractive lawn? Then start writing in your journal. Write down when you fertilized the lawn and the amount you applied. Document any insect, disease, or weed problems, and any pesticide applications. Staple your soil-test report to one of the pages. Your journal can become a teaching tool, especially when you need the assistance of a lawn-service company or county extension agent to help you diagnose a particular problem. The notes you take about weather conditions, fertilizing, watering, and any pest control applications are important clues that can help reveal the answer to a problem.

Planting

If you can justify the expense, install **tall fescue** or **Kentucky bluegrass** sod; you should have plenty of water available to help make it through the summer.

If you want a green lawn without sodding, then sow seed as early in the month as possible, mulch with weed-free straw, and keep the seedbed moist for a few weeks to speed-up establishment. Helping your lawn make it through the summer will be your greatest challenge.

If you can delay seeding until the fall . . . then wait.

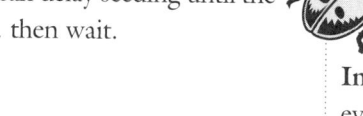

Watering

Newly seeded or sodded lawns should be watered frequently. As the seedlings emerge and the sod "knits" into the soil, gradually water less frequently but more deeply and less often.

Water established lawns as needed. One inch of water per week is adequate on clay soils. Apply one-half inch of water every third day on sandy soils.

Fertilizing

Do not fertilize established lawns at this time.

Mowing

Mow frequently, removing no more than one-third of the lawn height at a time. Leave the clippings on the lawn.

Pest Control

Insects: If your lawn looks wilted, even after watering, if it's been torn up by skunks, birds, and moles, or if parts have turned brown and feel spongy, check to see if you have an infestation of white grubs. See Warm-Season Lawns, August Insects on p. 187 for a description and controls.

The red imported fire ant was introduced into the U.S. as early as 1918. Because it's not native to this country, fire ants have no competitors, parasites, or predators to keep their numbers in check. They produce unsightly mounds and their painful stings pose a health threat, particularly to young children and older people. If fire ants have cropped up in your lawn or landscape, control them with the "two-step method" described in the Warm-Season Lawns chapter, April Insects on p. 178.

Diseases: Rust and dollar spot are fungal diseases that attack bluegrass and fescue lawns. Rust causes grass leaves to turn yellow before turning brown and dying. Take a close look at the leaves and look for red, orange, or brown spores. Heavy infestations cause thinning. Many varieties have good-to-moderate levels of resistance to rust, so this disease shouldn't be much of a problem. Collect infected grass clippings to prevent the spores from spreading to other areas of the lawn. Avoid keeping the grass wet for long periods by watering in the early morning.

Dollar spot produces small circular areas of straw-colored grass which range from 1 to 6 inches across. If you examine individual grass blades, you'll find straw-colored lesions with reddish-brown borders. Sometimes the lesions will extend across the blade while the leaf tip remains green. Early in the morning you may be able to spot a spider web–like growth over the infected lawn area. Dollar spot is more common during the spring and fall months. Maintain adequate levels of fertility, especially nitrogen, since this diseases favors "hungry" lawns. Fungicides are generally unnecessary.

Weeds: Identify weeds after they emerge to select an appropriate post-emergent herbicide labeled for your lawn. Post-emergent herbicides are most effective when the weeds are young and actively growing with air temperatures between 65 and 85 degrees F. Be sure the herbicide is labeled for use on your lawn.

Helpful Hints

Two basic lawn-management practices that can either "make" or "break" a lawn—opening it up to a weed infestation—are mowing and fertilizing.

- Always mow with a sharp mower blade. Sharp blades cut the grass cleanly, which ensures rapid healing and regrowth. When dull blades tear and bruise the leaves, the wounded grass plants become weakened and less able to ward off marauding weeds.

- **Mow** at the proper height for your lawn. For example, mow **tall fescue** at 3 inches during the summer months. By maintaining the appropriate height, you will allow the root system to fully develop, helping the grass tolerate summer heat and stress.

- Follow this mowing rule-of-thumb: Remove no more than one-third of the grass height at any one mowing. For example, when your **centipede** lawn reaches 3 inches in height, it's time to mow. Cutting off more than one-third at one time can stop the roots from growing, which is an open invitation to weeds.

- **Fertilize** lawn grasses with the right amount of fertilizer based on soil-test results and at the proper time of year. Cool-season grasses like **Kentucky bluegrass** and **tall fescue** should be fertilized in the fall.

- **Avoid** trimming grass with a weed-eater near the trunks of young trees and shrubs. The rapidly spinning monofilament line can easily damage the bark, exposing it to attack from insects and diseases. Maintain a shallow layer of mulch around the shrub and trees to suppress grass, eliminating trimming and protecting the trees.

Planning

Plan to get your lawn in shape to help it cope with this summer's heat and humidity. Here are a few techniques to help you toughen up your lawn while reducing your water bill:

1 Encourage the development of a deep root system by watering only when the need arises. Look for signs of moisture stress: folded or curled leaves, a dull bluish-gray color cast to the lawn, and footprints that remain in the grass long after you've walked over it. ***Water*** those areas that exhibit these symptoms first. If you want to be strict about watering, then irrigate only those areas that are important to your landscape, such as recreational areas and other parts of the lawn that get a lot of use. Do not water again until the signs of moisture stress recur.

2 ***Water*** late at night or early in the morning when dew has formed. Watering a lawn already moistened by dew will not encourage disease outbreaks. Besides, it will save you money. For example, at midday, in hot, dry and windy weather, 30 percent or more of the water evaporates. Watering at night or in early morning cuts evaporation in half, to 15 to 20 percent. Since it takes 640 gallons of water to irrigate 1,000 square feet with one inch of water, late-night and early-morning watering gives substantial savings in cost and in the amount of water you apply.

3 Gradually raise the mowing height by one-quarter to one-half as the temperature climbs this summer. A higher mowing height encourages deeper root growth and reduces heat stress.

4 Make sure that your mower blade is sharp. Grasses that are cut cleanly lose less water and heal more rapidly than leaves shredded by a dull mower blade.

5 Avoid a fast-food diet by using a slow-release fertilizer that contains $1/4$ to $1/2$ of its nitrogen in a "water insoluble" or "slowly available" form. These controlled-release nitrogen fertilizers are available at the rate the lawn grass can use them and do not quickly wash away.

Planting

Think twice before starting a cool-season lawn from seed. The seedlings won't have enough time to get settled in before the onset of hot summer weather. Consider installing sod, provided that you're willing to keep it well watered during its establishment and during droughty periods this summer.

Watering

Water your lawn on an as-needed basis to keep it green. Rely on the signs of moisture stress described in this month's Planning section to determine which parts of the lawn need to be watered to keep them green.

Fertilizing

Wait until fall to fertilize your cool-season lawn.

Mowing

Refer to p. 142 for suggested mowing heights for cool-season lawns. Maintain a sharp mower blade and recycle the grass clippings by leaving them on the lawn.

Pest Control

Insects: See April.

Diseases: Brown patch can start appearing in Carolina lawns this month. See next month's Diseases for more information about this fungal disease.

Dollar spot and slime mold may also be present. As the name suggests, slime mold is a slimy-looking fungus that may be yellow, white, gray, red, violet, or other colors. These slimy growths may be a few inches or up to several feet in diameter and live on the grass blades of your lawn. You may even find them on your shrubs during warm weather, especially during or after heavy periods of rain. These fungi are not harmful to the plants on which they reside. They feed on bacteria, other fungi, and decayed organic matter. If you're bothered by this fungus's presence, simply hose or brush it off the lawn.

Weeds: Pre-emergent herbicides to control crabgrass and goosegrass last for a period of time before losing their effectiveness. Therefore, a repeat application will be necessary for season-long control. Refer to the label to see when it has to be reapplied to control germinating weeds this summer.

Helpful Hints

Managing your lawn properly will help your lawn fight weeds naturally. Don't expect a weed-free lawn, however. We're dealing with Mother Nature, you know. Weeds will find a way to get a foothold, and when they do, learn to identify them to help you control them.

- If you find weeds in your lawn, figure out what sparked the invasion. If the basic cause is not corrected, weeds will continue to be a problem despite your many attempts to try to get rid of them. Weeds often appear as a result of poor management. They take advantage of thin or weak stands of grass.

- Select the best weed-control method. **Handpull** a few weeds rather than taking more drastic measures. Perennial weeds that come back year after year from underground plants parts can be handpulled when the soil is moist, making sure that you remove as much of the root system as possible—dandelion becomes a multiheaded hydra of leaves when you pop off the tops and leave the deep taproot behind.

- If you choose to use a herbicide, make sure that you read and following the label directions carefully. Select a herbicide that is labeled for your lawn grass and is labeled to control the weeds in your lawn.

Keep these mowing tips in mind:

- Do not remove or alter safety features of your lawnmower.

- Pick up debris that may damage your mower or be thrown by spinning blades.

- Family and pets should be completely out of the area you are cutting.

- Never clear clogged clippings with the motor running, and never mow barefoot or in sandals.

Planning

The best way to determine the fertilizer requirements of your lawn is by having your soil tested at least every three years through your local county cooperative extension service office. Plan to have your soil tested this month or next so you can be ready for fall. Maintaining the appropriate soil pH for your lawn grasses and applying only the minerals that are deficient in the soil will benefit the lawn and keep money in your pocket.

Planting

If you need to plant, install **Kentucky bluegrass** or **tall fescue** sod. Make sure you have plenty of water to help it get established and survive the summer.

Watering

Water your lawn when it show signs of moisture stress: bluish-gray color, footprints that remain in the lawn after walking on it, and wilted, folded, or curled leaves. During long, dry hot spells in the summer, you have two choices when it comes to watering your established lawn:

1 *Don't water.* Let the lawn turn brown.

2 *Water* the grass to keep it green.

When a **Kentucky bluegrass** lawn turns brown during a drought, it's a sign of dormancy. The leaves and shoots die, but buds in the crown and rhizomes (underground stems) generally remain alive and grow when more favorable conditions return.

Tall fescue has no means of escape like **Kentucky bluegrass.** Three weeks or more without rain in the summer can injure or kill **tall fescue.**

If reseeding or resodding is not an option, then water only when the lawn really needs it. Look for these signs of "thirst" before watering your lawn:

- **Footprinting.** Walk across your lawn. If your footprints remain in the grass very long, the lawn is dry and should be watered to prevent the grass from turning brown and going dormant.

- **Color test.** When a lawn is dry for a long time, it develops a dull bluish-gray cast.

- **Check the leaves.** During dry spells, grass leaves respond by rolling or folding the leaves.

- **Screwdriver test.** If the soil is very dry, it will be hard to insert a screwdriver into the lawn.

If any of these techniques show that your lawn is experiencing drought stress, apply about an inch of water per week.

Whatever option you choose—to water or not to water—stick with it. Flip-flopping between the two can weaken your lawn.

Fertilizing

Do not fertilize cool-season lawns at this time.

Mowing

If your mower was in the shop and the lawn grew so high that mowing it at the correct height would remove more than one-third its height, raise the mower height so you will remove no more than one-third of the lawn height. Gradually reduce the mower height, with one or two days between mowings, until you reach the correct height.

Pest Control

Weeds: Apply post-emergent herbicides as needed to control summer annual and perennial broadleaf weeds such as knotweed, lespedeza, and spurge. Do not apply post-emergent herbicides unless weeds are present, grass is actively growing, and the lawn is not suffering from drought stress. Finally, apply herbicides when the weeds are actively growing in warm conditions with adequate soil moisture. Applications during droughty conditions or whenever the weeds are not actively growing may result in poor control.

Continue to follow proper lawn-management practices by mowing at the proper height, mowing with a sharp mower blade, and removing no more than one-third of the grass height at each mowing. If you need to apply post-emergent herbicides, remember to follow label directions and *spot-treat* problem areas in the lawn. To avoid injuring the desirable grasses, avoid making herbicide applications when the air temperature exceeds 85 degrees F. and when the lawn grasses are stressed by drought or high temperatures.

Diseases: Brown patch or Rhizoctonia blight is a devastating disease that attacks most **fescue** and **bluegrass.** It's favored by high temperatures and high humidity. Look for circular, tan-colored dead patches several feet in diameter. Sometimes there's a tuft of green grass in the center that may be unaffected or may recover more rapidly than grasses at the margins, creating a "doughnut." This disease is most severe on grasses receiving high levels of nitrogen in late spring or summer. Collect and compost clippings from infected areas. Fungicides can be used to protect healthy grass from attack. Wait until fall to rake up dead areas and seed or sod.

Planning

If you water your lawn when you see signs of drought stress—footprints staying in the grass after you walk over it, a bluish-gray cast that turns back to green when the lawn is watered, and wilting, rolled leaves—or if you allowed the lawn to turn brown and dormant and are watering every three weeks during dry spells, apply the correct amount of water each time you irrigate. Apply an inch of water on clay soils. To do this, you need to calibrate your irrigation system so you'll know how much water you apply per hour and exactly when to stop watering. Follow these calibration steps:

1 For an in-ground home irrigation system, place several equal-sized coffee cans or other straight-sided, flat-bottomed containers randomly throughout the area to be irrigated. For above-ground, portable, hose-end sprinklers, containers should be arranged in a straight line away from the sprinklers to the edge of the water pattern.

2 Turn on the irrigation for 15 minutes.

3 Turn off the water, collect the cans, and pour all the water into one of the cans.

4 Measure the depth of water you collected.

5 Calculate the average depth of water by dividing the total amount of water in inches by the number of cans. For instance, if the total depth was 3 inches, and you used six containers, then the average depth would be $3/6$, or 0.5 inches.

6 Multiply the average depth by four to determine the application rate in inches per hour. For example, one-half inch multiplied by four equals 2 inches per hour. If you run the system for one hour, it will apply 2 inches of water; run it for half an hour, and it will apply 1 inch. If during irrigation water runs off the lawn, apply a half-inch, stop the system and let it soak in, then apply more.

Planting

Sod can be installed during hot weather as long as you provide sufficient water to keep the soil moist. Before laying the sod, moisten the soil to prevent the roots from coming into contact with excessively hot and dry soil. *Water* immediately afterwards to wet the soil below to a depth of 3 or 4 inches.

Watering

Newly seeded or sodded lawns cannot tolerate droughty conditions. Lawns established last fall by seed need attention to watering, as these lawns do not have an adequate root system established yet to survive an extended period of drought. At this stage of development, drought can kill the young crowns of the turf. Look for signs of "thirst" and water accordingly or water by the calendar, applying 1 inch of water during droughty periods to prevent the grass from dying. If you choose not to water, repairing bare patches or renovation will be in order this fall. About 1 inch of water per application each week is adequate for irrigated lawns. Do not discontinue watering in midsummer—*water* dormant lawns every three weeks in the absence of rain.

Fertilizing

Do not fertilize at this time.

Mowing

Start mowing a sodded lawn when it's firmly rooted and securely in place. If you haven't already done so, raise the cutting height of your mower a notch or two to put less stress on the turf. By increasing the height, you can also increase the depth of the root system.

Pest Control

Diseases: Brown patch attacks **fescues** and **bluegrass** and is encouraged by overwatering and overfertilizing with nitrogen. Collect and compost clippings from infected areas. Fungicides can be used to protect healthy grass from attack. Wait until fall to rake up dead areas, and seed or sod.

Pythium blight is a "hot-weather" (80 to 95 degrees F.) fungal disease that rapidly gobbles up large lawn areas. Infected leaves look water-soaked, are copper-colored, dark brown, or black in color, and feel greasy. Look for fungal strands during the evening or early-morning hours. Avoid spreading this disease when mowing. Collect the infected clippings and compost them. Fungicide are available.

To avoid pythium blight, postpone seeding until the arrival of cool temperatures in the fall. Avoid watering before dew forms at night or in the morn-

Helpful Hints

Here are some pointers to help you water efficiently:

1 If you have an in-ground, automatic sprinkler system, use the automatic position on the time clock when you are away from home for more than a few days. Using the automatic setting while you are at home, however, can overwater or underwater your lawn, depending on the weather. The system can be made more efficient by installing soil-moisture sensors in the lawn. These sensors will prevent the sprinkler valves from opening when they detect that the soil is moist.

2 When you're at home, set the time clock to "off" and manually turn on the in-ground system when the lawn needs water. The same applies to above-ground hose and sprinkler systems with irrigation clocks that screw onto the hose bibs. Turn on the system manually, and use the clock to shut it off when the right amount of water has been applied.

3 While the irrigation system is on, check the sprinkler heads for an even spray pattern. Examine the heads and replace those that leak or are damaged. Replace any worn nozzles. Make sure the sprinklers are delivering water to the lawn instead of the driveway or road.

4 Fix leaky hoses, spigots, and valves. A lot of water is wasted through leaky hose connections and worn-out spigots. A fairly slow leak—a faucet dripping one drop per second—will leak two gallons of water or more per day.

ing after sunrise, a practice which can prolong the time the grass blades are wet and susceptible to attack. Do not fertilize cool-season lawns in the summer months.

Weeds: During this time of the year it may seem as if the weeds are healthier and growing more vigorously than the lawn grass. See June.

Planning

The best place to be outside on a hot afternoon in summer is in the cool shade of a large tree. But although we appreciate the shade, most lawn grasses don't. Even the most shade-tolerant grasses need at least four hours of sunlight to survive.

In areas receiving less than four hours of sunlight, plant shade-tolerant ground covers or maintain a mulched area around the base of the tree. You can create a natural-looking low-maintenance area with mulch by allowing the tree's leaves to remain where they fall, replenishing the mulch layer for you.

If enough sunlight is available, then consider shade-tolerant grasses. **Fine fescues** are most tolerant of shade, followed by shade-tolerant varieties of **Kentucky bluegrass** (**A-34, Georgetown,** and **Glade**), and **tall fescue** (**Trident, Adventure,** and **Apache**).

When managing grasses in the shade, you'll have to adjust your maintenance practices. See the July Helpful Hint in Warm-Season Lawns on p. 185 for some tips.

Planting

If the lawn is overrun with weeds or if parts have thinned out or disappeared completely due to this past summer's drought, Mountain gardeners should plan to renovate now. Piedmont gardeners can wait until next month. Renovation is the step you should take before having to completely overhaul the lawn and start all over again from scratch.

Before you renovate, figure out how your lawn spiraled into decline. Improper mowing, watering, fertilizing, and pests can be disastrous. Too much shade, a lack of water during extended dry spells, or using a grass that's not adapted to your area can also lead a lawn down the path of needing renovation. After you came to terms with the problem that led to decline, follow these steps:

1. If your soil hasn't been tested in the past two or three years, submit a sample to your county cooperative extension service office.

2. Eliminate any undesirable weeds or lawn grasses that will compete with your new lawn. *Handpull* or use a herbicide. Some herbicides require a waiting period of four to six weeks before seeding, so plan accordingly.

3. *Mow* the area with a reel or rotary mower set at its lowest setting and collect the clippings. If a thick thatch layer is present in the **Kentucky bluegrass** or **fine fescue** lawn (greater than $1/2$ inch in thickness), *rake out* the thatch layer by hand. For large areas, use a vertical mower which can be rented from an equipment rental shop. This machine has revolving vertical blades that cut into the thatch layer and lift it to the surface. Set the machine so the blades cut into the upper $1/4$ to $1/2$ inch of soil. It leaves shallow grooves or slits in the soil surface. Rake up the debris and add it to the compost pile or mulch the vegetable garden. Seeds falling into the furrows created by the vertical mower are much more likely to germinate and grow.

Vertical Mower

4 If the soil is compacted, use a power-driven aerifier or core aerator to improve air and water movement into the soil (see September Planning). Core in several directions. Use the vertical mower to break up the cores.

5 Seed the bare areas. Use a blend of **tall fescue** cultivars, applying 6 pounds per 1,000 square feet. **Kentucky bluegrass** can be seeded at 1 1/2 to 2 pounds per 1,000 square feet (be patient with **Kentucky bluegrass** since it may take up to three weeks for the seedlings to appear).

6 Distribute the seed with a rotary or drop-type spreader, applying half the total amount in one direction and the other half at right angles to the first. *Rake* the seed into the soil to ensure good seed-to-soil contact. (Instead of broadcasting the seed, you can see if your equipment rental dealer has a slit seeder—a machine that cuts furrows and deposits the seed in the soil.)

7 Cover the area with clean straw to conserve moisture and enhance germination.

8 *Fertilize* the lawn one month after renovating.

9 *Mow* the grass when it grows one-third higher than its recommended height.

Care for Your Lawn

If your **Kentucky bluegrass** lawn feels spongy and is unthrifty-looking, take a look at the thatch layer. See September, p. 158–59.

Watering

Water dormant lawns every three weeks in the absence of rain, or take your chances with the understanding that reseeding may be necessary in the fall.

Fertilizing

Established lawns can be fertilized *next* month.

Mowing

Continue to mow your lawn regularly, removing no more than one-third of the grass height at each mowing.

Pest Control

Insects: If your lawn looks wilted, even after watering, if it's been torn up by skunks, birds, and moles, or if parts have turned brown and feel spongy, check to see if you have an infestation of white grubs. See Warm-Season Lawns, p. 187 for their description and control.

Diseases: Look for brown patch disease on **tall fescue.** *Avoid* this disease next year by fertilizing and watering properly.

Weeds: It is time to apply herbicides to your lawn for winter annual or perennial weeds that germinate or form rosettes in turf during the fall. Check herbicide labels before using, and select an appropriate chemical for the weed types and lawn type in your yard.

If annual bluegrass and other winter weeds were a problem in your lawn last spring, you will have them again unless you control them this fall. The seeds are sitting there waiting to germinate this month. Apply a pre-emergence herbicide to prevent them from appearing this fall.

Planning

Lawns need air to breathe.

When a clay soil becomes compacted, closing up the air-filled pore spaces, the lawn will decline. Besides choking the roots for air, compacted soil reduces the movement of water and nutrients to the roots. Soon the grass plants weaken, making them less able to compete with weeds and slow to recuperate from injury. Eventually the lawn thins out, giving rise to goosegrass and prostrate knotweed: two notorious weeds that thrive in compacted soils.

Make plans to help your lawn breathe easier this fall by aerifying your lawn—create pores or cavities that will loosen up the soil and create pore spaces that will admit air, water, and nutrients.

The simplest and cheapest way to aerify a small lawn is with a spading fork. Push the tines into the soil as far as you can (at least 4 inches) and rock the fork back and forth to enlarge the holes. This movement will loosen up the soil and make room for new grass roots. The only limitation to using a spading fork is that at the same time you are making a hole you may be forcing soil particles around the hole closer together, causing more compaction.

Larger lawns require a power-driven core aerator or aerifier, which can be rented at lawn-and-garden supply centers. The working parts of these machines are spoon-shaped tines or hollow tubes. As the tubes are driven into the lawn, cores of soil are removed from the ground and strewn across the lawn. The holes that result increase the amounts of air, water, and nutrients that are available to the roots, making it easier for your lawn to breathe.

Cool-season grasses should be aerified in the fall when there is less heat stress and danger of invasion by weedy annuals. Allow at least four weeks of good growing weather to help the plants recover.

Planting

In the Piedmont and Mountains, seed thin, bare areas.

1 Pull out any remaining grass or weeds. Loosen up the soil with a rake or shovel.

2 Hand-sow a blend of at least two varieties.

3 *Rake in* the seed lightly.

4 *Mulch* with weed-free straw and keep the patch moist.

5 Gently water the newly seeded area. Keep it moist but not flooded.

Mowing

Don't retire the lawn mower when the growth of your lawn slows down this fall. As long as the grass continues to grow, it should be mowed.

Care for Your Lawn

During the fall, remove leaves by raking, blowing, or bagging when mowing to prevent smothering of the turf. Grass will grow long after deciduous trees have dropped their leaves. Collect the leaves and shred them for mulch around trees and shrubs, or recycle them into the compost pile.

If your **Kentucky bluegrass** lawn feels spongy and is unthrifty-looking, take a quick look at the thatch layer. Thatch is a dense, spongy collection of living and dead grass stems and roots lying between the soil surface and green grass leaves in established lawns. Cut out a pie-shaped wedge of sod from your lawn with a knife or spade. If you have a thatch problem where the layer exceeds ¹/₂ inch in thickness, you need to dethatch—physically remove the thatch from your lawn. Use a dethatching rake for small areas or a vertical mower for larger lawns. To reduce the accumulation of thatch, follow these practices:

- *Fertilize* according to soil-test recommendations, being sure to avoid applying excessive amounts of nitrogen.

- *Mow* your lawn at the proper height and mow frequently.

- Monitor the soil pH and keep it at the recommended level for your particular turfgrass. Acidic soils hamper the activity of earthworms, insects, and microbes that can break down thatch.

- If you use pesticides, use them sparingly and locally to control specific pest problems. This will minimize the destruction of earthworms and other thatch-decomposers.

Watering

Water the lawn if necessary, relying on the symptoms of moisture stress as your guide.

Fertilizing

Fertilize **Kentucky bluegrass** or **tall fescue** according to the results of a soil test. In the absence of soil-test recommendations, use a 3:1:2 analysis (such as 12-4-8 or 16-4-8) fertilizer where ¹/₄ to ¹/₂ of the nitrogen is slowly available (look for "water insoluble nitrogen" or "slowly available nitrogen" on the label). Apply ¹/₂ or 1 pound of nitrogen per 1,000 square feet of lawn. If you accidentally spread fertilizer on the sidewalk, driveway, or road, sweep it up and return it to the lawn.

Mowing

Mow often enough that no more than one-third of the grass height is cut. *Recycle* grass clippings by leaving them on the lawn.

Pest Control

Insects: Before treating your lawn for grubs, sample several damaged areas in your lawn to get an average of the number of grubs per square foot to decide if control is necessary. Lawns can tolerate lower or higher

numbers of other white grubs, depending on the health of the lawn and the kind of grub. Submit the grubs to your cooperative extension service office for identification to help you decide if an insecticide application is warranted. See Warm-Season Lawns, p. 187.

Weeds: If annual bluegrass (*Poa annua*) and other winter annuals have been a problem in the past, gardeners in in the Mountains can apply a pre-emergent herbicide early this month—Piedmont gardeners later in the month—to control the germinating seeds before they appear. Annual bluegrass germinates in late summer and early fall when temperatures drop consistently into the mid-70s F. A pre-emergent herbicide forms a barrier at or just below the soil surface and kills the emerging seedlings when they grow and come into contact with the herbicide. Look for annual bluegrass in shady or moist areas.

Planning

As you rake up the fallen leaves from your lawn, plan to recycle them as mulch or compost. For a fine-textured mulch, shred the leaves with a lawn mower or a leaf shredder. Finely cut leaves look more attractive and tend to stay where you put them.

Compost them. To compost leaves, researchers recommend building piles at least 4 feet in diameter and 3 feet in height. To keep the piles to a manageable size, make them no larger than 5 feet high and 10 feet wide. You can compost leaves by themselves, or add fresh vegetable peelings, grass clippings, or other kitchen or yard trimmings.

To speed up the composting process, shred the leaves before putting them into the pile. Be sure to avoid adding meat or grease, which may cause odors and attract pests. Pay particular attention to moisture and air: keep the ingredients moist enough so you can squeeze water droplets from a handful of leaves, and aerate or supply air to the pile by turning the materials. Turn the pile once a month during warm weather. In cool weather turn it less frequently, preventing too much heat from escaping. To convert the leaves to compost fairly quickly requires the addition of nitrogen to the pile. Add a nitrogen-containing fertilizer such as 10-10-10. Good natural substitutes for synthetic fertilizers include horse or cow manure, bloodmeal, or cottonseed meal.

Mix this crumbly, earthy-smelling "black gold" into heavy clay soil to improve drainage and make the soil easier to cultivate. Compost helps sandy soils retain water and nutrients.

Planting

In the Piedmont there's still time to reseed bare areas or start a new lawn, *but hurry.* Try to get it completed by mid-month. To fill in bare spots in your lawn.

1 Loosen the soil to a depth of $1/2$ inch with a rake. If you have the gusto, use a shovel to break up the top 6 inches of soil.

2 Sow the seed and work it in lightly.

3 Gently water the newly seeded area. Keep it moist but not flooded.

4 *Mulch* lightly with weed-free straw to keep the area moist.

5 Keep the patch moist until the seedlings emerge.

6 After a month, *fertilize* the patch lightly to encourage growth.

Care for Your Lawn

Core-aerate **tall fescue** that is subject to heavy traffic on clay soils, minimizing compaction and improving rooting.

Watering

Newly seeded or sodded lawns should be watered frequently. As the seedlings emerge and the sod "knits" into the soil, gradually water less frequently but more deeply.

Fertilizing

Wait until next month to fertilize the lawn.

Mowing

Mow often enough so that no more than one-third of the grass height is cut. *Recycle* grass clippings by leaving them on the lawn.

Pest Control

Insects: If fire ants have cropped up in your lawn or landscape, control them with the "two-step method" described in the Warm-Season Lawns chapter, April Insects on p. 178.

Diseases: "Fairy rings" can be found in all types of grasses. They may appear as a ring of mushrooms or simply as a dark-green ring of lush grass. The ring may vary from a few inches to several feet in diameter. Fairy rings are caused by soil-inhabiting fungi that feed on old roots, stumps, and thatch. Fairy-ring fungi are not plant parasites, but they can cause the lawn to dry out because their fungal bodies make the soil repel water. Grass inside the ring is usually in a state of decline. On young rings the grass on the inside of the ring may be dead. On old rings there may be a dead band of grass a few inches to several feet wide forming a partial or complete ring.

Fairy rings are difficult to control. You can be patient and allow them to disappear over time. Watering the ring to saturate the soil for several hours and over several days may help. As a last resort, you can replace the infested soil occupied by the fairy ring with clean soil.

Helpful Hint

If you'd like to grow moss (but were afraid to ask your neighbor how since he's been trying to get rid of it for the past five years), rest easy, because it's a "passalong" plant. With your neighbor's permission, "borrow" some moss by carefully cutting out small sections and transplanting them to a moist, shady spot. Lay the sections a short distance away from each other and moisten the moss patches lightly until they become established. The pieces should eventually fill in to create a velvety-green, seamless carpet. You can even grow moss on concrete planters and steppingstones, and along garden walls to give them an aged, weathered look. Here's how:

- Grind the moss into small particles. Pour about a quart of buttermilk into a bucket and add the ground-up moss, along with a handful or two of composted cow manure.

- Stir thoroughly until the concoction becomes soupy.

- Rub the concrete surface with a steel brush. This will roughen the surface and give it a weathered appearance.

- Finally, brush the solution onto the concrete. Moss will gradually begin to grow on it, making it look aged. Be advised, however, that for several weeks following this treatment the concrete could be aromatic, to say the least. Hey, it's just a small price to pay for beauty.

Weeds: *Handpull* or *spot-treat* chickweed, henbit, and other winter annuals with a broadleaf herbicide. Use a herbicide labeled for your lawn grass and for the weeds you're trying to control.

Planning

Although "a rolling stone gathers no moss," expect moss to collect in the moist, shaded areas of your lawn. In addition to shady places, mosses are especially fond of acidic (low pH) soils with low fertility, poorly drained or wet soils, or combinations of these. These primitive, nonflowering plants spread by producing dust-fine spores that are carried on the wind and alight on moist ground, rocks, bricks, or tree trunks. The spores germinate and form a network of green threads that soon develop into tiny matted plants. Most grow from only 1/4 inch to 2 inches high.

Although mosses are harmless—their only requirement is moisture—folks either court them or hate them. I love the velvety, cushiony look and feel of moss. Mosses are cultivated as ornamentals in Japanese gardens. A famous 13th-century garden in Kyoto called Saiho-ji ("Moss Temple") has over forty species and varieties of rolling green mosses spread over 4¹/₂ acres. The mosses come in light and dark shades of green, often highlighted with splashes of bronze, gold, and gray.

If you're planning to rid your lawn of moss by raking it out and then reseeding, be aware that in most cases, the moss will return. Only when you make the growing conditions less appealing to the moss and more favorable for the lawn grass will you be able to halt the moss's advance.

Before you choose to fight a "turf war" with moss, figure out your chances of winning. If your moss-covered lawn gets less than four hours of sunlight a day, it will be too shady for turfgrasses. You're going to lose the battle unless you can improve sunlight penetration by selectively pruning tree limbs. If there's always going to be insufficient sunlight, your best bet is to cut your losses and ditch the grass. If you really dislike moss, plant shade-tolerant ground covers or mulch with leaves, needles, or wood chips. Ideally, extend the mulch layer to the drip line or outermost branches of the tree.

If your lawn is receiving adequate sunlight but still seems to be losing ground to moss, follow these steps to improve the health, density, and appearance of your lawn:

- Test your soil at least every three years, and *fertilize* according to the results of your soil test and at the proper time. Maintain a soil pH between 5.8 and 6.5 for **tall fescue** and **Kentucky bluegrass.**

- Improve poorly drained areas by regrading to direct water away from the site.

- Cultivate compacted, heavy clay soils with a core aerifier—a machine that removes plugs of soil. You can rent, purchase, or contract this service through lawn care companies. For small areas, use a spading fork to punch holes in the soil to improve drainage.

- *Mow* grasses growing in the shade at the top of their recommended mowing height range to promote deep rooting and to leave as much leaf area as possible to manufacture food.

Planting

Install sod as long as the soil isn't frozen.

Watering

Do not allow newly sodded areas to dry out. When the sod has "knitted" or rooted into the soil, reduce the frequency of irrigation and water deeply as the roots begin to penetrate the soil.

Fertilizing

Fertilize **Kentucky bluegrass** or **tall fescue** according to the results of a soil test. Fertilizing in the fall promotes root development without excessive top growth. With a strong root system, your lawn will be better able to withstand drought conditions next summer. See September "Fertilizing."

Pest Control

Diseases: Rust and dollar spot are fungal diseases that attack **bluegrass** and **fescue** lawns.

Rust causes grass leaves to turn yellow before turning brown and dying. Take a close look at the leaves and look for red, orange, or brown spores. Heavy infestations cause thinning. Many grass varieties have good-to-moderate levels of resistance to rust, so this disease shouldn't be much of a problem. Collect infected grass clippings to prevent the spores from spreading to other areas of the lawn. Avoid keeping the grass wet for long periods by watering in the early morning.

Dollar spot produces small circular areas of straw-colored grass which range from 1 to 6 inches across. If you examine individual grass blades you'll find straw-colored lesions with reddish-brown borders. Sometimes the lesions will extend across the blade while the leaf tip remains green. Early in the morning you may be able to spot a spider web–like growth over the infected lawn area. Dollar spot is more common during the spring and fall months. Maintain adequate levels of fertility, especially nitrogen, since this diseases favors "hungry" lawns. Fungicides are generally unnecessary.

Weeds: Pull young, emerged weeds now while the task is easier and the weather is comfortable. By eliminating the weeds before they set seeds, you'll also reduce next year's problem.

Helpful Hint

Small low spots in the lawn can be raised by carefully removing the turf and filling in the low spots with soil. Use your spade to cut out the low spot, going down about 2 inches deep. Angle your blade under the sod to cut the roots cleanly. Lift up the sod and fill in the spot with soil. Replace the sod and keep it moist until it knits into the soil.

DECEMBER

Planning

Make plans to winterize the lawn mower before putting it away for the winter. Nothing could be more exasperating next spring than a lawn mower that won't start. The secret to getting it to start on the first (or second) pull next spring is to winterize it.

1 *Run the engine dry.* Untreated gasoline stored for long periods can cause a gummy buildup in the carburetor that can make it impossible to start after a few months. Run the engine until it stalls. Alternatively, you can add a small amount of gasoline stabilizer to the fuel tank and run the engine for a few minutes to distribute it with the fuel.

2 *Drain and replace the oil.* Disconnect the wire from the spark plug for safety. Change the oil at least once a year (refer to your owner's manual) and check the oil level each time you use the machine. Recycle the used oil.

3 *Clean the air filter.* Foam-element air filters should be removed and cleaned with hot, soapy water. Before replacing it, pour a couple of tablespoons of clean engine oil onto it and distribute it by squeezing the foam.

4 *Oil the spark plug.* Remove the spark plug and pour a tablespoon of clean engine oil into the hole. Replace the spark plug and pull the starter cord a couple of times to crank the engine and distribute the oil. This will protect the engine from corrosion during the winter.

5 *Clean and store the engine by brushing the cooling fins to make sure they're not plugged.* Scrape off any dirt or grass clippings on the underside with a screwdriver, putty knife, or wire brush. If the blade is dull, remove and sharpen it or replace it.

Planting

Sod can be installed as long as the soil is not frozen.

Watering

If dry weather persists and the lawn shows signs of drought stress, apply an inch of water per week in the absence of precipitation. Newly seeded or sodded lawns should be watered frequently. As the seedlings emerge and the sod "knits" into the soil, gradually water less frequently but more deeply and less often.

Fertilizing

Do not fertilize the lawn at this time.

Mowing

You may still have to mow this month. Continue practicing the "one-third rule": Do not remove any more than one-third of the height at each mowing.

Pest Control

Weeds: *Handpull* or *spot-treat* chickweed, henbit, and other winter annuals with a broadleaf herbicide.

Warm-Season Lawns

Perhaps you've dreamt of the perfect lawn: an emerald-green carpet that never needed mowing, fertilizing, or watering . . . in sun or shade, summer or winter, it stayed green every day of the year. Sorry, but you can enjoy this grass only in your dreams (unless you call Astroturf® grass, of course).

But don't despair. You can achieve a lawn that looks good and is functional and still have your weekends free. You just have to understand its needs and then try to meet them.

Keep in mind that each maintenance practice influences another. Your fertilizing practices affect how often you mow, and mowing height affects how often you need to water and how many weeds you will have. Become familiar with some basic turf establishment and maintenance practices.

In the Carolinas we can grow either cool-season, cool-climate grasses or warm-season, warm-climate grasses. Cool-season grasses (**Kentucky bluegrass, perennial ryegrass, tall fescue,** and **creeping red fescue)** grow well during the cool months (60 to 75 degrees Fahrenheit). They are adapted to the Piedmont and the Mountains. **Tall fescue** grows in the northern reaches of the Coastal Plain in North Carolina. See the Lawns, Cool-Season chapter (p. 139) for information about growing cool-season grasses in the Carolinas.

Warm-season grasses (**bermudagrass, centipedegrass,** and others) thrive in hot weather, looking their best when the temperatures are 80 to 95 degrees F. They go dormant and turn brown when the weather cools. They can be grown in the Piedmont and the Coastal Plain. Refer to January Planning, p. 172–73, for a description of these warm-season grasses. Refer to the Planting Chart (p. 171) to help you select the right turfgrass for your lawn.

Starting a Lawn

Depending on the grass, a warm-season lawn can be started by seed or sod, or with grass pieces called sprigs or stolons. Whatever method you choose, follow the pre-planting steps outlined in Starting a Lawn in the Cool-Season chapter on p. 140.

Seeding

Common **bermudagrass** and **Japanese zoysiagrass** (*Zoysia japonica*) can be seeded from April through July. Here's how:

1. Apply the seed with a drop-type or rotary spreader to get uniform distribution. Sow half the required amount in one direction and the other half at right angles to the first to help ensure good coverage. For very small seed like **centipedegrass** or **bermudagrass,** mix the seed with a carrier such as corn meal or grits to distribute the seed evenly.

Warm-Season Lawns

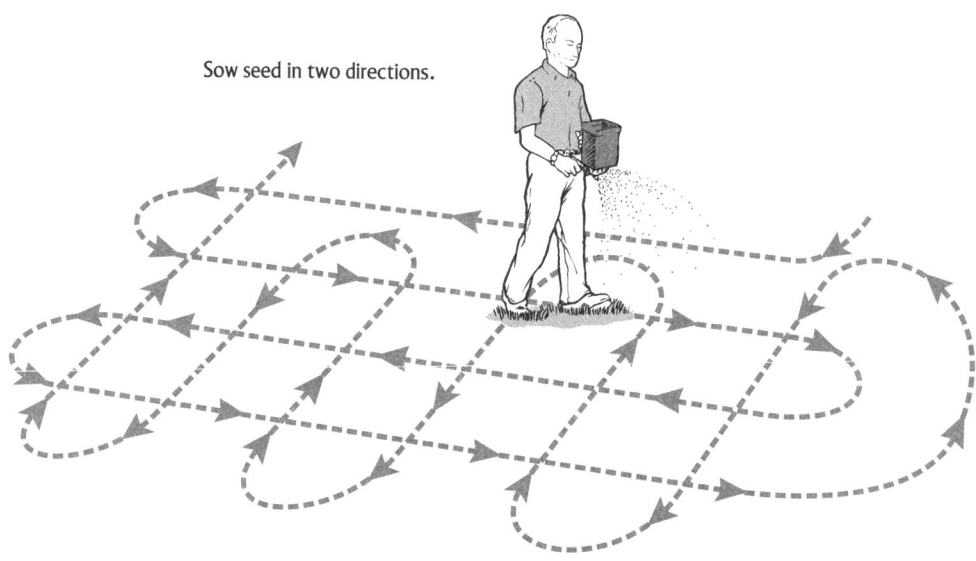

Sow seed in two directions.

2 Lightly rake the seeds into the top ¼ inch of soil. Then roll the seedbed with a light or empty lawn roller (water-ballast roller) to ensure good seed-to-soil contact.

3 *Mulch* the seedbed to prevent soil erosion, retain moisture, and prevent crusting of the soil surface. The most commonly used mulch is straw—it is important to use weed-free straw. Use enough weed-free straw so that one-half to three-quarters of the bare ground is covered. If it's not spread too thickly, straw can be left to decompose.

4 *Water* the lawn after seeding. Expect to water a few times a day for several weeks until the seedlings emerge and become established. As the seedlings mature and the root system develops, reduce the frequency of watering, but make sure you water deeply to wet the entire root zone.

5 *Mow* the lawn when the grass is one-third higher than the desired height. For example, if you want to maintain your **centipedegrass** lawn at 2 inches, mow the grass when it reaches a height of 3 inches.

Warm-season grasses that do not produce seed can be sodded, plugged, or sprigged. *Sod* can be installed as long as the soil temperature remains above 55 degrees F for several weeks, usually during April through September. Sprigging or plugging can be done from April through July. Prepare the soil as you would for seeding. Refer to p. 146 to learn how to sod a lawn.

Plugging involves planting small pieces of sod—plugs—about 2 inches in diameter or larger on 6-inch or 1-foot centers. Plugs can be purchased in trays or they can be cut from sod with a spade or axe. **Centipedegrass, St. Augustine-grass,** and **zoysiagrass** are often plugged by digging a hole, putting in the plug, and then tamping it into place. You can even repair bare

Warm-Season Lawns

spots in your lawn by cutting out plugs from your own lawn. *Water* immediately after planting to wet the soil beneath the plugs to ensure rooting into the prepared soil. Water often enough so the plugs don't dry out. Deeper, thorough watering can then be done as the roots begin to penetrate the soil.

out. The goal is to water often enough to keep the seedbed moist but not waterlogged, until the plants can develop sufficient root systems to take advantage of deeper and less frequent watering.

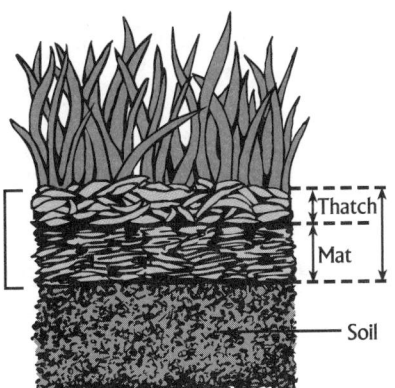

Plugs are normally spaced on 6- to 12-inch centers.

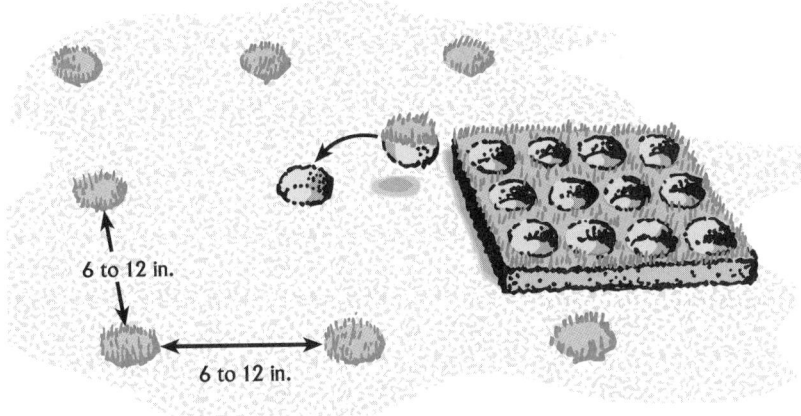

6 to 12 in.

6 to 12 in.

Sprigging is the planting of sprigs—above-ground and below-ground grass parts called stolons and rhizomes. They can be purchased by the bushel or obtained by mechanically shredding or hand-shredding a piece of sod. The sprigs are either planted in rows in small areas called space planting or, for larger areas, broadcast randomly over the prepared area and covered lightly with soil. It's important that part of the sprig protrudes above the soil surface and part of it is buried or "set." *Water* lightly and frequently so the sprigs don't dry

As with seeding, sodding, or plugging, sprigging requires regular watering to help the grass roots become established.

Thatch Control

If you cut out a pie-shaped wedge of sod from your lawn and examine it, you may find a layer of thatch. Thatch is a dense, spongy collection of living and dead grass stems and roots lying between the soil surface and green grass leaves in established lawns. **St. Augustinegrass, hybrid**

bermudagrass, and **zoysiagrass** tend to develop thatch at a faster rate than **centipedegrass.**

Thatch originates from old stems, stolons (above-ground stems), roots, and rhizomes (below-ground stems) shed by grasses as new plant parts grow. Unlike grass clippings, which decay quickly, the sloughed-off parts contain high levels of lignin (hard-to-decompose cell wall material) and decay very slowly, collecting on the soil surface faster than they decompose.

A shallow thatch layer (under $1/2$ inch) actually benefits the lawn.

- Thatch acts as a natural cushion, enabling the lawn to endure wear and tear.

- It also works as a mulch by retaining moisture and insulating the soil from temperature extremes.

Warm-Season Lawns

Unfortunately, thatch can become a thick destructive layer, affecting the health, vigor, and appearance of your lawn. It causes problems when it exceeds $1/2$ inch in thickness. The grass develops roots within the thatch layer, where it's unable to obtain adequate moisture and minerals. The thatch also provides a habitat for destructive insects and disease-causing organisms.

To remove thick thatch layers, use a dethatching rake for small areas or a vertical mower for larger lawns. A vertical mower with revolving straight fixed blades is a good choice. The blades cut into the thatch layer and lift it to the surface where it can be raked up and added to the compost pile or used as a mulch in the vegetable garden.

To reduce the accumulation of thatch, follow these practices:

- *Fertilize* according to soil-test recommendations, and be sure to avoid applying excessive amounts of nitrogen.

- *Mow* your lawn at the proper height, and mow frequently.

- *Aerify* your lawn in late spring and summer with a machine that creates "pores" in the lawn by the action of spoons or tines mounted on a drum or reel. As the machine rolls over the lawn, it removes cores of soil from the ground. The earthen cores or plugs are deposited on the lawn and contain microorganisms that help to break down the thatch.

- Monitor the soil pH and keep it at the recommended level for your particular turfgrass. Acidic soils hamper the activity of earthworms, insects, and microbes involved in breaking down thatch.

- If you use pesticides, use them sparingly and locally to control specific pest problems, thus minimizing the destruction of earthworms and other thatch-decomposers.

Watering

Refer to Watering in the introduction to Cool-Season Lawns chapter on p. 141.

Fertilizing

Fertilize your lawn based on the results of a soil test. See Fertilizing in the Cool-Season chapter on p. 141.

Fertilize warm-season grasses in late spring and summer, making the first application at least two or three weeks after the lawn fully greens up. Use the chart on p. 169 as a guide.

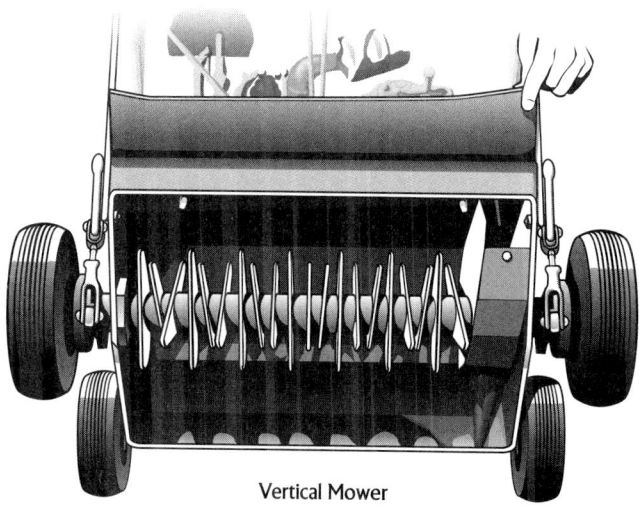

Vertical Mower

Warm-Season Lawns

Suggested Calendar for
Fertilizing Warm-Season Lawns in the Carolinas

Lawn Grass	Month of application[1]	Total pounds of Nitrogen per 1,000 sq. ft. of lawn per growing season per year[2]
Bermudagrass (common and hybrid)[3]	April, May, June, July, or August	2 to 5
Carpetgrass	April, June, or August	$1/2$ to 1
Centipedegrass[4]	April, June, or August	$1/2$ to 1
St. Augustinegrass	April, May, June, July, or August	2 to 3
Zoysiagrass	April, June, or August	1 to 3

FOOTNOTES:

[1] For high-maintenance lawns, apply 1 pound of nitrogen per 1,000 square feet; $1/2$ pound of nitrogen per 1,000 square feet is fine for low-maintenance lawns and on sandy soils with little organic matter.

[2] The total yearly amounts of nitrogen are suggested guidelines. The higher amounts are suited for lawn owners interested in higher quality, and for lawns growing in sandy soils or in coastal areas with longer growing seasons. In the absence of a soil test, use a complete fertilizer with a 4:1:2 or 3:1:2 ratio except for **centipedegrass** (see footnote 4 below). Use a slow- or controlled-release fertilizer. Acting like timed-release capsules, the nutrients are gradually made available to the plant. Look for one with at least one-half of the total amount of nitrogen listed as "water insoluble nitrogen." A slow-release fertilizer is a good choice, especially in sandy soils, which tend to leach, or near shallow water tables, to reduce the number of fertilizer applications and the threat of water contamination.

[3] Dormant lawns overseeded with **ryegrass** (see September Planning and Planting on p. 188) can be fertilized in November and February with 1 pound of nitrogen per 1,000 square feet per application.

[4] Established **centipedegrass** requires a low-phosphorus, high-potassium fertilizer such as 1-1-2 or 1-1-3. Phosphorus is normally not needed on established **centipedegrass** lawns unless recommended by soil-test results. Overfertilizing **centipedegrass** often results in pest problems and a disorder called "centipedegrass decline" (see May Helpful Hint on p. 181).

Lawns, Warm-Season

Mowing

Two kinds of mowers are used for mowing turfgrasses: rotary mowers and reel mowers. Rotary mowers have a whirling blade that cuts the grass at high speeds in machete-like fashion. They can be used to cut lawns down to an inch. Reel mowers have a series of blades that cut the grass like scissors. The blades press the grass against a bedknife to slice the grass, giving the lawn a highly finished look. Reel mowers are a good choice for hybrid **bermudagrass** and **zoysiagrass** lawns which have to be maintained at low cutting heights. Follow these basic rules of proper mowing:

1. Mow with a sharp mower blade. Sharp blades cut the grass cleanly, which ensures rapid healing and regrowth. When dull blades tear and bruise the leaves, the wounded grass plants become weakened and are less able to ward off invading weeds or to recover from disease or insect attacks.

2. Mow your lawn regularly. A good rule of thumb is to remove no more than one-third of the grass height at any one mowing. For example, if you are maintaining your **centipede** lawn at 2 inches, mow the lawn when it is about 3 inches high. Following the one-third rule will produce smaller clippings, which will disappear quickly by filtering down to the soil surface.

3. Mow at the proper height. See Guidelines for Mowing Height chart below:

Pest Control

The secret to thwarting pests is to work with nature. Once you select an appropriate grass suited to your location, create conditions for the grass to thrive with proper establishment and maintenance. Healthy, well-managed grass can resist invasion from weeds and attacks from insects and diseases. As they say: "An ounce of prevention is worth a pound of cure."

If problems occur, identify the problem before taking action. If you need help, contact your cooperative extension service in North or South Carolina.

Guidelines for Mowing Height[+]

Lawn Grass	Mowing Height (inches)[+]
Bermudagrass, Common **Hybrid**	1 to 2 3/4 to 1 1/2
Carpetgrass	1 to 2
Centipedegrass	1 to 2
St. Augustinegrass	2 to 3
Zoysiagrass	3/4 to 1 1/2

[+] Measure the height of the mower on a level surface and adjust it to the proper height.

Carolina Warm-Season Lawns

Turfgrass Planting Chart

Lawn Grass	Common Bermuda	Hybrid Bermudagrass	Carpetgrass
Area Best Adapted	Piedmont and Coastal Plain	Piedmont and Coastal Plain	Coastal Plain
Planting Time	Late spring to midsummer	Late spring to midsummer	Late spring to midsummer
Method of Planting	Seed, sprigs[1], or sod Unhulled seed: 2 to 3 lbs./1,000 sq. ft. Hulled seed: 1 to 1½ lbs./1,000 sq. ft	Sprigs[1] or sod	Seed: 2 to 4 lbs./1,000 sq. ft.
Tolerance to Drought	G	E	P (prefers wet sites and acid soil)
Salt	G	G	P
Shade	G to F	P	G
Traffic	E	G	G to P

Lawn Grass	Centipedegrass	St. Augustinegrass	Zoysiagrass
Area Best Adapted	Piedmont and Coastal Plain	Piedmont and Coastal Plain	Piedmont and Coastal Plain
Planting Time	Late spring to midsummer	Late spring to midsummer	Late spring to midsummer
Method of Planting	Seed, sprigs, plugs[2], or sod Seed: ¼ to ½ lbs./1,000 sq. ft.	Seed, sod or plugs[2] Seed: 1 to 2 lbs./1,000 sq. ft.	Seed, sprigs[1], plugs[2], or sod Seed: 1 to 2 lb./1000 sq. ft.
Tolerance to Drought	G	G	G
Salt	P	G	G
Shade	G	G to F	G to F
Traffic	P	F	E

E = Excellent; G = Good; F = Fair; P = Poor

[1]Broadcast 3 to 5 bushels of sprigs per 1,000 square feet of lawn (1 sq. yd. of sod pulled apart yields 1 bushel of sprigs)

[2]Using 2-inch-square plugs planted on 6-inch "centers" (6 inches from the center of one plug to the center of the next one), 12 square yards of whole sod would be needed to establish a 1,000-square-foot lawn. Likewise, a 12-inch "on center" spacing would require 3 square yards of sod per 1,000 square feet of lawn.

Note: One square yard of sod yields 324 (two-inch-square) plugs.

Planning

If you want to change your lawn, spend some time this month learning about the many different kinds of warm-season grasses that you can choose. All share the common feature of tolerating hot summers and mild winters.

Common **bermudagrass (*Cynodon dactylon*)** grows rapidly from seed to form a lawn in less than a year. It's extremely drought tolerant, rejoices in hot weather, handles wear-and-tear well, and tolerates salt spray so it can be grown on the coast. It's got a few drawbacks, however. It does poorly in shade, even light shade. It's also very aggressive. **Bermudagrass** spreads by both above- and below-ground runners that make weeding flower and shrub beds an endless battle (hence its other common names of wiregrass or devilgrass).

Hybrid bermudagrasses are more refined than common. Whereas common **bermudagrass** produces a rather open turf with unsightly seedheads, the improved selections—**Tifway (Tifton 419)** and **Tifway II**—have finer leaves, darker green color, and are thicker. They also require more frequent fertilizing and mowing to keep them in shape. **Midiron** and

Vamont are coarse-leaved, cold-tolerant cultivars. **Tifgreen (Tifton 328), Tifgreen II,** and **Tifdwarf** are finer-bladed grasses that are used on golf courses, football fields, and other recreational areas.

Centipedegrass (*Eremochloa ophiuroides*) is widely grown in the Carolinas and is especially suitable for people who want a dense, decent-looking lawn that requires little mowing and fertilizing. **Centipede** has a lighter green color than most grasses (Granny Smith apple-green) and grows slowly. It can be grown in full sun to part shade. Because **centipedegrass** only produces above-ground runners called stolons, it can be easily controlled near flower beds and walkways. Although **centipede** requires little effort, it has no tolerance for neglect or mismanagement. In either situation, it may succumb to a disorder called "centipede decline." The grass may fail to green-up in the spring or begin to grow and die in late spring and summer. See the May Helpful Hint on p. 181 for more information about centipede decline.

Zoysiagrass (*Zoysia* spp.) forms a very dense, attractive lawn in full sun and partial shade. In the winter it turns a beautiful beige. **Zoysiagrasses** grow very slowly compared to other grasses. This is a disadvantage when it comes to establishment, which can take up to two years when plugged (2-inch plugs on 6-inch centers). Also, it recovers slowly from injury. **Zoysiagrass** forms thatch readily (thatch is a spongy accumulation of dead, decaying plant matter on the soil surface), especially when it's mowed too high or infrequently, or when it's heavily fertilized. Mowing the tough, wiry leaves requires a sharp mower blade. The best quality can be achieved with a reel-type mower.

Two popular **zoysiagrass** cultivars are **Meyer,** the **zoysiagrass** often advertised as the "super" grass in newspapers and magazines. It has good cold tolerance and spreads more rapidly than most other **zoysias,** but has a coarse texture. **Emerald zoysia** is one of the most beautiful **zoysiagrasses,** fine textured and having less winter hardiness than **Meyer,** but darker green in color and more shade tolerant.

St. Augustinegrass (*Stenotaphrum secundatum*) or **Charleston grass** is widely grown along the coast because of its tolerance to salt spray and its ability to grow in shade. This fast-growing grass has large flat stems and broad coarse leaves. It has an attractive blue-green color and forms a fairly dense turf. It spreads along the ground with above-ground stems called stolons. Although it's an aggressive grower, it can be easily confined to the lawn.

St. Augustinegrass has a few problems. It can become thatchy when it's heavily fertilized or watered frequently. Some cultivars are susceptible to cold damage. A major insect pest of **St. Augustinegrass** is chinch bugs, whose feeding causes the leaves to wilt and turn brown. However, chinch bug–resistant cultivars are available.

Carpetgrass (*Axonopus affinis*) is ideally suited for wet, poorly drained, acid (pH 4.5–5.5) soils where ease of establishment and care is more important than quality.

Planting

Delay planting warm-season grasses until the air temperature stays consistently above 60 degrees F.

Watering

Dormant and overseeded lawns may have to be watered this month if it's been dry and warm and windy conditions prevail. See September Planting on p. 188 for information about overseeding.

Fertilizing

Do not fertilize dormant lawns.

Mowing

Maintain **ryegrass**-overseeded **bermudagrass** lawns at a height of 1 inch. Dormant lawns do not have to be mowed—but make sure your mower will start on the first pull this spring. Service your lawn mower yourself or take it to a lawn repair shop. See the Cool-Season Lawns chapter, February Planning, p. 145.

Pest Control

Weeds: Prevent winter annuals such as common chickweed and henbit from going to seed by handpulling. *Handpull* wild garlic when the soil is moist to remove the entire plant—bulb and all. If you leave the bulb behind, it will resprout.

Helpful Hint

Avoid heavy traffic on dormant lawns. Dry grass is easily broken and the crown of the plant may be severely damaged or killed.

Planning

Before you fertilize your lawn in the next few months, plan to calibrate your spreader. Calibrating your spreader enables you to apply the right amount of fertilizer to your lawn. It helps you avoid the mistake of applying too much, which can harm the plants and the environment, or too little and not achieve the results you expect. Follow these steps to calibrate a rotary or cyclone spreader.

1 Gather the following materials:

- Rotary spreader (check to see that the parts are in working order)

- Bucket

- Hand-held calculator

- Tape measure at least 50 ft. long

- Scale for determining weight

- Fertilizer

2 Unlike a drop-type spreader that distributes a uniform amount of fertilizer across its width, a rotary spreader slings the fertilizer out in a wide, uneven pattern. More fertilizer falls in the center and less at the edges. About 2/3 of the entire application width—called the "effective width"—receives a uniform amount of fertilizer.

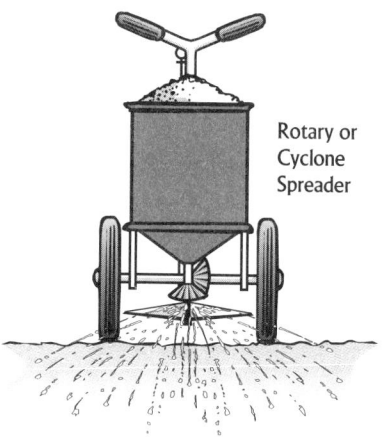

Rotary or Cyclone Spreader

Here's how to measure the effective width of your spreader.

- Find a hard surface where you can measure the width of the fertilizer pattern.

- Place a small amount of fertilizer into the spreader's hopper.

- Walk a short distance at a regular pace and then stop.

- Measure the application width of the fertilizer band. Multiply the width by 2/3 or 0.66. For example, if the fertilizer is cast out in a 12-foot-wide swathe, the effective width is 8 feet (0.66 × 12 ft.). This 8-foot-wide band receives an even amount of fertilizer. An area two feet on either side of this band receives less fertilizer.

- Sweep up the fertilizer and return it to the bag.

3 Knowing the effective with of your spreader makes the rest of the calibration process easier.

4 When you're ready to fertilize your lawn, find a flat portion to calibrate the amount delivered by your spreader. Mark off an area that measures 1,000 square feet. In our example, the effective width is 8 feet—so the length must be 125 feet to create a 1,000-square-foot test area (1,000 sq. ft./8 ft.).

5 To apply 1 lb. of nitrogen per 1,000 square feet with a 16-4-8 fertilizer, you need to spread 6 lb. of fertilizer (100/16). To deliver it uniformly to avoid any skips, make two passes. Apply half the total amount in one direction and the other half at right angles to the first. *Calibrate the spreader based on one-half the application rate or 3 lb. of 16-4-8 fertilizer.*

6 Weigh some fertilizer, say about 10 lb., and put it in the hopper with the spreader in the "closed" position.

7 Set your spreader according to the fertilizer label which may specify the setting for your spreader. If it's not listed, start at a low setting to avoid applying too much.

8 Start walking about ten feet behind the starting point

you marked earlier. Open the spreader when you reach the starting line when you're walking at a "normal" pace.

9 Walk at a normal pace and close the hopper when you cross the finish.

10 Weigh the remaining fertilizer in the spreader and subtract the final weight from the starting weight to determine how much fertilizer you applied over the 1,000-square-foot area. For example, if you poured in 10 lb. fertilizer at the start and 8 lb. was left over, then you spread 2 lb. of fertilizer over the 1,000-square-foot area.

11 At the setting you tested, you applied less nitrogen than you need. So go back to step 6 and repeat the process with the spreader set at a higher setting. Move your calibration test site to another part of the lawn to avoid applying too much fertilizer to that area. Once you've found the correct setting that applies 3 lb. of 16-4-8 per 1,000 square feet, record it in your gardening journal for future reference.

To calibrate a drop-type spreader, follow the same steps. To make it easier, however, collect the fertilizer in a "catch pan" secured beneath the spreader openings. This catch pan is a V- or box-shaped trough made of cardboard or a piece of aluminum guttering. Weigh the fertilizer after the test run to see how much was applied.

Drop-Type Spreader

Planting

Delay planting warm-season grasses until the daytime temperature stays consistently above 60 degrees F.

Watering

Dormant and overseeded lawns may have to be watered this month if it's been dry and warm and windy conditions prevail.

Fertilizing

Do not fertilize dormant lawns.

Overseeded **bermudagrass** and **zoysiagrass** lawns can be fertilized this month. Use a fertilizer recommended by soil-test results. Do not apply a fertilizer containing phosphorus and potassium if adequate levels are already present in the soil. See the Fertilizer Chart on p. 169 for suggested rates.

Mowing

Overseeded **ryegrass** lawns maintained at 1 inch should be mowed when the grass is $1^1/2$ inches tall.

Pest Control

Weeds: If your lawn has a history of weed invasions, determine why the weeds invaded and correct the problem. Weeds are often found in lawns with a thin or weak stand of grass. The most common causes of a poor lawn are using a grass that's not adapted to your region or improper mowing, watering, and fertilizing. Other factors that affect the condition of the lawn include insects, diseases, compacted soil, and thatch. *Handpull* winter annuals. Treat wild garlic with a broadleaf herbicide when the air temperature is above 50 degrees F.

Planning

If your lawn is overrun with weeds or if it has thinned out as a result of last summer's drought, make plans to renovate it next month or in May. Renovation allows you to replace your lawn without having to rototill it up. Follow these steps:

1. If your soil hasn't been tested in the past three years, submit a sample to your county cooperative extension service office.

2. Eliminate any undesirable weeds or lawn grasses that will compete with your new lawn. *Handpull* them or use a nonselective herbicide such as glyphosate (Roundup®, Kleen-up®) or glufosinate (Finale®). Some herbicides require a waiting period of four to six weeks before seeding, so plan accordingly.

3. *Mow* the area with a reel or rotary mower set at its lowest setting, and collect the clippings.

4. If a thick thatch layer is present (greater than $1/2$ inch in thickness), *rake out* the thatch by hand. For large areas, use a vertical mower which can be rented from an equipment rental shop. This machine has revolving vertical blades that cut into the thatch layer and lift it to the surface. Set the machine so the blades cut into the upper $1/4$ to $1/2$ inch of soil. It leaves shallow grooves or slits in the soil surface. *Rake up* the debris and add it to the compost pile or mulch the vegetable garden. Seeds falling into the furrows created by the vertical mower are much more likely to germinate and grow.

Vertical Mower

5. Seed or plug the bare areas. Use a rotary or drop-type spreader to apply the seed, applying one-half of the total amount in one direction and the other half at right angles to the first. *Rake* the seed into the soil. Plant plugs on either 6-inch or 12-inch centers. Instead of buying plugs, cut out plugs from established areas with a spade or specially designed plugging tool and plant them in the bare areas.

6. Cover the seeded area with mulch to conserve moisture and enhance germination.

7. Apply water immediately after planting and keep the soil moist until the seedlings or sprigs become established. Gradually cut back on the frequency of watering but water longer to encourage deep rooting.

8. *Mow* the grass when it's $1/3$ higher than the desired height.

9. *Fertilize* the lawn 1 month after planting to speed-up establishment.

Planting

Wait until next month to plant warm-season grasses.

Care for Your Lawn

Do not burn the dead leaves and thatch from dormant lawns. In addition to harming or killing the grasses, this can be a fire hazard.

Fertilizing

Wait until next month to fertilize hybrid **bermudagrass** and **zoysiagrass.**

Watering

Dormant lawns may need to be watered to prevent them from drying out, especially when warm windy weather prevails.

Pest Control

Insects: If your lawn is riddled with fire ant mounds, wait until they become active before treating them with the "two-step method" described in next month's Pest Control.

Mole crickets are serious lawn pests in the sandy soils of the Coastal Plain. Both the tawny mole cricket and the southern mole cricket were accidentally introduced to the United States in the early 1900s from South America. The tawny mole cricket is dark brown and can reach 1 1/2 inches in length; southern mole crickets are smaller and grayer. Both species possess the formidable digging claws on their front legs that earn their name. Mole crickets damage lawns by tunneling through the soil and uprooting plants, causing them to dry out and die. The tawny mole cricket actually feeds on grass, while the southern mole cricket is primarily a carnivore, feeding on insects and earthworms.

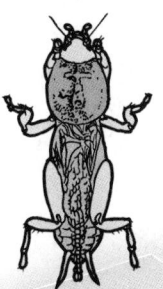

Mole Cricket

Most of the damage occurs in late summer and fall as nymphs reach maturity. The overwintering adults will be tunneling in late winter and spring. The damage subsides in the spring when eggs are laid and the adults die. It's usually midsummer before further damage is noted.

Right now, identify the problem areas where adults are present. These are the areas where most of their offspring will be found in late June and July. You can control the adults with an insecticide, but it's best to wait the summer to control the young nymphs which are most sensitive to insecticide applications.

Diseases: Brown patch attacks warm-season grasses in the spring as the lawn emerges from dormancy, or in the fall as they're going dormant. Collect infected clippings and compost them. Avoid overfertilizing, especially with nitrogen during the fall or spring. Water during dry spells to keep the grass healthy, but avoid overwatering. Fungicides will protect healthy grass from becoming infected.

Weeds: Early this month, Coastal Plain gardeners can apply a "crabgrass preventer" or pre-emergent herbicide to control summer annuals such as crabgrass and goosegrass. Piedmont gardeners can wait until later this month to apply a pre-emergent herbicide. Crabgrass seed germinates when the day temperatures reach 65 to 70 degrees F. for four or five days; it coincides with the time when **forsythia** and **crabapples** are in bloom. Goosegrass germinates about three or four weeks after crabgrass.

Prevent winter annuals such as Carolina geranium, common chickweed, and henbit from going to seed by handpulling, mowing off the flowers, or spot-treating with a broadleaf herbicide. Identify weeds after they emerged to select an appropriate post-emergent herbicide. Post-emergent herbicides are most effective when the weeds are young and actively growing with air temperatures between 65 and 85 degrees F. Be sure the herbicide is labeled for use on your lawn and your lawn has fully greened up and is actively growing.

Planning

To maintain a healthy, attractive lawn, start writing in your journal. Write down when the lawn came out of dormancy and when you fertilized and the amount you applied. Document any insect, disease, or weed problems, and any pesticide applications. Staple your soil-test report to one of the pages.

Your journal can become a teaching tool, especially when you need the assistance of a lawn-service company or county extension agent to help you diagnose a particular problem. The notes you took about weather conditions, fertilizing, watering, and any pest control applications are important clues that can help reveal the answer to a problem.

Planting

Repair bare patches or replant large areas using seed or sprigs when the average daytime temperatures stay above 60 degrees F. Refer to the Planting Chart on p. 171 for suggested rates.

Care for Your Lawn

Examine the depth of the thatch layer in your lawn by cutting out a pie-shaped wedge of sod from your lawn with a knife or spade. If the thatch layer exceeds $1/2$ inch in thickness, physically remove thatch from the lawn by dethatching. Wait until the lawn comes out of dormancy and is actively growing. Use a dethatching rake for small areas or a vertical mower for larger lawns. See Thatch Control in the introduction (p. 167) for more information.

Watering

Water newly seeded, plugged, or sodded lawns to encourage rapid establishment.

Fertilizing

Wait at least two or three weeks after your lawn has completely greened up before fertilizing according to soil test-recommendations. See the Fertilizer Chart on p. 169 for recommended rates.

Mowing

Before **St. Augustinegrass** comes out of dormancy, lower the mowing height to remove the tops of the dead grass blades.

Pest Control

Insects: If fire ants have cropped up in your lawn or landscape, control them using the "two-step method":

Step 1. Broadcast a fresh-bait insecticide over the entire landscape. A fire ant bait consists of a pesticide on processed corn grits coated with soybean oil. While it can be used on individual mounds, it's best to distribute them widely in your landscape. They're less expensive than individual mound treatments and they control colonies even when mounds aren't visible. Apply the bait when the workers are foraging for food. In the spring and fall, this is during the warmer daylight hours. In the summer, apply the bait in late afternoon or evening when the ants are foraging. Distribute the bait with a handheld seed spreader. Make one or two passes over the area at a normal walking speed to apply the recommended rate. Most mounds that receive this slow-acting bait treatment will eventually be eliminated.

Step 2. No sooner than seven days after applying the bait, treat only those mounds that pose a threat to you and your family. These are mounds located near walkways, play equipment, and other areas where your paths cross. Use an approved fire ant insecticide product following label directions. If you use a soluble powder, distribute it evenly over the mound. Liquid concentrates—chemical products that are diluted with water and then applied to the mound—must be applied in sufficient volumes to penetrate the entire nest. Before using any of these pesticides, read and follow the label directions carefully.

Look for the burrowing and tunneling activity of mole crickets in the Coastal Plain. Mark these areas for control with an insecticide in late June and July.

If your lawn looks wilted, even after watering, check to see if you have an infestation of white grubs. See Warm-Season Lawns, August Insects on p. 187 for a description and controls.

Diseases: Watch out for brown patch and dollar spot. Dollar spot commonly attacks **bermuda** and **zoysiagrass,** and occasionally **centipedegrass** and **St. Augustinegrass.** This fungal disease attacks the leaf blades. Symptoms include small circular areas of straw-colored grass which range from 1 to 6 inches across. If you examine individual grass blades you'll find straw-colored lesions with reddish-brown borders. Early in the morning look for a spider web–like growth over the infected area. Dollar spot is more common in the spring and fall months. Maintain adequate levels of fertility, especially nitrogen, since this diseases favors "hungry" lawns.

Spring dead spot is a fungal disease that primarily attacks **bermudagrass** lawns. Look for dead circular patches of grass in the spring as the **bermudagrass** comes out of dormancy. Patches may be 2 or 3 feet across. These areas often look like "doughnuts," where healthy grass grows in the center of dead areas. Cut out the dead areas and replant them after thoroughly mixing the soil under the patch or, better yet, after removing the soil and replacing it with clean soil from another part of the landscape. To manage this disease, avoid excessive nitrogen fertilizer applications in late summer and fall. Aerify lawns to reduce thatch buildups naturally. *Dethatch* lawns with thatch layers greater than 1/2 inch in thickness. Fungicides have demonstrated best control when applied in the fall.

Weeds: Pull weeds now while the task is easier and the weather is comfortable. By eliminating the weeds before they set seeds you'll also reduce next year's problem.

Florida betony (*Stachys floridana*) is a fast-spreading cool-season perennial weed that's often called "rattlesnake weed" because it produces white, segmented tubers that resemble a rattlesnake's tail. It emerges from seeds and tubers during the cool, moist months of fall. It grows and spreads rapidly throughout the winter months. From late spring to early summer the Florida betony bears white to pink trumpet-shaped flowers. Growth stops in response to the onset of high summer temperatures and the plant becomes nearly dormant.

Pull or dig out all plant parts, especially the tubers, when the soil is moist. Hoe or cut the top growth down to soil level repeatedly to "starve" the plant. Spot-treat with a recommended herbicides that's labeled for your lawn and for controlling Florida betony.

Planning

Sodding gives you an instant lawn in the shortest time when compared to seeding or sprigging. It can be done as long as the soil temperature is higher than 55 degrees Fahrenheit. If you're planning on sodding your lawn, follow the steps outlined in the March Planting Cool-Season Lawns chapter, p. 146.

Watering

Keep the newly seeded or sprigged areas moist by frequently sprinkling the area. See May Planning in the Cool-Season Lawns chapter, p. 150, to learn how to strengthen your lawn to reduce your water bill this summer.

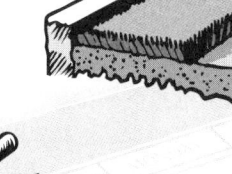

Sod Placement

Planting

See April.

Fertilizing

St. Augustinegrass can be fertilized this month with a slow-release nitrogen fertilizer, which will help reduce chinch bug and gray leaf spot problems.

Care for Your Lawn

After your lawn has come out of dormancy and greened up, measure the thickness of the thatch layer. *Dethatch* if necessary. See Thatch Control in the introduction on p. 167.

Mowing

Mow your lawn at the recommended height with a sharp blade. Avoid cutting more than one-third of the height or the plant may be stressed, exposing it to a weed invasion.

Pest Control

Insects: In the Coastal Plain look for the tunneling and burrowing activity of mole crickets. Mark these areas for treatment with an insecticide in late June and July.

Southern chinch bugs are notorious pests of **St. Augustinegrass** that may also attack **bermudagrass, centipedegrass,** and **zoysiagrass** but cause them less harm. Damage is mainly caused by the nymphs, which suck sap from the grass and inject a toxin that causes the leaves to turn yellow and die. As the grass dies, the chinch bugs move to healthy grass, leaving the killed grass in their wake. As they feed, they cause the dead areas to slowly enlarge. Chinch bug damage is usually greatest during hot, dry weather, and in sunny areas rather than in the shade. High levels of nitrogen and thick thatch layers predispose turfgrasses to chinch bug attacks.

Chinch Bug

Because chinch bug damage can be easily confused with drought (chinch bugs cause the leaves to turn a yellowish-orange straw color, while drought makes the leaves turn a grayish-brown straw color), it's best to sample the edge of the patch to confirm your suspicions. Here's how to sample for chinch bugs by flushing them out with water:

1 Cut out both ends of a coffee can and push one end down into the yellowed grass at the edge of the yellowed area.

2 Fill the can with water. If chinch bugs are present, adults and nymphs will float to the top within 10 minutes. Take action if you find 25 to 30 insects per square foot.

Chinch bugs can be controlled with an insecticide. To manage these pests, follow a balanced fertilization program according to the results of a soil test. Use a slow-release nitrogen fertilizer to reduce chinch bug problems. Remove thatch layers that exceed 1/2 inch in depth.

Diseases: Watch for brown patch—circular patches of brown grass up to several feet in diameter. Collect infected clippings and compost them. Remove dead areas and replant the bare spots with plugs taken from healthy areas.

Look out for gray leaf spot on **St. Augustinegrass.** Collect infected clippings and compost them.

Weeds: Pre-emergent herbicides to control crabgrass and goosegrass last for a period of time before losing their effectiveness. A repeat application will be necessary for season-long control. Refer to the label to see when it has to be reapplied to control germinating weeds.

Helpful Hint

"Centipedegrass decline" usually occurs in the spring when parts of the lawn fail to come out of dormancy. Sometimes parts of the lawn start to green-up and grow, but then die in late spring and summer. Several factors cause centipedegrass decline, including a high soil pH, high amounts of nitrogen and phosphorus applied the previous year, heavy thatch buildup, nematodes, and diseases that make the grass injury susceptible. Here are some ways of controlling centipedegrass decline:

1 Maintain the appropriate soil pH for **centipedegrass.** A pH between 5.5 and 6.0 is best. A pH above 6.0 can result in an iron deficiency, causing the lawn to turn yellow. A pH below 5.0 can make magnesium and calcium unavailable to the grass.

2 **Fertilize** properly. See the Fertilizing Chart on p. 169. Avoid late-summer applications, which can predispose **centipedegrass** to winterkill. Follow soil-test results before applying phosphorus.

3 **Control thatch.** Roots grow in a thatch layer and become vulnerable to drought stress and winter injury. Avoid excessive nitrogen fertilization, which encourages the rampant growth that results in thatch buildup. Remove excessive thatch with dethatching equipment like a vertical mower.

4 **Mow properly.** Mow often enough that no more than a third of the leaf is removed; let the clippings lie on the lawn.

5 If there are areas in the lawn which fail to green-up in the spring or begin to grow and then die (centipede decline), renovate the lawn. Follow the renovation steps described in the March Planning, p. 176.

Identify weeds after they emerged to select an appropriate post-emergent herbicide labeled for your lawn. Grassy summer annuals to watch out for include crabgrass, goosegrass, and sandbur. Dallisgrass and bahiagrass are perennial grasses that may be present.

Post-emergent herbicides are most effective when the weeds are young and actively growing and the air temperature is between 65 and 85 degrees F.

Planning

The first bagging mowers made their debut on American lawns in the early 1950s. Somehow, collecting and removing grass clippings and putting them into garbage bags with the trash caught on. But you should really plan to recycle your grass clippings as you mow. Returning your grass clippings to the lawn saves time, energy, and money—and look at recycling grass clippings as a way of fertilizing your lawn. Grass clippings contain about 4 percent nitrogen, $1/2$ to 1 percent phosphorus, 2 to 3 percent potassium, and smaller amounts of other essential plants nutrients. This is basically a 4-1-3 fertilizer.

Planting

There's still time to renovate a lawn—if possible, determine what led to a lawn's demise. Correct any mistakes to your lawn-care plan to avoid future renovations.

Install sod or plant plugs or sprigs of warm-season grasses.

Care for Your Lawn

Dethatch your lawn with a vertical mower if the thatch layer measures more than $1/2$ inch. *Mow* the lawn afterward to remove any further debris, and then water thoroughly to prevent the exposed roots from drying out.

Watering

Apply an inch of water on clay soils once a week and $1/2$ inch on sandy soils every three days. Calibrate your irrigation system to apply the correct amount of water: too much water will be wasteful and too little produces shallow-rooted plants (see July Planning in the Cool-Season Lawns chapter on p. 154).

Fertilizing

For improved quality, *fertilize* bermudagrass and zoysiagrass this month with a nitrogen fertilizer (see the Fertilizer Chart on p. 169). Keep in mind that this application will encourage growth, which translates into higher maintenance.

Mowing

For the most attractive look, *mow* bermudagrass and zoysiagrass with a reel-type mower. Allow the clippings to lie on the lawn.

Pest Control

Insects: Mole crickets damage lawns by tunneling through the soil and uprooting plants, causing them to dry out and die. The tawny mole cricket actually feeds on grass, while the southern mole cricket is primarily a carnivore, feeding on insects and earthworms.

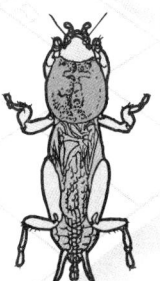

Mole Cricket

Beginning late this month, sample areas where you previously observed damage from mole crickets in the spring. Early in the morning or late in the afternoon, mix 2 tablespoons of liquid detergent in 1 gallon of water and pour it over a 1- to 2-foot-square area. The detergent solution irritates the mole *crickets, forcing them to the surface. Newly hatched mole crickets are only about $1/4$ inch long and tend to disappear quickly after coming to the surface, so watch very closely for two to three minutes. If small mole crickets appear, apply an insecticide following label directions. Irrigating dry soil twenty-four hours before applying the pesticide will cause mole crickets to move into the moist soil, making them easier targets.*

Be on the lookout for nematodes. Nematodes are microscopic, soil-inhabiting, eel-like worms that feed on turfgrass roots. They are more commonly found in coarse-textured sandy soils than fine-textured clay soils. Nematode-infested roots cannot take up water or fertilizer as well as healthy ones. The infested lawn grass wilts easily and lacks normal green color. High nematode populations result in severe yellowing. The damage usually occurs in irregularly shaped or circular areas. There are several kinds of nematodes, including sting, ring, stubby root, root-knot, and lance. **Centipedegrass** is especially susceptible to damage by ring nematodes. Lance nematodes are often found on **St. Augustinegrass.**

If you suspect nematodes, confirm your suspicions by having your soil analyzed by the North Carolina Department of Agriculture Agronomic Division or the Agricultural Service Laboratory at Clemson University. Samples can be submitted through your county extension office. If nematodes are a threat, the best defense is to keep your lawn healthy. The healthier the plant, the less susceptible it will be to light or moderate nematode attacks. *Fertilize* annually according to soil-test results, irrigate during dry spells, and *mow* at the proper height. These measures can help the turfgrass cope with the infestation.

Learn the identity of the nematodes to see if you can replace the susceptible grass with a resistant one. For example, in areas infested with ring nematodes, St. Augustinegrass can be used in place of centipedegrass. In the future, add organic matter prior to lawn establishment to improve soil structure and moisture retention in sandy soils. This not only creates a better growing environment for the turfgrass, but also a better habitat for the natural predators of the nematodes.

Diseases: Look for gray leaf spot on **St. Augustinegrass.** Infected leaves and stems have small, oblong, tan lesions with purple borders. The gray spores can sometimes be seen during warm, wet weather. When severe, the entire lawn may look scorched.

Collect the infected clippings while mowing, and compost them. Gray leaf spot can be controlled with fungicides. During the growing season use moderate amounts of nitrogen fertilizer, preferably one that contains $1/4$ to $1/2$ of the nitrogen in a slow-release form.

Weeds: *Spot-treat* summer annual broadleaf weeds such as knotweed, lespedeza, and spurge with a post-emergent herbicide. Perennial grasses that may be lurking in your lawn include dallisgrass and bahiagrass. The weeds should be actively growing and the lawn should not be suffering from drought stress.

Helpful Hint

For easier lawn maintenance, eliminate the hard-to-mow spaces. Eliminate acute angles in beds and borders. Combine single trees or shrubs into a large planting connected with ground covers.

Planning

If you plan to irrigate your lawn this summer, water wisely and efficiently:

1 If you have an in-ground, automatic sprinkler system, use the automatic position on the time clock when you are away from home for more than a few days—but using the automatic setting while you are at home can overwater or underwater your lawn, depending on the weather. The system can be made more efficient by installing soil-moisture sensors in the lawn. These sensors will prevent the sprinkler valves from opening when they detect the soil is moist.

2 When you're at home, set the time clock to "off" and manually turn the in-ground system on when the lawn needs water. The same applies to above-ground hose and sprinkler systems with irrigation clocks that screw onto the hose bibs. Turn the system on manually, and use the clock to shut it off when the right amount of water has been applied.

3 While the irrigation system is on, check the sprinkler heads for an even spray pattern. Examine the sprinkler heads and replace those that leak or

are damaged. Replace any worn nozzles. Make sure the sprinklers are delivering water to the lawn instead of the driveway or road.

4 Fix leaky hoses, spigots, and valves. A lot of water is wasted through leaky hose connections and worn-out spigots. A fairly slow leak—a faucet dripping one drop per second—will leak 2 gallons of water or more per day.

Planting

The quickest way to convert a piece of bare ground into a lush lawn is with sod. Purchase freshly harvested sod and lay it down on a well-prepared bed. Refer to the steps outlined in the Cool-Season Lawns chapter, March Planting (p. 146).

Watering

Apply 1 inch of water per week to clay soils. On sandy soils apply $1/2$ inch of water every third day. Clay soils should be watered until runoff occurs; wait 30 minutes for the water to soak in and then continue watering until you've applied an inch.

Fertilizing

See May.

Mowing

A brown or grayish cast over lawns can be caused by dull or improperly adjusted mower blades that tear grass blades rather than cutting them. If you haven't already done so, raise the cutting height of your mower a notch or two to put less stress on the turf. By increasing the mowing height you will also increase the depth of the root system.

Pest Control

Insects: Sample areas where you previously observed damage from mole crickets in the spring. Early in the morning or late in the afternoon, mix 2 tablespoons of liquid detergent in 1 gallon of water and pouring it over a 1- to 2-foot-square area. The detergent solution irritates the mole crickets, forcing them to the surface. Newly hatched mole crickets are only about $1/4$ inch long and tend to disappear quickly after coming to the surface, so watch very closely for two to three minutes. If small mole crickets appear, apply an insecticide following label directions. Irrigating dry soil twenty-four hours before applying the pesticide will cause mole crickets to move into the moist soil, making them easier targets.

Diseases: Watch for gray leaf spot on **St. Augustinegrass.** Collect infected clippings and compost them. Use a slow-release nitrogen fertilizer to reduce gray leaf spot problems.

Weeds: If you need to apply post-emergence herbicides, remember to follow label directions and spot-treat problem areas in the lawn. To avoid injuring the desirable grasses, avoid making herbicide applications when the air temperature exceeds 85 degrees F. and when the lawn grasses are stressed by drought or high temperatures.

Helpful Hint

Growing turfgrass in the shade can be challenging. Even the most shade-tolerant grasses need at least four hours of sunlight to survive. If there's insufficient light, switch to a shade-tolerant ground cover or maintain a 2- to 3-inch layer of mulch instead of a lawn. If enough sunlight is available, then consider shade-tolerant grasses. **St. Augustinegrass** is the most shade-tolerant, followed by **zoysiagrass, centipedegrass,** and **carpetgrass. Bermudagrass** is the least shade-tolerant of the warm-season grasses. When managing grasses in the shade, you'll have to adjust your maintenance practices:

1   **Mow** grasses in the shade about $1/2$ to 1 inch higher than normal. The shaded grass needs as much leaf surface area as possible to take advantage of any available light. Continue to mow on a regular schedule, never removing more than one-third of the height.

2   **Fertilize** grasses growing in shaded areas with only one-half to two-thirds as much nitrogen as grasses growing in full sun. Fertilize them at the same time as you fertilize the turfgrass growing in the sun—just use less fertilizer. Reducing the amount of nitrogen to grasses in shade reduces the chances of diseases.

3   As with the rest of the lawn, grasses in shady spots should be watered when they show signs of drought stress. **Water infrequently but deeply, and only when absolutely necessary.** Light, infrequent watering encourages shallow roots and increases disease problems associated with turf growth in shade.

Planning

This is an appropriate month to learn more about xeriscaping, a term which means "dry landscaping." It combines water conservation techniques with good old-fashioned commonsense gardening. Although the idea originated in the western United States where yearly rainfall is a mere fraction of what we get in the Carolinas, the same water-saving principles can be used in our own landscapes. The seven basic xeriscape principles can be found in Trees, July Planning, on p. 298. You can create practical, functional lawn areas with drought-tolerant lawn grasses (Principle 2). Common **bermudagrass** ranks number one in drought tolerance. Think about reducing the size of the lawn to save water. For example, try joining trees into beds with shrubs and ground covers. Consider eliminating hard-to-irrigate lawn areas such as narrow strips between a walkway and a building, or irregularly shaped areas. Plan to incorporate these water-saving principles into the design and maintenance of your landscape to lower water use and save money.

Planting

Avoid seeding or sprigging in late summer or early fall because the plants may be killed by cold weather. If you have to plant now, sod early this month to get the plants settled in before they go dormant with the first frost.

Watering

Don't water the entire lawn. Consider only those areas that need water. Look for signs of thirst to identify highly drought-prone areas: high spots, sandy locations, and areas adjacent to sidewalks, patios, and driveways.

Fertilizing

Follow April guidelines. Avoid overfertilizing **centipedegrass,** which can lead to centipede decline (see May Helpful Hint) as a result of excessive thatch.

Mowing

Continue to *mow* your lawn regularly, removing no more than one-third of the grass height at each mowing.

Pest Control

Insects: Sample areas where you previously observed damaged from mole crickets in the spring. Early in the morning or late in the afternoon, mix 2 tablespoons of liquid detergent in 1 gallon of water and pour it over a 1- to 2-foot-square area. The detergent solution irritates the mole crickets, forcing them to the surface. Newly hatched mole crickets are only about $1/4$ inch long and tend to disappear quickly after coming to the surface, so watch very closely for two to three minutes. If small mole crickets appear, apply an insecticide following label directions. Irrigating dry soil twenty-four hours before applying the pesticide will cause mole crickets to move into the moist soil, making them easier targets.

If your lawn looks wilted, even after watering, if it's been torn up by skunks, birds, and moles, or if parts have turned brown and feel spongy, check to see if you have an infestation of white grubs. White grubs are the immature larvae of scarab beetles, a family that includes Japanese beetles, masked chafers, and May and June beetles. They have plump, cream-colored, C-shaped bodies and distinctive yellow to brown heads. Most have rather long life cycles, lasting from several months to three years.

The Japanese beetle is the most common of these pests. Adult females lay their eggs in the soil around July. Two weeks later the grubs hatch and begin feeding on grass roots. Heavily infested lawns can be rolled back like a carpet. The most serious damage occurs in September and October before hibernation and during April and May before the larvae pupate to become adults.

Sample several damaged areas in your lawn to get an average of the number of grubs per square foot and to decide if control is necessary. Go to the edge of a damaged patch of grass and with your spade or knife, make cuts on three sides of a 12-inch square. Pry this flap back and examine the roots and upper 3 inches of soil for white grubs. (Heavily infested patches can be lifted and rolled back like a throw rug.) Count the number of grubs in this area. Move on to another patch and count the number of grubs you find. After sampling the edges of several dead or dying areas, determine the average number of grubs per square foot. Most healthy lawns can tolerate at least five to seven

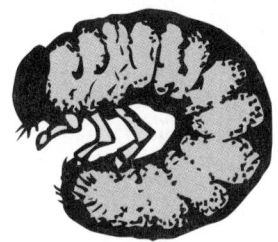

White Grub

Japanese beetle grubs per square foot. If your average count is higher, then an insecticide may be needed to save the lawn from further damage. The insecticide may need to be watered-in so it can reach the grubs as directed by the label instructions.

A long-term biological approach to managing Japanese beetle grubs is with milky disease (Milky Spore Powder Japanese Beetle & Grub Control®), a naturally occurring bacterium (*Bacillus popilliae*) that primarily infects Japanese beetle grubs; it will not work as well against other types of white grubs. When the Japanese beetle grubs become infected with milky disease, they eventually die, releasing billions of spores into the soil to infect future generations of grubs. Best results are achieved when your neighbors treat their lawns at the same time.

The best time to apply milky disease is now or in the spring when the grubs are feeding near the soil surface. Be patient—it takes up to three years for milky disease to become established. Once it does, it will suppress the numbers of grubs in your lawn. During its establishment period, do not treat the lawn with a chemical insecticide—the insecticide will keep the grub population at a very low level, preventing the buildup of the bacteria.

Diseases: Check for gray leaf spot disease on **St. Augustinegrass.** Collect infected clippings and compost them. Use a slow-release nitrogen fertilizer to reduce gray leaf spot problems.

Weeds: See July.

Planning

If you expect a green lawn year-round, skip the green spray paint and plan to overseed with a cool-season grass. Perennial ryegrass (*Lolium perenne*) and **annual ryegrass** (*Lolium multiflorum*) are the commonly used cool-season grasses that provide green color during the winter months after warm-season grasses have long turned brown and dormant. Contact your cooperative extension service office for a list of recommended **ryegrass** varieties that will perform well in your region. **Perennial ryegrass** is more expensive, but offers a higher-quality look when mowed. It's also more tolerant of cold, disease, and drought than is **annual ryegrass.** These strengths allow perennial ryegrass to live somewhat longer than annual ryegrass, which makes it a burden in the spring when you want the warm-season lawn to overtake the **ryegrass.**

Bermudagrass lawns tolerate overseeding better than **centipedegrass, St. Augustinegrass,** or **zoysiagrass.**

Overseeding is best done on a lush and healthy lawn. Never overseed turfgrasses growing in moderate to heavy shade. If you do, the **ryegrass** will survive and linger into summer, competing with the turf awakening from dormancy for sunlight, moisture, and nutrients. Often it results in a thinned-out lawn that's easily invaded by weeds.

Planting

The best time to overseed is two or three weeks before the expected first frost or when the soil temperature drops below 75 degrees F. Here's how to overseed your **bermudagrass** lawn:

1 *Mow* the lawn closely.

2 Use a power rake to remove any excess thatch and to open up the lawn to get good seed-to-soil contact.

3 Use a rotary or drop-type spreader to apply 5 to 10 pounds of **ryegrass** seed per 1,000 square feet. Sow half the seed in one direction, the other half at right angles to the first.

4 After seeding, rake the ground with a stiff broom to make sure the seed is in contact with the soil. Follow-up by "topdressing" (applying a shallow layer) the seed with compost.

5 *Water* the lawn lightly two or three times a day until the seeds germinate.

6 When the lawn becomes established, water only when necessary to prevent the **ryegrass** from wilting.

7 After the second mowing, fertilize with 1 pound of nitrogen per 1,000 square feet, using a complete fertilizer, such as 16-4-8.

Care for Your Lawn

If your lawn feels spongy and unthrifty-looking, take a quick look at the thatch layer. Cut out a pie-shaped wedge of sod from your lawn with a knife or spade. If the thatch layer exceeds 1/2 inch in thickness, plan to dethatch—physically remove the thatch from your lawn—next spring after the lawn comes out of dormancy and is actively growing. *Rake up* leaves that fall on the lawn to prevent them from matting down and harming the grass.

Watering

Water as needed. Apply 1 inch of water per week to clay soils. On sandy soils apply 1/2 inch of water every third day. Clay soils should be watered until runoff occurs; wait 30 minutes for the water to soak in, then continue watering until you've applied an inch.

Fertilizing

Do not fertilize at this time. Heavy amounts of nitrogen can predispose warm-season lawns to winterkill. Often potassium is recommended to increase winter hardiness and drought tolerance. Recent research, however, has shown that making additional applications of potassium when already adequate levels are present in the soil can cause other nutrients, namely calcium and magnesium, to become deficient. Follow soil-test results to apply only the minerals that are deficient. Do not lime **carpetgrass** and **centipedegrass** unless recommended by soil-test results.

Mowing

Raise the mowing height of your lawn by 1/2 inch several weeks before the first expected frost. Don't retire the lawn mower when the growth of your lawn slows down this fall. As long as the grass continues to grow, it should be mowed. An overseeded lawn requires the same maintenance as a permanent lawn. Make sure the mower blade is sharp to cut the **ryegrass** cleanly. The lawn will need to be mowed regularly, removing no more than one-third of the height each time you mow.

Pest Control

Insects: Before treating your lawn for grubs, sample several damaged areas in your lawn to get an average of the number of grubs per square foot to decide if control is necessary. Lawns can tolerate lower or higher numbers of white grubs, depending on the health of the lawn and the kind of grub. Submit the grubs to your cooperative extension service office for identification to help you decide if an insecticide application is warranted. See August Insects on p. 187.

Scout for adult mole crickets in the Coastal Plain and treat if necessary.

Examine the yellowish to brownish spots in your **St. Augustinegrass** lawn for chinch bugs. Use the coffee can technique (see May Insects) to sample for them at the edge of the damaged area.

Diseases: Dollar spot or brown patch may be present. Refer to the Diseases sections in April and May to learn how to manage these fungal diseases.

Weeds: If annual bluegrass (*Poa annua*) and other winter annuals have been a problem in the past, gardeners in the Piedmont can apply a pre-emergent herbicide early this month (Coastal Plain gardeners later in the month) to control the germinating seeds before they appear. A pre-emergent herbicide forms a barrier at or just below the soil surface and kills the emerging seedlings when they grow and come into contact with the herbicide. Annual bluegrass germinates when the air temperatures drop consistently to the mid-70s. Look for it in shady or moist areas.

Planning

The best way to determine the fertilizer requirements of your lawn is by having your soil tested at least every three years through your local county cooperative extension service office. Plan to have your soil tested in the next few months so you'll be ready next spring. Maintaining the appropriate soil pH for your lawn grasses and applying only the minerals that are deficient in the soil will benefit the lawn and keep money in your pocket.

Planting

If you want to overseed your lawn with **ryegrass** in the Coastal Plain, start working on it early this month.

Watering

Water as needed to prevent moisture stress. Pay attention to the signs of "thirst" described in Watering in the June, Cool-Season (p. 152) before irrigating.

Fertilizing

Do not fertilize at this time.

Mowing

Remove tree leaves from the lawn to reduce lawn problems. Compost them or shred them to use as mulch around your flower or shrub border.

Pest Control

Insects: If fire ants have cropped up in your lawn or landscape, the best approach at control is the "two-step method." See April Insects, p. 178, for information about this method.

Examine the yellowish to brownish spots in your **St. Augustinegrass** lawn for chinch bugs. Use the coffee can technique (see May Insects, p. 180–81) to sample for them at the edge of the damaged area.

Diseases: Fairy rings can be found in all types of grasses. They may appear as a ring of mushrooms or simply as a dark-green ring of lush grass. The ring may vary from a few inches to several feet in diameter. Fairy rings are caused by soil-inhabiting fungi that feed on old roots, stumps, and thatch. Fairy ring fungi are not plant parasites, but they can cause the lawn to dry out because their fungal bodies make the soil repel water. Grass inside the ring usually is in a state of decline. The grass on the inside of young rings may be dead. On old rings there may be a dead band of grass a few inches to several feet wide forming a partial or complete ring.

Fairy rings are difficult to control. You can be patient and allow them to disappear over time. Watering the ring to saturate the soil for several hours and over several days may help. As a last resort, you can replace the infested soil occupied by the fairy ring with clean soil.

Brown patch or Rhizoctonia blight is a devastating disease, especially on **St. Augustinegrass** in the fall. See November Diseases.

Weeds: Florida betony is a cool season perennial weed that emerges from seeds and tubers during the cool, moist months of fall. Throughout the winter months it grows and spreads rapidly and can reach heights of less than 2 feet.

Spot-treat with herbicide while it's actively growing this month. See April Weeds for more information.

Planning

As you rake up the fallen leaves from your lawn, plan to recycle them as mulch or compost. For a fine-textured mulch, shred the leaves with a lawn mower or a leaf shredder. Finely cut leaves look more attractive and tend to stay where you put them. To compost leaves, researchers recommend building piles at least 4 feet in diameter and 3 feet in height. To keep the piles to a manageable size, make them no larger than 5 feet high and 10 feet wide. You can compost leaves by themselves, or add fresh vegetable peelings, grass clippings, or other kitchen or yard trimmings.

To speed up the composting process, shred the leaves before putting them into the pile. Be sure to avoid adding meat or grease, which may cause odors and attract pests. Pay particular attention to moisture and air. Keep the ingredients moist enough so you can squeeze water droplets from a handful of leaves. Aerate or supply air to the pile by turning the materials. During warm weather, turn the pile once a month. Turn it less frequently in cool weather to prevent too much heat from escaping. To convert the leaves to compost fairly quickly requires the addition of nitrogen to the pile. Add a nitrogen-containing fertilizer such as 10-10-10. Good natural substitutes for synthetic fertilizers include horse or cow manure, bloodmeal, or cottonseed meal.

Mix this crumbly, earthy-smelling "black gold" into heavy clay soil to improve drainage and make the soil easy to cultivate. Compost helps sandy soils retain water and nutrients.

Planting

Postpone seeding, plugging, or sodding until next spring.

Care for Your Lawn

Rake up any fallen leaves.

Watering

Dormant lawns may need to be watered to prevent them from drying out, especially when warm windy weather prevails.

Fertilizing

Dormant, overseeded **bermudagrass** and **zoysiagrass** lawns can be fertilized this month. Use a fertilizer recommended by soil-test results. Do not apply a fertilizer containing phosphorus and potassium if adequate levels are already present in the soil.

Mowing

Overseeded **ryegrass** lawns should be mowed between 1 and 2$^{1}/_{2}$ inches high.

Pest Control

Diseases: Brown patch or Rhizoctonia blight is a devastating disease, especially on **St. Augustinegrass** in the fall. Look for circular, brown dead patches in the lawn. Take a close look at the infected grass plants at the edge of the dead area and you'll find rotting leaf sheaths near the crown at the soil surface. *Rake up* dead areas and remove the infected grass. Reduce the occurrence of this disease by not overfertilizing in the fall or spring when the disease is likely to appear.

Weeds: Treat wild garlic with a broadleaf herbicide when the air temperature is above 50 degrees F. *Handpull* wild garlic when the soil is moist to remove the entire plant—bulb and all. If you leave the bulb behind, it will resprout.

Planning

If you want to give your dormant lawn and yourself a rest this winter, plan to winterize your mower. If you've overseeded your lawn, *skip this section* because your mower won't be resting this winter. Follow these steps to get your mower to start on the first (or second) pull next spring:

The secret to getting it to start on the first (or second) pull next spring is to winterize it.

1 *Run the engine dry.* Untreated gasoline stored for long periods can cause a gummy buildup in the carburetor that can make it impossible to start after a few months. Run the engine until it stalls. Alternatively, you can add a small amount of gasoline stabilizer to the fuel tank and run the engine for a few minutes to distribute it with the fuel.

2 *Drain and replace the oil.* Disconnect the wire from the spark plug for safety. Change the oil at least once a year (refer to your owner's manual) and check the oil level each time you use the machine. Recyle the used oil.

3 *Clean the air filter.* Foam-element air filters should be removed and cleaned with hot, soapy water. Before replacing it, pour a couple of tablespoons of clean engine oil onto it and distribute it by squeezing the foam.

4 *Oil the spark plug.* Remove the spark plug and pour a tablespoon of clean engine oil into the hole. Replace the spark plug and pull the starter cord a couple of times to crank the engine and distribute the oil. This will protect the engine from corrosion during the winter.

5 *Clean and store the engine by brushing the cooling fins to make sure they're not plugged.* Scrape off any dirt or grass clippings on the underside with a screwdriver, putty knife, or wire brush. If the blade is dull, remove and sharpen it or replace it.

Planting

Wait until next spring to seed, plug, or sod your lawn. You and your lawn should take the month off.

Watering

If the month has been dry, periodic watering may be necessary to prevent the grasses from drying out, especially when the weather is warm and windy.

Fertilizing

Do not fertilize dormant lawns.

Overseeded **bermudagrass** lawns can be fertilized this month. See February Fertilizing on p. 175.

Mowing

Mow your overseeded **bermudagrass** lawn at 1 inch before the grass gets taller than $1^1/2$ inches. Dormant **bermudagrass** that has not been overseeded need not be mowed.

Pest Control

Weeds: *Handpull* or *spot-treat* chickweed, henbit, and other winter annuals with a broadleaf herbicide.

Perennials

Perennials give the garden an air of dependability and versatility. They come in a wide array of crayon colors and have a flowering season that spans winter to fall. Best of all, perennials grow fuller and more beautiful with each passing year.

Though often referred to simply as "perennials," technically these plants are "herbaceous perennials," so called because of the soft and fleshy stems that differentiate them from woody trees and shrubs. The top growth of most perennials is killed by freezing fall temperatures. The below-ground portions—crown and roots—survive over the winter months and produce new growth in the spring. Although bulbs have a similar growth pattern, they are classified separately because of their unique system of storing food in thick, bulblike structures.

Unlike their annual cousins, perennials come back year after year. They have a shorter flowering period, however, generally lasting only three to five weeks (many annuals bloom for three to five months).

Before you flip back to the Annuals and Bulbs chapters or move on to Roses or Shrubs, be aware that this shorter blooming period is not a shortcoming. Perennials deliver more than just flowers: they offer an endless variety of leaf shapes and colors and interesting outlines and textures. They're constantly changing, too. You can expect a different look in each season before, during, and after flowering. Even in the winter months, perennials like **maidenhair grass** or **coneflowers** provide architectural interest with their leaves, stems, and seedheads.

Planning

Picking the right perennials requires planning. Before you buy and plant perennials:

1 Know the growing conditions in your landscape. Use the base map you created as described in the introduction (p. 10), which familiarizes you with the above- and below-ground features of your landscape.

2 Know the growing requirements of your perennials. Match their needs to the growing conditions in your landscape. Use these criteria to winnow the list of candidates to some really worthwhile selections.

Hardiness: Select perennials that are cold hardy in your area—able to survive the winter with little or no protection. See the cold-hardiness map on p. 13. Remember that these hardiness zones are only guidelines, since microclimates and soil drainage often determine how hardy and long-lived a perennial will be in any given landscape. Heat hardiness is also important. Plants native to climates that have cool summers will not tolerate hot, dry summers. Attempting to grow them in a landscape outside their "comfort zone" will result in disappointment.

Soil conditions: Generally, most perennials prefer well-drained soil. In fact, more perennials are killed during the winter by wet, poorly drained

Perennials

conditions than by cold temperatures. If the site is naturally wet and improving drainage would be prohibitively expensive, then by all means cultivate moisture-loving perennials in that part of the garden.

Sun exposure: Determine the amount of sunlight an area receives and match perennials to those light levels.

3 Learn about the ornamental attributes of various perennials. Here are a few characteristics to look for.

Eye-catching flowers, leaves, and fruits: Perennials are dynamic, ever-changing plants that are capable of offering more than one season of interest. In most cases, many cultivars of a given species are available, greatly extending the size and/or color range of the species.

Time and length of bloom: To create a season-long display of color, know when your perennials will flower—you will be able to create a parade of color from a variety of perennials throughout the season. If

you're looking for long-flowering perennials, there's usually a catch: in order for them to bloom continuously, you'll have to deadhead them (remove the spent flowers) repeatedly or cut them back.

Height and size of mature plants: Knowing their eventual height and spread will help you select the right number of plants and to space them strategically to avoid an overcrowded or overplanted look.

4 Learn about the maintenance requirements of your perennials. If you prefer a low-maintenance approach, avoid perennials that require staking, frequent dividing, and regular deadheading, as well as those that are invasive reseeders.

5 Whenever possible, choose plants that are resistant to or at least not bothered by serious pests that may wreak havoc in the garden.

Refer to mail-order catalogs, perennial plant encyclopedias, and gardening magazine articles to help you do a background check on your perennials.

Soil Preparation

Because of their perennial nature, prepare the planting bed right the first time. Refer to Annuals, Preparing the Soil (p. 25) for details on good soil preparation.

Planting

Purchase perennials in containers or as dormant bare-root plants. You can grow them from seed, but starting with established plants will give you quicker satisfaction.

In the Carolinas, plant container-grown perennials year-round. Fall is the best time to plant, which gives the perennials sufficient time to become established before the onset of hot, dry summer weather. For fall plantings, especially in the Mountains, allow at least six weeks before hard-freezing weather occurs.

However, you'll usually find the best selection of perennials in spring. Gardeners faced with the prospect of a hot summer following closely on the heels of spring should plant early, then be prepared to coddle the plants with regular watering during the summer months.

Perennials

Here's how to plant a container-grown perennial:

1 Hold your hand over the top of the pot with the plant stems between your fingers. Tip the pot over and gently tap the plant into your hand. If the roots are circling around the rootball, loosen them to encourage growth into the surrounding soil. The tangled roots of large-rooted **hostas** and **daylilies** can be teased apart with your fingers. Use a knife, pruning shears, or sharp spade to score the sides of the rootballs of fine-rooted perennials; make three or four shallow cuts to encourage root growth along the length of the ball.

2 *Dig* a hole as wide as the rootball and the same depth.

3 Set the plant in the hole so the crown is at or slightly above ground level.

4 Cover and firm the soil lightly around the plant.

5 Water thoroughly to settle the soil around the roots. Depending on the weather and rainfall, you may need to *water* daily for the first few weeks. *Mulch* with a 2- to 3-inch layer of compost to conserve moisture and suppress weeds, spreading a 1/2-inch layer near the crown but not covering it.

6 During the next few weeks, keep the plants well watered to help them become quickly established. After that, begin cutting back, eventually watering on an "as-needed" basis. Test the soil and rootball to see if they're moist.

Fertilizing

If the soil is properly prepared at the start, supplemental fertilization may not be necessary for several years after planting. Let the perennial's growth rate and leaf color guide you in your fertilizing decisions—and rely on soil-test results. If the bed is already highly fertile, a soil test will save you from the undesirable results of overfertilizing, which leads to a lot of leafy growth at the expense of flowers.

In the absence of a soil test, use a complete balanced fertilizer that contains nitrogen, phosphorus, and potassium, such as 10-10-10. Most fertilizer recommendations are based on nitrogen, which is an important element in plant growth and is often the one most likely to be deficient in the soil. Apply 1 pound of nitrogen per 1,000 square feet (up to 2 pounds can be applied if you use a slow-release fertilizer). If your perennials are growing in a bed, follow the steps outlined in Fertilizing in Vines and Ground Covers on p. 311 to determine the right amount of fertilizer to apply.

Apply the fertilizer when the new shoots emerge and, if necessary, once or twice again during the growing season.

Water the bed after application so the fertilizer enters the soil and is available to the plant. Wash any fertilizer off the foliage to prevent fertilizer burn.

Watering

Perennials vary in their watering needs, but most require an ample moisture supply at least when they are actively growing. Seedlings or newly planted perennials should be watered daily for the first few weeks, depending on the weather and rainfall. After that, begin cutting back, eventually reaching an "as-needed" basis.

Perennials

When they become established, *water* less frequently. Established plants may need to be watered once a week in clay soils that hold more water than sandy soils. Sandy soils may need to be watered twice a week. Instead of following the calendar, *water* when the top 2 or 3 inches of soil feels dry. When you do water, water deeply to encourage deep rooting.

Dividing

Perennials are divided to control their size, invigorate them, and to increase their numbers. Short-lived perennials or old perennials that have become crowded with sparse flowers can be kept vigorous and blooming through division. After dividing, the vigorous younger sections are replanted so they'll flower more prolifically.

A general rule-of-thumb is to divide spring- and summer-blooming perennials in the fall, and fall-flowering perennials in early spring when the new shoots have emerged. Exceptions to this rule are fleshy-rooted perennials such as **peony** (*Paeonia*) and **oriental poppy** (*Papaver orientale*), which should be divided in the fall.

Mountain gardeners in the higher elevations can wait until spring to divide, since the rigors of winter may kill the young divisions before they have time to become established. Gardeners in the milder areas of the Carolinas can divide through fall and into early winter. It is most important to divide the plants when they're not flowering.

Pruning

Pruning is not often associated with herbaceous perennials, but deadheading to remove spent flowers, pinching stems or buds, and cutting back leggy plants are all aspects of pruning. Pruning improves the appearance of the plants, extends their bloom period or encourages repeat-flowering, controls diseases by improving air movement, and increases the size and number of flowers.

Pest Control

To manage pests, practice Integrated Pest Management, or IPM. This common-sense approach focuses on establishing and maintaining healthy plants and understanding pests. When pest control is necessary, start with the least-toxic solutions such as handpicking the pests or dislodging them from the plant with a strong spray of water. Potent chemical pesticides are con-sidered only as a last resort, when the pest populations exceed acceptable levels of damage. You must decide if the plant should be saved with a pesticide application, or composted. Follow this IPM approach to reduce or avoid pest damage:

- Select and properly plant well-adapted species and cultivars, especially those that have disease resistance.

- Maintain them properly by meeting their needs for light, water, and nutrients.

- Inspect for pests regularly. It's easier to control small outbreaks than to wait to be surprised by full-scale attacks. If you have to, prune out affected plant parts or completely remove the plant from the bed.

Many disease problems can be prevented:

- Provide good soil drainage to prevent and control soilborne diseases that cause root and stem rots.

- To help reduce disease outbreaks, keep the leaves dry when watering and maintain enough room between plants for good air circulation.

- Clean up any fallen leaves and remove any spent flowers. They can harbor pests.

Carolina Perennials

Common Name (Botanical Name)	Hardiness Zones	Light Exposure*	Bloom Period	Comments
Aster (*Aster* spp. and hybrids)	5 to 8	Sun	Late summer, fall	Choice perennials for fall flowers, which come in a wide range of colors; however, some species will bloom in the summer and reflower in the fall if deadheaded immediately after the flowers have faded.
Black-eyed Susan or Coneflower (*Rudbeckia* spp.)	3 to 9	Sun to partial shade	Summer, fall	Tolerant of hot and dry situations, these coneflowers provide a range of yellow to gold flowers from early summer to fall: Goldsturm (*R. fulgida* var. *sullivantii* 'Goldsturm'); three-lobed coneflower (*R. triloba*); and Autumn Sun cutleaf coneflower (*R. lacinata* 'Autumn Sun').
Blanketflower (*Gaillardia* × *grandiflora*)	2 to 9	Sun	Summer	Daisylike flowers appear from early summer and sporadically until frost. Drought, heat, and salt tolerant. Short-lived, so divide every 2 to 3 years to maintain vigor.
Blue wild indigo (*Baptisia australis*)	4 to 8	Sun to partial shade	Spring	Easy to grow; adapted to poor, low-fertility soils. 'Purple Smoke' has dusky violet flowers.
Coneflower, Purple (*Echinacea purpurea*)	3 to 8	Sun to partial shade	Summer	Tough, heat- and drought-tolerant; produces long-lasting blooms throughout the summer.
Coralbells (*Heuchera* species and hybrids)	3 to 8	Partial shade	Late spring to early summer	Intensive breeding efforts have resulted in hybrids with richly colored, textured leaves.
Daisy, Shasta (*Chrysanthemum* × *superbum*)	4 to 9	Sun	Spring, summer	Can be short-lived, so divide every 2 to 3 years. 'Alaska' and 'Becky's Daisy' are two long-blooming cultivars.
Daylily (*Hemerocallis* spp. and hybrids)	7 to 9	Sun	Spring to fall	Among the most widely grown perennials in the Carolinas. Array of cultivars offers a rainbow of flower colors from late spring to early fall.
Gaura (*Gaura lindheimeri*)	5 to 9	Sun, partial shade	Summer	Does best in hot, dry locations. 'Swirling Butterflies' and 'Siskiyou Pink' are two exceptional cultivars.
Hosta (*Hosta* spp. and hybrids)	3 to 8	Partial shade/shade	Summer	Most popular perennial for shady areas. With over 100 species and more than 1,400 registered cultivars, the choices are seemingly endless.
Lantana (*Lantana camara*)	8 to 10	Sun	Summer to fall	Spectacular flower displays from late spring to early fall. 'Miss Huff' and 'Mozelle' are hardy lantanas in 7b.
Lenten roses (*Helleborus orientalis*)	4 to 9	Partial shade to shade	Late winter to early spring	Long-lived and durable, produces nodding, roselike flowers above dark evergreen foliage. Self-sows readily. Breeding programs have resulted in a wide array of hybrids with remarkable variations in flowers and leaves.

*Partially shaded area receives four hours or less of direct sunlight per day.

Carolina Perennials

Common Name (Botanical Name)	Hardiness Zones	Light Exposure*	Bloom Period	Comments
Cheddar pinks (*Dianthus gratianopolitanus*)	5 to 8	Sun, partial shade	Late spring to early summer	'Bath's Pink' and 'Tiny Rubies' (double bright pink) are good selections. 'Firewitch' produces magenta flowers that persist for about 4 to 6 weeks in the spring, and scattered blooms throughout the summer.
Russian sage (*Perovskia atriplicifolia*)	3 to 9	Sun	Mid- to late summer	Large open bushy plant. Above the grayish-white stems spikes of lavender-blue flowers appear in mid- to late summer.
Phlox (*Phlox* spp.)	4 to 8	Sun to partial shade	Early spring and summer	Moss phlox (*P. subulata*) creates a blanket of blue, pink, purple, or white flowers in early spring. Spotted phlox (*P. maculata*) is more powdery mildew resistant than garden phlox (*P. paniculata*), whose spectacular blooms have no equal. Both require deadheading to prolong their bloom.
Pincushion flower (*Scabiosa columbaria*)	3 to 8	Sun to partial shade	Late spring to fall	Deadhead spent blooms to keep plants blooming. Flowering ceases in hot summer weather and resumes when cooler weather arrives. 'Butterfly Blue' and 'Pink Mist' are two outstanding cultivars.
Sage (*Salvia* spp. and hybrids)	5 to 10	Sun to partial shade	Summer to fall	Many species native to the southwest, Mexico, and Central America. They're noted for their heat- and drought-tolerance and magnificent flowers which attract hummingbirds and butterflies. Well-drained soil is critical to their survival. Some such as Mexican bush sage (*S. leucantha*) bloom only in the fall. For color from summer until frost consider these salvias: Indigo spires—dark violet-blue flowers that fade to deep blue in the fall; Blue anise sage (*S. guaranitica*)—brilliant violet-blue; Brazilian bog sage (*S. uliginosa*)—sky-blue flowers through most of the season except a brief "floral rest" during the hottest part of summer; and Texas sage (*S. greggii*)—red, pink, raspberry, peach, white, and yellow. Salvias should not be cut back until the spring when new growth emerges.
Stokes' aster (*Stokesia laevis*)	5 to 9	Sun to partial shade	Summer	Easy to grow; tolerates heat and drought.
Stonecrop (*Sedum* spp. and hybrids)	4 to 9	Sun to partial shade	Summer	Variety of shapes and sizes, but all have succulent leaves and showy clusters of tiny star-shaped flowers. They form neat mounds of fleshy leaves. Some varieties bloom in late spring; others bloom until frost. Autumn Joy (*Sedum* × 'Autumn Joy') is the most popular, blooming in midsummer until frost.
Yarrow (*Achillea* spp.)	4 to 9	Sun to shade	Summer	Durable plants with fine-textured, ferny leaves. Fairly drought resistant; long-blooming. Flowers can be dried for arrangements.

*Partially shaded area receives four hours or less of direct sunlight per day.

Carolina Perennials

Ornamental Grasses

Common Name (Botanical Name)	Hardiness Zone	Light Exposure*	Height	Comments
Blue fescue (*Festuca glauca* 'Elijah Blue')	4 to 7	Sun	8 in.	Powdery blue leaves with flower stalks that rise up to 18 in. and change from blue-green to buff color. Needs well-drained soil; dislikes heat and humidity.
Blue switchgrass (*Panicum virgatum* 'Heavy Metal')	5 to 9	Sun	4 ft.	One of several outstanding cultivars for borders or accent plants with powder-blue leaves that turn bright yellow in the fall.
Karl Foerster feather reed grass (*Calamagrostis* × *acutiflora* 'Karl Foerster')	6 to 9	Sun	4 ft.	Arching green leaves give rise to green flowers tinged with purple in early summer. Flowers dry to golden spikes in the fall which can be appreciated in the landscape or in dried arrangements; prefers moist soils. Fall-blooming reed grass (*C. brachytricha*) is reported to be heat-tolerant.
Fountain grass (*Pennisetum alopecuroides*)	5 to 9	Sun	3 ft.	Easy-to-grow grasses produce soft, bottlebrush-like spikes that range from white to cream, pink to red, and black to brown.
Maiden grass (*Miscanthus sinensis*)	6 to 9	Sun	10 ft.	Some of the showiest and most beautiful of the flowering grasses. They produce silky tassels that mature into fluffy plumes that last well into winter.
Pampas grass (*Cortaderia selloana*)	7 to 10	Sun	4 to 6 ft.	Tough, durable, grass that has become a fixture in the southeast. The razor-sharp leaves make spring cleanup an adventure. Dwarf and variegated cultivars are available.
Red Baron blood grass (*Imperata cylindrica* 'Red Baron')	5b to 9	Sun to partial shade	18 in.	Bright-green leaves turn progressively redder as the season progresses; provide shade from the hot afternoon sun in the Coastal Plain.

Sedges

Common Name (Botanical Name)	Hardiness Zone	Light Exposure*	Height	Comments
Sedges (*Carex* spp.)	5 to 9	Partial shade to shade	12 to 18 in.	Unknown, underused relatives of ornamental grasses with finely-textured leaves that prefer moist conditions.

*Partially shaded area receives four hours or less of direct sunlight per day.

Planning

As you design your perennial garden, you can take the traditional route and plan for perennials in island beds or borders. An island bed can be viewed from all sides. A perennial border is often called a mixed border because it can include annuals, shrubs, and trees to create a variety of colors and textures. A border is usually backed up to a wall, fence, or hedge. It should be wide enough to accommodate a generous helping of plants; this means it should be at least 8 feet in width, including a 2-foot space in the back to allow for air movement and room for you to maintain the planting.

Perennials can also be used in other ways—

Pockets of color: Light up your landscape with long-blooming perennials. Tuck them in around your shrubs to add color and texture, and use them alone or in concert with annuals and bulbs to add some pizzazz to the front of your home, along walkways, or on the corners of your patio.

Ground covers: Evergreen **daylilies, hellebores,** and **wild gingers** (*Asarum*) can be used to cover large areas of ground.

Containers: Perennials can be grown with annuals and bulbs in containers to bring color where you want it—on the front porch, deck, or patio, or near the swimming pool. Select compact, long-blooming perennials such as **'Stella de Oro' daylily, goldmoss** (*Sedum acre*), and the **Galaxy series** of **yarrow.**

Planting

For the cost of a commercial packet of seed, you can produce hundreds of seedlings—for less than the cost of a single potted transplant. Many cultivars won't come true from seed, which means that the offspring will not be identical to the parents and, in most cases, will be inferior to the parents. These cultivars must be propagated vegetatively—by stem or root cuttings or by division. There are some varieties, however, that will come true from seed (see the Helpful Hint on the opposite page).

In the warmer parts of the Coastal Plain, start perennials from seed late this month. Perennial seeds often require a specific chilling period before germination can occur. To learn about any special treatment required to overcome dormancy and induce germination, follow the packet instructions prior to sowing the seeds.

Starting perennial seeds indoors is similar to the seed-starting technique described for annuals in the January Planting section on p. 30. Some perennials will germinate readily—in one to two weeks or less than a month. Others, however, will germinate randomly over an extended period of time that can range from days to several weeks and sometimes several months. This most commonly occurs with perennial seeds that have special pregermination requirements. Refer to the seed packet for instructions. Some seeds have thick seed coats **(wild blue indigo, lupine,** and perennial **sweet pea)** and need to be soaked in water or scratched with a file so water can be absorbed or imbibed by the seed. Other seeds, particularly perennials from temperate regions, need to be stratified, or exposed to moist chilling conditions for a specified time period (check the seed packet for the length of cold exposure); otherwise, they won't germinate.

Seeds such as **bleeding heart** (*Dicentra*), **columbine** (*Aquilegia*), and **garden phlox** can be overwintered outdoors in a cold frame (see October Planting on p. 218 for more information). Seeds can be stratified in the refrigerator in milder areas of the Carolinas. Here's how:

1   *Fill* a plastic bag with damped milled sphagnum peat moss or

vermiculite, and place the seeds in the bag. *Label* the bag with the date and the name of the seeds.

2 Place the bag in the refrigerator at 40 degrees Fahrenheit for the required period of time, usually between six to eight weeks. After the required cold treatment, *sow* the seeds in trays or pots and move them to a cool location (less than 70 degrees F) in bright, indirect light so that germination will occur.

Care for Your Perennials

Mountain gardeners should inspect their perennials to see if any have been heaved out by the freezing and thawing of the soil. Firmly press them back down into the soil to prevent them from freezing or drying out. To reduce frost-heaving, maintain a layer of mulch around your perennials to insulate the soil.

Helpful Hint

Many seed-propagated cultivars will not come true, which means the offspring will not be identical to the parents. There are a number of cultivars, however, that can be successfully propagated from seed. Here is a short list of some of these perennial cultivars:

- **Summer Pastels yarrow (***Achillea millefolium***'Summer Pastels')**
- **Alaska** and **Snow Lady Shasta daisies (***Chrysanthemum* × *superbum* 'Alaska' and 'Snow Lady')**
- **Baby Gold goldenrod (***Solidago canandensis* 'Baby Gold')**
- **Blue Bouquet speedwell (***Veronica spicata* 'Blue Bouquet')**
- **Early Sunrise, Sunray,** and **Sunburst tickseed (***Coreopsis grandiflora* 'Early Sunrise', 'Sunray', and 'Sunburst')**
- **Fugi series, Sentimental Blue,** and **Shell Pink balloon flower (***Platycodon grandiflorus* 'Fugi' series, 'Sentimental Blue', and 'Shell Pink')**
- **Gay Butterflies butterfly weed (***Asclepias* × 'Gay Butterflies')**
- **Queen Victoria cardinal flower (***Lobelia cardinalis* 'Queen Victoria')**

easily, enough moisture is present. If the medium feels slightly moist but water is difficult to squeeze out, add water.

Fertilizing

Do not fertilize perennials at this time.

Pruning

Ornamental grasses don't have to be trimmed back just yet. As long as they haven't been damaged by buffeting winter winds, ice, or snow, enjoy their glorious winter foliage.

Watering

Determine the need for watering seed-propagated perennials by squeezing the top half-inch of medium between your thumb and forefinger. If water squeezes out

Pest Control

Diseases: Damping off is a serious disease that attacks and kills seeds and seedlings. See Annuals, February Diseases on p. 33 for a description and control.

Planning

Design your garden on paper before planting—it's easier to move plants on paper with an eraser than in the garden with a trowel or shovel! Refer to your base map described in the Introduction (p. 10), which will show the planned location of your perennial garden as well as its size and shape.

1 Make an outline of the bed on graph paper that has a grid of $1/4$-inch squares, each square representing one foot. *Divide* and label the length of the bed into three sections: "tall" on one end, "medium" in the center of the bed, and "short" in the front. To create a bed with spring, summer, and fall interest, use three sheets of tracing paper and start designing backwards: from fall to summer to spring and from the back of the border to the front.

2 Label your first sheet Fall, and use your pencil to plant fall-blooming perennials. Draw them as bubbles or blobs to scale, accounting for their eventual mature spread. Since late-summer- and fall-blooming perennials are usually the tallest perennials in the garden reach-ing over 3 feet in height, focus on the "tall" section in the back first. Then intersperse a few "medium" and "short" growers in the middle and front of the bed. Identify each bubble with the name of the plant, and color it with the plant's predominant color of bloom.

Take a second sheet of tracing paper and label it Summer. Most summer-blooming peren-nials are in the middle height range, between 2 to 3 feet tall. Plant a few taller ones in the back and some shorter ones in the front. Label and color the bubbles.

Take your last sheet of tracing paper and label it Spring. Focus on the front of the border because a majority of these plants are low-growing, gener-ally under 2 feet. When you've created a spring-blooming pat-tern in the front, fill in the center and back rows with other spring-flowering plants.

Finally, after you've moved your plants around and have arrived at the best design, draw up your master plan. Trace your fall and summer displays onto the Spring sheet, or transfer all of them to a fresh sheet of tracing paper. This final design will be your buying and plant-ing plan.

You don't have to buy all of these plants at once. Over a period of two or three years you can start them from seed, buy transplants, or acquire them as trades or passalong plants. In the meantime, fill in the vacancies with annuals.

Planting

Start perennials from seed. See last month's Planting (p. 200) for detailed sowing instructions. *Divide* and *replant* summer- and fall-flow-ering perennials as their new growth emerges. These include **asters, chrysanthemums,** and **Shasta daisies.**

Care for Your Perennials

Mountain gardeners should inspect their perennials to see if any have been heaved out by alternating freezing and thawing of the soil. Firmly press them back down into the soil to prevent them from freezing or drying out. To reduce heaving, maintain a layer of mulch around your perennials to insulate the soil.

Fertilizing

Seedlings growing in soil-less mixes need to be fertilized when the first true leaves appear. *Feed* at every other watering with a water-soluble fertilizer in order to promote faster growth until the plants are ready to plant outdoors. *Water* between feedings with plain water.

Pest Control

Diseases: Damping-off can be a problem on seedlings. See February Annuals on p. 33 for a description and controls.

Weeds: Control any winter annual weeds such as bittercress, common chickweed, and henbit by hand-pulling. Suppress them with a shallow layer of mulch.

Watering

Do not allow the pot or flats to dry out. If they're uncovered, *check* them daily and *water* as needed.

Pruning

Cut shorter ornamental grasses to 4 to 6 inches in height and **pampas grass** from 6 to 12 inches in height. When pruning back the **pampas grass,** wear gloves and cinch the top-growth with rope to make removal easier.

Trim away any dead leaves or stems from **asters, coreopsis,** and **rudbeckia.** Avoid damaging the crown of new leaves at the base. Wait until new growth emerges before cutting back **lantana** and **salvia.**

Planning

When designing a perennial garden, it's easy to go overboard and end up creating a complex border comprised of a multitude of plants. This can be a problem especially if you're faced with a shoe-string budget. Try staring perennials from seed, trade plants with neighbors, purchase less-expensive plants at the beginning, and grow perennials that are good reseeders.

Planting

Plant perennials when they become available from local nurseries or when they arrive in the mail from catalog orders. Plant dormant bareroot plants soon after receiving them. Here's how:

1 Remove the plastic wrapping and shake the packing material loose from the roots. Soak the roots in a bucket of water at least an hour before planting.

2 *Dig* the planting hole wide enough to accommodate the roots when they're spread out.

3 Create a cone of soil in the bottom of the hole and tamp down the top firmly. This will prevent the plant from settling too deeply.

4 Set the plant over the cone and drape the roots evenly over the top.

5 *Backfill* the hole. Work the soil in among the roots with your fingers. If the perennial has settled too deeply, *lift* it gently to raise the crown to the proper level.

Dig up, divide, and replant established perennials if they've become too crowded and flowering has been sparse. Some fast-growing perennials need to be divided between one and three years after planting—these include **aster, astilbe, beebalm, boltonia, garden mum, garden phlox, rudbeckia, Shasta daisy,** and many others. To avoid interrupting flowering, dig up summer- and fall-blooming perennials when the new growth is a few inches high.

Divide ornamental grasses before new growth emerges. *Cut back* the old culms to within 4 to 6 inches of the ground and use a sharp shovel or large knife to slice one or more wedges out of the crown. Immediately plant them elsewhere.

Uncover the trays or pots overwintered outdoors, and move them to a cold frame for protection from freezing temperatures. The perennial seedlings will emerge over a range of weeks (sometimes longer). *Transplant* tray-grown seedlings to individual pots after they've developed their first set of true leaves.

Care for Your Perennials

Press back any perennials that may have frost-heaved over the winter. Maintain a 2-inch layer of mulch around your perennials. Keep the mulch away from the crowns to avoid rot.

Watering

Keep newly planted perennials moist (do not let them dry out).

Fertilizing

Most perennials benefit from a boost with fertilizer as new growth begins in the spring. Select a slow-release fertilizer according to soil-test results. Follow the label directions regarding the amount and frequency of application. *Water* the fertilizer in to make it available to the plants.

Pruning

As new growth emerges, *prune away* any dead, winter-killed leaves and shoots, and compost them or bury them in the vegetable garden.

Cut back Russian sage (*Perovskia atriplicifolia*), leaving 6 to 12 inches of woody stem. *Pinch out* the tips of the new growth that results, or cut it back by half when it reaches a foot in length to produce a denser, sturdier specimen.

Cut back the dormant winter foliage of warm-season ornamental grasses within a few inches of the ground before the new shoots emerge. Cool-season grasses such as **blue fescue** (*Festuca glauca* 'Elijah Blue') and **blue lyme grass** (*Leymus arenarius*) can be sheared, generally removing no more than one-third of their height.

Pest Control

Insects: Flower thrips damage **bellflower, daylily,** and **peony** flowers with their feeding. *Remove and discard* thrips-infested flowers.

Diseases: Damping off can be triggered by sustained waterlogged conditions in the growing medium.

Helpful Hint

How many perennials will you need to plant in a given area?

The following chart shows the number of plants per square foot for a given spacing:

Spacing (inches)	Spacing Multiplier (# of Plants per Sq. Ft.)
12	1
15	0.64
18	0.44
24	0.25
36	0.11

Assume the bed measures 48 square feet (8 feet long and 6 feet wide) and you want to plant the perennials 15 inches apart. To determine the number of plants needed for the bed, use this equation:

Area of Bed × Spacing Multiplier = Total # of plants

In our example, the perennials will be spaced 15 inches apart, so

48 square feet × 0.64 = 31

Space 31 perennials 15 inches apart to occupy a 48-square-foot bed.

Avoid overwatering. Water your seedlings only when the surface of the medium feels dry.

Inspect the newly emerging leaves of your **daylilies** for reddish-brown streaks and browned-out spots. They could be afflicted with a disease called leaf-streak.

This fungus overwinters in dead, infected leaves, so collect and discard diseased or dead leaves to reduce the chances of future outbreaks.

Weeds: *Handpull* winter annuals such as henbit and common chickweed to prevent them from going to seed. Maintaining a 2-inch layer of mulch will suppress weeds.

In some cases you can rely on a preemergent herbicide to reduce the amount of handweeding required. See Vines and Ground Covers, May Weeds, on p. 325 for more information.

APRIL

Planning

Some perennials become top-heavy and require support to prevent them from bending or toppling over. They include **delphinium**, **snowbank boltonia** (*Boltonia asteroides* 'Snowbank'), **gaura, peony, sneezeweed, balloon flower,** and **culver's root** (*Veronicastrum virginicum*). Plan to support these plants early in their growth before they get too tall and floppy. There are a wide variety of materials you can use such as specially designed peony rings, tomato cages, and plastic or bamboo stakes. Position the stakes so the plants will eventually hide the supports. When securing their stems, tie the soft twine into a figure eight to avoid binding a stem.

To avoid staking some perennials altogether, select compact, lower-growing cultivars or prune (by pinching or cutting back) them at least eight weeks before flowering to keep their height in check. See the Pruning section to learn more about this approach.

Planting

Condition or *harden-off* the seedlings started indoors. Gradually expose them to outdoor conditions by moving them to a cold frame or a porch for at least a week before planting in the garden.

When planting ornamental grasses, follow this general rule of spacing: *Place plants as far apart as their eventual height.* This means that grasses that top out at 3 feet can be planted 3 feet apart from center to center.

Plant container-grown perennials as described in the Planting section (p. 194–95) in the introduction to this chapter.

Care for Your Perennials

Clean up plants and flower beds.

Watering

Keep newly planted perennials well watered during the first few weeks to help them get quickly established.

Fertilizing

Apply a slow-release fertilizer when the new shoots emerge. Follow the label directions regarding the amount and frequency of application. Water afterwards to make the minerals available to the roots.

Pruning

Pinching involves the removal of $1/2$ to one inch of each shoot, up to 2 inches of shoot tips. Pinched perennials produce more but smaller flowers than plants that haven't been pinched. Pinching will stagger the bloom period of plants, particularly **garden mums,** and will prevent them from growing tall and straggly. Plants that respond well to pinching include **aster, beebalm, garden mums, Gateway spotted joe-pye weed** (*Eupatorium maculatum* 'Gateway'), **pink turtlehead** (*Chelone lyonii*), **spike speedwell** (*Veronica spicata*), **Autumn Joy sedum,** and others.

Pest Control

Insects: Watch out for aphids and whiteflies on **chrysanthemums, coreopsis, sedum, verbena,** and others (see p. 213). Snails and slugs may be a problem on **hosta, ligularia, bear's breeches** (*Acanthus mollis*), and other perennials. See the Pest Appendix on p. 366 for descriptions and controls.

Look for columbine leaf miners. The larvae tunnel between the upper and lower leaf surfaces, producing telltale grayish-white serpentine trails. There are several generations of larvae and adults per year.

Control leaf miners by crushing the larvae inside the leaf before they become too disfigured or by cutting off the leaf altogether and removing it from the garden. For heavy infestations, cut columbines to the ground after flowering. New growth will soon emerge.

At the end of the growing season, remove any debris near the base of your plants to reduce next-year's overwintering offspring. Not all columbines are equally susceptible to this pest. The native **American columbine** (*Aquilegia canadensis*), for example, is reported to be less susceptible to leaf miner attack.

Diseases: Botrytis blight (*Botrytis paeoniae*) attacks **peony** buds, causing them to turn black and shrivel up. This fungal disease also attacks flowers stalks, leaves, and leaf petioles.

Remove and dispose of infected plant parts as soon as you spot them. If necessary, apply a fungicide in the spring as new shoots emerge.

Helpful Hints

Some gardeners crave perennials that bloom longer than the norm of a month. They may have an endless variety of leaf shapes and colors in the garden, but they've got to have flowers too! Fortunately, there are a number of long-blooming perennials that can extend the flowering season for several months. With periodic deadheading, the following perennials can be expected to bloom for two months or more:

- **Yarrow,** such as **'Coronation Gold'** and **'Fire King'**
- **Clara Curtis chrysanthemum**
- **Moonbeam** and **Zagreb threadleaf coreopsis** (*Coreopsis verticillata* **'Moonbeam'** and **'Zagreb'**)
- **Purple coneflower** (*Echinacea purpurea* **'Bright Star'** and **'Magnus'** among others)
- **Baby Cole blanketflower** (*Gaillardia* × *grandiflora* **'Baby Cole'**)
- **Whirling Butterflies gaura** (*Gaura lindheimeri* **'Whirling Butterflies'**)
- Reblooming **daylilies,** including *Hemerocallis* **'Bitsy'**, **'Stella de Oro'**, and **'Happy Returns'**
- **Russian sage** (*Perovskia atriplicifolia*)
- **Garden phlox** (*Phlox paniculata*)
- **Goldsturm black-eyed susan** (*Rudbeckia fulgida* var. *sullivantii* **'Goldsturm'**)
- **Butterfly Blue pincushion flower** (*Scabiosa* **'Butterfly Blue'**)
- **Sunny Border Blue longleaf veronica** (*Veronica longifolia* **'Sunny Border Blue'**)
- **Clump verbena** (*Verbena canadensis* **'Abbeville'**, **'Homestead Purple'**, and several others)
- **Goodness Grows speedwell** (*Veronica* × **'Goodness Grows'**)

Weeds: *Handpull* bittercress, chickweed, henbit, and other winter annuals before they go to seed.

Pre-emergent herbicides are available for many of the more common perennials. These herbicides kill germinating weed seedlings before they appear. See Annuals, March Weeds on p. 35 for tips on selecting a pre-emergent herbicide.

Planning

If you're serious about growing perennials well, start a journal this month. It will document your observations, thoughts, and plans for the future. Some of the following items can be noted in your journal:

- Blooming dates for each variety

- Condition of the flowers, leaves, and overall health of your perennials

- Pest problems: insects, diseases, weeds

- Kinds of pesticides used and when they were applied

- Plants that need to be moved or replaced because they turned out to grow larger than you expected or more demanding than you had planned

Your journal can become a teaching tool, especially when you need the assistance of a county extension agent, Master Gardener, or a garden center staff person to help you diagnose a particular problem. The notes you took about weather conditions, fertilizing, watering, and any pest control applications are important clues that can help reveal the answer.

So start writing.

Planting

It's not too late to plant perennials as long as you're willing to pamper them, helping with regular watering to speed up their establishment before hot summer weather arrives.

Care for Your Perennials

Begin staking tall-growing plants when they reach one-third of their mature height. Place the stakes close to the plant, but take care to avoid damaging the root system. Secure the stems of the plants to stakes in several places with paper-covered wire or other materials that will not cut into the stem. Tie the twine into a figure eight to avoid binding the stem. Summer- and fall-flowering perennials often require support. Some plants, however, can simply be pruned back lightly in midsummer to reduce their height and encourage branching and sturdiness. **Swamp sunflower** (*Helianthus angustifolius*) can be handled this way. See June Pruning (p. 211) for more information about this technique.

Watering

When watering, *apply* sufficient moisture to soak the soil deeply, wetting the root zone of your plants. Instead of following the calendar, *water* when the top 2 or 3 inches of soil feels dry.

Fertilizing

Evaluate your perennials for color and growth to determine the need for fertilizer. To encourage more growth, *fertilize* with a slow-release fertilizer.

Helpful Hint

You can create a cutting garden of flowering perennials so you can enjoy the flowers indoors as well as outdoors. Some popular perennials that can be grown in a cutting garden are **black-eyed susan (*Rudbeckia* spp.), aster, astilbe, bellflower (*Campanula*), chrysanthemum, gayfeather (*Liatris*), Globe thistle (*Echinops*), peony, phlox, purple coneflower (*Echinacea purpurea*), Shasta daisy,** and **yarrow (*Achillea*).**

Pruning

In the spring, when new shoots in a clump of **garden phlox** reach 8 to 10 inches tall, *thin out* all but four or five of the well-spaced healthy ones to allow good air circulation. Thinning helps prevent disease, especially powdery mildew, improves the appearance of the plants, and produces sturdier stems.

Some spring-flowering perennials should be sheared after flowering, cutting them back by one-half. Among them are **cheddar pinks** (*Dianthus gratianopolitanus* 'Bath's Pink'), **evergreen candytuft** (*Iberis sempervirens*), and **moss phlox** (*Phlox subulata*). **Garden chrysanthemums** can be sheared when the new growth reaches 4 to 6 inches in length. Shearing an inch off the top will delay flowering and encourage bushiness and the production of a lot of flower buds.

Pest Control

Insects and mites: Aphids, spider mites, and whiteflies can be a problem. Spider mites are especially fond of **chrysanthemums, coneflowers, daylilies,** and **phlox** (see p. 213).

Reseeding Perennials

Perennials that reseed themselves produce volunteers that can be transplanted to other parts of the garden or traded with friends and neighbors. Sometimes, they can produce more seedlings than you care to have which makes them behave like weeds. The following perennials reseed freely so keep that in mind if you're going to introduce them into your garden. Deadheading them before they release their seeds is one way of reducing their offspring.

- **Blackberry lily (*Belamcanda chinensis*)**
- **Phlox**
- **Columbine (*Aquilegia*)**
- **Four-o-clock (*Mirabilis jalapa*)**
- **Hardy begonia (*Begonia grandis*)**
- **Lenten rose (*Helleborus orientalis*)**
- **Fountain grass (*Pennisetum alopecuroides*)**
- **Northern sea oats (*Chasmanthium latifolium*)**
- **Patrinia**
- **Plume poppy (*Macleaya cordata*)**
- **Purple coneflower (*Echinacea purpurea*)**
- **Shasta daisy (*Chrysanthemum* × *superbum*)**
- **Zebrina (*Malva sylvestris* 'Zebrina')**

Diseases: Avoid leaf spot diseases by watering your perennials from below and limiting contact with the leaves. Proper spacing with plenty of air movement will reduce fungal infections.

Weeds: *Handpull* weeds when they're young. Try not to put off this chore until next weekend. Hoeing and maintaining a shallow mulch layer will also help.

Planning

When you planned your garden, you probably chose perennials for their flowers, bloom time, and other features. But have you thought about selecting perennials for their ability to attract beneficial insects? Beneficial insect predators and parasites such as lady beetles, lacewings, syrphid flies and tachinid flies prey on harmful insects including aphids, caterpillars, and mites. In general, the larvae feed on insects and mites while the adults feed on nectar and pollen—either exclusively or to supplement their diet when insects or mites are in short supply. Some of the perennials found by researchers to attract beneficial insects include: **fernleaf yarrow** (*Achillea filipendulina*), **basket-of-gold** (*Aurinia saxatilis*), **feverfew** (*Chrysanthemum parthenium*), **stonecrop** (*Sedum kamtschaticum*), **Peter Pan European goldenrod** (*Solidago virgaurea* 'Peter Pan'), and **spike speedwell** (*Veronica spicata*).

To keep beneficial insects in your landscape, plan to have flowering perennials in bloom all season long to provide them with a ready supply of nectar and pollen.

Planting and Transplanting

Many perennials can be propagated by rooting softwood stem cuttings, including **balloon flower, beebalm, chrysanthemum, penstemon, phlox, salvia,** and **veronica.** (Softwood stems are mature and firm but not yet hardened and woody.) Here's how to do it:

1 Use a sharp knife or razor blade to take 3- to 6-inch-long cuttings of terminal growth. Make an angled cut just below a node—the point where the leaf joins the stem. Remove the lowest leaf or two.

2 Dip the cut end into a rooting hormone suited for herbaceous plants.

3 *Fill* a small pot with equal parts of peat moss and perlite. Use a pencil to poke a hole in the medium before inserting the cutting. This prevents the rooting powder from being scraped off.

4 When you have inserted all the cuttings, *water* them well, and place the pots in a plastic bag closed at the top with a twist-tie.

5 Set the pots in a bright location, but not in direct sunlight. When the cuttings have produced small new leaves, move them to the garden. Instead of transplanting them to their permanent home, move them to a "halfway house" for rooted cuttings—a small makeshift nursery where they can be spaced out in easy-to-tend rows and won't be forgotten or neglected. After a few weeks, when they've grown large enough to hold their own, move them to their permanent spot in the garden.

Continue planting perennials; with the onset of hot, dry weather, however, be prepared to be on call with adequate water throughout their establishment period. *Continue to move to the outdoors perennials that you grew from seed.* Depending on their size, it may be better to transplant them to your home nursery where they can receive the attention they deserve rather than risk moving them to their permanent place in the garden where they can be forgotten. Better yet, *transplant* them in the fall when the weather becomes cooler and less stressful.

Plant **Shasta daisy, coreopsis,** and **coneflower** from seed. *Sow* them directly in the garden or in trays or pots. Seeds will take two to three weeks to emerge. When seedlings are 2 to 3 inches high, *thin* the plants to about 6 inches apart, or *transplant* them from pots into individual containers.

 Watering

Water recently planted perennials which are especially vulnerable to heat and drought stress. *Water thoroughly* to encourage deep rooting.

Fertilizing

If you used a slow-release fertilizer early in the season, check the label and evaluate the growth and appearance of your perennials to see if a second application is warranted.

Pruning

Pinch out the terminal growth of fall-blooming **garden chrysanthemums**. Repeat the pinching each time a lateral bud sends out a shoot—pinch as soon as the new shoot has about three sets of leaves. This will increase the number of blooms and produce stockier, bushier plants. To produce fewer but larger blooms, *disbud* **chrysanthemum** flowers—see August Pruning (p. 214). **Autumn Joy sedum** tends to flop over in midseason, especially when sited in partial shade. *Pinch out* the growing tips or *cut back* the stems to a foot to encourage branching and the production of a lot of flowers.

Deadhead **achillea, bellflower, baby's breath** (*Gypsophila paniculata*), **columbine, Butterfly Blue pincushion flower** (*Scabiosa* × 'Butterfly Blue'), **spike speedwell** (*Veronica spicata*), and **salvia** to lateral or side buds. After the side buds finish flowering, cut the stems down to the basal leaves at the crown.

To avoid staking late-flowering plants such as **asters, joe-pye weed,** or **Summer Sun heliopsis** (*Heliopsis helianthoides* 'Summer Sun'), prune them back to one-third their height. This will give them a fuller and more compact growth habit that won't require support.

Pinch out the growing tips of other late-summer- and fall-flowering plants such as **snowbank boltonia, swamp sunflower** (*Helianthus angustifolius*), and **sneezeweed** (*Helenium autumnale*). They will produce many smaller flowers without any noticeable loss in height.

Cut back **amsonia** and **baptisia** after flowering by one-third to one-half their height; otherwise, they will continue to grow with abandon and will splay apart in late summer.

 Pest Control

Insects and mites: Be on the lookout for aphids, slugs and snails, spider mites, and thrips. *Handpick Japanese beetles* and discard them in a jar of soapy water. Neem can be applied to the leaves to reduce feeding by the adults. Use other insecticides for heavy infestations.

Diseases: Avoid overhead watering and remove spent flowers and dead or dying leaves. Look for signs of powdery mildew on your **garden phlox** and **beebalm**. Infected leaves have a grayish-white powder on both sides of the leaves. Heavy infestations can cause the leaves to become curled and eventually yellow and die.

Remove any infected plants and discard them. Thin out the plants to improve air movement. Fungicides can be applied when the symptoms appear and until they're gone. In the future, select varieties resistant to powdery mildew (see p. 217, September Diseases).

Weeds: *Handpull* or hoe out any weeds to prevent them from stealing water and nutrients from your perennials. Suppress their emergence with a layer of mulch.

Planning

Take advantage of the cool temperatures inside to catch up on writing in your garden journal and reading about perennials. If you haven't kept up with regular entries, plan some time this month to sit down and record your observations of the performance of your plants, any pest problems, control measures, and thoughts about what needs to be done as summer closes and gives way to fall. Write down the names of any plants that need to be composted or given away. And find some good books about perennials and learn more about the design aspects of perennial borders. Learn how to use color, form, and texture to create a living portrait in your landscape.

Planting

Any planting done now should be done with caution. Keep plants moist until they settle in. Mountain gardeners can divide **daylilies** after they finish blooming. See p. 202, February Planting, for details. Plants with fleshy roots—such as **butterfly weed** (*Asclepias*), **gas plant** (*Dictamnus*), and old-fashioned **bleeding heart** (*Dicentra spectabilis*)—can be propagated from root cuttings. Some perennials, such as **oriental poppy**

(*Papaver orientale*), can be propagated from root cuttings. Wait until the oriental poppies are fully dormant in midsummer (at this point the foliage will have died, so you will need to mark the location of the crowns beforehand). Here's how to propagate them from root cuttings:

1. Rake the soil away from the crown to expose a few pencil-thick side roots. *Cut* these off cleanly with a knife and replace the soil. *Do not remove more than a few roots from each crown.*

2. *Cut* each root into 2- to 3-inch lengths and plant them horizontally in a flat containing moist sand or peat moss.

3. *Cover* the flat with a layer of clear plastic to keep the roots moist, and put the flat in a cool, shaded location. Callus tissue will form on the cut ends, and roots and shoots will develop from adventitious buds along the roots.

4. Several weeks after sprouting, *transplant* the young plants to a protected location.

The seeds of many perennials can be sown either in pots or directly in the garden. Although it may take seed-propagated perennials from two to three years to bloom

from seed, some will bloom in less than a year. Start the following perennials now outdoors in a partially shaded location, or indoors in trays or pots (next year you can sow a second crop indoors in early spring for flowering the same season):

- **Butterfly weed** (*Asclepias tuberosa*)

- **Large-flowered tickseed** (*Coreopsis grandiflora*)

- **Maltese cross** (*Lychnis chalcedonica*)

- **Purple coneflower** (*Echinacea purpurea*)

- **Red valerian** (*Centranthus ruber*)

- **Shasta daisy** (*Chrysanthemum* × *superbum*)

- **Spike speedwell** (*Veronica spicata*)

- **Oxeye daisy** (*Heliopsis helianthoides*)

- **Violet sage** (*Salvia* × *superba*)

- **Yarrows** (*Achillea*)

Care for Your Perennials

Stake tall-growing late-season bloomers before they topple over.

Fertilizing

After pinching or pruning your perennials, *fertilize* them to speed up their recovery. If you use a slow-release fertilizer, now is the time to make your second application of the season according to label directions (your first application should have been applied in the spring at planting or when the new shoots emerged. *Water* afterwards to make the nutrients available to your plants.

Watering

During periods of low or no rainfall, *water* plants (especially new plantings or perennials that have been fertilized) when they need it, and not by the calendar. When you do water, do a thorough job so water penetrates the soil deeply. Wait until the soil becomes dry in the upper inch or so before watering again. To learn how to water efficiently, refer to the July Helpful Hint in Roses on p. 241. Summer- and fall-flowering perennials such as **daylilies** need an ample supply of water to encourage flowering. *Inspect* the mulch in flower beds. If wind, rain, and natural decay have reduced its thickness to an inch or less, *apply* more mulch to raise the level to 2 to 3 inches—but leave only about a

1/2-inch-thick layer around the bases of the plants. Perennials that have been cut back heavily should be kept moist to support the emerging growth.

Pruning

To ensure flowers this season, gardeners who've been shearing their **mums** should make their last cuts in early July in the Mountains and no later than early August elsewhere. Continue to *deadhead* spent flowers to improve appearance and prolong the blooming period of certain perennials such as **beebalm, black-eyed susan, daylilies, monkshood** (*Aconitum*), **purple coneflower, perennial salvia** (*Salvia nemerosa*), **spotted phlox** (*Phlox maculata*), **Stokes' aster,** and **yarrow** (*Achillea*). Shear **Moonbeam threadleaf coreopsis** (*Coreopsis verticillata* 'Moonbeam') for a second bloom.

Pest Control

Insects and mites: Aphids, spider mites, and whiteflies continue to be on the prowl this month. They can be washed from plants with a strong stream of water. Insecticidal soap, insecticides, and miticides will keep their numbers in check.

Watch out for Japanese beetles this month. Adults emerge as early as mid-May in the Coastal Plains. Their highest numbers occur this month. Thankfully, there's only one generation a year.

Diseases: Southern blight attacks a number of perennials, especially **artemisia, aster, columbine, coralbells, liatris, phlox, salvia,** and **Shasta daisy.** This soil-borne disease occurs during periods of high temperatures (80 to 90 degrees Fahrenheit) and in moist soils. The fungus attacks the stem at soil level and moves up the stem rapidly, killing the tissues as it ascends. The leaves turn yellow and wilt, and eventually the entire plant collapses. Look on the infected stem for dozens of brown, mustard seed–sized sclerotia—the "seeds" of the fungus. *Remove and discard infected plants. Leave the area fallow for six months or longer. Fungicidal soil drenches can be used to treat the soil when a shorter fallow period is used.*

Leaf diseases may show up during wet weather. *Trim away heavily infected leaves and compost them.*

Weeds: Continue handpulling weeds out of the flower beds. With proper spacing, your perennials should be able to shade out the soil naturally and keep the weeds at bay.

AUGUST

Planning

This is a good month to update your gardening journal and make plans for improvements this fall and next year. What were the most troublesome insects and diseases this season? Perhaps you need to make plans to dig out some perennials and replace them this fall.

Think about the perennials that seemed to "take a lickin' and keep on tickin'." Also, take notes about those perennials that looked attractive while requiring little attention to deadheading, staking, and pest control. Did any of the perennials tolerate droughty conditions better than others? Spend some moments over the next few months pondering these features and documenting them in your journal.

Over the past few months you may have saved newspaper and magazine clippings of articles written by local garden writers who tout certain perennials. Perhaps you wrote down comments from friends, or saw high-performing perennials that grabbed your attention in private or public gardens or in botanical gardens. Find all of the notes you wrote on the backs of credit card receipts, napkins, and road maps, and compile them into your gardening journal so you can act on them next growing season.

Planting

Any planting done now should be followed with regular watering, keeping the soil moist in order to speed up establishment. Mountain gardeners can divide or move perennials to other parts of the garden, paying attention to watering and mulching after planting.

Care for Your Perennials

If you're going on vacation this month, have someone take care of your flower beds while you're away. See Annuals, July Planning (p. 42) for some helpful suggestions.

Pruning

Deadhead **phlox** to prevent the flowers from going to seed. The seedlings do not come true to the color of the parent, and often their sheer numbers overtake a planting, giving you the impression that the flowers from the parents have magically changed color. ***Disbud* chrysanthemums** to produce fewer but larger blooms. Most mums, except spray types, respond well to disbudding. To disbud, pinch off the side buds that form in the angles of the leaves along the main stems.

Leave only the large top bud. *The plant will channel its energy into this bud, which will develop into impressive proportions.*

Watering

During periods of low or no rainfall, *water* plants—especially new plantings—when they need it, and not by the calendar. When you do water, do a thorough job so water penetrates the soil deeply. Wait until the soil becomes dry in the upper inch or so before watering again.

Avoid irrigating your perennials with an overhead sprinkler. In addition to wasting water and watering weeds, wetting the leaves will encourage diseases to infect them.

Container-grown flowers can dry out quickly, especially when located in full sun. Feel the soil in containers at least once a day to check for moisture. When water is necessary, *apply* it long enough so that it runs out the drainage holes. Keep in mind that clay pots, which allow water to be lost to evaporation from the walls of the pot, will need to be watered more often than plastic pots—and small pots will dry out faster than large planters.

Mulch to decrease weeds and conserve moisture. Inspect the mulch in flower beds. If wind, rain, and natural decay have reduced its thickness to an inch or less, *apply* more mulch to raise the level to 2 to 3 inches. Mulch conserves moisture, suppresses weed growth, and makes those weeds that do grow easier to pull out.

Fertilizing

Be cautious about fertilizing. Unless the leaves look pale or off-color, fertilizing won't be necessary. Avoid excessive fertilization. It produces the soft, succulent growth favored by pests.

Never skimp on building up the natural fertility of the soil with applications of organic mulches such as compost.

Pruning

Trim away any dead, damaged, diseased, or insect-infested leaves.

To improve their appearance, *deadhead* the spent flowers from **garden phlox, obedient plant (*Physostegia virginianum*), perennial salvia, pincushion flower, purple coneflower,** and **sneezeweed.**

Helpful Hints

- If you have a friend who is new to gardening and is interested in trying perennials, introduce him or her to these "no fuss-no muss" beauties: **Autumn Joy sedum, balloon flower, butterfly weed, daylily, Goldsturm coneflower, hosta, Lenten rose, purple coneflower, southern shield fern,** and **threadleaf coreopsis.** They not only look terrific–they're great confidence-builders too.

- Create a theme garden with perennials. It could be a single-color theme garden (such as a "white" garden with white-flowered plants); a butterfly and hummingbird garden; an evening garden with flowers and leaves that can be appreciated in the twilight hours; or a scented garden with fragrant perennials. Plans for these and other theme gardens can be found in perennial plant encyclopedias and other reference books. A number of reference books have sample designs for these gardens so you can make substitutions of plant materials to fit your design. Adapt the existing design and plant list to suit your site.

Pest Control

Nematodes are microscopic organisms that live in the soil and attack the roots of plants. They are commonly found in coarse-textured sandy soils. See Roses, July Pest Control on p. 240 for more information.

Insects and mites: Be on the lookout for aphids and spider mites. Plants infested by spider mites have faded, stippled leaves. Remove these pests with a strong spray of water from the hose. Resort to a pesticide if their numbers are high and damage is great.

Diseases: Fungal leaf spots, powdery mildew, and other diseases could be afflicting your perennials. Evaluate the extent of damage to determine if a fungicide application is necessary. Remove and discard heavily infested plants.

Weeds: Control weeds by hand-pulling and maintaining a shallow layer of mulch. Prevent the weed from going to seed by removing the flowers. Any seeds that can be eliminated now will not have to be dealt with next year.

Planning

Summer usually takes it toll on gardeners and on the plants in the garden. As late summer approaches and you feel as bedraggled as your garden, you can gain inspiration from fall-flowering perennials. **Garden mums** (*Chrysanthemum × morifolium*) have long been the mainstay of the fall garden and are available in a wide array of heights, flower forms, and colors. But there's more than mums. Consider **asters** such as 'Monch' (*Aster × frikartii*), **Autumn Joy sedum**, **ironweed** (*Vernonia altissima*), **Confederate hibiscus** (*Hibiscus mutabilis*), **joe-pye weed** (*Eupatorium purpureum*), **goldenrod** (*Solidago* 'Golden Thumb' and 'Peter Pan'), **Japanese anemone** (*Anemone hupehensis*), **swamp sunflower** (*Helianthus angustifolius*), *Salvia guaranitica*, and the tender **Mexican sage** (*Salvia leucantha*).

Ornamental grasses also make great choices for the fall and winter garden with their plumes of flowers and shimmering leaves. Some great choices include **Red Baron blood grass** (*Imperata cylindrica* 'Red Baron'), **Heavy Metal switch grass** (*Panicum virgatum* 'Heavy Metal'), **Morning light maidenhair grass** (*Miscanthus sinensis* 'Morning Light'), and **Karl Foerster feather reed grass** (*Calamagrostis × acutiflora* 'Karl Foerster'). Make plans to learn more about these and other late-season flowering plants that will thrive in your corner of the Carolinas. Look for these and other plants in your garden center or mail-order catalogs, and plan to weave them into your landscape.

These are just a few of the perennials that will lift your garden and your spirits this fall, so plan to get them in your garden.

Planting and Transplanting

Establish new perennial flower beds: *dig, divide, and replant* overcrowded beds of **beebalm, daylilies, cheddar pinks, Shasta daisies,** and **threadleaf coreopsis.** Spread a liberal amount of organic matter over the area and mix it into the soil at least 6 to 8 inches deep. Space divisions at least 1 foot apart in all directions so that root competition will not be a problem for several years.

Cool-season ornamental grasses can be planted now to take advantage of the cool temperatures, allowing the roots to become established before spring's burst of growth.

Astilbe is not a long-lived perennial, so divide it every three or four years to maintain vigor. When replanting divisions, leave three or four "eyes" in each section, and replant so the eyes are about $1/2$ inch below the soil surface.

Now is the time to move perennial plants started from seed in midsummer to the home nursery row or to their permanent spot in the garden. Follow this general guideline for spacing plants: small plants under 1 foot tall or front-of-the-border plants should be spaced about 12 to 18 inches apart. Plants of intermediate size (1 to $2^1/2$ feet tall) should be placed at least 18 to 24 inches apart (three or four plants per 10 square feet), and larger plants should be spaced roughly 3 feet apart.

Care for Your Perennials

Pull out stakes and remove cages as plants finish for the year. Clean the stakes and cages and store them where you can locate them next spring.

Watering

Fall is the driest season in the Carolinas. Keep newly-set-out transplants well watered to help them establish quickly.

Fertilizing

Fertilizing is not necessary this late in the season. Allow the perennials to go dormant so they can tolerate the winter weather.

Pruning

Deadhead **silvermound artemisia** (*Artemisia schmidtiana* '**Nana**') to remove the flowers. It tends to decline after flowering, so channeling the plant's energy to the leaves will prevent them from self-destructing.

Pest Control

Insects: Check for evidence of snails and slugs. Set out baits or traps for them as the weather turns cooler and wetter.

Diseases: Remove infected leaves and clean up fallen leaves and discard them. Fungicides may not be warranted this late in the season. Make a note in your gardening journal about varieties that were highly susceptible to powdery mildew, and consider replacing them with more resistant cultivars next year. Powdery mildew–resistant **garden phlox** cultivars include **Bright Eyes**, '**David**', '**Eva Cullum**, **Franz**

Helpful Hints

Herbaceous **peonies** are long-lived plants (even outliving gardeners!) that sport gorgeous flowers in white, pink, or red in double, semi-double, or single forms (depending on the cultivar). Even when out of flower, their attractive leaves command attention. **Peonies** can't be grown throughout the Carolinas, however, because of their need for cold temperatures and disdain of extended hot and humid conditions. Depending on the cultivar, **peonies** require a certain number of hours of temperatures below 40 degrees Fahrenheit to come out of dormancy, grow, and bloom normally.

To cultivate **peonies** at the edge of their heat hardiness in 7b and the northern half of 8a, select early- to mid-season cultivars and single or Japanese flower forms. Early-blooming cultivars enable you to avoid warm, humid weather and accompanying diseases, particularly gray mold or botyrtis blight. Late-flowering semidoubles and doubles with their thick collection of petals tend to hold moisture, which fosters fungal infection.

Some herbaceous perennials that have performed well in zone 7b include the double-flowering **Red Charm, Felix Crousse,** and **Highlight.** Double pink-flowered perennials include **Raspberry Sundae, Sarah Bernhardt, Mrs. Franklin D. Roosevelt, Mons. Jules Elie,** and **Gene Wild.** Double white perennials include **Carolina Moon, Festiva Maxima, Shirley Temple, Duchess de Nemours,** and **Gardenia.** Some good single-flowered performers include **Mikado** (red), **Westerner** (pink), and **Jan van Leeuwen** (white).

Schubert, Natascha, Robert Poore, and 'Starfire'. The following beebalm cultivars are less prone to infection by powdery mildew: 'Claire Grace', 'Colrain Red', 'Elsie's Lavender', 'Jacob Cline', 'Marshall's Delight', 'Raspberry Wine', and 'Vintage Wine'.

Weeds: Don't turn your back on the weeds in your flower beds. Summer annual weeds like crabgrass and goosegrass have matured and are going to seed. Winter annual weeds like annual bluegrass, chickweed, and Carolina geranium are germinating. Hoe them out or handpull them now.

Planning

With the onset of cooler temperatures, begin planning the expansion of old beds, the creation of new ones, or the rearrangement of plants in the beds. Refer to your journal to help you decide if beds need to be expanded, reduced, or planted with new perennials. When starting new beds, have the soil tested through your cooperative extension service office. Test old flower beds every three years.

Planting

Herbaceous **peonies** can remain undisturbed for many years. When they become overcrowded, however, and blooms are few and far between, they will have to be divided. **Divide** them when the leaves and shoots are killed by frost. Mountain gardeners should be aware that peonies need six to eight weeks to develop roots before the ground freezes.

1 **Cut** the foliage to within 4 inches of the ground. Then use a spading fork to gently **lift** each clump.

2 Set the clumps on a tarp or piece of newspaper and allow them to **air-dry** for an hour or so. This will make it easier to brush the soil off the root and crown.

3 Examine each plant carefully before dividing it with a sharp knife. Your goal is to make divisions that have at least three stout roots and three to five dark-red "eyes" or growth buds each. Smaller divisions will take longer to bloom. The outer edges of the clump typically yield better divisions than the woody center.

4 Allow the divisions to cure in a warm, dry place for a day or two. **Plant** the cured divisions in a well-drained fertile bed, allowing 3 feet between plants. Dig each hole 2 feet wide and 18 inches deep, and mix compost or well-rotted manure into the bottom. Position the division and backfill the hole so the eyes are no more than $1/2$ to 1 inch below the surface. **Peonies planted too deeply will never bloom.**

5 Water the newly planted divisions well, and **mulch** lightly with compost or shredded leaves.

Ferns can be planted or transplanted in fall. Hardy ferns are best divided in early fall or very early spring before new growth emerges. Ferns such as **hayscented fern** (*Dennstaedtia punctilobula*) and **ostrich fern** (*Matteuccia struthiopteris*) have branching rhizomes on or near the soil surface. These can simply be cut; make sure, however, that you have a growing tip and one or two intact fronds. Replant the divisions at the same level.

Other species such as **cinnamon fern** (*Osmunda cinnamomea*) develop a tangle of rhizomes and roots—you will have to dig up the whole clump and do your best to separate individual plants from the mass. Occasionally ferns develop multiple crowns that can be cut apart and planted individually. The important thing is not to cover the crowns of the new transplants with more than $1/2$ inch of soil, and to keep them well watered until they are established. A shallow layer of mulch throughout the growing season will help retain moisture in the soil.

There's still time to **dig, divide, and replant** crowded perennials. In the higher Mountain elevations, wait until spring, as winter may kill the young divisions before they have time to become established. Look for perennials that have grown out-of-bounds or have declined due to overcrowding and have developed a ring of growth with an empty center.

Care for Your Perennials

Before the first freeze, take cuttings of **Confederate rose (*Hibiscus mutabilis*),** a fall-blooming perennial that's marginally hardy in zone 7b, where the top growth will get winter-killed and resprout from the crown the following spring. The flowers can be either single or double, depending on the cultivar. The peony-like flowers go through subtle color changes like light pink to red; others change in chameleon-like fashion, opening white, changing to pink, and finally turning a deep crimson red.

If you're concerned that the plant will not survive the upcoming winter, or if you choose to share this plant with friends, it roots very easily from cuttings taken in the fall. They root easily in water, and they can be potted up after rooting. *Transplant* them outside after the last freeze in spring to an area in full sun or partial shade.

Watering

Add mulch to your perennial border. A 2-inch layer of weed-free straw or chopped leaves will help conserve soil moisture, protect the root system, and reduce plant loss from soil heaving during

Helpful Hints

- As you divide your perennials and replant them, don't forget the passalong features of plants, which means you can give them to a friend or swap for another desirable plant for your garden.

- Some perennials, such as **butterfly weed (*Asclepias*), euphorbia, oriental poppy,** and **gas plant (*Dictamnus albus*),** resent division. **Hellebores** are difficult to move when they're more than a few years old; fortunately, they reseed with abandon, allowing you to transplant or share the offspring with friends.

the winter. Keep new plantings watered if the weather is dry. Established gardens may need water as well so they won't go into winter with sufficient moisture. Rake up fallen leaves, shred them with a mower, and use them as mulch around your perennials.

Fertilizing

Do not fertilize this late in the season. Allow the perennials to go dormant so they can tolerate the winter weather.

Pruning

Cut back the **peonies** hard after the first frost, and compost the trimmings to reduce the chances of disease outbreaks.

Prune perennials when their tops are nipped by cold. Some perennials produce seeds that are attractive to birds. Leave these plants standing as long as there are still seeds in them.

Pest Control

Diseases: Clean up the dead leaves from around your perennial flowers. If left on the ground, leaves and stems can harbor diseases and provide convenient places for pests to spend the winter.

Weeds: Hoe or handpull any weeds in the beds to prevent them from going to seed, and to prevent the younger weeds from settling in for the winter. *Mulch* with a shallow layer to suppress emerging weeds.

Planning

Plan to plant and maintain perennials that offer winter interest. You can keep your perennial garden looking attractive while nourishing birds with perennials that offer attractive leaves, stems, and seedheads. Ornamental grasses are at the top of the list with their brightly colored seedheads and leaves that turn to yellow, orange, red, or purple with the onset of cooler winter temperatures. See the Helpful Hint on p. 221 for others.

Planting

Continue to set out perennials in the Piedmont and Coastal Plain if any good selections are available from garden centers. Mountain gardeners can set out or transplant no later than four to six weeks before the ground is expected to freeze. Late-planted perennials will benefit from a 3- to 5-inch layer of mulch after the ground freezes to protect them from being lifted by the freezing and thawing of the soil. *Lift and move* perennial volunteer seedlings to a new location. If they're not crowded, leave them alone.

Start perennial seeds that need to be stratified or exposed to moist chilling conditions for a specified time period (check the seed packet for the length of cold exposure); other-

wise, they won't germinate. Stratification is a survival mechanism that prevents seeds from germinating in the fall when they can be killed by harsh winter temperatures. Only after being exposed to conditions that mimic winter can they overcome the seed's internal mechanism that inhibits it from germinating. Seeds such as **amsonia (*Amsonia tabernaemontana*), gas plant (*Dictamnus albus*), monkshood (*Aconitum* spp.),** and **turtlehead (*Chelone* spp.)** can be stratified in a cold frame for the specified period of time. Here's how:

1 *Sow* the seeds in pots or trays. *Label* each container with the plant's name and the date of sowing.

2 Move the pots and trays to an unheated porch, garage, or cold frame where they can be exposed to outdoor temperatures but protected from snow, wind, and rain. Cover the pots or trays with plastic wrap to prevent the potting medium from drying out. They should be exposed to cold temperatures of less than 40 degrees Fahrenheit for four to eight weeks.

3 As springlike weather arrives, the seeds will start sprouting, usually when the temperatures are between 45 and 60 degrees F. Different species will germi-

nate at different times. Some may appear in very early spring, others in late spring, while a few may take up to a year or more. Do some research beforehand to know how much time you'll have to commit. Once the seedlings emerge, remove the plastic, and *water* them to keep them from wilting.

4 As seedlings sprout, move the pots to a cool location (below 70 degrees) with bright indirect sunlight.

5 When seedlings have grown a second set of true leaves, *thin* or *transplant* them to prevent overcrowding. If you don't need many plants, *thin* to one seedling per pot by cutting off extras with scissors. If you want a lot, *transplant* the seedlings one per container into 2¼- or 3-inch-wide plastic pots filled with a moist, peat-based potting mix. Use a fork to gently lift seedlings out of containers and *tease them apart.* Handle seedlings by the leaves to avoid damaging their stems.

6 Water the seedlings and place them out of direct sun for a few days to recover. After a week, put them in a place that receives morning sun. Begin feeding the seedlings once a week with a dilute (half-strength) liquid fertilizer.

7 *Plant* in the garden by late summer or early fall. Some slower-growing species may not be large enough to move yet. Keep them in a cold frame over the winter, and set them out the following spring.

Plant **peonies** now in the Piedmont and Mountains. For best results, choose a variety that blooms in early to mid-season. **Peonies** are long-lived, reliable, and extremely cold-hardy (zones 3 to 7) plants that produce magnificent flowers in spring and early summer and attractive compound leaves throughout the season. Gardeners who want to grow **peonies** in the warmer parts of zones 7 and 8a should refer to the September Helpful Hints, p. 217. *Plant* dormant bare-root herbaceous peonies so the "eyes" or buds on the division are covered by no more than 1½ to 2 inches of soil. In milder areas, the eyes should be no deeper than ½ to 1 inch below the soil surface. **Peonies** planted too deeply will never bloom. *Plant* container-grown **peonies** so the top of the rootball is less than an inch below the soil surface.

Care for Your Perennials

There's still time to *dig, divide, and replant* crowded perennials.

Look for perennials that have grown out-of-bounds or have declined due to overcrowding and have developed a ring of growth with an empty center. *Divide* peonies when the leaves die back (see October Planting, p. 218).

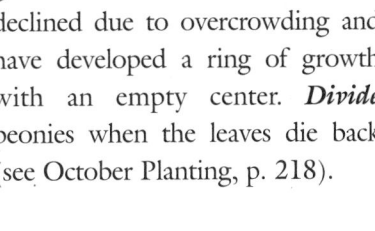

Watering

Keep newly planted transplants well watered to help them get established.

Fertilizing

Fertilizer is not needed at this time of year.

Pruning

Reduce **peony** botrytis blight and powdery mildew on **beebalm** and **phlox** by trimming away and disposing of old, dead stems.

Avoid pruning **Monch's aster, ferns, salvias, mums,** and other marginally hardy plants so the crowns will be insulated during cold weather. Prune them when new growth emerges in the spring. Plants such as **leadwort** (*Cera-*

tostigma plumbaginoides) that also emerge late in the spring should not be pruned; the old stems and leaves will let you know where they are so you won't accidentally damage them by digging.

Perennials with winter interest should not be pruned until winter takes its toll and turns the growth to mush.

Pest Control

Diseases: See October (p. 219).

Weeds: *Handpull* any young winter annuals, or cover them with a shallow layer of compost. Weeding is never fun, but the cooler temperatures can make it more bearable.

Helpful Hint

Some perennials have showy seedheads that last well into winter if you don't tidy them up and remove them. Some of these are **blackberry lily (***Belamcanda chinensis***), coneflowers (***Echinacea*** and ***Rudbeckia***), grapeleaf anemone (***Anemone tomentosa***), swamp hibiscus (***Hibiscus coccineus***), and yarrow.**

Planning

As you pore over the catalogs or read gardening magazines, jot down the names of perennials that are worth growing in your garden. Start a "wish list" of perennials in your gardening journal. Some information that should be included:

- Name (Common name and botanical name) and cultivar

- Expected bloom time (for example, early spring, midsummer, early fall)

- Cold/heat hardiness

- Flower color

- Ornamental characteristics (flowers, leaves, seedheads)

- Height and spread

- Pest problems

- Additional comments (self-sows, requires staking, needs regular deadheading, etc.)

Cut out the pictures of perennials from catalogs and paste them in your journal of favorites. This will help you identify perennials and quickly visualize them.

These are just a few of the features of each plant that can be included. Information about these plants can be found in mail-order catalogs, perennial plant encyclopedias, and other reference books.

Planting

Seeds that need an exposure to cold temperatures can be sown this month and set outdoors.

Care for Your Perennials

Late-planted perennials in the Mountains and the colder parts of the Piedmont where the soil freezes should be mulched to insulate the soil and reduce the occurrence of frost-heaving.

Watering

Keep newly planted transplants well watered to help them get established.

Fertilizing

Do not fertilize your perennials at this time.

Pruning

Continue to *cut back* the dead, damaged, or dying perennial top growth that offers no winter ornamental interest or food for birds. Cut down to within 2 to 3 inches of ground level or just above the new foliage at the base.

Perennials such as **coneflower, heliopsis**, and **black-eyed Susan**, whose seedheads offer food for birds, are best left unpruned until late winter.

Pest Control

Diseases can be carried over the winter on plant parts and infect the plants in spring. Remove all fallen leaves and dead stems form the perennials before mulching.

Helpful Hint

Join a garden club, become a Master Gardener with the Cooperative Extension service, or volunteer at a local botanical garden or arboretum. Share your gardening experiences with others and refine your gardening skills with other super-charged gardeners. It's also a good way of sharing your excesses with like-minded gardeners who are willing to share their bounty.

Roses

No other flower stirs up as much emotion in the Carolinas as the rose. Most of us love to give roses and we love to receive them; we're divided, however, on the issue of growing them in our gardens. Some gardeners will grow roses with the thought that beauty has its price ("no pain, no gain"). They devotedly dust, spray, deadhead, prune, feed, mulch, and otherwise defend and nurture these garden bluebloods. Other Carolina gardeners avoid roses for this very reason, seeing them as fussy and temperamental, unable to flourish without human support. It should be understood that roses fall into two categories. Any gardener can enjoy some member of this royal family if choices are made knowledgeably:

- The *high-maintenance/high-performance* types demand a certain level of doting that includes preventative pesticide applications, regular feeding, and primping. Your efforts will be rewarded with blemish-free leaves and exquisite flowers.

- The *easy-care* types are suitable for gardeners who love roses but aren't interested in intensive management. These include not only the eye-catching **old garden roses** discovered in old cemeteries and abandoned homesteads but also the modern **hybrid teas, grandifloras, and climbers.** They are vigorous and more tolerant of pests than are other kinds of roses. Though less demanding, they can still produce magnificent flowers.

Planning

Roses have three basic requirements:

1 **At least six hours of direct sunlight each day:** An ideal location receives full sun in the morning and shade from the late-afternoon sun. Sunlight is important for the production of flowers; the flowers can quickly fade, however, if exposed to sun all day.

2 **A well-drained, fertile location:** See January Planting on p. 228.

3 **Room to grow:** Whether you plant them in groups or among flowers or shrubs, give roses room to spread their limbs and roots. Avoid shoe-horning them into overcrowded plantings—airflow is critical for drying off rose leaves to discourage diseases.

Once you've found the right spot, the next step is to pick the right roses for your garden. More than 20,000 cultivars of roses have been divided into three groups by the American Rose Society: **old garden roses, modern roses,** and **species roses.** These are further subdivided into classes. How you use these roses in your landscape—in flower borders, hedges, or on trellises—will dictate the classes of roses you'll select. But don't forget to choose for flower color, fragrance, and durability too.

Planting

Plant bare-root and potted roses in the spring or fall. Selection is usually best in the spring.

Whether you buy your roses at a garden center or from a mail-order company, select a grade No. 1 rose. Look for the grade on the tag.

Plant bare-root roses soon after buying them or receiving them in the mail. Unwrap and soak the roots in a bucket of water for a few hours before planting. Then follow these planting steps:

Roses

1 **Dig** the planting hole about 12 inches deep and at least 2 feet wide for **hybrid teas** and other large rosebushes.

2 Create a cone of soil in the bottom of the hole and **tamp down** the top firmly. This will prevent the rose from settling too deeply.

3 Set the plant over the cone and **drape the roots** evenly over the top. The bud union should be about an inch above the soil surface. Lay your shovel handle across the hole to help gauge the correct depth.

4 **Backfill** the hole. Work the soil in among the roots with your fingers. If the rose has settled too deeply and the bud union is below soil level, grasp the canes close to the crown and lift it gently to raise it to the proper level.

5 To protect the canes from losing too much moisture as the roots are developing, hill up dry mulching materials like wood chips or shredded leaves over the top of the plant so only a few inches of the canes are showing. Once the new shoots begin to emerge, **remove** the mulch from the canes.

Potted roses are typically bare-root plants that have been potted up by the nursery. They can be set in as late as summer, but it's best to plant them in the garden as early as possible so that they will be established before summer's heat and humidity arrives. Follow these steps:

1 **Dig** a hole only as deep as the container and at least three times the diameter of the pot. If soil at the bottom of the hole is loose, **firm** it with your hand.

2 Adjust the depth of the rose so the graft union is at least 1 inch above the soil surface. The graft union is the knobby swollen knot where a bud from the flowering variety was grafted or more accurately budded onto a rootstock of another variety.

3 **Remove** the plant by cutting away the bottom and sides of the container.

4 If the roots are growing around the rootball, use a sharp knife to score the rootball shallowly in three or four places. **Cut** from the top down to the bottom.

5 **Backfill** the hole and **water** to settle the soil.

Whether planting a potted rose or a bare-root rose, apply a shallow 2- to 3-inch layer of mulch to conserve moisture, suppress weeds, and keep the soil cool.

Watering

To speed up establishment, water newly planted roses often enough to keep the roots moist during the first few weeks. Gradually reduce the frequency but not the depth of watering: *water your roses deeply to encourage deep rooting.*

Fertilizing

Take the guesswork out of fertilizing your roses—rely on a soil test. Follow soil test results to see what nutrients and micronutrients (elements needed in small quantities such as iron, manganese, zinc, and others) are lacking. With that in mind, you can make a sound decision when searching for the right fertilizer for your roses.

If you're interested in exhibiting prize-winning roses, contact the Carolina Rose Society for fertilizing programs and recipes that will maximize the performance of your roses.

Pruning

Roses have to be pruned. But before you flip to the next chapter, understand the reasons why:

- *To keep them healthy.* Remove dead, damaged, or diseased growth when discovered, at any time of year.

Roses

- *To shape and direct their growth.* **Climbing** and **rambling roses** must be pruned so their canes can be secured to trellises or arbors. Roses with a bush-type habit benefit from having their shoots directed away from the center of the plant.

- *To encourage more blooms.* Pruning repeat-blooming roses such as **hybrid teas** that produce flowers on current-season's shoots encourages flushes of new growth on which flowers are produced.

- *To keep them confined to their allotted space.* Some roses can be given 3 feet, but in short time they'll scramble for three more. Pruning keeps them in their place so they won't crowd their neighbors.

Pruning can be intimidating, not only because of the thorns but also because of the uncertainty of what and where to cut. It's really not a complicated process. Pruning roses involves three basic cuts:

- **Thinning** is the removal of a shoot at its point of origin on the stem, back to another side branch, or at the base. These cuts open up the plant to improve air movement and sunlight penetration.

- **Cutting back** or **heading back** is pruning back to a bud on the stem. This cut encourages branching by stimulating a few buds behind the cut to grow.

- **Shearing** is an intense form of heading back where multiple cuts are made to produce dense growth. **Miniature roses** and **floribundas** grown as hedges are commonly sheared.

Although pruning methods vary among different classes of roses, they all follow these general rules:

- Use sharp tools to make clean cuts for rapid healing of wounds.

- Always begin by pruning out dead, damaged, and diseased wood (the "3 D's"). *Head* or *cut back* the canes to at least an inch below darkened or discolored areas, making sure you cut back to healthy green wood. Examine the pith or center of the cane. If it's brown, continue pruning back until the pith looks white.

- *Angle* each cut. *Point* your shears at a 45-degree angle towards the center of the shrub, sloping the cut downward from the bud. The dormant bud should be at the top of the angle.

- Make pruning cuts above a bud or branch that faces away from the center of the plant.

- *Remove* the lower of any crisscrossing canes that rub together. Rubbing produces wounds that are open invitations to pests.

- *Prune out* suckers—growths that emerge from below the bud union on grafted roses—at their point of attachment on the rootstock.

- *Thin out* any spindly, weak branches and any canes growing into the center of the bush.

- Allow the natural habit of the plant to guide your cuts.

Pests

Roses are troubled by a wide range of pests; some varieties, however, are more susceptible than others. The easy-care roses listed on the Planting Chart (p. 226–27) are more vigorous and better able to withstand attacks than others, provided you plant and maintain them properly.

To manage rose pests, learn to identify them and follow an Integrated Pest Management approach to deal with them (see the Pest Control in the introduction to Shrubs chapter, p. 253). For information on the intensive culture of exhibition-quality blemish-free roses, contact a consulting rosarian at the Carolina Rose Society.

Carolina Roses

Old Garden Roses	Class	Color	Comments
Mutabilis	China	Yellow blend	Flowers darken with age: opening yellow and changing to orange, pink, and finally to red; introduced before 1894.
Old Blush	China	Medium pink	One of the South's oldest roses and one of the parents crossed by John Champneys of Charleston which gave rise to the Noisette class of roses; introduced in 1752.
Alister Stella Gray	Noisette	Light yellow	Blooms heavily in the spring and sporadically throughout the summer on nearly thornless canes; introduced in 1894.
Lamarque	Climbing Noisette	Yellow-white blend	Fragrant flowers are borne steadily throughout the season; introduced in 1830.
Duchesse de Brabant	Tea	Light pink	Bears fragrant flowers steadily; introduced in 1857.
Mrs. B. R. Cant	Tea	Light pink	Flowers continuously; introduced in 1901.

Species Roses	Class	Color	Comments
White Lady Banks (*Rosa banksiae* var. *banksiae*)	Species	White	Fragrant flowers appear in abundance in early to late spring in full sun or partial shade on thornless canes. Yellow Lady Banks (**R. banksiae** 'Lutea') is a double yellow flowering form; introduced in 1824.
Rugosa Rose (*Rosa rugosa*)	Species	White, pink, red	Tough durable roses sprouting fragrant flowers, attractive crinkled leaves, and colorful hips; heat and cold hardy. Their salt-tolerance makes them suitable for *North Csrolina*'s coastal areas; introduced in 1892.

Modern Roses	Class	Color	Comments
Peace	Hybrid Tea	Yellow blend	World's most famous rose, the long-lasting nearly perfect yellow flowers are edged with pink.
Gold Medal®	Grandiflora	Medium yellow	Considered one of the best grandiflora roses. Fragrant golden-yellow flowers with a hint of red at the tips.
Betty Prior	Floribunda	Medium pink	Fragrant blooms resemble dogwood; flowers heavily.
Gene Boerner	Floribunda	Medium pink	Vigorous and free-flowering with long-lasting blooms.

Carolina Roses

Modern Roses	Class	Color	Comments
Iceberg	Floribunda	White	Best white flower in its class; continuous bloom on nearly thornless canes.
Livin' Easy	Floribunda	Orange blend	Steady bloomer with glossy green leaves.
Nearly Wild	Floribunda	Medium pink	Blooms all season long.
Sexy Rexy®	Floribunda	Medium pink	Continuous display of lightly scented flowers.
Sunsprite	Floribunda	Deep yellow	Steady bloomer; performs best in the cooler regions of the Piedmont and Mountains.
The Fairy	Polyantha	Light pink	Low and compact grower, blooms well into fall.
New Dawn	Large-flowered Climber	Light pink	Fragrant flowers appear with abandon in early summer followed by late-summer repeat bloom.
Pride 'n' Joy™	Miniature	Orange blend	Flowers fade to salmon pink.
Starina®	Miniature	Orange-red	Flowers occur singly and in clusters.

Modern Shrub Roses	Class	Color	Comments
Abraham Darby®	Shrub	Orange-pink	David Austin English rose that combines an old-fashioned look and fragrance with the everblooming habit of a modern rose.
Carefree™ series	Shrub	Pink	Repeat-flowering; Carefree Wonder™ rates highly.
Dream™ series	Shrub	Orange, pink, red, yellow	New millenium introduction; I trialed them for one season and was impressed with their care-free, season-long blooms.
Meidiland™ series	Shrub	Pink, red, or white	Showy and tough repeat-flowering roses suited for a low-maintenance landscape.

Planning

Whether you plan to sprinkle a few roses amongst your perennials and shrubs or have thoughts of producing an everblooming rose border, sit down and take the time to select the right roses for your purpose. Aside from saving you money and sleep, along with alleviating frustration, choosing roses that match your site and your management style will pay big dividends in beauty. Unless you're willing to commit to a regular pesticide program, select durable, easy-care roses.

As you swoon over the colorful catalogs, compile a list of roses that you "just gotta have." Before you mail in your order, compare your list with varieties recommended by the Carolina District Rose Society. Take a look at the *Handbook for Selecting Roses,* a booklet published annually by the American Rose Society (American Rose Society, P.O. Box 30,000, Shreveport, Louisiana 71130-0030; 318-938-5402; http://www.ars.org). It covers both **old garden** and **modern roses** that are evaluated by rosarians across the country. The scores will give a clue to how your choices measure up against others in their class. If it turns out some varieties you have picked have not been tested by the rosarians in the Carolina District Rose Society,

you may enjoy taking it upon yourself to give it a trial in your own garden.

Consider All-America roses as well. All-America Roses Selections, Inc. (AARS) is a nonprofit research organization founded in 1938 for the purpose of evaluating and identifying roses that stand head-and-shoulders above others. Six types of roses can vie for the All-America title each year: **hybrid teas, floribundas, grandifloras, miniatures, climbers,** and **landscape roses.** AARS roses are evaluated in test gardens throughout the U.S. by commercial rose producers. They are scored on such characteristics as vigor, growth habit, hardiness, disease resistance, and flower production.

Before you order, make sure you've got enough room in your garden. Order the plants early and they will arrive at the right time for your area.

Planting

It's time to prepare the site for your roses:

1 For individuals or groups of roses, *dig* and *work the soil*

thoroughly over as large an area as possible. Before digging, make sure the soil is dry enough to work. If soil sticks to the shovel or your shoes, wait a few days to allow the soil to dry. Digging wet clay soil can ruin soil structure, making it more suitable for making bricks than growing roses.

2 *Spread* a 2-to 4-inch layer of organic matter such as compost on the soil surface. *Add* limestone to increase the soil pH of acidic soils or sulfur to decrease the pH of alkaline soils as recommended by the soil-test results. Roses can tolerate a soil pH between 5.5 and 7.0; a pH of 6.2 to 6.8, however, would be ideal. *Mix* these materials into the bed 8 to 12 inches deep. Allow the bed to settle for a few days before planting.

3 Coastal gardeners can select and plant bare-root roses at the middle of the month or later. When selecting a bare-root rose, look for these features:

- *Three or more sturdy canes that show no signs of shriveling or discoloration.*

- *Healthy-looking roots that are well distributed around the plants.*

- *Dormant, leafless canes.* A bare-root rose that has leafed out is in jeopardy, because the leaves are demanding sustenance from the roots. If you choose to purchase plants in this state, *plant* them immediately if the conditions are favorable, or pot them up and *transplant* them later when more favorable conditions exist.

Remember that a grade No. 1 rose will be a better investment than lower grades (which are indicated by higher numbers).

Plant bare-root roses as discussed in the Planting section in the introduction (p. 224).

Space plants according to their growth habit and mature spread. Follow these general spacing guidelines: **hybrid teas** and **grandifloras,** 3 to 4 feet apart; **floribundas,** 2 to 3 feet. **Climbers** need 8 to 12 feet between plants, and **miniatures** between 18 and 24 inches. **Species, shrubs,** and **old garden roses** can be spaced 5 to 6 feet apart.

Coastal gardeners can move their roses to other spots in the garden now. Unless the conditions are dry enough so you can work the soil without damaging its structure, Piedmont gardeners can wait until next month.

Helpful Hint

Finding disease-resistant roses requires careful study and observation. Speak to consulting rosarians with the Carolina District Rose Society, which includes twenty local rose societies in both North and South Carolina. Reach them through the American Rose Society. Ask your county cooperative extension agent about University-based rose variety trials. Finally, monitor other gardens for disease-free varieties that remain healthy and vigorous all season long without being sprayed. These are the ones likely to be resistant to local diseases.

Care for Your Roses

Mountain gardeners should check the winter protection on their roses. If the mulch has been scattered or blown away to expose the crown of the plant, particularly at the bud union, put it back in place.

If you have **miniature roses** indoors as gift plants, they need bright light. Move them to a south-facing window or place them under fluorescent lights.

Pest Control

Insects: Mites can be a problem on **miniature roses** growing indoors. Use insecticidal soap to get rid of them. Before doing so, *check* the label to see if your plant is listed. You may have to test a small area first for signs of injury. It may take seven to ten days for injury symptoms to appear. If your plant shows sensitivity to insecticidal soap, rinse the soap off once the mites are killed.

Apply a dormant horticultural oil in late winter or early spring before bud-break to smother overwintering insects and their eggs. Read the label for cautions on high and low temperature limits at the time of application.

Planning

Roses can be interplanted with annuals, bulbs, and perennials. Winter-blooming annuals and spring-flowering bulbs can fill in around the stark-looking canes of roses that are dormant or easing into growth. During the growing season, roses can bloom at the same time as perennials to create an eye-catching display of color. When roses have finished bearing their first round of flowers and are gearing up for another growth flush, flowering perennials can fill in those voids so your bed or border will always be in bloom.

Planting

Plant bare-root roses as discussed in the Planting section in the introduction (p. 223–24).

If you have to delay planting for a week, store the plants in a cool (above-freezing), dark location such as a refrigerator or garage. Keep the roots moist with sawdust, compost, or peat moss.

To store them temporarily for more than a week, "heel-in" (cover the roots of dormant plants with soil for a short period) the roses in the garden. Pick a well-drained spot and dig a trench about 12 inches deep and wide enough to accommodate the roots. Lay the rose down at a 45-degree angle, and cover the roots and most of the length of their canes.

Greenhouse-grown **miniatures** should be protected from frost and planted after weather has warmed and the chance of freeze injury is past.

Care for Your Roses

Cut and divide outdoor-growing **miniature roses** when they're dormant in the Piedmont and Coastal Plain. Wait until March or April in the Mountains. See Care for Your Roses, April, p. 234)

Pruning

Prune roses that produce flowers on current-season's growth before new growth begins. Valentine's Day is often the recommended pruning time for Coastal Plain gardeners; Piedmont gardeners can wait until the end of the month or early March. Others prune when the **forsythia** is in full bloom. I wait for the rosebuds to start swelling and becoming plump before pruning.

Prune everblooming roses now, including bush roses such as **hybrid teas, grandifloras,** and **floribundas. Miniatures** and repeat-flowering **climbers** that produce flowers on current-season's growth may also be pruned (see March Pruning, p. 232, for instructions). In the Mountains, wait until next month or April, after the coldest part of winter has passed.

Hybrid teas and **grandifloras** are grown for their magnificent flowers. **Hybrid teas** produce single flowers on long stems, while **grandifloras** send up clusters of large flowers on strong, straight stems. *Prune* both classes to outward facing buds to develop an open, bowl-shaped habit.

1 Select three to six of the most vigorous, well-spaced canes (pencil size in diameter or thicker) from **hybrid teas,** and up to eight from **grandifloras.**

2 *Remove* the older canes that are brown or gray at the base.

3 Reduce the length of the canes by one-third or one-half. Generally, do not cut them back lower than 18 inches unless they've been damaged by pests or cold. Alternate the height of these final cuts to outward-growing buds to give your rose an informal look rather than an unnatural-looking "flat top."

Floribundas and **polyanthas** are grown for their grand display of flower clusters. They need a lighter-handed approach that will encourage the production of gobs of flowers all season long.

1 Lightly *head back* the canes either just below where they flowered or down to one-third their length. *Cut back* twiggy clusters to a strong bud. When grown as a hedge they can be sheared with hedge clippers to remove one-third to one-half of their height.

2 *Thin out* the twiggy growth on the inside of the plant.

3 *Remove* a few of the spindly canes at the base to make room for the remaining canes. To produce the maximum number of flowers, leave more canes than you would for **hybrid teas** and **grandifloras.**

Repeat-blooming old garden roses, species, and **shrub roses** that flower on current-season's wood should be pruned right before growth begins in late winter or early spring. They can be tip-pruned throughout the growing season to encourage the production of flower-bearing side shoots.

Watering

Water newly set plants at planting. Keep the soil moist but avoid excessive watering, which can inhibit root growth.

Pest Control

Insects and mites: Apply a dormant oil spray as described in January Pest Control, p. 229. Cane-boring insects such as square-headed wasps and small carpenter bees bore into the pith of cut rose stems, leaving a telltale hole in the tip. The attacked cane wilts and dies back. These pests are not as common as rose aphids and Japanese beetles, so control them only when high numbers are present. After pruning your roses, paint the cuts on stems larger than 1/4 inch in diameter with wood glue or shellac to block borers from entering.

Diseases: *Remove* any of last year's leaves that remain after pruning. Overwintering leaves could harbor disease spores. Apply a fresh layer of compost over the old mulch. Watch for and control blackspot and powdery mildew on rose foliage.

After pruning, apply fungicides to control blackspot on susceptible roses. Powdery mildew–susceptible varieties can be treated with a fungicide (neem oil, lime-sulfur, or others) at the first sign of the disease.

Cankers are brown to black discolored areas on canes and are caused by various fungi. These dead areas often encircle the cane completely and kill all growth above the canker. Sometimes they elongate and extend all the way down to the crown, killing the entire plant. These fungi enter healthy canes through wounds caused by winter injury or improper pruning cuts.

Use sharp tools to produce clean cuts that will heal rapidly. Prune out infected canes, cutting back to healthy tissue. Look at the pith or center of the cane and continue pruning back until the pith looks white. If you cut into diseased canes, disinfect your pruning shears with Lysol®, which is less corrosive than the traditional mixture of water and household bleach (4 parts water to 1 part sodium hypochlorite). This will prevent diseases from spreading to other canes.

Planning

If you have little room for roses in your landscape, plan to go vertical with climbing roses. Allow your budget to dictate the kind of support you need for your climbers. Use existing structures in your landscape such as lampposts, clothesline posts, or porch columns. You can even sink an 8-foot pressure-treated 4×4 about 18 inches into the ground and train a climber onto it. Or link two or three posts together with chain or heavy rope to create a festoon. *Train* the flexible canes of **rambling roses** along the chain so blooms will appear along its length.

Planting

Plant potted roses when they become available in the Piedmont and Coastal Plain. Plant them as early as possible to get them settled in before summer's heat and humidity arrives. In the Mountains, plant dormant bare-root roses about four weeks before the last expected freeze. At the higher elevations in the North Carolina Mountains, where the temperature may drop to zero degrees F, wait until after the last freeze before planting.

Care for Your Roses

Remove the winter coverings from your roses when the **forsythia** is in full bloom. Even **forsythia,** however, can be fooled by sudden blasts of cold air, so be prepared to protect your roses if an unexpected cold-air mass moves in. Get indoor-grown **miniature roses** ready for planting outdoors. Acclimate them gradually to the outside air. After the last freeze, *plant* them in the garden or in outdoor containers.

Watering

Water newly planted roses often enough to keep the roots moist during their first few weeks. Gradually reduce the frequency but not the depth of watering—deep watering encourages deep rooting.

Fertilizing

Fertilize roses after pruning and before they leaf out. Follow soil-test results to supply the necessary nutrients. Use a slow-release fertilizer that contains at least one-third of its total nitrogen in a slowly-available form.

Pruning

Miniature roses are the easiest class to prune. These dense, low-growing roses with small stems, leaves, and flowers range in height from 6 to 18 inches. Use a hedge clipper to trim the tops to about a foot above the soil (height will vary according to variety). Afterwards, use pruning shears to remove any twiggy growth from the center to increase air movement.

Despite their name, **climbing roses** cannot climb but rather lean, relying on their sharp thorns to give them a foothold and to secure their canes to the support. The goal for pruning and training **climbing roses** is to produce a "skeleton" or basic framework of upright canes or "trunks" that bear flower-bearing side shoots. Create this framework by training the shoots onto a support during the first few years. Keep the shoots or "trunks" spaced far apart to allow for air movement and sunlight penetration. When training a **climbing rose** onto a support, keep this rule-of-thumb in mind: orient the shoots horizontally so they will produce flowers along their length. *Follow these guidelines when pruning climbing roses:*

1 Allow **climbers** to become established during the first few years so they produce long, sturdy canes. Don't prune them back too heavily or you can cause climbing sports to revert back to their bush form. Secure the canes with soft twine or green tie-tape. Tie the twine into a figure eight to avoid binding the stem.

2 In early spring before new growth emerges in everblooming climbers, shorten lateral or side shoots to two or three buds.

3 After flowering, examine the framework of vertical canes. *Thin out* thick, brown woody canes that bear few flowers and have less growth compared to the other canes. Since climbing sports do not produce as much vigorous growth as bush roses, try not to remove more than one of the skeletal canes a year. In addition to removing a cane at its base, you can cut back one of the oldest canes to a new side branch to encourage further growth from the base. Fill each vacancy with a flexible new shoot that's growing from the crown at or just above the bud union.

4 On once-blooming **climbers** that produce their heaviest crop of flowers on previous season's growth, *deadhead* the faded flower stems to three or four pairs of leaves. Remove some of the oldest wood at the base as well, provided that you have enough younger canes to replace it.

5 To encourage repeat flowering on everblooming climbers, *head back* the side shoots that have flowered to the lowest pair of five-leaflet leaves close to the main stem.

In many cases, **ground cover roses** are just **climbers** in disguise. Instead of being trained upright, they've been spread to grow along the ground. The objective is to encourage as much ground-covering growth as possible. Tip-prune the ends of the shoots before new growth begins on everblooming roses and after the major flush of bloom from once-bloomers and most of the **old-fashioned roses.** *Thin out* bushy types of **ground cover roses** to prevent the plants from being choked with branches.

Pest Control

Weeds: *Handpull* winter annuals such as henbit and common chickweed to prevent them from going to seed. *Maintain* a 2- to 3-inch layer of mulch to suppress weeds.

Insects: Watch out for aphids and spider mites. Look for aphids clustered near the tips of new shoots and flower buds. Dislodge them with a strong spray of water early in the morning, giving the leaves plenty of time to dry before evening.

Diseases: Inspect your plant for signs of blackspot and powdery mildew. If your roses are plagued by these diseases, either follow a weekly fungicide spray program or plant disease-resistant roses. Although these roses may still get disease, they may be vigorous enough to outgrow infections.

Flower buds and flowers covered with a grayish-brown fuzz might be infected with gray mold, a springtime fungal disease that's active in cool, wet weather. It also attacks new shoots. Collect and discard the infected flowers and promptly prune out discolored canes back to healthy tissue. After pruning, treat plants with a recommended fungicide to protect the wounds.

Planning

If you're serious about growing roses, plan to start a journal this month. Document your observations, thoughts, and plans for the future. Some of the following items can be noted in your journal:

- Bloom dates for each variety.

- Condition of the flowers, leaves, and overall health of your roses.

- Pest problems such as insects, diseases, and weeds.

- Pesticides used, and when they were applied.

- Plants that need to be moved or replaced because they turned out to be "a lotta-care" roses.

Your journal can become a teaching tool, especially when you need the assistance of a county extension agent or a consulting rosarian to help you diagnose a particular problem. The notes you took about weather conditions, fertilizing, watering, and any pest control applications are important clues that can help reveal the answer.

So start writing.

Planting

When planting **climbing roses** next to a wall, place them at least 2 feet away from it. Plant potted roses when the soil is dry enough to be worked.

Pruning

Prune roses to buds that point outward. This encourages good air and sunlight penetration. Dark-colored canes indicate dead wood. Cut back an inch below these darkened areas. If the center of the cane is discolored, cut back further until white pith is exposed. If there are no live buds, *remove* the entire cane or branch.

Care for Your Roses

Divide dormant **miniature** rosebushes that have produced a lot of woody, unproductive growth. Dig them up, then gently twist or cut apart the clumps. Trim away any old woody growth and *replant* the divisions like new bushes.

Loosely tie **climbing roses** to trellises with broad strips of material such as soft twine or nylon. Use a figure-eight tie between the cane

and the trellis so that the tie won't put pressure on or otherwise injure the cane. Do not use wires; they can damage canes.

Last-year's mulch may contain fungal disease spores that can infect your rosebushes. If you haven't done so already, apply fresh mulch to blanket the old mulch. Keep the layer between 2 and 3 inches thick. If you prefer to remove the old mulch, apply it to other areas of the landscape not occupied by roses, or bury it in the garden.

Watering

To prevent water from running off, it is helpful to create a temporary berm, or dike, around newly planted roses in clay soil. *Remove* the berm when the roses become established. Whenever you irrigate, keep the leaves dry to reduce the growth and spread of diseases.

Fertilizing

Fertilize once-blooming roses in early spring before growth begins. Repeat-blooming roses should be fertilized only if necessary. Evaluate the growth and appearance of the plant to decide if fertilizing is necessary. When using a fast-release fertilizer, time your application after each flush of bloom. Only one or two applications may be necessary during the season if you use a slow-release fertilizer. Refer to the fertilizer label for the rate and frequency of application. *Water* afterwards to make the nutrients available to the rose.

Pruning

Remove suckers arising from below the graft union of roses. Cut them off where they attach to the rootstock. If you're not sure of the extent of winter injury, wait until the buds "break" (new growth emerges). *Remove* any dead wood above the bud.

Pest Control

Insects and mites: Inspect your roses for rose aphids and spider mites. See March, p. 233, for controls.

Nematodes: Nematodes are microscopic organisms that live in the soil and attack the roots of plants. They are commonly found in coarse-textured sandy soils, more often than fine-textured clay soils. See July Pest Control on p. 240 for more information.

Helpful Hint

Roses can be rooted by taking softwood cuttings in late spring and summer. This means taking stems from current-season's growth:

1. Fill a 6-inch pot with equal parts of moist peat moss and perlite.

2. Select a stem that has just flowered and is about the diameter of a straw. **Remove** it from the plant.

3. Count upward two or three pairs of leaves from the bottom of this cutting, and make a cut ¼ inch above the topmost bud.

4. Wound the bottom end of the stem with a razor blade or sharp knife by making a ½- to 1-inch vertical slit through the bark on the side opposite the top bud. Roots will emerge from along the edges of the wound.

5. Dip the lower end in a rooting hormone (contains indole-butyric acid or IBA) to encourage uniform rooting. Tap off the excess.

6. Using a pencil, make a hole in the rooting medium and insert the cutting. **Remove** leaves that may be buried in the medium. Firm the medium around it and settle them in with a fine spray of water.

7. Put the pot in a plastic bag and move it to a shaded location outside against the north wall of your house or under a tree. Alternatively, you can sink the pot in the ground in a shaded location and cover the cuttings with a clear plastic 2-liter soda bottle whose bottom has been removed. The soil should be watered to prevent the cuttings from drying out.

8. Open up your mini-hothouse occasionally if there's too much condensation inside. You can unscrew the cap of the soda bottle.

9. The cuttings should root in a month and will send out new leaves if you've been successful. To see if they've rooted, give the stem a gentle tug. If it resists, it has rooted. **Remove** the bag. Pot up the cuttings in individual pots and keep them moist and shaded. Gradually expose the rooted cuttings to stronger light to harden them off. After a couple of weeks, **transplant** them.

Planning

Plan to water your roses efficiently this summer when hot weather arrives. The general recommendation is to apply 1 to 2 inches of water on a weekly basis. One inch of water is equivalent to applying 5 to 6 gallons of water to a 3-foot-square area with the rosebush in the center. With clay soils, which hold more water than sandy soils, apply this amount once a week; with sandy soils, however, it's best to split it into two applications of 3 gallons, each spaced a few days apart. Adjust the amount to account for rainfall and prevailing weather conditions. If the weather has been cloudy and rains have been adequate, watering may not be necessary. Rely on common sense and observation:

- *Check* the soil. A sandy soil that's dry to a depth of 2 to 4 inches indicates a need for water. In clay soil, simply not being able to dig easily down to 2 to 4 inches is enough to know that it's dry.

- Look at your roses. If the leaves are grayish-green in color and slightly wilted, moisture could be lacking. Waiting until the roses are completely wilted before watering can affect the health and survival of your roses.

Planting

A potted rose makes a great gift for Mother's Day. Refer to the Planting section of the introduction (p. 223) for details.

Pruning

Old garden roses, species, and **shrub roses** come in a wide range of sizes and shapes. Generally, allow the natural shape of the plant to guide your pruning cuts. Hold off on pruning them until they've achieved a decent size, perhaps after the second or third growing season. Here are a few pruning tips:

- *Shorten* long, vigorous canes by up to one-third to encourage production of flower-bearing side shoots.

- *Tip-prune* last year's lateral or side shoots to 6 inches in length.

- On established plants, *remove* one or two of the oldest canes that produce few, if any, flowers, maintaining a balance between old and new growths.

To avoid pruning flower buds, remember that one-time bloomers or roses that produce their heaviest flush on old wood should be pruned after flowering in the spring. For shrub roses that produce attractive hips or rose fruits, such as hybrid **rugosa roses,** prune only some of the shoots, preserving some of the hip-bearing branches.

As befits their name, **ramblers** (forerunners of today's large-flowered climbers) will ramble and scramble hither and yon if allowed. They'll do it beautifully, however, even though they generally bloom only once in early summer. Pruning and training a **rambler** is akin to housebreaking a pet: start early and be consistent or you'll be left with a mess.

1 When the flowers fade, deadhead the flowering shoots by cutting them back to three or four leaf pairs.

2 **Ramblers** tend to sprout more new canes than most **climbers,** and it's the one-year-old canes that produce flowers. So make room for new canes by taking out one-third of the oldest canes—provided that you have enough young replacements. Before removing any of the oldest canes, take a look at the new ones. Some canes will emerge from the base, but others will sprout higher up on older wood. Prune out the oldest wood that has little or no new growth.

3 *Tie* the vigorous new canes to their supports. Since **ramblers** have long flexible canes, try spiraling them around arches or pillars, or festoon them through chains. Bend them sideways to encourage flowering along their length.

4 Finally, cut back any wayward limbs that have outgrown their space.

Once-blooming **climbers** produce their heaviest crop of flowers on last-year's growth, so prune them after flowering:

1 *Deadhead* the faded flower stems to three or four pairs of leaves.

2 Examine the framework of vertical canes. *Thin out* thick, brown woody canes that bore few flowers and had less growth compared to the other canes. Before doing so, make sure you have enough younger canes to replace the ones you remove.

3 Tie in younger canes growing from the crown at or just above the bud union to fill in the openings.

Deadheading is a form of pruning that involves the removal of dead or spent flowers during the season to improve a rose's appearance and to remove potential harboring sites for disease organisms. Deadheading also encourages the production of more flowers on **remontant** or repeat-flowering rose varieties. To deadhead, remove the flower by making a diagonal cut ¼ inch above the first compound leaf that has five leaflets, otherwise known as a "five." (Roses produce compound leaves containing three, five, and seven leaflets.) On young,

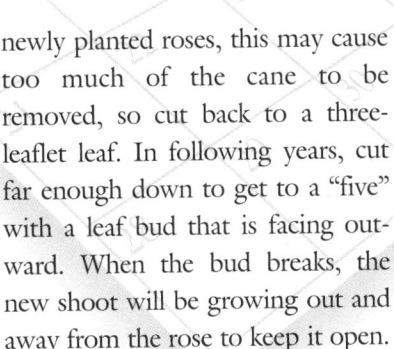

Deadheading

newly planted roses, this may cause too much of the cane to be removed, so cut back to a three-leaflet leaf. In following years, cut far enough down to get to a "five" with a leaf bud that is facing outward. When the bud breaks, the new shoot will be growing out and away from the rose to keep it open.

Watering

See April, p. 234.

Fertilizing

See April, p. 234.

Pest Control

Insects and mites: Be on the lookout for damage caused by rose aphids, spider mites, and flower thrips. Take necessary action if their feeding is more than you or your roses will tolerate.

Diseases: Leaves attacked by blackspot and powdery mildew should be picked up and discarded. To improve the effectiveness of fungicide sprays, practice good sanitation: clean up any fallen leaves and faded blooms, prune out dead, damaged, and diseased canes, and replace mulch each spring.

Planning

As part of your summer vacation plans, why not find some time to visit private and public gardens that feature roses. Seeing those extraordinary roses in the flesh that you've seen only in catalogs can be a priceless inspiration.

Some notable rose gardens are the All-America Rose Selections Public Gardens. These accredited gardens showcase those three or four exceptional roses selected from thousands each year. Winners of this coveted title are chosen from six types of roses: **hybrid teas, floribundas, grandifloras, miniatures, climbers,** and **landscape roses.** Here are the AARS gardens in the Carolinas:

- North Carolina Biltmore Estate in Asheville

- Tanglewood Park Rose Garden in Clemmons

- Fayetteville Rose Garden at Fayetteville Technical Community College

- Raleigh Municipal Rose Garden in Raleigh

- Reynolds Rose Gardens of Wake Forest University in Winston-Salem

- South Carolina Edisto Memorial Gardens in Orangeburg

Don't forget your camera and gardening journal. Enjoy!

Planting

If you happen to see a variety that you like in your local nursery or garden center, buy it—but be careful. Although container-grown roses can be transplanted this month, you need to pay careful attention to watering and mulching. Such roses are under a lot of stress from heat and humidity and can easily be forgotten when stuck somewhere in the landscape. It may be better to keep it in the container close to the house so that it can get the attention it needs. Plant it in the fall when weather becomes more favorable.

Care for Your Roses

Climbing roses may not produce canes near the base after a period of years. If removing some of the oldest canes doesn't spark any growth, try *notching.* Make a cut above a bud near the base of the plant by slicing one-third of the way through a stem. This tends to force that bud into growth.

Watering

Keep the following "ground rules" in mind when watering your roses this summer:

- Newly planted roses need to be watered often enough to prevent the soil from drying out as they settle into their new surrounding. Reduce the frequency of watering gradually, but continue to water deeply to encourage the development of a deep, extensive root system.

- Roses on sandy soils will require more-frequent watering than roses on clay soils.

- Roses will need more water when the temperatures are high than when they're cool.

- *Water* deeply and infrequently, wetting as much of the root zone area as possible. Roots may extend to a depth of 6 to 12 inches. The goal is to produce deeply rooted plants. Shallow, frequent sprinklings on established plants encourage shallow rooting.

- Keep the leaves dry by applying water to the soil surface. Fungal diseases such as blackspot rely on moisture to infect and spread.

- *Mulch* your roses with a 2- to 3-inch layer. Organic mulches—compost, pine needles ("straw"), shredded leaves, and wood—conserve moisture, suppress weeds, and supply nutrients as they decompose. Keep the mulch a few inches away from the crown.

Fertilizing

Avoid excessive fertilization. It produces the soft, succulent growth favored by pests. Try to grow your roses on the "lean and mean" side. Evaluate the quality and quantity of flowers and shoots produced by your roses, and decide if a boost of fertilizer is warranted. Never skimp on building up the natural fertility of the soil with applications of organic mulches such as compost. If you used a slow-release fertilizer early in the year, *check* the label and evaluate the growth and appearance of your everblooming roses to see if a second application is warranted. Supplement mulch with well-rotted horse or cow manure to add nutrients.

Pruning

Cut few if any flowers during the first blooming season after planting. By removing only flowers and not stems you will encourage plants to develop into large bushes by fall, at which time some flowers and stems may be cut. *Deadhead* flowers as soon as they have passed their peak. If allowed to remain on the plant, the flower heads will develop seedpods (also called hips) that draw heavily on the plant's food supply. Always use sharp pruning shears and cut on a downward slant from the bud. *Remove* any spindly shoots or suckers originating below the graft union, or any damaged, diseased, or dead canes. To produce specimen flowers on **hybrid tea** or **garden roses,** *remove* flower buds that have developed on shoots other than the main one. Allow only one flower bud to develop and mature on each main shoot. *Prune* once-flowering **climbers** and **ramblers** that bloom on last year's growth. *Thin out* any of the oldest canes to make room for new ones from the base. Long canes that have to be removed should be cut out in a piecemeal manner. Cut the cane into 8- to 12-inch sections and *remove* them one at a time. It's far easier to deal with the cane in short bites than to wrestle all of its length out at once. Head back any wayward canes to keep them confined to their support. Refer to May Pruning on p. 236 for more details.

Pest Control

Insects and mites: Pests to watch for include rose aphids, spider mites, thrips, and Japanese beetles. *Handpick* Japanese beetles and discard them in a jar of soapy water. Neem can be applied to the leaves to reduce feeding by adults. Use other insecticides for heavy infestations.

Diseases: Be on the watch for blackspot and powdery mildew. To head off disease resistance when using synthetic fungicides, switch back and forth between different kinds.

Weeds: Handpull weeds when they're young and easier to remove. *Suppress* their growth with a shallow layer of compost.

Planning

This is the perfect month to find a soft chair, a cool drink, and another good book (besides this one). It's time to kick back and enjoy the beautiful fruits of your earlier labors. The book you select might offer the lore of roses. The beautiful flowers, the exquisite fragrances, the nutritious rose hips, all set among vicious thorns, is the stuff of poetry and novels. Much has been written since roses were first cultivated during the Shen Nung dynasty in China (2737–2697 B.C.). Use these summer doldrums to learn more about the less-strenuous side of roses. It can add a new dimension to your enjoyment of them.

Planting

If you must plant potted roses now, *water them thoroughly* to settle them in. Keep them well watered to speed up their establishment. If you can, delay the project until fall, when the temperatures are cooler and less stressful for the rose and you.

Care for Your Roses

Roses may take a rest, as you should, when the daytime temperatures ease into the 90s. Plants in full summer sun are especially affected. Unless you're willing to push them with adequate water and fertilizer, give 'em a break.

Do not fertilize unless the plants are growing vigorously and showing "hunger" signs. Prune off faded flowers and cut back any weak canes to prepare the plant for a long blooming spell in the fall.

Watering

See May Planning, p. 236.

Fertilizing

Do not fertilize your roses unless you are willing to support their growth with regular watering. Water is necessary to making the fertilizer available to the roots, but it is important to keep that new growth healthy and alive. In the hotter parts of the Carolinas, roses can be rested this month. When the cooler fall temperatures arrive, you can resume feeding and water them for a fabulous fall display.

Pest Control

Insects: The following insects are active now, along with their telltale signs: Japanese beetles skeletonize leaves and feed on flower buds and flowers; rose aphids occur in clusters near the tips of shoots and their feeding causes leaves to become wrinkled, sticky, and sometimes coasted with a black sooty mold; spider mites cause yellow or bronze stippling on the leaf surface; thrips damage flower buds, creating streaks or spots on the open blooms and brown edges on flower buds that fail to bloom.

Nematodes: Nematodes are microscopic organisms that live in the soil and attack the roots of plants. They are more commonly found in coarse-textured sandy soils than in fine-textured clay soils. One type, the root-knot nematode, produces small galls or swellings on the roots. Nematode-infested roots cannot take up water or fertilizer as well as healthy ones. The plants may be weak-looking, stunted, and wilted. Their leaves turn yellow or off-color and drop off earlier than normal.

If you suspect nematodes, have your soil assayed by the NC Department of Agriculture Agronomic Division. South Carolina residents can submit soil samples to the Agricultural Service Laboratory at Clemson University. Submit samples

Helpful Hint

Follow these steps to conserve water by using it more efficiently while maximizing its effectiveness:

1 Amend the soil prior to planting. Use organic matter such as shredded leaves, compost, well-rotted manure to help the soil hold on to moisture, especially in sandy soils, and to improve aeration of clay soils. Work the soil as deeply as possible to encourage deep rooting.

2 Mulch. Apply a 2- to 3-inch layer of organic materials to reduce water evaporation from the soil. Use whatever is inexpensive and available such as compost, pine needles or "pine straw," shredded leaves, bark, or wood.

3 Fertilize moderately. Fertilization requires watering to make the nutrients available to the plant. It also encourages growth which, in turn, needs to be supported by more water. Consider using slow-release fertilizers that produce moderate growth. Fertilize moderately according to soil-test results. Use natural fertilizers with "slowly available" or "water-insoluble" nitrogen and synthetic fertilizers containing slow-release nitrogen, such as urea formaldehyde or sulfur-coated urea. The nitrogen in these types of fertilizer does not quickly wash away, and it provides green color without causing excessive leaf growth.

4 Use drip irrigation for efficient watering. These systems use emitters, drip collars, or drip tubing to apply water right to the soil surface. Another advantage is that they keep the leaves dry and thus avoid foliar diseases. On clay soils, where run-off can occur when watering with a hose, this waste of water is greatly reduced. Coastal gardeners who have saline water will benefit from drip-irrigation systems. They use less water to moisten the root zones of your plants, putting less salt in the soil. Planting raised beds will also make it easier to flush out accumulated salts with irrigation water and rainfall.

5 Water deeply. Encourage the growth of deep, extensive roots by watering to a depth of 6 to 12 inches.

6 In addition to relying on rain gauges and weather forecasts, serious water-conservationists may want to invest in devices that measure moisture tension—the amount of force holding water to the soil particles. As the soil dries, the moisture tension increases, making it more difficult for the plant to absorb water. These devices detect when a critical level is reached beyond which the plant will become stressed. With this information, you can irrigate and avoid the crisis. Among these instruments are tensiometers, gypsum moisture blocks, and neutron probes.

through your county extension office. If nematodes are a threat, the best defense is to keep the plants healthy. Add organic matter such as compost, com- *posted pine bark, or peat moss to improve soil structure and moisture retention in sandy soils. This not only make a better growing environment for the* *plant but also creates a favorable environment for the growth of natural predators of the nematode.*

Planning

The cool early mornings and evenings during the "dog days of August" are a fitting time to plan on renovating beds and preparing new ones. Plan—don't plant, unless you're in the Mountains and the daytime temperatures are inviting enough to work the beds. In the Piedmont clay soils, which may require a pickaxe this month, wait until next month or October before getting to work. If your roses were planted in low spots and aren't thriving, now is the time to consider moving them in the next few months when they're dormant, building raised beds, or installing drainage tiles to carry away excess water. Determine the roses that will have to be moved in the next couple of months. Mark the ones to be transplanted with colorful tape.

Planting

Potted roses can be planted in the Mountains. They ought to have plenty of time to get established before cold weather arrives. Pay attention to regular watering during the first few weeks after planting. Water is the most important "soil amendment" when establishing plants.

Care for Your Roses

If you rested your roses last month, Mountain and Piedmont gardeners can jump-start everbloomers into growth for a fall-flowering display. Coastal Plain gardeners can wait until later this month or early next month.

Watering

See May Planning, p. 236.

Fertilizing

Depending on the fertility of your soil, everblooming roses may require a little boost from a fast-release fertilizer. Follow label directions to determine the amount to apply.

Pruning

Remember the 3 D's when visiting the garden: damaged, diseased, or dead twigs must go.

Remove any suckers from the rootstocks of grafted plants. The leaves on these shoots will look different from the variety.

Pest Control

Insects and mites: Inspect your roses for Japanese beetles, rose aphids, and spider mites. Evaluate the extent of injury and decide on the level of control. Should you resort to handpicking Japanese beetles? Or is the infestation bad enough that you should cover the roses with cheesecloth or netting? Are they present in such high numbers that chemical control is the best course of action?

Coastal Plain gardeners confronted with root-knot nematodes (see July Pest Control on p. 240 for more information) should plant roses grafted onto *Rosa fortuniana*, a rootstock highly recommended for sandy southeastern soils. This heat-tolerant rootstock is resistant to root knot nematodes. Unfortunately, roses on these rootstocks can be difficult to find. Your best bet is to buy them from catalogs that specify the rootstock used.

Diseases: Watch out for blackspot and powdery mildew. Warm, humid days and cool night temperatures favor the growth of powdery mildew.

Rose mosaic virus is the most common viral disease of roses. Symptoms usually occur on new growth: crinkly deformed leaves, misshapen buds and flowers, leaves with blotches of yellow, ring patterns of light green to yellow lines on the leaves, or a mottling of different shades of green on the leaf. Rose mosaic virus makes a rose less vigorous, reduces the size and number of flowers, and sometimes deforms them. The plant is stunted and the bud graft may fail, killing the top variety and leaving the rootstock.

Rose mosaic is systemic, meaning that it can be found in all parts of the plant except the few cells at the tips of the growing points. Infected plants may decline in vigor and become stunted so your only course of action is to remove them. Pruning away the afflicted parts will not remove the virus from your rose. There are no chemicals that cure a virus-infected plant or any

Helpful Hints

A simple way of propagating roses, particularly **shrub roses** that have long, pliable stems, is by layering:

1 **Bend** one of the lowest stems to the ground in early spring.

2 **Wound** the underside of the stem and cover it with soil. Hold it in place with a piece of wire bent to a hairpin shape and pushed into the ground. Do not bury the shoot tip.

If you layer now, the shoots will usually be rooted by the end of the growing season. Then you can sever from the parent and transplant. Shoots layered later in the summer should be left through the winter and separated in the spring.

that protect plants from becoming infected. This particular virus spreads through the propagation of infected plants, as when virus-infected plant material is budded or grafted to a healthy plant. Since there is little natural spread of rose mosaic viruses, plants that develop mosaic symptoms in the rose garden do not need to be replaced as long as their growth is acceptable.

The only control for viruses is prevention: avoid purchasing plants showing mosaic symptoms. The industry is taking steps to rid rose cultivars of viruses. The plants are extensively tested to be sure that the virus cannot be detected in the treated material. Plants that pass the test are used to propagate virus-free stock.

Weeds: Handpull grassy and broadleaf weeds from your rose beds. *Maintain* a shallow mulch layer to suppress their growth.

Planning

Make plans this month to order roses for delivery in December on the Coast, and early next year elsewhere. As the saying goes, "the early bird gets the worm." Select roses for their flowers, fragrance, and ability to withstand the rigors of summer heat and humidity. Disease resistance should be as important as the appearance of the plant. Refer to your gardening journal to help you make the right selections and to avoid those plants that couldn't measure up in your garden. Some companies have deadlines for accepting orders, so once you've ogled the photographs, start in on the bland-looking order form and make a notation in your calendar.

Planting

It is a good time to plant roses. Look for roses that you can purchase as replacements, or other good roses that deserve to be in your garden.

Care for Your Roses

Continue tying up the canes of climbing roses, securing them sideways to encourage horizontal growth.

Watering

Fall is one of the driest seasons in the Carolinas. Whenever you water, keep the leaves dry to reduce the growth and spread of diseases.

Fertilizing

Stop fertilizing roses six weeks before the average first freeze date in your area to allow the new growth to harden off, preparing the roses for their winter rest.

If you didn't do so last month, Piedmont and Coastal gardeners can fertilize everblooming roses with a fast-release fertilizer if necessary. *Water* afterwards to make the nutrients available to the roses.

Pruning

Roses in the Piedmont and Coast areas can be deadheaded and pruned to encourage new growth now that the cooler temperatures of fall are on the way. In the Mountains, stop deadheading roses so the seedpods, or rose hips, will mature. Instead, grab faded petals in your hand and pluck them from the hip. The colorful hips add an attractive feature to the win-

ter garden. Producing them also encourages the rose to focus its energy on "hardening off," in anticipation of winter dormancy.

Pest Control

Insects and mites: Rose aphids and spider mites may still be active. Evaluate the extent of injury and decide if pest control measures are warranted. Use a water wand to wash mites off of plants on a weekly basis, preferably early in the morning.

Diseases: Clean up fallen rose leaves. They can harbor disease and insect pests over the winter if allowed to remain on the ground. Keep the rose plants clean, and the area around their feet clean and free of debris. During the growing season, pick up and remove fallen leaves.

Weeds: keep the area around the roses free of weeds to eliminate any overwintering hideouts for two-spotted spider mites.

Helpful Hints

Growing roses near walkways or front porches creates a hazardous situation for passersby who may find themselves pierced by thorns. Fortunately, not all roses are equipped with body-piercing thorns. Botanically, they're not thorns, they're prickles—but they hurt anyway. For these situations, consider thornless or nearly thornless roses. Your children will be out of harm's way, and weeding won't be a bloody venture. Roses that have smooth or nearly thornless canes are: **Lady Banks Rose** (species; white and yellow-flowered varieties); **swamp rose (*R. palustris*); prairie rose (*R. setigera* var. *serena*); Zephirine Drouhin** (bourbon; cerise pink); **Paul Neyron** (hybrid perpetual; pink); and **Marie Pavie** (polyantha; creamy-white). Experiment with these and other thornless roses as well. Thorny roses do have their place in your landscape. They can be used as barriers to prevent people from taking shortcuts through your garden, or to keep your neighbor's roaming dog on his side of the hedge. Unfortunately, deer are unfazed by them.

Try growing a rose using seed from the hips that you find on your plants in the fall. Just be aware that the seedlings, especially those of hybrid roses, will not be identical to the rose from which you collected the seed. You may get lucky and end up with your own new, highly sought-after rose. Here's how to collect and sow the seeds:

1   **Harvest** the ripe hips soon after they turn color. Though the color varies according to species and cultivar, expect the hips to change to red, yellow, or orange. Collect them soon after they color up: the longer you allow them to ripen, the more dormant the seeds will become, further delaying germination.

2   **Slice** each hip from top to bottom in two or three places with a knife; **peel** each section open to expose the seeds. **Soak** the seeds in water for twelve to twenty-four hours. **Drain** the seeds, then **mix** them with equal parts of moistened sphagnum peat moss and vermiculite in a plastic bag. Seal the bag and place it in your refrigerator crisper for about three months, which is usually adequate for hybrid rose seeds. This exposure to cool temperatures is called **moist-chilling** or **stratification** and is necessary to encourage uniform germination.

3   After this conditioning, take the seeds out of the refrigerator and **sow** them in a seed flat, which is basically a shallow wooden, plastic, or aluminum container with drainage holes. Use the same medium you used for stratification. Move the flat to a sunny location offering bright indirect sunlight. This can be a room maintained at 65 to 70 degrees Fahrenheit, outdoors on the north side of your house, or in a cold frame. The seedlings can be transplanted when they develop two or three sets of true leaves (the leaves that follow the first "seed leaves" or cotyledons). Use 3-inch pots and treat them as potted roses.

During the first few months, the seedlings often produce tiny flowers. You will have to wait until the roses mature to see the true size and form of the flowers. You may want to cull out some of the seedlings on the basis of flower color alone. The seedling roses can be transplanted outdoors.

Planning

Identify beds whose soil will have to be tested. Soil testing is best done every two or three years. Contact your cooperative extension service office for soil-testing materials. You can take samples this month, or wait until the cooler fall weather arrives. This is also a good month to think about creating new beds, keeping in mind the three basic requirements of roses:

1 Six hours of direct sunlight per day.

2 A well-drained, fertile location.

3 Room to grow.

Plan on creating narrow beds, about 4 to 5 feet wide, so you can reach the plants from both sides. This will make chores like deadheading, watering, fertilizing, and pest control easier. Gaining access from the sides will also prevent you from walking inside the bed and compacting the soil.

Mountain gardeners who live where the temperatures reach 10 degrees Fahrenheit should plan to put their roses to sleep under protective blankets of soil or mulch. This will protect them from freezing temperatures and the seesawing weather patterns of winter, which can tease a dormant bud into waking up too early. Make plans to find and stock-pile dry mulching materials such as wood chips, shredded leaves, and evergreen branches.

Planting

Fall is a good season for planting in the milder areas of the Carolinas. Coastal gardeners and those in warmer parts of the Piedmont can even plant throughout late fall and into winter if temperatures are mild. The welcome cooler temperatures are important to us, and also to the roses. It lets them concentrate on producing roots and settle in as the tops slow down and become dormant. Follow the steps in the Planting section of the introduction (p. 224).

Now is a good time to move roses that have outgrown their location. Piedmont and Coastal gardeners can postpone moves until next month or December, depending on how mild the temperatures are. Here's how to do it:

1 *Cut out* all dead wood and twiggy undergrowth.

2 With soft twine such as jute, slowly draw the canes together into a bundle. You can cut them back, but if it has taken many years to produce this growth, you may want to save it.

3 Use a spade to *cut* the roots, starting 1 or 2 feet from the center of the rose, getting as much of the rootball as possible. The size of the rootball will depend on how much you or a friend can physically manage. Drive the spade as deep as it will go.

4 Using a spading fork (it has four straight prongs), *lift up* the rose. *Cut* any stubborn roots with pruning shears or your spade.

5 *Slide* the rootball onto a tarp that's about 6 square feet, or large enough to allow you to wrap up the rootball to prevent it from falling apart. If the rose is dormant and the temperatures are cool, you can shave or shake off some of the soil (in most cases all of it) and treat the plant like a large bare-root rose.

6 *Transplant* the rose into its new location as soon as possible. If you take the bare-root approach, protect the roots from drying out. *Moisten* them with water or *cover* them with wet newspaper during the move.

7 The site should be prepared as discussed in the introduction (p. 223). After planting, *water it in* to settle the soil and follow

up with a 2- to 3-inch layer of mulch. You can keep the canes secured with twine for protection from damaging winter winds, or the twine can be removed now.

Care for Your Roses

If your **climbing roses** are in an exposed location, tie them up firmly with broad strips of rags so that the wind will not whip them against the trellis and bruise the bark. Roses grown in containers need to be put in the ground, container and all, in a protected area of the landscape. *Mulch* with a layer of compost.

Watering

Water newly planted roses if there's insufficient rain. Fall can be dry time in the Carolinas. Water deeply and infrequently.

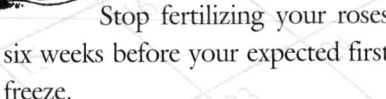

Fertilizing

Stop fertilizing your roses six weeks before your expected first freeze.

Pruning

Stop deadheading spent flowers. *Remove* petals with your hand to allow the rose hips to form, which helps trigger winter dormancy.

Pest Control

Spider mites: Sorry, but they can still be active in the warmer parts of the Carolinas. Since your roses will shed their leaves soon, control may not be necessary. Controlling the overwintering eggs with a dormant horticultural oil this fall when the rose goes dormant may be all that's needed.

Diseases: Rake and clean up the garden to get rid of blackspot spores that can overwinter on the leaves. If powdery mildew is a problem, control may not be necessary, since we're approaching the end of the season and leaves will be shed.

Planning

Update your gardening journal and make plans for improvements next year. What were the most troublesome insects and diseases this season? Were there problems with the pest control measure you selected? Perhaps you need to make plans to dig out some roses and replace them early next year.

Think about the roses that seemed to "take a lickin' and keep on tickin'." Was it the rose itself, or could its performance also be attributed to the growing environment—plenty of air circulation, diligent removal of infected leaves, adequate water and fertility? Spend some time pondering these factors, along with others, and document them in your journal.

Planting

It is still time to plant and move roses. *Water* them thoroughly and *mulch* to keep them from freezing.

Care for Your Roses

Prepare your roses for winter by allowing rose hips to form. If you haven't done so already, have a soil test taken of your rose beds. At least every two or three years, have your soil tested through your cooperative extension service to determine soil pH and fertility levels. **Miniature roses** need lots of light to bloom indoors. Give them at least four hours of direct sunlight from a south-facing window, or put them under cool-white fluorescent lights to receive at least sixteen hours of light daily. The tops of the plants should be 2 to 4 inches below lights.

Watering

As cold weather sets in, reduce water, but do not allow roses, especially those that have recently been planted, to dry out completely. Plants need water during dry spells, even during the winter months.

Fertilizing

Do not fertilize at this time of the year.

Miniature roses growing indoors under artificial lights can be fertilized with a liquid water-soluble fertilizer to encourage flowering.

Pruning

Allow the hips to signal dormancy. It's not necessary to prune back rose plants to make them attractive in winter. If you do this before a freeze, you may awaken dormant buds, which will produce new growth that will only be killed by freezing temperatures. Even gardeners along the warmer coast should wait until January (at the earliest) to begin pruning roses. If a rose's height will put it in peril of being damaged by strong winter winds, prune back only after a freeze.

Pest Control

Spider mites: Spider mites are a serious pest of **miniature roses,** especially indoors. To reduce their numbers, bathe each plant once a week under running water, washing the undersides of leaves as well as the tops. Their population can also be checked with applications of insecticidal soap.

Diseases: Clean up rose beds. Rake fallen leaves and compost them, or bury them in the vegetable garden.

Helpful Hints

To help your roses survive the winter, gardeners, particularly Mountain gardeners, need to keep in mind:

The plants should go into the winter in a vigorous state. Plants stressed by drought or lack of fertility, or those defoliated by pests, are more inclined to succumb to cold then robust plants.

Roses should be grown in a well-drained location. Roses will not tolerate "wet feet," especially during the winter months.

Winter winds can dry out the canes of exposed roses, loosen a rose's footing, or bruise canes as they're jostled by the wind. You can plant roses near walls or fences or erect temporary windbreaks of burlap, or the canes may benefit from staking or being tied down. **Plant** the roses at a distance that is at least four to six times their mature height from the windbreak.

Mountain gardeners are faced with the freezing and thawing of the soil, frost-heaving, that can lift up plants, causing them to dry out. Carefully **push down** any plants and **maintain** a mulch layer to moderate soil temperatures.

Own-rooted roses are varieties grown from cuttings. **Old garden roses** are typically grown on their own roots, as are some **modern roses.** Own-rooted roses offer an advantage in the Mountains where winters are very cold. If the top is lost to winter cold, but the rootstock survives, the variety won't be lost. New growth will arise from the roots. When you lose the top of a grafted rose, what's left is a rootstock designed for durability rather than for beauty.

Pruning will begin early next year. Assemble your pruning tools and equipment. If you need any of these tools, put them on your Christmas wish list. **Tools needed for pruning:**

- pruning shears. The proper tool for most pruning is a sharp clean set of bypass pruners with curved blades that cut with a scissorlike action and give the cleanest cut. Pruning shears cut canes up to $1/4$ inch in diameter. The bypass types are preferred over anvil pruners. These have a single cutting blade that, when cutting, presses the stem against a flat piece of metal (anvil). They should not be used for roses because they crush the stem being cut.

- long-handled lopping shears (12- to 18-inch-long handles) to cut out thick canes up to one-half inch in diameter. Select bypass types with lightweight metal alloy handles.

- a keyhole saw about 7 to 8 inches long with a thin pointed tip allows you to maneuver into tight corners. It can be used to cut very large canes ($1/2$ inch diameter or greater) near the crown. **Remove** large stubs close to the bud union.

- thorn-proof gloves with gauntlet-type cuffs to protect your hands and forearms when pruning.

- hedge shears to prune **miniature roses** or **floribunda** hedges.

- spray bottle of Lysol®. Use it to disinfect tools when cutting into cankers or canes infected with crown gall disease. It's less corrosive than bleach.

Planning

Look at this month as a time of reflection. Review what happened during this past year. If this was your first year growing roses and you've been pleased by your performance and theirs, make plans to get better.

Planting

Weather permitting, Coastal Plain and Piedmont gardeners can plant bare-root roses or move roses to other parts of the landscape.

Care for Your Roses

Roses that are newly planted in the fall will benefit from winter protection, especially in the higher elevations in the Mountains and valleys. Late-summer and early-fall-planted roses also need to be protected. Tender roses such as **teas, Chinas,** and **Noisettes** should be protected with mulch to protect their roots and above-ground canes:

1 ***Prune out*** any dead or diseased canes.

2 ***Mound*** the plant with dry materials like wood chips, leaves, or pine needles 1 to 2 feet high and as wide at the base of the plant. Carefully ***shake*** the mulch into the center of the plant around each cane.

3 To keep the mulch contained, surround the shrub with chicken wire that's been staked into place and fill this cylinder with mulch.

When the buds of **miniature roses** have started to open, bring them into living areas to enjoy. After the flowers fade, return them to a bright location receiving at least four hours of direct sunlight, or position them beneath artificial lights. Shear away dead flowers and allow about six weeks for a new flush of flowers to develop.

Watering

Keep **miniature roses** well watered to encourage the production of new shoots and flowers.

Fertilizing

Do not fertilize roses this month. **Miniature roses** growing indoors can be fed with a liquid houseplant fertilizer.

Pruning

Winter winds can aggravate tall-growing **hybrid teas,** breaking their canes and injuring their roots as they're tossed about by the wind. Wait until they're dormant to cut them back to 3 feet, thereby lessening their chances of getting tousled by the wind.

Pest Control

Spider mites: Watch out for spider mites on indoor **miniature roses.** Use insecticidal soap to control them. Heavily infested roses should be quarantined to prevent the mites from infesting other plants.

Insects: Apply a dormant oil spray early in the month, before new growth emerges, to control overwintering insect and spider mite eggs.

Diseases: Blackspot overwinters on fallen leaves and canes. Rake out the leaves and compost them or bury them in the flower border or vegetable garden away from any roses.

Weeds: *Handpull* any young winter annual weeds, or cover them with mulch. Weeding is never fun, but the cooler temperatures can make it more bearable.

Shrubs

Shrubs are a gardener's best friends. For starters, they come in a dizzying array of shapes, sizes, forms, and colors. Some have soft, naturally billowy forms, others sport showy, fragrant flowers or brightly colored berries, and still others deliver stunning fall color. Some shrubs can be used as ground covers with their wide-spreading branches and low growth habit, while other, taller-growing shrubs can be pruned to look like small trees.

Shrubs can be used in a variety of ways: foundation plantings, flower borders, screens, hedges, and stand-alone "look-at-me" accent plants. They also lend themselves to being sheared and clipped into geometrical, sometimes whimsical shapes.

Like best friends, shrubs are always there through each changing season. For year-round appeal, unite shrubs and other plants in your landscape—small trees, ground covers, perennials, and annuals—to match and contrast leaf colors and textures, forms, and flowers.

Planning

Before you introduce any new shrubs into your landscape, refer to the planning process described in the introduction to this book (see p. 10). Once you've determined where you want your shrubs, select shrubs that match the conditions in your landscape. Pay attention to the following factors.

Light requirements: Does your site have full sun, partial sun, or shade? What do the shrubs prefer?

Drainage: In general, plants prefer well-drained soils. Plants like **azaleas** and **boxwoods** will wilt and die in a constantly damp low spot faster than you can say *Phytophthora* (that's the root rot that preys on plants intolerant of "wet feet"). If you have such "hog wallows," choose shrubs that are adapted to boggy conditions. These include **anisetree (*Illicium*)**, **Virginia sweetspire (*Itea virginica*)**, and **summersweet (*Clethra alnifolia*)**.

Temperature: Will the shrubs be exposed to freezing temperatures or extreme heat?

Space limitations: What is the eventual mature height and spread of the shrub? How fast will it grow? In limited spaces, select smaller, more compact shrubs over the vigorous growers that soon engulf windows and porches.

Function: Shrubs can be used in a variety of ways:

- screen or hedge
- ornamental interest—flowers, leaves or fruit
- food for wildlife—berries, acorns, seeds, and nectar

Low maintenance: Several qualities can mean a plant does not require a lot of maintenance:

- drought tolerance
- pest resistance
- slow growth rate

Consider native shrubs (and their domesticated cultivars), whose ability to thrive in your area for centuries gives them reason enough to be part of a low-maintenance landscape.

Planting

To learn how to plant shrubs, refer to Planting in the introduction to the Trees chapter on p. 281.

Fertilizing

Newly planted shrubs can be fertilized after they've become

Shrubs

established. That may take months or longer, depending on their size. Once established, fertilizer applications can stimulate growth and help shrubs fill in to their allotted space in the landscape.

Shrubs that have already "filled-in" won't have to be fertilized on a regular basis. Replenishing the mulch at their roots with compost or other "recyclable" organic materials will provide them with a steady diet of minerals. If your shrubs are growing in a lawn that is fertilized, do not add additional fertilizer.

Apply fertilizer when it will be readily absorbed by the roots of your shrubs and when the soil is moist, which can be any time from late spring after new growth emerges up to early fall. However, if water is unavailable or when the shrubs are stressed by drought during the summer months, do not fertilize at all because their roots will be unable to absorb the nutrients.

Fertilize based on the shrub's appearance (see March Fertilizing, p. 262) and according to soil-test results. Most fertilizer recommendations are based on nitrogen, which is an important element in plant growth and often the one that's most likely to be deficient in the soil. Apply 1 pound of nitrogen per thousand square feet of root zone area. Up to 2 pounds can be applied with a slow-release fertilizer.

In the absence of a soil test, use a complete fertilizer with a ratio of 3-1-2 or 3-1-3, such as 12-4-8 or 15-5-15. **Palms** benefit from fertilizers that also contain magnesium and other micronutrients, such as manganese, particularly palms growing on the Outer Coastal Plain, where micronutrient deficiencies are common.

Apply fertilizer to the shrub's root zone area (area occupied by nutrient and water-absorbing roots), which can extend beyond the drip line or outermost branches. See Fertilizing in the Trees chapter, p. 282, for more information.

Since most of a shrub's roots are in the top foot of soil, evenly broadcast the fertilizer with a handheld spreader or a rotary or cyclone spreader over this root zone area. Sweep any fertilizer off the branches and water afterwards to make the nutrients available to the roots. If the shrub's root zone area is confined by a sidewalk or driveway, reduce the root zone area accordingly.

How Much Fertilizer?

If your shrubs are growing in a bed, follow the steps outlined in Fertilizing in Vines and Ground Covers, p. 311, to determine the right amount of fertilizer to apply.

Watering

Not all established shrubs have to be watered during hot, dry summer months. Drought-tolerant shrubs can withstand long periods without rain or irrigation.

See the ground rules for proper watering in the Watering section in the Introduction to this book on p. 17.

Refer to the May Planning section, p. 266, to learn more about efficient watering methods.

Pruning

Pruning is a basic maintenance requirement for shrubs; it improves their health and appearance and keeps them in bounds. Not all shrubs have to be pruned, however. **Barberry, cotoneaster, gardenia, mahonia,** and **pittosporum** rarely need to be pruned if given enough space to develop their natural size. Some multistemmed shrubs such as **deutzia, forsythia,** and **nandina** must have their older stems removed entirely, a few at a time each year. This keeps them youthful and vigorous. Others, such as **mountain laurel, rose-of-Sharon,** and **viburnum** already have an attractive natural shape that may require the occasional removal of wayward branches that detract from their beauty.

Shrubs

There are two basic pruning cuts: heading or heading back involves removing a portion of a branch back to a bud or branch. Heading stimulates a flush of new shoots just below the cut making the plant look more dense. When you shear your **yaupon holly** or **boxwood** hedges, you're making a bunch of heading cuts (Figure 1).

A thinning cut is the removal of a branch back to where it joins the limb or trunk. Thinning opens up the center of the shrub to sunlight and reduces the number of new shoots that sprout along the branches. A lot of growth can be removed by thinning without dramatically changing the shrub's natural appearance or growth habit and giving it the "just-pruned" look (Figure 2).

When you prune, follow two basic rules:

1 Spring-flowering plants that bloom before June 1 can be pruned right after flowering; they bloom on last-year's growth. So pruning shrubs such as **forsythia, quince,** and **azalea** now will give them time to develop new flower buds for next year. There are a few exceptions to this rule, such as **oakleaf hydrangea** and certain **azalea** cultivars that bloom after June 1, even into July, but on last-year's wood.

2 Summer-flowering shrubs produce flower buds on current-season's shoots. They can be pruned in late winter before new growth emerges. A few of these summer-flowering shrubs are **beautyberry, butterfly bush,** and **glossy abelia.**

Prune out dead, damaged, or diseased wood at any time of year.

Pest Control

Experts have developed a common-sense approach to pest management. It brings Mother Nature into the battle on the gardener's side by integrating smart plant selection with good planting and maintenance practices and an understanding of pests and their habits. It starts with growing strong, healthy plants that by themselves can prosper with minimal help from you. As in Nature, an acceptable level of pests is accommodated. Control is the goal, rather than elimination. This is called Integrated Pest Management, or IPM for short. And it can work for you. It can be summarized in these steps:

(Figure 1)
Heading Back

(Figure 2)
Thinning

Shrubs

1 Select shrubs that are adapted to your region and that have few pest problems. Refer to the Planting Chart (p. 255–57) as a start, visit local nurseries and garden centers, and consult with your county cooperative extension service agent.

2 Start with healthy, high quality, pest-free plants.

3 Select the right location.

4 Properly plant, fertilize, mulch, and water the plants. Avoid overfertilizing, which encourages a lot of succulent growth that is attractive to insects and susceptible to disease. Overfertilization can also contaminate streams, lakes, and groundwater.

5 Watch for and learn to identify pests. At least once a week, walk through your landscape and examine your shrubs for problems. Inspect the undersides of the leaves and the shoots. If you spot a problem and can't identify it yourself, take a sample to your garden center or cooperative extension service office for assistance.

6 When trouble strikes, turn to nonchemical controls first. Insects such as aphids can be hosed off with a strong spray of water; others such as Japanese beetles can be handpicked.

7 Sometimes it is necessary to resort to more-potent but least-toxic measures such as insecticidal soap and *BT.*

8 You may have to occasionally resort to more potent pesticides, especially when you feel the damage is more than you or your shrubs can tolerate. Consider spot-treating heavily infested plants instead of making a blanket application that can destroy beneficial insects such as ladybugs, predatory mites, and green lacewings. Use recommended pesticides and apply according to label directions. Foraging honeybees and other pollinators are sensitive to these insecticides, so treat the plants in early morning or late evening when no bees are present.

9 Keep your garden clean. *Remove* damaged, dead, or pest-ridden stems or branches whenever you see them. *Clean up and discard* any infected flowers and leaves.

Carolina Shrubs

Deciduous

Common Name (Botanical Name)	Hardiness Zones	Light Exposure	Comments
Azalea (*Rhododendron* spp. and hybrids)	Varied	Partial shade	Many species, cultivars, and hybrids sporting stunning flowers and outstanding fall color.
Bottlebrush buckeye (*Aesculus parviflora*)	5 to 8	Sun to shade	Summer-flowering native; suckering growth habit (9 to 12 ft. high and 15 ft. wide). Leaves turn bright yellow in fall.
Butterfly bush (*Buddleia davidii*)	5 to 9	Sun	Dozens of cultivars offering a wide range of color in summer (10+ ft. high/6 to 8 ft. wide).
Dwarf fothergilla (*Fothergilla gardenii*)	5 to 9a	Sun to partial shade	Native to the Coastal Plain, grows 3 to 5 ft. high and wide and bears fragrant, fluffy, white bottlebrush-like flowers in spring. Yellow to orange to red fall color.
American fringetree or Old-Man's Beard (*Chionanthus virginicus*)	4 to 9	Part shade to sun	Multistemmed shrub or small tree 12 to 15 ft. high and wide. White, fleecy flowers in spring. Chinese fringetree (*C. retusus,* zones 5b to 9b, 20 ft. high and 15 ft. wide), its Asian counterpart, produces a blizzard of white flowers in spring.
Hydrangea (*Hydrangea* spp.)	See Comments	Sun or partial shade	Many species with showy flowers, others have attractive fall color. Some notable species include oakleaf hydrangea (*Hydrangea quercifolia,* zones 5 to 9), bigleaf or French hydrangea (*Hydrangea macrophylla,* zones 6 to 9), whose flower color is often related to soil pH: pink flowers with alkaline pH, Pee Gee hydrangea (*Hydrangea paniculata* 'Grandiflora', zones 3 to 8), and smooth hydrangea (*Hydrangea arborescens* 'Annabelle', zones 4 to 9).
Sweet pepperbush (*Clethera alnifolia*)	5 to 9	Sun or shade	Fragrant summer-flowering native with attractive clusters of upright flower spikes, long-lasting golden yellow fall color.
Rose-of-Sharon (*Hibiscus syriacus*)	5 to 8	Sun or partial shade	Old-fashioned trouble-free shrub; 8 to 12 ft. high and 6 to 10 ft. wide. Consider the National Arboretum introductions.
Deciduous Hollies (*Ilex* spp. and hybrids)	Varied	Sun to partial shade	Exciting species and hybrids showing off brightly colored red or gold berries in fall and winter. For the female to set large numbers of fruit, a male holly that flowers at about the same time must be nearby.
Viburnum (*Viburnum* spp. and hybrids)	5 to 7 (8)	Sun to part shade	Evergreen to deciduous shrubs or small trees; many noted for showy flowers, colorful berries, or brightly colored fall leaves.
Chastetree (*Vitex agnus-castus*)	7b to 9	Sun to partial shade	Longlasting spikes of purple, pink, or white flowers in summer on new growth; 10 to 15 ft. high and 8 to 10 ft. wide.
Old-fashioned Weigela (*Weigela florida*)	4b to 9a	Sun to part shade	Popular during Victorian times; renewed interest with the introduction of new top-quality hybrids. Wide range of flower colors in late spring from white to deep pink and even red to yellow; 6 to 9 ft. tall with an equal or greater spread. 'Wine and Roses', 'Minuet', and 'Bristol Ruby' are a few exceptional cultivars.

Carolina Shrubs

Evergreen

Common Name (Botanical Name)	Hardiness Zones	Light Exposure	Comments
Azaleas (*Rhododendron* spp. and hybrids)	Varied; species- and cultivar-dependent	Part shade	Numerous species, hybrids, and cultivars offer flowers from spring through fall.
Glossy abelia (*Abelia ×grandiflora*)	6a to 9a	Sun or shade	Semi-evergreen shrub (sheds its leaves) in the colder Mountain areas. Bears pale pink flowers in spring, summer, and fall.
Boxwood (*Buxus* spp.)	5 to 8	Sun to partial shade	Creates the "backbone" or year-round structural dimension of the landscape. Numerous dwarf species and cultivars with unique forms and colored leaves are available.
Rhododendron (*Rhododendron* spp.)	Varied	Part shade	Enormous variety of species and thousands of garden hybrids and cultivars.
Camellia (*Camellia japonica*)	7 to 9	Partial shade	Signature plant of Southern gardens. Flowers appear from late winter to early spring. Sasanqua camellia (*C. sasanqua*) has smaller flowers in fall to early winter.
Indian or Yeddo hawthorn (*Rhaphiolepis umbellata*)	(7b) 8 to 10	Sun to part shade	Late-winter and early-spring clusters of fragrant star-shaped flowers in shade of white and pink; salt tolerant. Look for cultivars resistant to Entomosporium leaf spot such as 'Blueberry Muffin', Eleanor Taber™, 'Georgia Charm', 'Georgia Petite', and 'Olivia'.
Holly (*Ilex* spp.)	Varied	Sun and partial shade	Good choices for hedges or foundation plantings. Popular choices include Stokes Dwarf and Nana Yaupon holly (*I. vomitoria*), Japanese holly (*I. crenata*), 'Dwarf Burford', 'Carissa', and 'Rotunda' Chinese hollies (*I. cornuta*).
Anisetree (*Illiciun* spp.)	7 to 8 or 9 depending on species	Sun to shade (depending on species)	Versatile group of tough, low-maintenace shrubs with anise-scented leaves, including hardy anise shrub (*I. parviflorum*), Florida anisetree (*I. floridanum*), and Japanese anisetree (*I. anisatum*).
Chinese juniper (*Juniperus chinensis*)	4 to 9 depending on cultivar	Sun	Many cultivars sporting a wide array of forms and sizes: Pfitzer juniper (*J. chinensis* **'Pfitzeriana'**), 'Hetzii', Hollywood juniper ('Torulosa'); Parson's juniper (*Juniperus davurica* **'Parsonii'**) and *J. virginiana* 'Grey Owl'.
Mountain laurel (*Kalmia latifolia*)	5 to 9	Sun or shade	Spectacular in bloom with large clusters of bell-shaped flowers ranging from pure white to pink to red in early summer.
Chinese fringe-flower (*Loropetalum chinense*)	7 to 9	Sun or part shade	Large shrub or small tree blanketed with creamy-white flowers in early to mid-spring. Look for the magenta- and pink-flowered forms (*L. chinense* var. *rubrum*) either with mature burgundy leaves—'Burgundy', 'Fire Dance', 'Ruby', and 'Zhuzhou Fuchsia'—or mature green leaves such as 'Blush'.

Carolina Shrubs

Evergreen

Common Name (Botanical Name)	Hardiness Zones	Light Exposure	Comments
Southern waxmyrtle (*Myrica cerifera*)	7b to 10	Sun to part shade	Can be trained as a shrub or small tree (15 to 20 ft. high and 20 to 25 ft. wide) with olive green leaves; only female plants produce the small waxy gray-green berries.
Heavenly bamboo (*Nandina domestica*)	6 to 9	Sun to shade	Not a true bamboo; develops into an unbranched shrub reaching 6 to 8 ft. with an equal spread. Noteworthy for the fine-textured leaves, showy flowers and fruit that persist well into winter, and brilliantly colored leaves. Numerous dwarf and medium forms with compact habit and colorful leaves such as 'Fire Power' (2 ft. high and wide); Harbor Dwarf (tight mound to 2 ft.); and Moonbay (upright to 2 ft.).
Oleander (*Nerium oleander*)	8b to 11	Sun to part shade	Summer-flowering shrub or small tree that produces clusters of pink, red, yellow or white flowers on the terminal ends of current season's growth; 15 ft. high and 10 to 12 ft. wide; dwarf oleander typically reaches a height of only 6 ft. at maturity. Tolerates salt spray, brackish water, and alkaline soil. All parts of the oleander plant are poisonous, so wear gloves when pruning and dispose of the trimmings separately. Do not burn them as toxic fumes will be produced.
Osmanthus (*Osmanthus* spp.)	7a to 9b depending on cultivar	Sun to part shade	Large shrub or small multistemmed tree (15 to 20 ft. high and 6 to 10 ft. wide). A few notable species include Fortune's osmanthus (***Osmanthus × fortunei,*** zones 7 to 8; 9 to 12 ft. high and 15 to 20 ft. wide); fragrant tea olive (*O. fragrans* 7b to 8; 10 to 12 ft. high and 10 to 14 ft. wide); and holly osmanthus or false holly (*O. heterophyllus,* zones 7 to 9; 6 to 12 ft. high/5 to 10 ft. wide). Look for eye-catching variegated cultivars.
Japanese pittosporum (*Pittosporum tobira*)	7b to 11	Sun to part shade	Large shrub or small tree 10 to 15 ft. high with a greater spread; spoon-shaped leathery leaves occurring in whorls on the stems; fragrant white flowers in spring. Good for screens, hedges, and foundation plantings.
Chinese podocarpus (*Podocarpus macrophyllus* var. *maki*)	7b to 11	Sun to part shade	Often trained as a dense hedge or screen with needlelike leaves although it can be grown as a tree (30 to 40 ft. high and 20 to 30 ft. wide). Several variegated forms are available.
Japanese cleyera (*Ternstroemia gymnanthera*)	7 to 9	Part shade to shade	New leaves are red-bronze in spring, olive in summer, and wine-colored in winter; 8 to 15 ft. high with half the spread. Salt tolerant—good for coastal areas.
Needle palm (*Rhapidophyllum hystrix*)	7a to 8b	Sun or part shade	Most cold-hardy palm in the world. Forms a low mound; tolerates sandy or clay soils. Purchase seed-grown, nursery-propagated plants.

JANUARY

Planning

As you examine the garden-ing catalogs arriving this month, begin making entries in your gar-dening journal. As you look at the gorgeous photographs of attractive shrubs, check to see if they come with the added bonus of pest resistance. Try to avoid adding another plant to your landscape that will result in a battle with pests during the hot, humid summer months! Have you forgotten about your fights with **euonymus** scales, *Entomosporium* leaf spot on **red tips,** and lace bugs on **azaleas** and **cotoneasters?** You can always practice "tough love" gar-dening by getting rid of the infested plants, but this can quickly become an expensive practice. Use the cata-logs as a starting point, and continue your search for pest-resistant plants in magazines and reference books, and during visits to local nurseries and garden centers.

Planting

Set out container-grown and balled-and-burlapped shrubs when the soil is not frozen. Follow the step-by-step planting instructions out-lined in the introduction to Trees (p. 281). If you were unable to move established shrubs last fall, you can transplant them now while they are dormant.

Care for Your Shrubs

Protect newly planted evergreens from winterburn by shading them on the south and southwest sides with temporary burlap screens or snow fences. Established ever-greens may also require similar

Evergreen Shrub Protection

sun and wind protection to prevent the leaves from turning brown and scorched. This is especially impor-tant in the Mountains where the soil can freeze and remain frozen on sunny days. When this hap-pens, the leaves continue to transpire or lose water, but the roots cannot replace the lost moisture from the frozen soil. Winterburn can also occur when the sun thaws the leaves, which then refreeze rapidly when the sun is blocked or at sunset when the leaf temperature drops quickly.

Fertilizing

Do not fertilize at this time.

Watering

During winter thaws, ***water*** fall-planted and established ever-greens, especially those on the south and west sides of the house. ***Mulch*** newly planted shrubs with a 2- to 4-inch layer of compost, and keep them well-watered.

Pruning

Remove any broken storm-damaged limbs. Use pruning shears, loppers, or a saw to make clean cuts. Any major pruning should be reserved for next month or after the coldest part of winter has passed.

Delay pruning or removing cold-damaged plants. Sometimes they'll sprout from the stems or from the roots, depending on the plant and the extent of injury. Be patient. It may take until May or June before new leaves sprout from the seemingly lifeless branches.

Summer-flowering plants that can be pruned later this month in the Coastal Plain after the coldest part of winter has passed include **butterfly bush, glossy abelia** (*Abelia × grandiflora*), **fragrant tea olive** (*Osmanthus fragrans*), **smooth hydrangea** (*Hydrangea arborescens*), and others. They produce flowers on current-season's growth.

Pest Control

Insects and mites: Apply dormant horticultural oil sprays on small landscape trees to smother overwintering insect eggs, aphids, mites, and scale insects. Be sure to spray the trunk, branches, stems, and both sides of the leaves thoroughly. Read the label for any precautions regarding the recommended high and low temperature limits at the time of application. Special equipment (or a professional) will be required to treat large trees.

Helpful Hint

Ice damage to woody plants occurs when high winds break heavily coated branches. Evergreens are more susceptible to snow damage than are deciduous plants because they have more leaf surface for accumulating snow. Ice and snow can damage your evergreens by their weight or if they are removed carelessly. A branch that breaks or becomes damaged by bending downward can be invaded by canker-producing fungi, leading to the death of the limb the following season.

Shrubs that would collapse underneath heavy snow loads can be protected. Place a crate or a wooden box with slats over the plants to catch any accumulating snowfall. During the winter, lift off snow with an upward sweep of a broom. When removing snow from walks and driveways, avoid piling the snow around the root zone areas of plants, which can produce waterlogged conditions when the snow melts.

Ice can be more troublesome than snow because it cannot be easily brushed off without damaging the limbs. Allow ice to melt naturally.

The limbs of valuable plants can be protected from ice breakage with flexible supports. Consider looping a bicycle tire inner tube around the trunk and branches. Or you can create horizontal supports by securing bungee cords throughout the framework of the tree and attaching their ends to bamboo poles or posts oriented on the outside of the tree.

At the end of winter, examine your plants and **prune out** any broken or dead limbs.

Before you prune out a limb that looks dead, scrape the bark with your thumbnail and look at the underlying tissue. A green layer indicates living tissue.

Cut back or **thin out** any damaged shoots by pruning within 1/4 inch above a live bud or just outside the branch collar.

Planning

In the colder areas of the Carolinas, plan to bring a touch of springtime indoors. Spring-flowering woody plants (whose flower buds were produced on last year's growth) can be forced into early bloom indoors once their dormancy requirements have been met. While the time varies between species, at least eight weeks of temperatures below 40 degrees Fahrenheit is generally sufficient.

Branches from shrubs are easier to force than those from trees, and the nearer the time is to the shrub's normal blooming, the more rapidly the forced branches will bloom.

Some readily forced branches include those of **bridalwreath spirea** (*Spiraea prunifolia*), **Cornelian-cherry dogwood** (*Cornus mas*), **border forsythia** (*F. × intermedia*), **honeysuckle** (*Lonicera*), **service-berry** (*Amelanchier*), and **spicebush** (*Lindera benzoin*). Follow these steps:

1 Cut the branches on a day when the temperature is above freezing, being careful not to disfigure the plant.

2 **Cut** the branches 6 to 18 inches long; longer branches are easier to use in floral arrangements.

3 Bring the branches indoors and make a second cut on a slant just above the previous cut. Make several 1-inch-long slits in the end of each stem as well.

4 Place the stems in a container to which a floral preservative has been added, covering up to one-third of the stems. You can make your own by mixing 2 tablespoons of fresh lemon or lime juice, 1 tablespoon of sugar, and $1/2$ tablespoon of household bleach in a quart of water. Place the container in a cool, dark location.

5 When the buds begin to show color, **move** the branches to the light, but keep them away from direct sunlight. Cool temperatures will prolong the life of the flowers when they appear.

Planting

Bare-root deciduous shrubs can be planted while they're dormant, about a month before the last average freeze in your area. See Trees, February Planting on p. 288.

Plant container-grown and balled-and-burlapped shrubs anytime, except when the soil is frozen and when severely cold weather prevails.

Care for Your Shrubs

Watch for signs of heaving among your small shrubs; the freezing and thawing of the ground can force shallow-rooted plants out of the soil. Replant any that have been heaved, and mulch with 3 to 4 inches of organic material to reduce fluctuations in soil temperature.

Fertilizing

Don't be too hasty to fertilize your shrubs. Wait until at least budbreak—when new growth emerges in the spring. See p. 262 to determine if fertilizing is necessary.

Watering

Water newly planted shrubs. Keep the soil moist but avoid overwatering, which can inhibit root growth.

Pruning

Shrubs can get a new look or be renewed when they have outgrown their location (perhaps they were mistakenly planted along the foundation of a house and have begun to engulf the windows or house), have been seriously damaged or neglected, or have become "leggy" with most of their leaves clustered at the top revealing bare or leafless stems below. There are two approaches.

1 The drastic approach is to *cut back* the plant to within 6 to 12 inches of the ground before spring growth begins. Most broadleaf shrubs, including **azaleas, camellias, privets, glossy abelia, Japanese cleyera,** and **nandina,** respond well to this treatment. When the new shoots emerge, *pinch out* the tips and *thin out* some of the new shoots to make some room and to begin developing a strong framework.

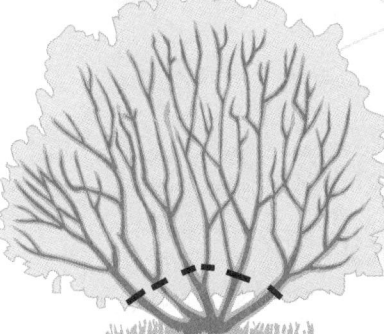

Severe heading back renews overgrown shrubs.

2 A milder tactic is to stretch renewal pruning over a period of three years. This works well for multiple-stemmed plants such as **forsythia** and **spirea.** In the first year, remove one-third of the oldest stems. In the following year, take out one-half of the remaining old stems and head back long shoots that grew from the previous pruning cuts. In the third year, remove the remaining old wood and head back the long new shoots.

Thin out one-third of the oldest stems.

Summer-flowering shrubs such as **butterfly bush** and **beautyberry** can be cut back to within 6 inches or a foot since they bloom on current-season's growth. Wait to prune spring-flowering shrubs until after they bloom.

Watering

If severe cold is forecast for your area, *water* evergreens before the soil freezes. The roots are not able to take up moisture when the soil is frozen.

Pest Control

Use dormant oil sprays on landscape plants to smother overwintering insects and mites before the plants leaf out. See January Pest Control, p. 259.

Diseases: Camellia flower blight is a fungal disease that attacks only the flowers of **Japanese camellia (*Camellia japonica*).** Follow these steps to manage this disease: 1) Pull off all affected flowers and *discard* them. At the end of the flowering season, rake up and destroy all fallen blossoms and other plant debris. 2) This disease requires community-wide attention. Fungal spores are produced over the length of the **Japanese camellia** flowering season in late winter and spring and can travel one-half mile or more from the source. Educate your neighbors about this disease and encourage them to pick up and *discard or destroy* diseased flowers. 3) A fungicidal drench can offer some degree of control, but it will be futile if your neighbors are not controlling this disease in their own gardens.

Weeds: Control any winter annual weeds such as bittercress, common chickweed, and henbit by hand-pulling. *Suppress* them with a shallow layer of mulch.

MARCH

Planning

Take a look at the shrubs near the foundation of your house and in your landscape. Dense shrubs should not be planted close to the foundation or siding, or in front of foundation vents, because they can obstruct air flow around and beneath your home, which can lead to moisture problems. Make plans to prune these shrubs or move them to another corner of the landscape. If you move them to south- or west-facing walls to insulate your house from summer's heat, keep them away from foundation vents and at least 4 feet from the foundation.

Be sure to keep shrubs away from the compressor on your split-system air conditioner. While the shade cast by the shrubs can reduce energy consumption, they should be planted far enough away so they won't obstruct air flow or service.

Planting

Plant balled-and-burlapped or container-grown shrubs. Follow the step-by-step instructions in the Trees introduction, p. 281.

Ground-layering is a simple way to propagate shrubs that have long pliable stems (such as **forsythia** and **winter jasmine**) or difficult-to-root plants (such as **rhododendron**). Here's how to do it:

1 Before growth begins, *bend* one or two young, healthy stems to the ground.

2 *Wound* the underside of the stem and cover it with soil. Hold it in place with a piece of wire bent to a hairpin shape and pushed into the ground. *Do not bury the shoot tip.*

3 If you layer now, the shoots will usually be rooted by the end of the growing season. Then you can sever the plant from the parent and transplant it. Shoots layered later in the summer should be left through the winter and separated in spring.

Watering

Water newly planted shrubs every few weeks in dry weather. *Check* the moisture in the rootball and surrounding soil before watering (see Trees, October Watering on p. 304).

Fertilizing

Evaluate the growth and appearance of your shrubs to decide if fertilizing is necessary. Look for these signs of "hunger" or deficiency in minerals: stunted growth, smaller than normal leaves, poor leaf color, early leaf drop. Be aware that these same symptoms of poor growth can be the result of the following causes: heavily compacted soil; stresses induced by insects, diseases, and weeds; or adverse weather conditions. Before you fertilize, determine the cause of the problem and correct it. Having your soil tested is one way of getting to the "root" of the problem. Rely on soil-test results to supply the minerals that are deficient in the soil.

Pruning

To create a hedge, start shearing plants during their early years to encourage compact growth.

1 *Prune* young one- to two-year-old plants to within a foot of the ground.

2 During the growing season, head back the tips of the shoots to encourage branching below the cuts.

Heading back the tips of the shoots encourages branching below the cuts to maintain a desired height and width.

3 Once a hedge reaches the desired height, choose an informal or formal look. An informal-looking hedge requires little care; you simply maintain the natural growth habit of the hedge. Prune only to remove dead, diseased, or damaged wood, and occasionally head back the shoots to maintain the desired height and width.

The formal look requires regular shearing during the growing season. When maintaining a formal hedge, follow these two rules-of-thumb:

1 *Clip* the hedges when the new growth is green and succulent.

Helpful Hint

To calculate the correct spacing for shrubs, add the plants' ultimate spreads and divide by two; the answer will tell you the proper distance between them at planting time. If plants at first appear to be too far apart, you can interplant these permanent plantings with temporary "filler" plants. Bulbs such as **daffodils, alliums, lilies,** and **crinums** or annual bedding plants can be used to fill in the gaps.

2 *Shape* the plants so the base of the hedge is wider than the top. A hedge with a narrow base becomes "leggy" over time because the top shades out the bottom, causing the stems to lose their lower leaves and show their knees.

Prune summer-flowering shrubs before new growth starts. Wait until spring-flowering shrubs bloom before pruning them.

Pest Control

Insects and mites: Apply a dormant horticultural oil spray on dormant landscape plants. See January Pest Control, p. 259.

Watch out for the "cool-weather" mites: southern red mites which attack **azaleas, camellia, Japanese** and **American hollies,** and rhododendron and spruce spider mites which feed on **arborvitae, false cypress, juniper, spruce,** and other conifers. They attack in the spring and fall—at higher Mountain elevations they may be active all summer long. See p. 267 for controls.

Look for small cone-shaped objects hanging from the branches of your **arborvitae, cedars, junipers,** and **Leyland cypress.** These are the nests of bagworms, which contain from 500 to 1,000 eggs that will hatch next month and into June. *Remove* the bags and *discard* them.

Weeds: Handpull winter annuals such as bittercress, common chickweed, and henbit to prevent them from going to seed. Maintain a 2- to 4-inch layer of mulch to suppress weeds.

A preemergent herbicide can reduce the amount of handweeding required. Pre-emergent herbicides kill germinating weed seedlings before they appear. See Annuals, March Weeds on p. 35 for tips on selecting a pre-emergent herbicide.

Planning

When planning shrub borders or foundation plantings, look for shrubs that bear edible fruits. In addition to **figs**, **'Wonderful' pomegranate** (*Punica granatum* 'Wonderful'), and **pineapple guava** (*Feijoa sellowiana*), my favorite shrub for year-round beauty is the **blueberry** (*Vaccinium*). Look for creamy-white or pink flowers in spring; deep-blue fruit in summer; orange, red, and yellow fall color; and rosy-pink stems in winter.

Rabbiteye and **southern highbush blueberries** can be grown in the Piedmont and dry, sandy soils of the Coastal Plain. Only the **highbush blueberry** can be cultivated in the Mountains, because it has the ability to survive cold winter temperatures of 10 degrees Fahrenheit and lower. **Blueberries** are acid-loving shrubs that can be grown like **azaleas** and **rhododendrons.** Use them in borders and hedges, and as backgrounds for perennial plantings. For highest yields, plant at least two varieties of **rabbiteyes,** and cross-pollination will occur.

Planting

Continue planting container-grown shrubs, following the step-by-step instructions in the Trees chapter, p. 281. Pay strict attention to watering to help them get established.

Care for Your Shrubs

Do not be too quick to pull out shrubs that are damaged by cold. You can *cut back* the dead branches above the ground, but leave the roots in place until June. Sometimes it takes a few weeks of warm weather for the new shoots to be jump-started into growth. *Check* mulched areas, and replace or replenish where needed.

Fertilizing

For blue flowers on your **French** or **mophead** and **lacecap hydrangeas,** maintain a soil pH between 5 and 5.5. An acid soil increases the availability of aluminum, which turns the flowers blue. Apply aluminum sulfate or sulfur to reduce the pH to this ideal range when you see new growth emerging (wait until next month to do this in the Mountains).

Fertilize palms with a slow-release fertilizer that has a 3-1-3 analysis, such as 18-6-12. Apply according to label directions. Broadcast or scatter the fertilizer under the canopy or bed area.

Watering

To prevent water from running off when watering, sometimes it's necessary to create a temporary berm, or dike, around newly planted shrubs in clay soil. *Remove* the berm when the plants become established.

Pruning

If you aren't sure of the extent of winter injury, wait until growth begins before removing dead wood. *Prune* spring-flowering shrubs as their blossoms fade. Prune out dead, damaged, or pest-ridden branches first. Avoid using heading cuts to prune them into mushrooms or meatballs. Rather, use thinning cuts to remove renegade limbs and to accentuate their natural shapes.

To prune **forsythia, quince, sweet mockorange, nandina,** and other multistemmed shrubs, cut off a few of the older central stems right at ground level so new ones can spring up and take over.

Prune **azaleas** only if they require it. *Thin* wayward branches. *Cut back* branches that have just a ring of leaves at the top.

Pest Control

Insects: Watch out for aphids, whiteflies, and spider mites. See the Pest Appendix on p. 362–65 for descriptions and controls. Azalea lace bugs suck sap from the undersides of **azalea** leaves, creating damage that appears as stippled or blanched areas on the surface of the leaves. The underside of the leaf will be covered with splattered, brown or black, varnish-like patches of fecal material. Their feeding causes the leaves to turn pale green or yellow and fall off. In the Carolinas expect two or three generations of azalea lace bugs. Damage from this pest is most serious on azaleas growing in sunny locations. If yours are growing in full sun, try moving them to a location that receives only filtered sunlight or afternoon shade. This tactic should reduce the lace bug populations to tolerable levels.

If you choose to use an insecticide, start early in the season in order to destroy the first generation of nymphs. You can apply an insecticidal soap or pyrethrin at three- to four-day intervals for a minimum of three applications, making sure to spray the undersides of the leaves. (If there is no rain to wash the leaves, don't exceed three applications or you may damage the plants.)

Look for tea scales on the undersides of the leaves of **camellias** and **hollies.** They look like white waxy or cottony oval specks. Scale insects suck plant sap and exude a sticky honeydew that's often colonized by a sooty mold fungus which gives the leaves and stems a sooty appearance. The young scale insects are called "crawlers" and are about the size of the period at the end of this sentence. They scurry about before settling down to begin feeding. Shortly after they settle, they produce a protective shell or cover.

Heavy infestations cause leaf-drop. Light infestations can be scraped off the plant. Summer horticultural oil sprays and other pesticides can be used to control these pests.

Diseases: Azalea leaf gall is a fungal disease that infects the newly emerging leaves and flowers of **azaleas** in the spring. The fleshy galls begin as light green to pink thickened areas on the leaves and eventually turn chalky white as the spores are produced. Camellia leaf gall infects **sasanqua camellias** more often than **Japanese camellias.** In both cases, the gall containing the fungus eventually ruptures and disperse the spores to other plants.

Handpick the galls and discard them. Fungicides are available.

Entomosporium leaf spot is a disease that attacks **red tips** (*Photinia* × *fraseri*) and **Indian hawthorn** (*Raphiolepis indica*), causing severe leaf drop. This fungal disease attacks newly expanding leaves in spring and fall. To prevent its spread, follow these steps:

1 Prune only in the winter before growth begins. (Summer pruning encourages flushes of new growth, which are susceptible to attack.)

2 *Remove* infected twigs and leaves and rake up and *discard* fallen leaves.

3 Space plants far enough apart to encourage rapid drying of the leaves after rainfall; avoid wetting the leaves, since the fungus is spread by splashing water.

4 As a last resort, protect the new leaves with a fungicide. Because photinia produces several growth flushes a season, expect fungicide applications to be a regular gardening chore.

Weeds: Follow March guidelines, p. 263.

Planning

With summer around the corner, now is a good time to plan for watering shrubs efficiently when hot weather arrives. Take some time this month to consider which irrigation method is best suited to your situation.

If you're going to handwater, find a nozzle that breaks the water into rain-size droplets that won't wash the soil away as its applied. If you choose to automate so that you won't have to handle this chore, think about an irrigation system.

Some install-it-yourself systems allow you to turn the water on and off yourself or automatically, in various patterns and for any length of time. The simplest is a soaker hose, a fibrous tube that "sweats" or allows water to seep out all along its length. It is suitable for dense plantings.

Some systems have nozzles that deliver the water in a low, horizontal pattern that wets the base but keeps the plants dry.

The most efficient watering method is drip or trickle irrigation. Such systems use short tubes, called emitters, that come off a main water-supply hose and go directly to the base of the plant. This is generally the most expensive form of irrigation and the most complex to set up, but it has advantages. The weeds in the area are not watered, and evaporation from the soil is minimized. Drip systems can have problems with clogging from soil particles and/or mineral salts suspended in water taken from springs or wells. New designs address this problem: some include filters and self-flushing emitters. All these systems include a timer or can be operated using one that you purchase separately.

Purchase all of these at garden centers or shop the Internet.

Planting

Although shrubs are best planted in the fall, those which have been grown in containers can be bought now and planted throughout the summer months as long as you pay careful attention to watering. When the flowers fade on your Mother's Day **hydrangeas,** don't throw them out. *Plant* them in the garden where they'll get morning sun and afternoon shade.

Care for Your Shrubs

To prevent damage to shrubs while mowing, surround them with a ring of mulch. Apply the mulch as far as the dripline or outermost branches.

Watering

Avoid watering your shrubs with a sprinkler. In addition to wasting water and watering weeds, wetting the leaves will encourage disease outbreaks.

Fertilizing

Evaluate your shrubs for color and growth to determine the need for fertilizer. To encourage more growth, *fertilize* with a slow-release fertilizer. *Water* well immediately afterwards.

Avoid excessive fertilization. High levels of nutrients, particularly nitrogen, will encourage leafy shoot growth at the expense of flower bud production. Overfed shrubs produce a lot of growth that can be attacked by insects or diseases. Sometimes it has to be pruned away to keep the shrub confined to its allotted space in the landscape.

MAY

Pruning

As **French** or **lacecap hydrangeas** age, renew the plant to encourage the production of new shoots. Remove no more than one-third of the oldest shoots at the base immediately after flowering. They will be replaced by more-vigorous younger shoots, which will flower the following season.

Continue pruning spring-flowering shrubs as their flowers fade. The new growth that develops will mature over the summer and fall and produce flowers next spring.

Not all **azaleas** have to be pruned. If they've overgrown their location or have dead branches, they will benefit from careful trimming. Take out individual branches with thinning cuts, removing the oldest branches at the base.

Prune rhododendrons immediately after flowering. *Snap off* old flower trusses. Remove them carefully so you won't damage next-year's flower buds.

Pest Control

Insects and Mites: Be on the lookout for damage caused by aphids and spider mites. Take necessary action if their feeding is more than you or your shrubs can tolerate.

Blast these critters off with a strong spray of water from the hose. Get underneath the leaves to dislodge spider mites.

Boxwood leafminer is the most serious pest of boxwoods, with heaviest infestations occurring on **common box** (*Buxus sempervirens*), **littleleaf boxwood** (*B. microphylla*), and **Harland boxwood** (*B. harlandii*). The lemon yellow larvae feed inside the leaves, resulting in splotchy yellow puckered or blistered areas on the undersides of the leaves. Heavily infested leaves often drop prematurely. Severe attacks can weaken the plant, resulting in twig dieback and exposing the plant to diseases and winterkill in colder regions.

The best way to suppress infestations of boxwood leafminers is to apply a systemic insecticide to kill the young larvae inside the leaves. Alternatively, your susceptible boxwood hedge could be replaced with cultivars of **common box** (*Buxus sempervirens*), such as 'Suffruticosa' (**English boxwood**) and 'Argenteovariegata,' that escape serious attacks, or the **Chinese boxwood** (*B. microphylla* var. *sinica*) cultivars 'Morris Midget' and 'Morris Dwarf.'

Euonymus scale is a common pest of **euonymus**. These oyster-shaped brown or white, scaly insects suck plant sap from the leaves and stems. Heavy infestations cause the leaves to turn yellow and fall off. Eventually, entire branches may be covered, finally killing the plant.

Expect two or three generations of euonymus scale per year. Prune out heavily infested branches. Control the offspring called "crawlers" in April, May, and June with an insecticide. Acutus wintercreeper euonymus (Euonymus fortunei 'Acutus') is resistant to this pest.

Watch out for Japanese beetles in the eastern Carolinas.

Diseases: During long, wet springs, **azaleas** and **camellias** may be attacked by the leaf gall fungus, which causes the new leaves to become thick and fleshy. See April Diseases, p. 265.

Fireblight is a bacterial disease that attacks **cotoneaster, flowering quince,** and **pyracantha.** The new shoots suddenly wilt, turn brown, turn black, and die. *Prune out* the diseased branches several inches below the infection. Grow fireblight-resistant **pyracantha** cultivars such as 'Apache', 'Fiery Cascade', 'Mohave', 'Navaho', 'Pueblo', 'Rutgers', 'Shawnee', and 'Teton'.

Weeds: Poison ivy is dangerous all year round. See Trees, May Weeds on p. 295 for more information.

JUNE

Planning

As part of your summer vacation plans, why not find some time to visit private and public gardens in the Carolinas? These gardens can be inspirational and educational. Refer to the Appendix, p. 368–371, for their addresses. Don't forget your camera and gardening journal. Enjoy!

Planting

With the availability of container-grown plants, the planting season is limited only by extremely hot weather, frozen soil in winter, and your ability to water regularly. With the onset of hot, dry weather, you can plant, but be prepared to be on call with adequate water throughout the establishment period of your shrubs.

June and July is an ideal time to take semi-hardwood cuttings when the new green growth begins to harden and turn brown. When you snap the twig, the bark often clings to the stem.

Some of the plants that can be rooted now include broadleaf evergreens such as **azaleas, camellias, banana shrub (***Michelia figo***), osmanthus, magnolia, nandina,** coniferous evergeens like **Japanese**

plum yew (*Cephalotaxus* **species**), **podocarpus,** and many others. Here are some simple propagating steps:

1 *Remove* a strip of bark ¹/₂ to 1 inch long on one side of each cutting. Dip them in a rooting hormone suited for woody plants (available at most garden centers).

2 Stick them in a container of equal parts peat and perlite or coarse sand. First make a small hole with a pencil in the moist medium. Then put the cutting into the hole, making sure it's deep enough in the moist medium to hide the wound.

3 *Enclose* the container in a zip-top plastic bag or one that can be twist-tied off at the top. Or use a clear 2-liter soft-drink bottle with its bottom removed over the cuttings.

4 Place the pot in a shaded location. Keep the cuttings moist. *Check* the cuttings for roots by gently tugging at a few of them. When you feel resistance, it means they have rooted and you can safely remove the top of the bottle.

5 *Remove* the plastic bag and repot them in a medium composed of equal parts potting soil and peat moss.

6 Gradually expose the rooted cutting to stronger light to harden them off. After a couple of weeks, *transplant* them into the garden.

Watering

Water recently planted shrubs, which are especially vulnerable to heat and drought stress. Water thoroughly to encourage deep rooting. *Avoid* irrigating your shrubs with an overhead sprinkler. Besides wasting water and watering weeds, wetting the leaves encourages disease outbreaks.

Fertilizing

If necessary, *fertilize* your **palms** with a slow-release nitrogen fertilizer as described in April, p. 264. The goal is to maintain growth. If the soil is low in magnesium as determined by a soil test, apply the recommended amount of Epsom salts.

Pink flowers occur on **French** and **lacecap hydrangeas** with a soil pH between 6.0 and 6.5. In this pH range, aluminum becomes "tied up" or rendered unavailable in the soil and so is absent from the flowers. Use lime to increase the soil pH to this desirable range. To avoid having to maintain this pH, grow pink-flowering cultivars such as 'Forever Pink' and 'Pia'.

Pruning

Prune out dead, damaged, or pest-ridden branches immediately. When shearing your hedges, *shape* the plants so the base of the hedge is wider than the top. This will expose the entire hedge to create a dense screen of leaves. See March Pruning, p. 262–63.

If you shear your **boxwoods,** it's important that you *thin out* some of the interior branches to admit sunlight and air movement. Light encourages growth on the inner stems, and air circulation reduces the occurrences of fungal diseases.

Pest Control

Insects and mites: Pests to watch for include aphids, euonymus scale, spider mites, and Japanese beetles.

Two-spotted spider mites (pale yellow, sometimes green, brown or red) are "hot-weather" mites, becoming active during the heat of summer. They attack a wide variety

of shrubs. Also, watch out for Japanese beetles.

Evaluate the extent of njury and decide if pest-control measures are warranted

Gardenia and whiteflies go together like peanut butter and jelly. These tiny mothlike insects are a common pest of gardenias. Whiteflies feed by sucking plant sap from the leaves. Lightly infested leaves develop a mottled appearance while higher populations cause leaves to yellow, shrivel, and die prematurely. Heavy infestations result in sticky leaves covered with a thin black film of sooty mold, a fungus which feeds on the honeydew excreted by the whiteflies.

See the Pest Appendix on p. 365 for controls.

Other pests: Azalea stem borers infest **azalea, rhododendron, blueberry,** and **mountain laurel.**

Prune out the wilted twigs and discard them. Plants attacked year after year can be protected with an insecticide.

Nematodes are microscopic, soil-inhabiting eel-like worms that damage roots. They are more commonly found in coarse-textured sandy soils than fine-textured clay soils.

See Roses, July Pest Control on p. 240 for a description and controls.

Diseases: Be on the lookout for root rot caused by the fungus *Phytophthora*, which means plant destroyer.

See July, p. 271, for a description and controls.

When some gardeners find lichens growing on their shrubs, they often panic, thinking that their trees are under siege. Relax. See Trees, June's Helpful Hint on p. 297.

Weeds: *Handpull,* or use a herbicide to spot-treat water- and nutrient-stealing weeds from your shrub beds and borders. A makeshift cardboard shield can be used to protect your shrubs from accidental contact with the herbicide. Suppress their emergence with a layer of mulch.

Planning

In some front yards you'll see the same handful of shrubs used over and over. It reminds me of an eight-pack of Crayola crayons. Although there are so many wonderful colors available, the same eight crayons are always used. Take some time this month to look at the big box of 64. Increase your shrub vocabulary to learn about the tremendous diversity of shrubs that can be cultivated in your Carolina landscape. Crayons don't just come in green, but also come in sea green, spring green, yellow green, and olive green.

The same is true of shrubs. **Butterfly bush** (*Buddleia davidii*) has lavender flowers. But there are also cultivars of **butterfly bush** such as **Nanho Alba** (white flowers), **Nanho Blue,** and **Nanho Purple.** Take your pick.

Don't forget native "American-made" shrubs that deserve a place in the landscape. These plants were growing in North America when the Europeans first arrived and are still here, which is proof of their longevity and ability to adapt readily to our Carolina climate, soils, and pests. Besides, they make terrific plants for attracting songbirds, butterflies, beneficial insects, and other wildlife. Look for cultivars of native plants that will fit perfectly into your landscape.

Take it from your children: Once you use burnt sienna, salmon, or aquamarine, you won't want to go back to using the red, yellow, and blue in the box of eight.

Planting

If your summer vacation is the only time you can plant, then go ahead and set out container-grown shrubs. Keep the rootball and surrounding soil moist until they become established.

Watering

Water recently planted shrubs, which are especially vulnerable to heat and drought. Water thoroughly to encourage deep rooting. *Check* the rootball and soil before watering instead of relying on the calendar. Avoid overwatering, which can suffocate the plant roots, causing the leaves to wilt. It can also expose the shrub to attack from root rot, a deadly fungal disease that prevails in waterlogged conditions and attacks susceptible plants.

Established, drought-tolerant shrubs may not require water; other shrubs, however, may need to be watered during prolonged dry periods. These shrubs will benefit from an application of 1 inch of water per week.

Fertilizing

If your healthy-looking shrubs have already fitted into their allotted space, there's no reason to encourage any further growth with fertilizer.

If your shrubs are experiencing drought stress, water is what they need most. Wait until late fall to fertilize them when they'll be more receptive.

Pruning

Remove diseased, dead, or broken branches at any time.

Pest Control

Insects and mites: Be on the lookout for damage caused by aphids and spider mites. Take necessary action if their feeding is more than you or your shrubs can tolerate. Blast these critters off with a strong spray of water from the hose. Get underneath the leaves to dislodge spider mites.

The second generation of azalea lace bugs occurs in late July through September. The adults and nymphs have piercing-sucking mouth parts for sucking sap from the undersides of the leaves. Injury by their feeding results in stippled or blanched areas on the upper leaf surface. Azalea lace bugs also deposit black, tarlike feces (frass) and the skins of molting nymphs on the undersides of the leaves. Heavy infestations cause the leaves to turn pale green or yellow and fall off.

Damage from this pest is most serious on **azaleas** growing in sunny locations. If yours are growing in full sun, try moving them to a location that receives only filtered sunlight or afternoon shade. This tactic should reduce the lace bug populations to tolerable levels.

Apply an insecticidal soap at three- to four-day intervals for a minimum of three applications, making sure to spray the undersides of the leaves. If there is no rain to wash off the leaves, then do not exceed three applications or you may damage the plants. Other insecticides are available.

If you prefer not to use insecticides and find that you can't maintain your **azaleas** without them, consider replacing them with lace bug–resistant **azaleas** such as **'Cavalier'**, **'Dawn'**, **'Dream'**, **'Elsie Lee'**, **'Eureka'**, **'Macrantha'**, **'Marilee'**, **'Pink Fancy'**, **'Pink Star'**, **'Red Wing'**, **'Salmon Pink'**, **'Seigai'**, and **'Sunglow.'**

Watch out for Japanese beetles this month. These big slow-flying bugs, metallic green with bronze wing covers, skeletonize leaves, leaving only a lacy network of leaf veins after their feeding. They also feed on flowers. Pick them off and *discard* them into a jar of soapy water. Neem can be applied to the leaves to reduce feeding by the adults. Other insecticides can be used for heavy infestations. If you choose to use Japanese beetle traps, place them far away from your susceptible shrubs. Thankfully, there's only one generation a year.

Diseases: Look for shoot blight on rhododendron. The terminal bud and leaves turn brown, roll up, and drop. *Prune out* affected branches. Fungicides can be applied at the first sign of disease. There is no cure for infested plants.

Inspect your plants for *Phytophthora* root rot, a devastating fungal disease that attacks a wide variety of plants.

Look for wilted, dying plants. Scrape the bark near the crown and look for a reddish-brown discoloration where the fungus has moved into the stem. Examine the roots as well. The "outer skin" or cortex of the root can be slipped off easily like the paper covering from a straw. When you slice it open, a root rot–infected root is reddish-brown inside instead of a healthy white in color. When symptoms are evident, chemical fungicides are often ineffective in controlling this disease. Remove the infected plant. If you want to replant in this area, select root rot–resistant plants.

Weeds: Control weeds by hand-pulling and maintaining a shallow layer of mulch. Prevent the weed from going to seed by removing the flowers.

Planning

Take advantage of the cool temperatures inside to catch up on writing in your garden journal and reading about shrubs. If you haven't kept up with regular entries, plan some time this month to sit down and record your observations on the performance of your plants, any pest problems, control measures, and thoughts about what needs to be done as summer closes and gives way to fall. Write down any plants that need to be transplanted or given away.

Planting

Container-grown shrubs can be planted in the Mountains. They ought to have plenty of time to get established before cold weather arrives. Pay attention to regular watering during the first few weeks after planting. Water is the most important "soil amendment" when establishing plants.

Watering

Inspect the soil moisture of newly planted shrubs and trees. If the soil is dry near the rootball, give them a good soaking to wet the soil deeply.

Coastal gardeners who have saline water will benefit from drip-irrigation systems. They use less water to moisten the root zones of your plants, thus putting less salt in the soil. Planting your shrubs in raised beds will also make it easier to flush out accumulated salts with irrigation water and rainfall.

Fertilizing

If you want to fertilize your shrubs now, use a slow-release fertilizer to avoid encouraging the rapid, succulent growth which can be killed by early fall freezes. Otherwise, wait until next spring when new growth begins.

Pruning

Remove diseased, damaged, or dead branches from shrubs. No severe pruning should be done.

Pest Control

Insects and mites: Spider mites are very active during hot, dry weather. Their feeding injury results in discolored, bronze-colored leaves. *Check* for mites by tapping a branch onto a white sheet of paper and looking for moving specks.

Natural predators can control spider mite populations. You can wash off mites with a strong stream of water.

Redheaded azalea caterpillars devour entire leaves and completely defoliate branches. You can identify this caterpillar by its red head and yellow stripes. When disturbed, it curls backward in a defensive posture.

Handpick the caterpillars and discard them in a jar of soapy water. **Bacillus thuringiensis (BT)** *is a biological insecticide that will control younger caterpillars. Other insecticides are available and can be applied to control heavy infestations.*

Remove the silken-needle-covered bag of bagworms on pines, junipers, hemlocks, arborvitae, and other evergreens.

Other pests: Weak-looking, stunted plants may be infested with nematodes. Because some shrubs are susceptible to certain kinds of nematodes and resistant to others, determine the identity of the nematodes attacking your plants. You may be able to outsmart them by growing resistant shrubs.

See Roses, July Pest Control on p. 240 for a description and controls.

Diseases: Wilted, dying plants may be a symptom of *Phytophthora* root rot. See last month's Diseases (p. 271) for a description and controls. Although this fungal disease is often found in wet or poorly drained sites, it will attack plants in fairly dry sites if they are planted too deeply. Overwatering plants also favors attack from this disease. Here are some tips to avoid root rot:

1 Avoid planting in poorly drained sites.

2 Improve drainage in heavy clay soil by planting in slightly raised beds, or add organic matter such as composted pine bark to as large a planting area as possible.

3 Plant plants that are highly resistant to root rot. **Azaleas** resistant to *Phytophthora* root rot include 'Corrine', 'Fakir', 'Fred Cochran', 'Glacier', 'Hampton Beauty', 'Higasa', 'Merlin', 'Polar Seas', and 'Rose Greely'. Grafting can also be used to thwart *Phytophthora* root rot. For example, susceptible **Japanese camellia** cultivars can be grafted onto rot-resistant **sasanqua camellia** rootstock.

Weeds: See last month, p. 271.

Helpful Hints

• Oceanfront landscapes expose plants to challenging, often inhospitable growing conditions. Few inland plants can survive the salt spray, sand, and battering winds.

Select native coastal plants that are indigenous to the area. Plant them on the windward side of your property. Not only will they prosper in these natural conditions, they'll also keep your landscape in harmony with its surroundings. Hardy exotic plants that can set the stage for the less-conspicuous natives include **Japanese black pine, Indian hawthorn,** and **Japanese pittosporum.**

Tender plants can be planted on the leeward side of your home or in protected microclimates created by gazebos, arbors, and fences. These microclimates can provide shade and protection from the seaside elements. Here's a sample of shrubs that can be grown in these exposed, ocean-front environments:

Shrub	Hardiness Zone
Common oleander (*Nerium oleander***)**	(7b)8 to 10
Dwarf palmetto (*Sabal minor***)**	8b to 11
Dwarf pittosporum (*Pittosporum tobira* 'Wheeler's Dwarf')**	8a to 11
Dwarf yaupon holly (*Ilex vomitoria* 'Nana')**	7a to 9b
Groundselbush (*Baccharis halimifolia***)**	5 to 9
Indian hawthorn (*Rhaphiolepis indica***)**	7b to 10
Japanese cleyera (*Ternstroemia gymnanthera***)**	7 to 10
Wax myrtle (*Myrica cerifera***)**	7b to 11

• If you're looking for plants that tolerate acid soil, consider **azaleas, rhododendrons, blueberries, cranberries** (all members of the heath family), and **camellias**—all thrive at a pH of 4.5 to 6.0. Other shrubs include **fothergilla (***F. gardenii* and *F. major***), New Jersey tea (***Ceanothus americanus***), serviceberry (***Amelanchier***), summersweet (***Clethra alnifolia***),** and **sweet bay (***Magnolia virginiana***).**

SEPTEMBER

Planning

As summer's heat and humidity finally yields to the shorter, cooler days of autumn, pay a visit to those far corners of the garden that haven't seen a gardener's eye since the 4th of July. Begin a wholesale evaluation of your landscape and make notes about tasks that need to be completed this month. Look around, and start looking for plants that may be in decline and will have to be replaced.

If you need some ideas for plants, look at the North Carolina Association of Nurserymen Plant Introduction Program. Along with the J. C. Raulston Arboretum, these plants have been selected for their outstanding landscape attributes and their adaptability to the southeast.

Look for the Georgia "Gold Medal" winners as well. These shrubs are selected for outstanding multiseason features such as summer flowers, colorful leaves, durability, and adaptability to various soil types and climates; they are easy to grow, have few pest problems, and require minimal care.

Be adventurous by selecting a few new and delectable shrubs from the menu.

Planting

Fall is the prime-time planting season. Select healthy container-grown or balled-and burlapped shrubs and plant them properly in the right location in your landscape.

Care for Your Shrubs

As the leaves fall, rake them up, shred them, and use them as a mulch around your shrubs.

Fertilizing

If your shrubs have produced sufficient growth this year, fertilizing may not be necessary. If you choose to fertilize, rely on soil test results to apply the nutrients required by your shrubs.

For blue flowers on your **French hydrangeas,** maintain a soil pH between 5 and 5.5. Apply aluminum sulfate or sulfur to reduce the pH to this ideal range. To avoid having to adjust the pH, grow a blue-flowered hydrangea such as **'All Summer Beauty', 'Blue Wave',** or **'Nikko Blue'.**

Watering

Don't let the cooler temperatures deceive you. Fall tends to be the driest season in the Carolinas. Continue watering regularly, and remember that it's better to water established shrubs deeply once a week than lightly every day. Water newly planted trees shrubs to provide sufficient moisture and encourage rapid establishment.

Pruning

Prune out only branches that are dead, diseased, or broken. Hold off on major pruning such as rejuvenation until late winter. Pruning now will only stimulate tender, new growth, which can be killed by our first freeze.

Pest Control

Insects and mites: Aphids and spider mites may still be active. Evaluate the extent of injury and decide if pest control measures are warranted. Use a water wand to wash mites off plants on a weekly basis, preferably early in the morning.

Diseases: Clean up fallen leaves, which can harbor disease and insect pests over the winter if allowed to remain on the ground.

Weeds: Don't turn your back on the weeds in your shrub beds. Summer annual weeds like crabgrass and goosegrass have matured and are going to seed. Winter annual weeds like annual bluegrass, chickweed, and Carolina geranium are germinating. Hoe them out or handpull them now.

Geotextile or landscape fabrics are synthetic mulch underliners that are used to suppress weeds on a long-term basis. When placed on the soil surface and covered with mulch, they enhance the ability of the mulch to suppress weeds. See Vines and Ground Covers, November Weeds (p. 337) for more information about these weed barriers.

Animals: Rabbits and deer can be a problem. Various commercially available mammal repellents can be applied to your shrubs. See October Animals, p. 277, for a homemade repellent recipe.

Helpful Hint

Generally, most **Japanese camellia (*Camellia japonica*)** cultivars bloom throughout the winter and early spring months. They can be coerced into bloom earlier, however, around October, through a simple technique called "gibbing."

Gibbing involves the application of the natural plant hormone gibberellic acid to **camellia** flowers. This growth regulator "awakens" the flower buds, releasing them from their state of dormancy. As a result, the treated flower buds swell and open up earlier than normal.

For more than twenty-five years, **camellia** enthusiasts have gibbed buds. Gibbing allows you to hasten flowering, especially on cultivars that tend to flower during the winter months. And gardeners who battle camellia flower blight, a diseases that kills **camellia** flowers in the spring (see February Pest Control, p. 261), can avoid the disease by coercing their camellias to bloom earlier when the fungus is still dormant.

Giberellic acid can be purchased from the American Camellia Society (100 Massee Lane, Fort Valley, GA 31030; 912-967-2358). A 1-gram package will treat 1,000 flowers.

To gib your **camellia** flowers, look for plump, round flower buds at the tips of the branches. Right next to the flower bud should be a smaller, pointed vegetative or growth bud (it produces leaves and stems). Twist out the growth bud, leaving its base or "cup" intact. Then apply one drop of gibberellic acid to the cup. Now move on to the next flower bud. You can expect blooms to open three to twelve weeks following the treatment. Obviously, early-flowering **camellia** cultivars will respond faster than the later-blooming ones. Start gibbing the first of September and treat a few buds on each **camellia** at weekly intervals so flowers will be produced throughout the season. One gibbing rule of thumb: treat no more than ¼ of the buds on young **camellia** plants. (On older plants, gib as many you like.)

OCTOBER

Planning

Late-season flowering plants could be considered the "Rodney Dangerfields" of the plant kingdom. They don't get any respect. How can they? During the spring months when winter-starved gardeners are looking for a floral feast, they skip over these late bloomers for the sumptuous flowers of **azaleas** and a multitude of other spring bloomers. "You're doomed without blooms" is the credo of plant merchandisers.

Even when they reach their peak in late summer and fall, late-season flowering plants still don't get any respect. At this time of year, deciduous shrubs are sporting their fall colors. But give these late-summer treats a second look:

Holly tea olive (*Osmanthus heterophyllus*), **senna** (*Cassia corymbosa*), **Fortune's osmanthus** (*Osmanthus × fortunei*), **sasanqua camellia** (*Camellia sasanqua*), and **tea-oil camellia** (*C. oleifera*) are standard fare. **Japanese fatsia** (*Fatsia japonica*) are other fall-flowering choices. Learn more about these and other late-season flowering plants that will thrive in your corner of the Carolinas.

Planting

Fall is a perfect season for planting in the Carolinas. Gardeners in the Coastal Plain and in the milder parts of the Piedmont can even plant throughout late fall and into winter. The cooler temperatures allow the shrubs to settle in comfortably and concentrate on producing roots. Follow the steps in the Planting section of the Trees introduction, p. 281.

To minimize the look of open spaces between newly planted shrubs, plant cool-season annuals or perennial low-growing ground covers.

Now is a good time to move shrubs that have outgrown their location. Shrubs normally transplant more readily than trees, and deciduous trees more readily than evergreens. Small plants transplant more successfully than do large ones of the same species.

Piedmont and Coastal gardeners can postpone any moves until next month or December, depending on how mild the weather is. Mountain gardeners should be mindful of this transplanting rule-of-thumb: Allow at least four weeks of soil temperatures above **40** degrees F. after planting to give the shrub some time to settle in before cold winter temperatures. See next month's Planting (p. 278) to learn the step-by-step transplanting approach.

Watering

Fall is unusually dry in the Carolinas, so don't rely on Mother Nature to water newly planted shrubs. *Water* frequently, checking the soil and rootball before watering.

Fertilizing

To add nutrients, supplement mulch with well-rotted horse or cow manure.

Pruning

Don't shear now, it's too late. You'll have brown-edged leaves all winter and you may spark tender new growth that will be killed by the first freeze. If there are a few wayward branches, cut them back by hand. Wait until spring to do any major shaping. Continue to *prune out* dead, damaged, and diseased branches.

Pest Control

Insects and mites: Sorry, but spider mites can still be active in the warmer parts of the Carolinas. Control the overwintering eggs with a dormant horticultural oil this fall when the shrubs go dormant (see January Pest Control, p. 259).

Diseases: *Prune out* infected limbs and rake up dead leaves to remove any overwintering fungal diseases.

Weeds: Keep the area around your shrubs free of weeds to eliminate any overwintering hideouts for two-spotted spider mites.

Animals: If you'd like to make your own repellent, mix 2 tablespoons of homemade hot pepper sauce per gallon of water or blend 2 or 3 rotten eggs in a gallon of water and spray it on your plants. Dried ground red peppers, ground black pepper, or chili powder are other repellents that can be dusted on or near flowers. To be effective, they will have to be reapplied after rain or heavy dew, and quite often to new plant growth.

Be aware that some of the repellents designed for mammals may kill non-targeted, beneficial insects. Before choosing a course of action, weigh the benefits of the treatment versus the level of acceptable damage.

Helpful Hint

While the two commonly grown species of **camellia (*C. japonica*** and ***C. sasanqua*)** are hardy only in zones 7, 8, and 9, the Ackerman hybrids have *C. oleifera* in their parentage, making them extra cold hardy. They are the result of the work of Dr. William Ackerman, a research horticulturist at the U. S. National Arboretum. According to him, the hardiest of the group are the fall-blooming **'Winter's Rose'** (miniature, shell pink, formal double), **'Winter's Interlude'** (miniature, pink, anemone form), **'Winter's Beauty'** (medium, lavender pink, peony form), and **'Winter's Waterlily'** (medium, white, anemone to formal double). These have successfully weathered temperatures to -10 degrees F.

In zone 6 they should be planted in a well-drained location with northern or western exposure, ideally with an overstory of shade trees to offer protection from sun and winter winds. **Mulch** well with a 2- to 3-inch layer of pine needles or other organic matter. Ackerman recommends providing additional protection for newly planted **camellias** during their first two winters. In late fall (late November or early December), enclose each plant in a wire cage or surround it with stakes. Apply a 6-inch layer of dry leaves as mulch, and wrap the cage or stakes in a layer of Microfoam. This in turn should be wrapped in a layer of plastic film (clear if the plant is shaded, opaque white if not). In early spring, open the top for a few days before removing the blanket completely.

NOVEMBER

Planning

Identify shrub beds and borders whose soil will have to be tested. Soil testing is best done every two or three years. Contact your cooperative extension service agent for soil-testing materials. You can take samples this month or wait a couple of months when the cooler fall weather arrives.

Planting

This is a good month to plant and move shrubs. In the Mountains, mulch with compost, shredded bark, or shredded leaves soon after planting to keep the ground thawed so roots can become established. Now is a good time to move shrubs that have outgrown their location. Here's how to move a shrub:

1 *Tie up* the branches of wide, low-spreading shrubs with soft twine.

2 Use a ribbon to *mark* the side of the shrub that faces north so it can be properly oriented when planting.

3 Create a good-sized rootball. Shrubs less than 3 feet in height and deciduous trees less than 1 inch in trunk diameter (measured 6 inches above the ground) can be moved bare root. Bare root means that most or all of the soil is removed from the roots after digging the plant. Bare-root plants should be moved when they're dormant.

Shrubs greater than 1 inch in trunk diameter and all broadleaf and narrowleaf evergreens should be moved with the soil attached. The size of the ball should be large enough in diameter and depth to include as much of the fibrous and feeding roots as possible. It also depends on how much you or a friend can physically manage.

1 With your shovel, dig a trench around the shrub to create a rootball that's 12 to 14 inches wide. This will be adequate for deciduous shrubs up to 2 feet tall and sprawling evergreens with a spread of two feet.

2 Use a spade to dig under the shrub. Undercut all around the plant with the spade before rocking it.

3 Once the rootball is free, tip the shrub to one side and slide a tarp beneath it as far as possible. Then lay down the shrub in the opposite direction and pull the tarp all the way under the plant. Now slide the shrub out of the hole.

4 Use a shovel handle to measure the depth and width of the rootball to determine how wide to make the hole.

5 *Plant* the shrub so the rootball is a few inches higher than the surrounding soil.

6 *Backfill* around the plant, and tamp down the soil lightly with the end of your shovel handle to settle the soil around the roots.

7 *Water* the plant thoroughly, making sure the rootball and surrounding soil are completely wet.

8 *Water* it in to settle the soil, and follow up with a 2- to 4-inch layer of mulch.

Care for Your Shrubs

Rake up and compost fallen leaves and fruit around shrubs because this litter offers overwintering places for insects and diseases.

Broadleaved and tender evergreens exposed to drying winds and sun may need to be shaded on the south and southwest sides to reduce moisture loss and leaf injury. Enclose your evergreens in these exposed locations with a burlap screen.

NOVEMBER

Fertilizing

Do not fertilize shrubs that are displaying their fall colors—wait until next year.

Watering

If fall rains have been scarce in the Mountains where the ground freezes, keep broadleaf evergreens such as **hollies** and **rhododendrons** well watered. Give them a deep watering once every two weeks. Evergreens continue to lose moisture from their leaves all winter, but once the ground is frozen they'll be unable to take up enough water to replace it. Sending them into winter well watered reduces the potential for damaged foliage.

Pruning

Limit any pruning to the removal of diseased, damaged, or broken branches. Wait until after the coldest part of winter has passed next year before pruning summer-flowering shrubs.

Pest Control

Insects and mites: Watch out for the "cool-weather" mites: spruce spider mites which feed on **arborvitae, juniper, spruce,** and other conifers. They attack in the spring and fall, although at higher elevations they may be active all summer long.

Those small cone-shaped bags aren't the fruits of your **arborvitae** or **juniper.** They house the eggs of bagworms which have been feeding on your conifers. *Remove and destroy* bagworm bags on narrow-leaved evergreens. Eggs overwinter in the bags produced by the females and will hatch out next spring.

If there is any evidence of scale on shrubs, *spray* with dormant oil in late fall and again in early spring. See January Pest Control, p. 259.

Animals: To protect young trees against deer damage, there are a number of deterrents you can try. Remember, deer will become accustomed to any object, so alternating items will help. Hang bars of strong-scented soap, mesh bags filled with human hair, paper bags of dried blood (bloodmeal), or strips cut from white plastic bags on trees that are likely to be attacked. Chemical deer repellents also can be applied. Be sure to reapply any chemicals after two to three weeks of normal weathering.

DECEMBER

Planning

The best way to prevent winter damage to shrubs is to select hardy species. As you tinker with your landscape over the winter, plan to consult publications containing information on the climatic zones for the shrubs you are interested in planting. It is better to select cold-hardy species in the first place rather than attempt to protect tender plants later.

Planting

Continue planting container-grown and balled-and-burlapped shrubs in the Piedmont and Coastal Plain where the soil doesn't freeze and thaw during the winter months. Take hardwood stem cuttings of evergreens such as **boxwood, camellia, holly,** and **juniper** this month, and root them in a cool greenhouse or cold frame.

Care for Your Shrubs

Construct windbreaks around broad-leaved evergreens predisposed to winter damage. Drive four wooden stakes around the shrub, wrap it with burlap, and staple it to the stakes.

Helpful Hints

Hollies are either male or female. The males produce pollen while the female hollies produce fruit. Although some female hollies such as **Burford** will produce fruit without requiring pollination, other hollies need male pollen. Generally, the best pollinator for a female holly is a male of the same species. Distinguishing between male and female **holly (*Ilex* species)** plants is pretty straightforward once the plants begin to flower next spring.

Male plants produce profuse numbers of whitish flowers, each with four prominent stamens that stick up between the petals. When the anthers ripen and split open, you can see the sticky yellow pollen.

Female hollies, by contrast, produce fewer blooms, and each bloom has in its center a green, pealike pistil, which will develop into the berry, surrounded by four poorly developed, nonfunctional stamens.

Because hollies are insect-pollinated, it's possible to get fruit from a pair spaced as far apart as $1/8$ mile. But you will improve your berry set by locating the two sexes closer together. If this is not possible, place flowering male branches in a container of water and set them at the foot of a female plant.

Fertilizing

Do not fertilize shrubs this month.

Watering

Mountain gardeners should make sure their newly planted shrubs are well watered before the ground freezes.

Pruning

When cutting branches from **hollies** or other evergreen shrubs and trees for indoor decoration, maintain the natural form and beauty of the plant.

Limit pruning of other plants to the removal of damaged or dead branches.

Trees

In the Carolinas we're fortunate to be able to grow a wide variety of native and adapted trees. These living investments grow in value with each passing year and offer so much to our landscapes. They shade us during the summer, offer privacy, and hide unsightly views. They surround us with the seasonal beauty of their leaves and flowers, and their attractive bark and branch architecture.

There's something for the energy-conscious, too. Trees save energy and money. Deciduous trees (leafless in winter) can shade your home in the summer, then let in sun to warm it in the winter. The afternoon shade of trees planted on the southeastern and western sides can reduce temperatures inside the home by 8 to 10 degrees. Trees also provide food, shelter, and nesting for wildlife. Pollen and nectar for hummingbirds, butterflies, and bees are added bonuses.

Trees are permanent plants, so pay particular attention to their selection and proper placement in your landscape.

Planning

Before you introduce any new trees into your landscape, refer to the planning process described in the Introduction to this book, p. 10. Once you've determined where you want your trees, select trees that match the conditions in your landscape. Here are a few suggestions to help you select the right one:

- Look for trees well suited for the growing conditions in your landscape. Sun-loving trees should be sited in full sun; understory types should be located in partial shade.

- Know the ultimate size and growth rate of the tree, which is important in selecting the right location.

- Select trees for shade and multi-season interest. Look for those that excel in several seasons, offering flowers, fruit, attractive bark, fall color, and unique branching habits.

- Look for trees that have few insect or disease problems. Some are magnets for pests: **willows, silver maple, Siberian elm,** and **several cherries** (*Prunus* species).

Planting

Most trees are available in containers or as field-grown balled-and-burlapped trees. Follow these steps to ensure a good start for your new tree:

1 *Match* the tree to its location. In addition to light levels, be aware of drainage, salt spray (for coastal gardeners), and other factors that can affect the tree's growth.

2 Have your soil tested through your county cooperative extension service office.

Planting a Tree

Trees

3 Dig a wide, shallow hole at least two or three times bigger than the diameter of the rootball, but no deeper than the height of the ball. By making the hole as wide as possible, the roots will grow quickly into the loosened soil, thereby speeding up the plant's establishment in its new home.

4 Slip the plant out of the pot and examine the rootball. Shrubs or trees growing in containers may have roots circling around the outside of the rootball. If you plant it as is, roots will grow from the bottom of the rootball. You should encourage roots to grow along the entire length of the rootball. To do this, take a knife, pruning shears, or the end of a sharp spade and lightly score the rootball in three or four places. Make shallow cuts from the top to the bottom of the rootball. Gently tease the sides of the rootball apart. Now this "doctored" plant will produce new roots from these cuts all around the rootball.

5 Remove any wire or twine from balled-and-burlapped plants and cut away as much wrapping material as possible after placing it in the hole. **Remove** synthetic burlap entirely; it won't break down and ultimately strangle the roots.

6 Plant even with or slightly above the surrounding soil. Place the tree in the hole for fit. Lay your shovel across the hole. The rootball should be level with or slightly above the handle. If, in your zeal, you've gone too deep, shovel some soil back in. Compact it with your feet. You want a firm footing for the rootball so it won't later sink below the level of the surrounding grade. That can cause roots to suffocate. *In slowly draining soils, set the rootball an inch or two higher than the surrounding soil and cover it with mulch.*

7 Start backfilling—returning the soil to the planting hole. Tamp the soil lightly as you go, but don't compact it. When half the rootball is covered, add some water to settle out any air pockets and remoisten the rootball. Finish backfilling and water again. Do not cover the top of the rootball with soil.

8 Mulch. Apply 2 to 4 inches of organic mulch such as compost, leaf litter, shredded wood, or pine straw. Extend it to the outermost reaches of the branches. Leave a space of 3 inches or more around the trunk to keep the bark dry.

9 Water frequently. Water—not fertilizer—is the most important ingredient to helping trees get established.

Depending on the weather and rainfall, you may need to water daily for the first few weeks. After that, begin cutting back, eventually reaching an "as needed" basis by testing the soil and rootball for moisture. See October Watering on p. 304 for details.

Fertilizing

Newly planted trees can be fertilized after they become established, which may take months or longer, depending on their size. Once established, fertilizing can stimulate growth and help them fill into their allotted space in the landscape.

Established trees shouldn't be fertilized on a regular basis. Replenishing the mulch over their roots with compost or other "recyclable" organic materials provides them with a steady diet of minerals. If your trees are growing in a lawn that is fertilized, do not add additional fertilizer.

Apply fertilizer when it will be readily absorbed by the roots of your trees and when the soil is moist, which can be any time from late spring after new growth emerges up to early fall. However, if water is unavailable or when the trees are stressed by drought during the summer months, do not fertilize at all because their roots will be unable to absorb the nutrients.

Fertilize based on the tree's appearance (see May, Fertilizing on p. 294) and according to soil-test results. Most fertilizer recommendations are based on nitrogen: apply 1 pound of nitrogen per thousand square feet of root zone area; up to 2 pounds can be applied with a slow-release fertilizer.

Apply the fertilizer to the area occupied by the tree's roots, which is called the **root zone area.** It's roughly a circular area with the tree in the center. The outermost reaches of the root zone area defined by the radius of the circle can be 3 times the distance from the trunk to the outermost branches or drip line. For example, if the distance from the trunk of your tree to the drip line is 4 ft., the "feeder" or mineral–absorbing roots can extend an additional 8 ft. beyond the drip line. So, expect the roots to cover an area up to 12 ft. away from the trunk.

Since most of a tree's roots can be found in the top foot of soil, *broadcast* the fertilizer evenly over the root zone area with a rotary or drop-type spreader. (To learn how to calibrate your spreader to apply the right amount of fertilizer, refer to February Planning in the Warm-Season Lawns chapter on p. 174). If the tree's root zone is confined by a sidewalk or driveway, reduce the root zone area accordingly.

Calculate the amount you need to apply over the root zone area. First, calculate the root zone area with this formula:

Root Zone Area = $3 \times$ (root radius) $\times$ (root radius)

In the example given above, the Root Zone Area is:

3×12 ft. $\times 12$ ft. = 452 square ft.

Assuming you have a 16-4-8 fertilizer, determine the amount of fertilizer required to apply 1 pound of nitrogen per 1,000 square feet using this equation:

Root Zone Area/1,000 sq. ft. divided by the %N in the fertilizer bag equals the amount of fertilizer to apply over the tree's root zone area.

$$\frac{452 \text{ sq. ft.} \div 1{,}000 \text{ sq. ft.}}{16\%^*} = 3$$

Apply 3 lbs. (or 6 cups) of 16-4-8 evenly over the root zone area.

*16% = 0.16

Watering

Not all established trees have to be watered during hot, dry summer months. Drought-tolerant trees can withstand long periods without rain or irrigation.

Pruning

Trees and large shrubs are pruned to improve their health and their branching structure. The goal of pruning young trees is to create a strong structure of trunk and limbs to support future growth. The focus for pruning mature trees (usually by professionals) is to remove weak limbs to focus the tree's resources on the stronger remaining branches. See January Planning (p. 286) for more information.

Pest Control

Insects and diseases are two of the most serious threats to your trees' health. Plants that are weakened by unfavorable growing conditions will not be able to tolerate pest attacks. Select better-adapted plants and match them to the site, or concentrate on pest-resistant cultivars.

Even so, some pest-resistant trees that are planted correctly in the right location can still be attacked by pests. It's just nature. A tree ought to be able to support a few insects or diseased leaves if it is kept healthy and vigorous.

When pests strike, follow an Integrated Pest Management approach to their control, which is discussed in the Pest Control section in the introduction to Shrubs (p. 253–54).

Carolina Trees

Small Trees
(up to 30 ft. at maturity)

Common Name (Botanical Name)	Hardiness Zone	Height/ Spread	Comments
Crapemyrtle (*Lagerstroemia indica* and hybrids)	7 to 10	8–30 ft./ 6–25 ft.	Best in sun. Summer flowers come in all shades of white, pink, red, or lavender; exfoliating bark and attractive fall color. Dwarf forms are available (see p. 290). Recent crosses with Japanese crapemyrtle (*L. fauriei*) at the U.S. National Arboretum resulted in about 20 cultivars, most of which exhibit increased cold hardiness and better powdery mildew resistance (see p. 297).
Flowering dogwood (*Cornus florida*)	5b to 8b	20–30 ft./ 20–30 ft.	Part shade (particularly in the afternoon). Flowers consist of 4 showy bracts attached to a small head of yellow flowers. Bracts may be white, pink, or red depending on the cultivar.
Kousa or Chinese dogwood (*Cornus kousa* cultivars and hybrids)	5–8	15–20 ft./ 15–20 ft.	Sun to part shade. Attractive peeling bark, longlasting bracts, yellow or red fall color, and attractive red fruits. Less heat-tolerant than flowering dogwood. The Stellar® series are hybrids between flowering dogwood and kousa (p. 293, Diseases).
Holly (*Ilex* spp.)	See Comments	See Comments	Sun to part shade. Many species, hybrids, and cultivars with a variety of shapes and sizes including American holly (*I. opaca*), hardy in zones 5 to 9, 15 to 16 ft.; Yaupon (*I. vomitoria*) 7–10, 15–20 ft./15–20 ft.; 'Foster's Holly #2', 6–9, 15–30 ft./8–12 ft.; 'East Palatka', 7 to 9, 25–35 ft./10–15 ft.; and 'Nellie R. Stevens', 6 to 9, 15–30 ft./10–15 ft.
Japanese maple (*Acer palmatum*)	5 to 8 (depends on cultivar)	15–25 ft./ 15–25 ft.	Sun to shade (best sited in partial shade in the warmer extremes of its hardiness range). Beautiful and durable with four-season ornamental interest. Wide choice of cultivars
Paperbark maple (*Acer griseum*)	5 to 7	20–30 ft./ 15–25 ft.	Purple-brown bark peels away to reveal cinnamon-orange bark beneath. Bright red and orange fall color.
Jelly or Pindo palm (*Butia capitata*)	8a to 11	15–25 ft./ 10–15 ft.	Sun to part shade. Rounded canopy of graceful blue-green to silvery-green fronds that curve in toward the trunk.
Windmill palm (*Trachycarpus fortunei*)	7b to 10	15–35 ft./ 10–15 ft.	Sun (with adequate moisture) to shade (especially in warmer areas of its range). Good patio or courtyard palm.
Eastern redbud (*Cercis canadensis*)	4 to 9a	20–30 ft./ 15–30 ft.	Sun to partial shade in the warmer areas of its range. Many exceptional cultivars, particularly 'Forest Pansy'.
Japanese snowbell (*Styrax japonica*)	6 to 8z	20–30 ft./ 15–25 ft.	Sun to part shade. Outstanding white bell-shaped flowers in spring; 'Emerald Pagoda' is a most desirable cultivar.

Medium Trees
(30 to 50 ft. at maturity)

Common Name (Botanical Name)	Hardiness Zone	Height/ Spread	Comments
River birch (*Betula nigra*)	4 to 9a	40–50 ft./ 40–50 ft.	Sun to part shade. Attractive peeling or "exfoliating" bark; resistant to bronze birch borer. Heritage® has a salmon-white trunk. Dura-Heat™ has smaller leaves, shrubbier, more heat-tolerant.

Carolina Trees

Medium Trees
(30 to 50 ft. at maturity)

Common Name (Botanical Name)	Hardiness Zone	Height/ Spread	Comments
Eastern red cedar (*Juniperus virginiana*)	3b to 9a	40–50 ft./ 8–25 ft.	Best in full sun. Tough and dependable. Many choice cultivars are available. Blue berries are borne on female plants. May be local restrictions when planting near commercial apple orchards because it is the intermediate host for cedar-apple rust.
Chinese or Lacebark elm (*Ulmus parvifolia*)	5b to 9	40–50 ft./ 35–50 ft.	Sun to part shade. Beautiful peeling bark revealing mottled patterns of gray, green, orange, and brown.
Cabbage palm (*Sabal palmetto*)	8b to 11	20–30 ft./ 35–50 ft.	Sun to part shade. State tree of South Carolina. Very salt tolerant.
Persian parrotia (*Parrotia persica*)	5 to 8a (8b)	20–40 ft./ 20–40 ft.	Sun to part shade. Tough, beautiful tree with reddish purple young leaves maturing to a lustrous dark green, and then turning various hues of orange, red, and yellow.
Chinese pistache (*Pistache chinensis*)	6b to 9	25–35 ft./ 25–35 ft.	Sun (tolerates part shade). Orange inner bark, peeling bark; outstanding fall color; withstands heat and drought.
Yellowwood (*Cladrastis kentukea*)	4b to 8a	30–50 ft./ 40–50 ft.	Sun (for best flowering) to part shade. Takes 5 to 8 years to come into bloom, bearing fragrant chains of wisteria-like flowers in late spring; brilliant yellow fall color.

Large Trees
(50 ft. or taller at maturity)

Common Name (Botanical Name)	Hardiness Zone	Height/ Spread	Comments
Baldcypress (*Taxodium distichum*)	5 to 10	60–80 ft./ 25–35 ft.	Sun (tolerates part shade). Tough and adaptable deciduous conifer. Tolerates extremes of wet and dry conditions. Showy bronze or yellow fall color.
Ginkgo or Maidenhair tree (*Ginkgo biloba*)	3 to 8	50–75 ft./ 50–60 ft.	Sun to part shade. Yellow fall color and highly pest resistant. Males are used in landscapes. Females produce plum-shaped fruits in late summer and fall that are foul-smelling when ripe.
Dawn redwood (*Metasequoia glyptostroboides*)	5 to 8	70–90 ft./ 25–35 ft.	Sun, tolerates part shade. Tough and adaptable deciduous conifer; tolerates extremes of wet and dry conditions. Showy bronze or yellow fall color.
Live oak (*Quercus virginiana*)	(7b) 8 to 11	60–80 ft./	Statuesque tree; tough and long-lived. Salt-tolerant.
Red maple (*Acer rubrum*)	4 to 8	60–75 ft./ 25–35 ft.	Sun to part shade. Noted for brilliant fall color displays of red, orange, or yellow.
Southern magnolia (*Magnolia grandiflora*)	(6) 7 to 10a	60–80 ft./ 30–40 ft.	Several selections offer larger or smaller leaves, better or repeat blooming and increased hardiness.
Willow oak (*Quercus phellos*)	6 to 9	60–75 ft./ 40–60 ft.	Sun. Tough tree well adapted to urban conditions. Scarcely recognized as an oak with graceful willowlike leaves.
Japanese zelkova (*Zelkova serrata*)	5 to 8	50–80 ft./ 50–75 ft.	Sun. Tough, almost pest-free. Fall color is showy copper, orange, red, or yellow.

Planning

If you're planning on pruning your trees this winter, have a purpose in mind as described in the following steps:

1 *Thin out* dying, dead, or pest-ridden twigs and branches. *Thinning* is a term that describes the removal of a branch where it joins the limb or trunk. Thinning opens up the center of the tree to sunlight and reduces the number of new shoots that sprout along the branches. A lot of growth can be removed by thinning without dramatically changing the tree's natural appearance or growth habit and giving it the "just-pruned" look.

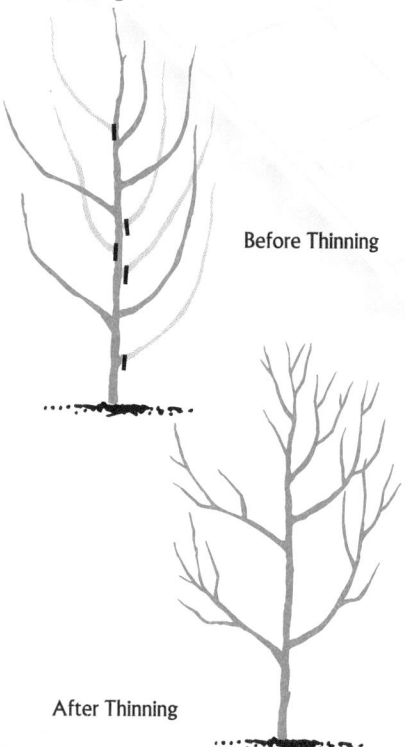

Before Thinning

After Thinning

Heading cuts are usually reserved for shrubs (see Pruning in the Shrubs chapter, p. 253) and are generally undesirable on mature trees. Young trees can be headed back to encourage branching on long leggy branches.

Never head back or "top" the limbs of mature trees: their structure is weakened or lost with the production of numerous snake-like sprouts, and the stubs that result are exposed to attack from insects and diseases.

2 Next, *remove* one of any two branches that are rubbing or crossing over another. Wounds develop on rubbing branches, creating entryways for invading insects and diseases.

3 *Remove* branches that form a narrow, V-shaped angle with the trunk. Branches that form an angle less than 45 degrees from the trunk (10 and 2 o'clock) are weakly attached.

4 *Remove* upright-growing side limbs that grow taller than the main trunk.

5 Do not coat the wounds with pruning-wound paints. *There is no scientific evidence that shows that dressing wounds prevent decay.*

Planting

If you purchased a live Christmas tree, plant it outdoors as soon as possible, especially if it has already been in the house for longer three days.

Care for Your Trees

If you staked your newly planted tree last fall, *check* the rubber straps and stakes. Make sure they're secured at the lowest point on the trunk to give the trunk a little room to move back and forth (encouraging the development of a strong, thick trunk). In the Mountains, the stakes may have to be hammered back into the ground if they've been heaved out of the soil by cold. Make a note in your journal to remove the straps in the spring after growth has started.

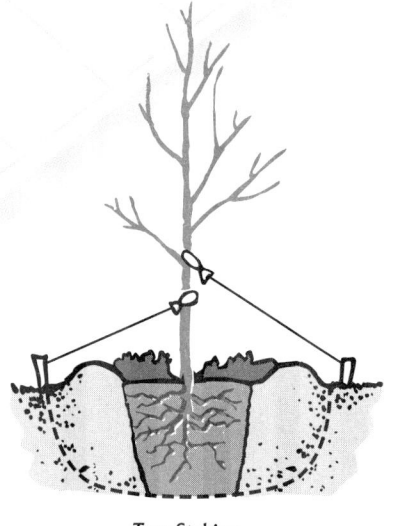

Tree Staking

Watering

During mild winter spells, water fall-planted and established evergreens, especially if the winter is dry. Pay particular attention to trees planted on the southern and western sides of your home. *Mulch* newly planted trees with a 2- to 3-inch layer of compost and keep them well watered.

Fertilizing

Don't be too hasty to fertilize your trees. Wait until at least budbreak—when new growth emerges in the spring. See p. 294 to determine if fertilizing is necessary.

Pruning

Start pruning after the coldest part of winter has passed. Gardeners in the Coastal Plain can start later this month, although it may be safer to wait until early next month. Piedmont and Mountain gardeners can wait until next month or March.

Helpful Hints

Mistletoe is a cherished Christmas decoration, but when you find it growing on your oaks, thoughts about kissing under the mistletoe on Christmas Eve last month are forgotten, and you will want to get rid of it. It is a pest that is half-parasitic: it has leaves to produce its own food, but it steals water and nutrients from its host. It can affect the growth and vigor of its host, exposing the tree to attacks by diseases and insects. In some instances, mistletoe can cause branches to die back, and heavy, shrubby mistletoes can break entire limbs. In other situations, mistletoe is simply a cosmetic problem, which affects only the appearance of the tree.

The only effective way to rid your tree of a mistletoe infestation is by pruning. Cut the infected limb 1 to 2 feet below the plant because mistletoe "roots" may extend up to a foot on either side of the point of attachment. Breaking off the tops (similar to plucking off the leaves of dandelions or wild garlic in the lawn) only encourages regrowth. **Pruning out mistletoe clumps from the uppermost reaches of trees should be left in the hands of certified arborists.** If you are a do-it-yourselfer, avoid butchering the tree with haphazard cuts which can kill the tree. Growth hormone sprays interrupt flowering or cause the shoots to fall off, but the mistletoe eventually resprouts and needs to be treated again.

Pest Control

Insects: Apply dormant horticultural oil sprays on small landscape trees before growth begins to smother overwintering insect eggs, aphids, mites, and scale insects. Special equipment or a professional will be required to treat large trees. See Shrubs, January Pest Control on p. 259 for more information.

Planning

Order fruit trees, or look for them in garden centers and nurseries in the milder areas of the Carolinas. Before you shop, do your homework. Be familiar with their growing requirements. In addition to full sun and a well-drained location, certain fruit trees require regular pruning, watering, and pest control to realize a full, blemish-free crop.

Fruit trees such as **peaches** require a certain number of chilling hours—hours at temperatures between 33 and 45 degrees Fahrenheit—for the dormant flower and leaf buds to awaken and develop normally. Varieties that require less than 750 hours are not recommended for North Carolina because they bloom too early and their flowers could be killed by frosts or freezes. South Carolina gardeners can grow varieties requiring more than 500 chilling hours.

For smaller landscapes, consider **apple** trees grafted onto size-controlling rootstocks. A grafted tree has the *scion,* or fruiting part, joined to a rootstock. These dwarfing rootstocks encourage earlier bearing on trees and also reduce their ultimate height. For example, a standard apple tree growing on its own roots will usually reach a mature height of 30 feet. If grafted onto a dwarfing rootstock,

however, the same variety may reach only 6 feet. This means that the trees can be planted closer together and can be pruned and picked without the use of ladders.

Various rootstocks offer widely different degrees of dwarfing. In catalogs the word "dwarf" is generally used to describe trees that are 50 percent or less of normal size, and semidwarf for those that are larger but less than full-size. To be sure of the rootstock you're getting, call the company for more details.

Planting

Bare-root, deciduous trees can be planted while they're dormant, about a month before the last average freeze in your area. Plant them as soon as possible after buying them or receiving them in the mail. Unwrap and soak the roots in a bucket of water at least twelve hours before planting. Broken roots should be pruned back cleanly to behind the break. Follow these steps for planting bare-root shrubs or trees:

1 *Dig* the planting hole wide enough so the roots can be spread out. Don't break or bend the roots to make them fit.

2 Create a cone of soil in the bottom of the hole and tamp down the top firmly. This will prevent the tree from settling too deeply.

3 Set the plant on top of the cone. *Drape* the roots evenly over the top. The topmost root should be positioned so it's just under the soil surface. Lay your shovel handle across the hole to help gauge the correct depth.

4 Work the soil in among the roots with your fingers. *Backfill* the hole halfway with soil, and water it in. Add the remaining soil and water again. If the tree has settled too deeply, grasp the trunk and lift it gently to raise it to the proper level.

5 *Mulch* with a 2- to 3-inch layer of compost, pine straw, or shredded wood.

Care for Your Trees

Ice and snow accumulation can damage your evergreens with their weight or if they are removed carelessly. See the January Shrubs Helpful Hint, p. 259.

Fertilizing

Don't be too hasty to fertilize your trees. Wait until at least budbreak, when new growth emerges in the spring. See p. 294 to determine if fertilizing is necessary.

Watering

Water newly planted trees. Keep the soil moist but avoid overwatering, which can inhibit root growth. If severe cold is forecast for your area, water evergreens before the soil freezes. The roots are not able to take up moisture when the soil is frozen.

Pruning

Begin pruning when the coldest part of winter has passed and before new growth begins. When pruning large, heavy limbs, follow the three-cut approach to prevent the branch from stripping bark away as it falls.

1 Make the first upward cut about a foot from the trunk and one-third of the way through the bottom of the limb.

2 Make the second downward cut from the top of the branch a couple of inches away from the

Limb Removal

first cut, farther away from the trunk. As the branch falls, the undercut causes the limb to break away cleanly.

3 Finally, *remove* the stub by making the last cut outside of the branch collar (a swollen area at the base of the branch). The collar region is the boundary between the trunk and the branch that acts as a natural barrier to decay-causing organisms. ***Never leave a stub. Stubs usually die and are entry points for decay-causing fungi.***

Avoid making "hat racks" out of your **crapemyrtles.** Follow these steps to produce a natural-looking tree form that accentuates the flowers, beautiful bark, and elegant structure:

1 *Remove* all broken and diseased limbs.

2 Next, thin out all of the side branches one-third to one-half way up the height of the plant.

3 *Remove* rubbing and crossing branches and shoots growing into the center of the canopy or upper part of the **crapemyrtle.** Make your cuts to a side branch or close to the trunk.

4 Head-back wayward and unbranched limbs. Make each cut above an outward-facing bud. This will encourage the development of branches behind the cut and make them fuller.

5 *Remove* dried-up seed clusters within reach. This will give the tree a more uniform appearance and look neater.

Pest Control

Insects and mites: See January, p. 287.

Examine your **Leyland cypress, arborvitae,** and **junipers** for the pine cone–shaped nests of overwintering bagworms. *Pick off* the egg-containing "bags" and discard them.

Planning

The first Friday following March 15 is Arbor Day in North Carolina. Make plans to plant a tree or support an organization that does.

Planting

Plant balled-and-burlapped or container-grown trees. Follow the step-by-step instructions in the introduction, p. 281. **Birch, black gum, dogwood, fir, hickory, magnolia, pecan, red oaks,** and **walnut** are best moved and planted in early spring while they're still dormant.

Care for Your Trees

Check the supports on newly planted trees. Remember that support stakes and anchor stakes are only temporary and should be removed within a year after planting. Allow some slack in the support so the trunk can move slightly, encouraging the development of a strong, thick trunk.

Mulch as far as the dripline or outermost branches, but leave a space of 6 inches between the trunk and the mulch to keep the bark dry.

Fertilizing

Fertilize trees only if necessary after they leaf out. Use a slow-release fertilizer that contains one-half of the nitrogen in a slowly available, water-insoluble form.

Watering

Newly planted shrubs will need watering every few weeks if the weather becomes dry. *Check* the moisture in the rootball and surrounding soil before watering. Gradually reduce the frequency but not the depth of watering: Deep watering encourages deep rooting.

Pruning

To keep **pines** sheared to form a dense hedge, you need to trim the new growth or "candles" each year. Timing is critical: do it when the new needles are about one-half the length of the old needles. Pruning the candles at this time will allow shoot buds to develop below the cuts. These will sprout next year.

Pines, most **junipers, spruces,** and **firs** should not be pruned back to older, bare branches because they will not produce new growth; the needleless branch usually dies.

Young **arborvitae, false cypress (***Chamaecyparis***), Leyland cypress,** and **yew,** however, can be cut back when they're dormant to one- or two-year-old wood that lacks foliage; dormant buds will sprout and fill in.

Trees that "bleed" or excrete sap profusely should not be pruned at this time. Although the bleeding is unsightly, it's not harmful. To minimize bleeding, *prune* the trees after the leaves green-up in the summer and the shoot stops growing. Some arborist have found that fall pruning minimizes bleeding, but this practice must be weighed against the possibility of making the trees susceptible to winter injury. The following trees "bleed" when pruned shortly before budbreak: **Birches (***Betula***), Elms (***Ulmus***), dogwoods (***Cornus***), European hornbeam (***Carpinus***), Honeylocust (***Gleditsia***), Magnolias (***Magnolia***), Maples (***Acer***), Silverbell (***Halesia***),** and **Yellowwood (***Cladrastis***).**

If your **crapemyrtle** grows too large and only heavy pruning will reduce it to the size you want, consider lower-growing crapemyrtles. **Crapemyrtle** shrubs that mature between 5 to 10 feet include **Acoma** (white flowers), **Pecos** (pink), and **Tonto** (red). These are also resistant to powdery mildew, a grayish-white fuzzy fungus that attacks and distorts the leaves. If these are still too tall, try **Hopi** (white), **Ozark Spring** (lavender), and **Victor** (dark red). They'll reach between 3 and 5 feet in height at maturity. Unfortunately, they are extremely susceptible to powdery mildew. For a mature height of less than 3 feet, try the slow-growing **Chickasaw** (pink-lavender), which is the smallest, reaching a height of 2 feet.

Some trees such as **Bradford pear** produce a lot of upright branches that grow too closely together on the trunk. As a result, they often split apart during snow-, ice-, and windstorms. *Thin out* the branches on young trees to give them more room. Shorten upright-growing limbs to prevent all of them from growing to the same size at one point on the trunk.

Pest Control

Insects and mites: Apply a dormant horticultural oil spray on dormant landscape plants to control overwintering insects and mites. See January, p. 287.

Look for the grayish-white webs or "tents" of Eastern tent caterpillars in the crotches of trees. They feed on the leaves of **crabapples, wild cherry,** and **apple,** but they aren't fussy. When these trees are scarce

Helpful Hints

Fruit trees require specialized training and pruning, which will vary according to the type, age, and variety of the fruit. However, the objective is the same: producing a strong framework of fruit-bearing limbs and shoots. Fruit trees need your attention. If you don't give it, you'll be left with an untrained, unruly tree with entangled masses of shoots and branches which produce little or no fruit and serve as a haven for insects and diseases. Consider the following tips when training and pruning fruit crops:

1 Before training or pruning a plant, visualize the results of your action. Training mistakes may easily be corrected, but once a branch is pruned out or removed it cannot be replaced.

2 Train as much as possible and remove as little as possible. Bending and tying shoots instead of cutting them out, especially on **apple** and **pear** trees, can induce early fruit production.

3 Use sharp pruning tools to make clean cuts.

4 Discard or compost pruned-out shoots and branches. These plant parts will serve as dwelling sites for insects and diseases and should be removed from the area to reduce pest populations.

Light pruning can be performed throughout the growing season to remove broken, injured, or diseased branches and to improve air circulation to control leaf diseases. Major removal of twigs and branches should be done during the dormant season, preferably before active growth begins in the spring.

you'll find them dwelling in **ash, birch, willow, maple,** and **oak** trees. Trees are rarely killed, but the damage is unsightly. To control them, wait until evening and wipe out the nests with a gloved hand, or wrap the nest around a stick and drop the whole nest into a container of soapy water. The bacterial insecticide **BT (*Bacillus thuringiensis*)** can be used to control the caterpillars when they're small.

Planning

Variety is the spice of life—which also applies to the landscape. Find time to increase your tree vocabulary by learning about a few trees this month. Plan to see and learn more about native American trees that have been growing in North America when the Europeans first arrived and are still here in our state. This is proof of their longevity and ability to adapt readily to our Carolina climate, soils, and pests.

Visit parks and preserves to see native plants in their natural habitats. Undisturbed areas near your home may also give you some ideas. See what grows well in your area. Take photographs of the plants and show them to knowledgeable people to help you identify them, or use a good field guide with color photos. Visit your local library and bookstores to find reference books on native trees. Become a member of a local native plant society. The members often swap plants and seeds and are knowledgeable about what grows best in your area.

When you have found some favorites, avoid the urge to dig up native plants from the wild. There are ethical, legal, and scientific consequences to this practice. It's better to purchase nursery-propagated natives from nurseries or mail-order catalogs.

Planting

It's not too late to plant container-grown and balled-and-burlapped plants. Pay careful attention to watering during their establishment phase.

Care for Your Trees

Avoid bumping into tree trunks with your lawn mower or whipping them with a nylon string trimmer. The resulting wounds can be colonized by fungal diseases or infested by borers which can eventually kill the tree.

Fertilizing

Fertilize palms with a slow-release fertilizer having a 3:1:2 analysis such as 18-6-12 or 15-5-10. Apply according to label directions. **Palms** benefit from fertilizers that also contain magnesium and other micronutrients such as manganese. This is particularly true of **palms** growing on the outer coastal plain where micronutrient deficiencies are common. **Broadcast** or scatter the fertilizer under the canopy or bed area.

Watering

Sometimes it's necessary to create a temporary berm or dike around newly planted shrubs in clay soil to prevent water from running off when watering. **Remove** the berm when the plants become established (see May Watering, p. 294).

Pruning

Repair the damaged or broken central leader of your **fir, pine,** or **spruce** to return the tree to its natural pyramidal shape. Begin by developing a new leader:

1 Select one of the topmost shoots and secure it upright to a wooden stake.

2 Shorten the nearby shoots by cutting off a third of their length to reduce competition with the new leader.

3 Work your way down and around the tree, cutting all branches back to a side branch or visible dormant bud.

Once you have reestablished a pyramidal shape, further pruning should not be necessary.

Pest Control

Insects and mites: Watch out for the "cool-weather" mites: southern red mites which attack **hollies** and **spruce,** and spider mites which feed on **arborvitae, juniper, spruce,** and other conifers. They attack in the spring and fall although at higher elevations they may be active all summer long.

Diseases: Dogwood anthracnose is a devastating fungal disease of **flowering dogwoods** (*Cornus florida*). It produces leaf spots and cankers on the twigs and trunk, eventually killing the tree. Fungicides can control this disease. **Dogwoods** that are resistant to dogwood anthracnose include *Cornus kousa* '**Steeple**' and the Stellar® hybrids (hybrids between **flowering dogwood** and **kousa dogwood**) **Stardust®, Stellar Pink®,** and **Celestial™**.

Many leaf diseases become active as the trees begin to leaf out. For example, apple scab will attack **apples** and **crabapples** as they come out of winter dormancy. It also affects petioles, blossoms, and fruit, but is most noticeable on the leaves and fruit. Velvety brown to olive spots develop on the undersides of the leaves as they emerge in the spring. Eventually the spots turn black with age and the leaf dies. While apple scab will not kill your

crabapple, severe leaf-drop two or three years in a row can weaken your tree and make it susceptible to injury from freezing temperatures. As with all diseases, reduce future infections by collecting and disposing of fallen leaves. Selectively *thin out* a few of the interior limbs to improve air movement and sunlight penetration to dry off the leaves quickly. Fungicides can be applied to your **crabapple** to prevent future infections. These sprays should be applied in early spring after the last flower petals have dropped and the green tips of leaf buds are showing. If you are unwilling to take on this battle or if your **crabapples** continue to languish and die, con-

sider planting cultivars that are resistant to scab and other diseases such as fireblight, cedar-apple rust, and powdery mildew. A few of these cultivars are '**Adirondack**', '**Autumn Treasure**', '**Callaway**', '**Centurion**', '**Donald Wyman**', '**Indian Summer**', '**Molten Lava**', and '**Tina**'.

Helpful Hints

Start training established trees and large shrubs with proper pruning cuts when they're young. Prune only small branches. If you didn't plant a high-quality tree with a strong trunk and well-spaced branches, you may have to prune regularly during its early years to improve its structure. Wait until they've had one full growing season before pruning them. Follow these proper pruning rules:

1 Cut the branch, but not the branch collar. The collar is a swollen area at the base of a branch just before it enters the trunk. It acts as a natural barrier to decay-causing organisms.

2 Do not make "flush cuts" close to the trunk. These cuts create wounds to trunk tissue, which lead to decay.

3 Never leave a stub. Stubs usually die and are entry points for decay-causing fungi. Always make your cut just outside the branch collar, the slightly thickened area at the base of the branch.

Planning

Spend some time this month updating your gardening journal and recording observations of some noteworthy spring-flowering trees, including their peak bloom periods and any pest problems. Use this information to begin making plans to add trees to your landscape, to make arrangements or replacements, and to correct any problems. Remember to keep a record of the varieties you grow. By knowing the specific name of each crop, you can ask for that variety next season if you like it, or avoid it if it wasn't up to par.

Planting

Trees are best planted during cooler seasons when the topgrowth has little demand for moisture from the roots. Container-grown plants, however, can be successfully transplanted on the heels of summer if you pay careful attention to watering them regularly during their establishment period.

Palms transplant best in spring and summer when they're actively growing. (When it's time to plant **tomatoes,** it's time to plant **palms.**) They prefer a well-drained, fertile, and slightly acidic to neutral soil. Cold-sensitive palms should be placed within 8 to 10 feet from the warm, southwest side of a brick wall so they will have a few extra warm degrees of protection in the winter. Tender palms should not be planted in exposed areas where they can be harmed by dry, cold winter winds.

Care for Your Trees

To prevent mower and string trimmer damage to tree trunks, surround them with a ring of weed-suppressing mulch.

Watering

Water newly planted trees to foster their establishment. Research has shown that the establishment period for trees takes 3 months per inch of trunk caliper (trunk diameter measured 6 inches above the ground) in hardiness zone 9, 6 months in zones 7 and 8, and 12 months in cooler regions. Gradually work into watering on a weekly or "as-needed" basis by testing the soil and rootball for moisture (see October Watering, p. 304).

Fertilizing

Look for these signs of plants that are "hungry" or deficient in minerals: stunted growth, smaller-than-normal leaves, poor leaf color, early leaf drop. If you want to encourage more growth, ***fertilize*** with a slow-release fertilizer. ***Water*** well immediately afterwards.

Pruning

Remove dead or diseased wood at any time. If you cut into diseased wood, disinfect your pruning shears with Lysol®, which is less corrosive than the traditional mixture of water and household bleach (sodium hypochlorite: 4 parts water to 1 part bleach). This can prevent the spread of disease to other branches.

The older leaves of **palms** die naturally and new leaves are produced from the growing point or "head" of the palm. ***Prune out*** old, dead palm fronds to tidy up the tree. Leave the leaf base attached to the trunk so the fibers of the trunk won't be torn away. Do not injure the growing point or the entire tree will die.

Pest Control

Insects: Aphids are soft-bodied insects often found clustered at the ends of tender new growth. They suck plant sap with their piercing-sucking mouth parts, causing the leaves to curl and become malformed. Aphids have many natural predators, including ladybird beetles, lacewings, and syrphid fly larvae. **Crapemyrtle** aphids can be controlled with summer horticultural oil, insecticidal soap, and other insecticides; however, specialized equipment may be required to treat large crapemyrtles. The *faurei* hybrids (hybrids between the Chinese *Lagerstroemia indica* and the Japanese *L. fauriei*) developed by Dr. Donald Egolf of the U. S. National Arboretum have moderate resistance to aphids. A few of these hybrids are 'Acoma', 'Biloxi', 'Caddo', 'Choctaw', 'Muskogee', 'Natchez', and 'Tuscarora'.

The adult **dogwood** borer is a clearwing moth that resembles a slender bee. The moth is attracted to weakened, stressed trees where it lays eggs on wounds, cankers, or pruning cuts. When the eggs hatch, the caterpillars bore into the bark and begin tunneling.

Dogwoods can be protected from attack with a pesticide application in late spring or early summer. As with all borers, timing is very important. The insecticide must be on the bark to intercept the newly hatched larvae before they burrow into the tree. Only wounded and cankered areas on the bark should be treated. There's no need to spray the healthy portions of the tree.

Watch out for bagworms on **arborvitae, blue spruce, juniper, hemlock,** and **Leyland cypress.** In addition to attacking needle-type evergreens, bagworms also feed on the leaves of many broadleaf shrubs and trees including **rose, sycamore, maple, elm,** and **black locust.** See Pest Appendix on p. 366 for a description and controls.

Watch out for the appearance of Japanese beetles in the eastern Carolinas.

Disease: Look for powdery mildew on **flowering dogwoods (*Cornus florida*),** a white powdery growth on infected leaves which may eventually drop. Most powdery mildews of landscape trees occur in late summer and do not pose any harm since they will be shedding their leaves shortly; **dogwoods,** however, become infected in early summer. Fungicides can control this disease. Dogwoods that are resistant to powdery mildew include the following: **kousa dogwood cultivars: 'Big Apple', 'China Girl', 'Gay Head', 'Greensleeves', 'Julian', 'Milky Way Select',** and **'Temple Jewel.'** The **Stellar** hybrids **Aurora®, Celestial™,** and **Stellar Pink®** are also resistant to powdery mildew.

Weeds: Poison ivy is dangerous all year 'round. You can get an irritation from the leaves, roots, berries, and even smoke when burning the vines. Learn to identify this deciduous vine with compound leaves comprised of three leaflets, hairy aerial roots along its stem, and cluster of white waxy fruit in late summer. Don't confuse it with **Virginia creeper (*Parthenocissus quinquefolia*),** which has five leaflets per leaf and climbs by tendrils with adhesive disks at its tips.

If you think you may have come in contact with poison ivy, wash immediately with soap and water and remove any clothes that may have the oil on them. Prevention is the best medicine for this ailment.

Planning

As part of your summer vacation plans, why not find some time to visit private and public gardens in the Carolinas? These gardens can be inspirational and educational. Refer to p. 368–69 for their names and phone numbers.

Don't forget your camera and gardening journal. Enjoy!

Watering

Water recently planted trees which are especially vulnerable to heat and drought. Water thoroughly to encourage deep rooting. *Mulch* with a 2- to 3-inch layer of compost to conserve moisture, suppress weeds, and moderate soil temperatures. Extend the mulch layer up to the drip line or outermost branches of the tree.

Pruning

When dead or damaged branches are found on shade trees, prune them out immediately. Summer storms can seriously damage trees in the landscape. Storm-damaged trees should be repaired when needed, rather than waiting for the dormant season. Hire certified arborists to remove large limbs damaged by storms.

Planting

With the availability of container-grown trees, the planting season is limited only by extremely hot weather, frozen soil in winter, and your ability to water regularly. With the onset of hot, dry weather, you can plant, but be prepared to be on call with adequate water throughout the establishment period of your shrubs. Unless you're willing to put in the time, wait until fall when the odds of successful establishment are in your favor.

Care for Your Trees

If mulch doesn't protect the bark of young trees from mower damage, resort to putting up stakes or guards.

Fertilizing

Fertilize trees based on need. If the trees are growing in a fertilized lawn, fertilizing may not be necessary. Time the application for the appropriate time for the grass. This is especially important for warm-season grasses, which may be subjected to winterkill if they're fertilized late in the fall or early in the spring. Since most of a tree's roots can be found in the top 12 inches of soil, the simplest way to fertilize them is with a rotary or cyclone spreader according to soil-test results.

Pest Control

Insects and mites: Be on the lookout for aphids, scale insects, spider mites, and dogwood borers. Monitor trees for Japanese beetles. Adults lay eggs in July and August and continually migrate to susceptible hosts. If only a few are present, pick them off by hand and discard them in a jar of soapy water. Neem can be applied to the leaves to reduce feeding by the adults. Use other insecticides for heavy infestations.

Keep bagworms at bay by applying the bacterial insecticide ***BT (Bacillus thuringiensis)*** as the larvae begin to feed and construct their bags. Heavy infestations may require an application of a systemic insecticide later in the season. Light infestations of bagworms can also be controlled by handpicking.

Remove the bags with scissors or a knife, and dispose of them by dropping them into a container of soapy water. Birds and parasitic wasps will work in concert with your efforts, and low winter temperatures can damage the overwintering eggs.

Diseases: Fireblight is a bacterial disease that attacks **apple, loquat, pear,** and other trees. *Prune out* the diseased branches several inches below the infection. If you cut into a diseased branch, disinfect your pruning shears with Lysol®, which is less corrosive than the traditional mixture of water and household bleach (sodium hypochlorite: 4 parts water to 1 part bleach). This can prevent the spread of fireblight to other branches or trees.

Powdery mildew is a grayish-white fungal disease that attacks the leaves, flowers, and shoots of older cultivars of **crapemyrtle.** *Prune out* heavily infested shoots. Fungicides are available; however, specialized equipment may be required to treat large crapemyrtles. Instead, consider growing the *faurei* hybrids—crosses between the Chinese *Lagerstroemia indica* and the Japanese *L. fauriei* developed by Dr. Donald Egolf of the U. S. National Arboretum: they are resistant to powdery mildew. They include 'Acoma', 'Apalachee', 'Biloxi', 'Choctaw', 'Comanche',

Helpful Hint

When some gardeners find lichens or Spanish moss on their trees, they often panic, thinking that their trees are under siege. **Relax.** Lichens are ominous-looking though harmless organisms that consist of a fungus and a green or blue-green alga which live in association with each other, looking like a single plant. Lichens often appear leafy or crusty and are colored gray, green, yellow, or white. They are typically found on dead or declining trees, on rocks, or on the ground. Their presence on failing trees is a sign, but never the cause, of poor plant health—the reduction of plant vigor has resulted in a more open canopy, which increases sunlight penetration and subsequent lichen growth.

You can remove the lichens from your tree with a stiff brush, but they will probably reappear if you do not determine the cause and correct it. Restoring your tree should increase the size and number of leaves and eventually lead to the gradual disappearance of lichens.

The gray strands of Spanish moss (*Tillandsia usneoides*) draping the limbs of **live oaks, pecans,** and **pines** pose no harm to the trees. Spanish moss is an **epiphyte,** which means that it's simply growing on the tree and using it for support as it collects minerals and water from the air. It's not stealing food (water or nutrients) from the tree–rather, it gives the tree an unmistakably Southern, genteel look.

'Hopi', 'Lipan', 'Miami', 'Osage', 'Pecos', 'Prairie Lace', 'Sioux', 'Tonto', 'Tuskeegee', 'Wichita', 'Zuma', and 'Zuni'.

Weeds: *Handpull* or use a herbicide to spot-treat water- and nutrient-stealing weeds. *Suppress* their emergence with a layer of mulch.

Planning

This is an appropriate time of year to learn about a landscape approach that combines water conservation techniques with good old-fashioned commonsense gardening. The result is a beautiful, water-efficient landscape. It's called *xeriscaping,* which means "dry landscaping." Although the idea originated in the western United States where yearly rainfall is a mere fraction of what we get in the Carolinas, the same water-saving principles can be used in our own landscapes. Here are the seven basic principles of xeriscaping:

1 *Careful planning and design.* Divide the landscape into "hydrozones" (areas within the design that receive low, moderate, or high amounts of water).

2 *Reducing lawn areas to functional spaces and growing drought-tolerant lawn grasses.*

3 *Preparing the soil well by using organic matter such as compost to improve soil structure.* Organic matter improves air and water movement and the ability of our soils to retain moisture and nutrients.

4 *Appropriate plant selection and grouping of plants with similar water needs.* Because xeriscapes have low-, medium-, and high-water-use "hydrozones," we can grow a wide variety of trees, shrubs, and flowers. These include drought-tolerant plants that can cope with extended periods of dry weather after they've become established. A xeriscape also has room for high-water-use annuals that need water to keep them blooming.

5 *Efficient watering methods such as drip and micro-sprinkler systems which help conserve water.*

6 *Mulching.* Blanket the soil around trees, shrubs, and flower beds with mulch to conserve moisture, suppress weeds, and enhance plant growth.

7 *Proper landscape maintenance.* Fertilize, prune, mow, and water the right way to produce healthy plants.

Research indicates that incorporating these principles into the landscape reduces water consumption by 30 to 60 percent or more. Thus xeriscaping lowers maintenance costs and increases the survival rate of landscape plants during droughty periods.

Planting

If your summer vacation is the only time you can plant, then go ahead and set out container-grown shrubs. Keep the rootball and surrounding soil moist until they become established.

Root semi-hardwood cuttings of **Bradford pear, crapemyrtles, redbud,** and **yaupon holly** to "passalong" to a friend. The current-season's shoots begin to harden and turn brown. When you snap the twig, the bark often clings to the stem. Here's how to take semi-hardwood cuttings of your favorite trees:

1 *Remove* a strip of bark about 1 inch long from one side of each cutting.

2 Dip each cutting in a rooting hormone for woody plants.

3 Stick the cuttings in a container filled with equal parts peat moss and coarse sand. Each cutting should be deep enough in the medium to hide the wound.

4 Finally, enclose the container in a polyethylene bag, tie the bag at the top, and place the cuttings in a shaded location.

5 *After a few weeks,* check the cuttings for roots by gently tugging at a few of them. When you feel resistance, it means they have rooted. Now you can safely remove the plastic bag and repot the young plants in individual pots in a mix of equal parts of potting soil and peat.

6 Gradually expose the rooted cuttings to stronger light to harden them off. *After a couple of weeks,* transplant them into the garden.

Watering

Water recently planted trees, which are especially vulnerable to heat and drought. *Check* the rootball and soil before watering instead of relying on the calendar. Avoid overwatering, which can suffocate the plant roots, causing the leaves to wilt. Excess water can also expose the tree to attack from root rot, a deadly fungal disease that prevails in waterlogged conditions and attacks susceptible plants (see September Diseases on p. 303).

Fertilizing

Do not fertilize at this time unless you've established a need for fertilizing, and only if you're willing to irrigate regularly afterwards to sustain the new growth.

Pruning

Remove diseased, dead, or broken limbs at any time.

Pest Control

Insects: Japanese beetles are highly attracted to some trees like magnets. A longterm solution is to substitute these Japanese beetle–prone trees with less palatable ones. Here are a few attractive ornamentals from a long list of Japanese-resistant trees: **arborvitae, ash, balsam fir, butternut, Chinese redbud, cryptomeria, dogwood, ginkgo, hazelnut, hemlock, hickory, hollies, Japanese pagodatree, magnolia, maples** other than Norway, **oaks** other than chestnut and pin, **smoketree, spruce, sweetgum, tamarisk, tuliptree, winter honeysuckle,** and **yew.**

Spines of sawdust an inch or more long sticking out of the trunk are a sure sign of the Asian ambrosia beetle. This aggressive pest first appeared in this country in 1974 in Summerville, South Carolina, and has now spread to other southeastern states where it attacks more than 100 species of trees. The 1/8-inch-long reddish-brown beetles typically invade young trees less than a foot in diameter. Because nearly the entire life cycle of the beetle is spent inside the wood, ambrosia beetles are difficult to control with insecticides. There are typically two generations of the beetle per year, and for trees that are younger than three years old, infestations are likely to be fatal. Spraying trunks and limbs with an insecticide in late February or March will help reduce infestations, but the only guaranteed way to kill all of the beetles is to *dig up and destroy an infested tree.* Older trees are likely to survive an attack, however, particularly if they are growing vigorously.

Remove bagworms from infested trees with scissors or a sharp knife. Bagworms are parasitized by several kinds of parasitic wasps, and insecticides are effective, particularly when applied when the bagworms are small.

Diseases: Powdery mildew attacks the leaves and shoots of the older **crapemyrtle** cultivars. See June Diseases, p. 297.

Weeds: *Handpull* any weeds. Use a shallow layer of mulch to suppress them.

Planning

Starting planning for fall-planting. Keep in mind the xeriscape principle: appropriate use of plant materials. Choose your plants thoughtfully and plant them in an environment that matches the plant's native habitat. There are plants that are highly adaptable and will perform well in a variety of situations. For example, **river birch** and **bald cypress** (*Taxodium distichum*) are native to low, wet areas, but they can be grown successfully on high ground.

Coastal residents will have a challenging time finding appropriate plants that will tolerate salt-laden ocean breezes near the beach. The challenge is especially great on the barrier island beaches where plants have to contend with poor sandy soils that have little ability to retain water or nutrients. *A good solution is to rely on native plants.* Examine the local habitat to see which indigenous plants can be used in the landscape. Native coastal plants not only perform better than most exotics but also keep the garden in harmony with its surroundings. However, not all of a coastal garden's plants have to be native. Hardy exotic plants can set the stage for the less-conspicuous natives. Here's a sample of trees that can be tolerate these exposed, ocean-front environments:

Common Name / (Botanical Name)	Hardiness Zone
Cabbage palmetto (*Sabal palmetto*)	8b to 11
Darlington's oak (*Quercus hemisphaerica*)	6 to 10
Live oak (*Quercus virginiana*)	7b to 11
Red cedar (*Juniperus virginiana*)	2a to 10b
Southern magnolia (*Magnolia grandiflora*)	6b to 10a
Southern red cedar (*Juniperus virginiana* var. *silicicola*)	8a to 10b
Windmill palm (*Trachycarpus fortunei*)	8a to 10b
Yaupon holly (*Ilex vomitoria*)	7a to 9b

Planting

Container-grown trees can be planted in the Mountains. They ought to have plenty of time to get established before cold weather arrives. Pay attention to regular watering during the first few weeks after planting. Gardeners in the milder areas of the Carolinas can plant now or wait until cooler weather arrives.

Watering

Inspect the soil moisture of newly planted shrubs and trees. If the soil is dry near the rootball, give them a good soaking to wet the soil deeply. According to research findings, mulch promotes faster growth of trees and shrubs than does grass or ground covers.

Fertilizing

Do not fertilize at this time unless you've established a need for fertilizing and you're willing to provide adequate moisture for roots to grow and absorb the applied minerals.

Pruning

Prune out dead, diseased, or broken wood. Hold off on major pruning until late winter. Major pruning now will only stimulate tender, new growth, which can be killed by our first freeze.

Pest Control

Spider mites are very active during hot, dry weather, especially on junipers, hollies, and many other ornamentals. Feeding injury results in discolored, bronze-colored leaves. *Check* for mites by tapping a branch onto a white sheet of paper and looking for moving specks. Natural predators can control spider mite populations. A strong spray of water from the hose applied to the undersides of the leaves will dislodge the adults during the growing season. An insecticidal soap, neem, or a miticide will also be effective, although repeated applications may be necessary.

Diseases: The leaves on deciduous trees will be falling in the next few months, so infected leaves may not require attention at this time since they're going to be shed very shortly.

Powdery mildew diseases attack a great many ornamentals, most often in late summer when the days are warm and nights are cool. Prevention is the first defense.

1 Grow powdery mildew–resistant varieties.

2 *Prune* plant for air movement and sunlight penetration.

3 Reduce fertilizer applications to avoid excessive, late-season growth.

Helpful Hints

- To have an insect identified, visit your local garden center or cooperative extension service office. Put the insect in a pill bottle and mail it or take it directly to the extension office. Isopropyl alcohol will preserve the insect, making identification easier.

- Plants can be used to reduce road noise. Solid barriers tall enough to screen the noise source from view are the best way to reduce the noise from high-speed car and truck traffic. Plantings of trees and shrubs will mitigate the noise from moderate-speed automobiles, found in suburban locations. Plants are better at absorbing high-frequency sounds, which are most bothersome to human ears, then they are at absorbing low-frequency sounds.

You will need to plant two or three rows of plants. Shrubs should be located adjacent to the traffic and be backed by taller trees. The planting must be sufficiently dense to screen the traffic from view. For year-round noise reduction, evergreens are the best choice. A mixture of plants—such as **arborvitae, spruce,** and **juniper,** as well as broad-leaved **holly** and **boxwood**—will ensure against a total loss if there is a disease or insect outbreak. If you plant fast growers for an "instant screen," be aware that many of these are weak-wooded and short-lived. Interplantings of longer-lived species will fill in the vacant spots when the fast growers die or have to be removed.

Recent research has shown greater noise reduction is obtained from a combination of trees and shrubs planted atop an earthen berm. Such combinations produce a noise reduction of 6 to 15 decibels immediately behind them, which the human ear will perceive as one-third as loud.

Cercospora leaf spot is a common disease of **crapemyrtles** that becomes noticeable this month and next. Diseased leaves have brown lesions that eventually turn yellow to red in color and then are quickly shed. Select resistant crapemyrtles.

The following cultivars are resistant to powdery mildew and Cercospora leaf spot: **Tuscarora, Tuskegee, Tonto,** and **Fantasy Japanese crapemyrtle.**

Planning

This fall plan to recycle your fallen leaves into mulch or compost. For a fine-textured mulch, shred the leaves with a lawn mower or a leaf shredder. Finely cut leaves look more attractive and tend to stay where you put them.

To compost leaves, researchers recommend building piles at least 4 feet in diameter and 3 feet in height. To keep them manageable, make the piles no larger than 5 feet high and 10 feet wide. Compost leaves by themselves, or add fresh vegetable peelings, grass clippings, or other kitchen or yard trimmings.

To speed up the composting process, shred the leaves before putting them into the pile. Avoid adding meat or grease, which may cause odors and attract pests. Pay particular attention to moisture and air. Keep the ingredients moist enough that you can squeeze water droplets from a handful of leaves. Aerate or supply air to the pile by turning the materials—during warm weather, turn the pile once a month. In cool weather, turn it less frequently to prevent too much heat from escaping. To convert the leaves to compost fairly quickly, add nitrogen to the pile. Add a nitrogen-containing fertilizer

such as 10-10-10 or a natural substitute such as horse or cow manure, bloodmeal, or cottonseed meal. *Mix this crumbly, earthy-smelling "black gold" into heavy clay soil to improve drainage and make the soil easier to cultivate. Compost helps sandy soils retain water and nutrients.*

Planting

Mountain gardeners can continue planting this month. Piedmont and Coastal Plain gardeners can wait until next month when the cooler temperatures make planting more enjoyable.

Pruning

Prune out dead or diseased wood from trees. Hold off on major pruning until mid- to late winter or even early spring before growth begins. Major pruning now will only stimulate tender, new growth, which can be killed by our first freeze. Any storm damage to large trees should be repaired by a certified arborist.

Wait until next year to prune your **crapemyrtles.** Research shows that late-summer, fall, and early-winter pruning may predispose woody ornamental plants, especially **crapemyrtles,** to cold injury. Delay pruning until late winter or early spring before budbreak.

Watering

Fall can be a very warm and dry month. *Water* newly planted trees. *Check* moisture in the rootball prior to watering.

Fertilizing

If your trees have produced sufficient growth this year, fertilizing may not be necessary. If you choose to fertilize, rely on soil-test results to apply the nutrients required by your trees. If they're showing their fall colors, wait until next year.

Pest Control

Insects: Fall webworm is a North American native insect that attacks more than 100 species of deciduous trees and shrubs, including **apple, ash, birch, cherry, linden, peach, sycamore, walnut,** and **willow.** It's one of the few American pests that has been introduced to Europe and Asia. Unlike the eastern tent caterpillar, which constructs similar webbed nests, the fall webworm does not become conspicuous until late summer and early fall. The green or yellow caterpillars spin webs near the ends of branches and feed on the enclosed leaves. The caterpillars do not leave the web nests until they are ready to pupate, which takes four to six weeks. Two generations hatch each year, the second being more conspicuous. Fall webworms are essentially a cosmetic nuisance. The defoliation typically involves only a few branches and occurs late in the season (by which time the tree is ready to shed its leaves naturally).

In most years, a large number of natural predators and parasitoids help to keep fall webworms in check. The bacterial insecticide *Bacillus thuringiensis (BT)* can be applied in June when the caterpillars are small and sprayed onto leaves next to the nest, on which the caterpillars will soon feed. Nests that are easy to reach can be pruned off or torn apart with a stick and the caterpillars dislodged with a strong stream of water. The simplest course of action, however, is to do nothing in the confidence that the fall webworms aren't doing your plants any real harm.

Diseases: Root rot caused by Phytophthora, which means plant destroyer, attacks a wide variety of plants including **dogwood, deodar cedar, Fraser fir, white pine,** and many others. Look for wilted, dying plants. Scrape the bark near the crown and look for a reddish-brown discoloration where the fungus has moved into the stem. These fungi are often found in wet or poorly drained sites. They'll attack plants in moderate to dry sites if they're planted too deeply. Overwatering plants in moderate to dry sites also favors these fungi. When symptoms are evident, fungicides are often ineffective in controlling this disease. Here are some tips to avoid root rot disease:

1 Avoid planting in poorly drained sites.

2 Improve drainage in heavy clay soil by planting in slightly raised beds, or add organic matter such as composted pine bark to as large a planting area as possible.

3 Use plants that are highly resistant to root rot.

Animals: Prepare now to protect your trees from deer and rodent feeding. Protect trees from deer with fencing or with repellents. Rabbits can be deterred by installing wire or plastic guards around the trunks of young shade trees and fruit trees. To discourage voles, pull the mulch away from the trunk about a foot.

Rabbits and voles will feed on the thin bark of young trees. To protect trees, shrubs, and ornamentals, use hardware cloth cylinders to keep voles away. A stiff wire-mesh hardware cloth is available at home centers and hardware stores. First use a shovel to cut the ground around the plant just enough to insert the wire cylinder. Then form the hardware cloth into a cylinder. The bottom edge of the cylinder should be buried at least 6 inches below the ground. If kept in place permanently, the mesh will girdle the tree's roots. To avoid injury, remove it after one or two years or bury it further away from the trunk without harming the feeder roots.

Planning

Deciduous trees light up the autumn skies with an assortment of fiery reds, oranges, and yellows. These colors result from the interaction of several pigments, including yellow xanthophylls, orange carotenoids, and red anthocyanins. The anthocyanins are manufactured by the conversion of sugars in the fall; the other pigments have been there all along but are not visible until the masking green chlorophyll has disappeared.

Okay, so maybe it's not that important to know where these brilliant colors came from. But it's good to know the names and cultivars of trees whose fall color would make an important addition to your landcape. Get your gardening journal and camera ready to take notes and pictures of some of your favorite trees.

Planting

Now and next month are excellent times to plant trees during the cooler temperatures of fall. In warmer areas, planting can continue into December. Trees planted in the fall can establish roots in the landscape soil before warm summer temperatures draw moisture from roots to stress the trees.

Remember to make the planting hole only as deep as the rootball. You can make it as wide as you like, but at least two to three times the diameter of the rootball. Purchase a high-quality tree with a strong trunk and well-spaced branches to avoid costly "training" by pruning.

Care for Your Trees

Do not become alarmed if your **yews, pines, arborvitae,** and **junipers** begin to shed their interior needles. It is natural for them to do so at this time of year.

Watering

Water evergreens thoroughly before the ground freezes in the Mountains. Evergreens continue to lose water by transpiring during the winter, but when the ground is frozen they cannot replenish the water.

In fall and early winter, don't forget to water newly planted trees to help them become established. A few weeks after planting, start cutting back on watering to every few days or longer, especially

with cloudy, rainy, or cool weather. Eventually, you can water on a weekly or "as-needed" basis by testing the soil and rootball for moisture. Here's how:

1 *Dig* a small hole in the loosened backfill soil just outside the rootball.

2 Squeeze a handful of the soil from the top and another from the bottom of the hole. If water drips between your fingers or the soil feels sticky, the soil is too wet. If it crumbles and falls from your hand as you open your fingers, you need to add water. If the soil stays together in your hand as you open your fingers, the moisture in the backfill is just right. But you'll still need to test the rootball.

3 Insert your fingers into the rootball. If it's dry, go ahead and water (water will squeeze out between your fingers if it's too wet).

Fertilizing

See September, p. 302.

Pruning

While you can still identify them easily, prune dead and diseased branched from trees and shrubs.

Pest Control

Insects: *Remove and destroy* bagworm bags on narrow-leaved evergreens. Eggs overwinter in the bags produced by the females and will hatch-out next spring.

Diseases: Old, fallen leaves contain the disease spores for next-year's plant infections. If you have disease-infected plants, prune out infected branches in the late fall and winter when the disease-causing organism is inactive. *Remove* any infected debris from around the plant's base and dispose of it.

Animals: To protect young trees against white-tail deer damage, there are a number of deterrents you can try. Remember, deer will become accustomed to any object, so alternating items will help. Hang bars of strong-scented soap or mesh bags filled with human hair on the outer branches with no more than 3 feet between them. Chemical deer repellents also can be applied. To be

Helpful Hints

- Over the course of their lives, trees sometimes develop holes in their trunks. Depending on the size of the cavity and the extent of decay, you may want to consult a certified arborist for advice. In general, cavities are no longer routinely filled now that it's known that trees compartmentalize wounds by creating chemical and physical barriers to contain the spread of infection. Over time, wound wood formed by callus tissue will develop along the edges of the cavity, forming a "callus roll" and strengthening the damaged trunk. Nevertheless, an arborist may decide to fill the cavity with urethane foam to prevent rainwater from accumulating. This soft, flexible foam forms a better bond with wood than the concrete that was used in the past. A piece of sheet metal can be tacked over the foam for cosmetic purposes if desired.

- Young trees can be inexpensively protected from rodents, string trimmers, and mowers with short, plastic tube-shaped tree guards. Each protector should be 6 to 12 inches tall and long enough to wrap around the entire trunk. Alternatively, you can purchase trimmer guards or make your own out of corrugated plastic drainpipe.

effective, repellents will have to be reapplied if there is rain or heavy dew; they will have to be applied often to new plant growth.

The only technique that ensures safety from deer is fencing. Both woven wire fences and multistrand electric fencing will do the job, but their construction can be elaborate and expensive. An alternative fencing material—$7^1/_2$-foot black plastic mesh—is nearly invisible and can be used to completely surround your plantings. To learn more about these and other techniques for keeping deer at bay, contact your local cooperative extension service.

Planning

When planning your landscape for trees, take advantage of a tree's winter interest. Bark, branches, and architectural forms give deciduous trees character. Look at the peeling or exfoliating bark of a wide variety of trees such as **crapemyrtle,** particularly **Natchez** and **Fantasy Japanese crapemyrtle** (*Lagerstroemia faurei* 'Fantasy').

Planting

Fall is the best time of year for moving trees. To ensure success, transplant trees when they're dormant. Where circumstances necessitate very late planting of trees, remember to mulch the area heavily to keep the ground thawed so roots can become established.

If you're planning on having a live balled-and-burlapped **Christmas tree,** dig a planting hole now before the ground freezes in the Mountains. Fill the hole with straw or hay to keep it from freezing. Store the soil in a garage or shed so you will have workable soil when you need it for planting the tree.

Care for Your Trees

Protect tender **palms** with tall, solitary trunks during the winter by tying up their leaves and wrapping the trunk with insulating blankets. Small specimens can be enclosed in wire circle and buried with pine straw. *Check* guy wires around newly planted trees to be sure hose sections still cover the supporting wires or ropes so they will not damage the trunks in windy weather. *Mulch* plantings to protect against winter cold.

Pruning

Do not be in a hurry to prune trees. Wait until next year after the coldest part of winter has passed.

Watering

Fall rains may be adequate for established trees. Newly planted trees, however, may require watering, especially in the Mountains where the ground freezes.

If fall rains have been scarce, water landscape evergreens thoroughly once every week or so until the ground freezes. Evergreens continue to lose moisture from their foliage all winter, but once the ground is frozen, they'll be unable to take up enough water to replace it. Sending them into winter well watered reduces the potential for damaged foliage.

Fertilizing

Do not fertilize trees at this time.

Pest Control

Diseases: *Remove* all mummified fruit from fruit trees, and rake up and destroy those on the ground. Rake and dispose of dropped **apple** and **cherry** leaves. Good sanitation practices reduce reinfestation of insects and diseases the following season.

Insects: Inspect trees and shrubs for bagworm capsules and the silvery egg masses of tent caterpillars. *Remove and destroy* them to reduce next year's pest population. If there is any evidence of scale on trees and shrubs, spray with dormant oil in late fall and again in early spring.

Animals: See December.

Helpful Hint

If you want to purchase a live Christmas tree, choose one that will thrive in your area, and make sure you know where you're going to plant it. Here are some choices for Carolina gardeners: Zone 6–**Colorado spruce, Norway spruce, white fir (** *Abies concolor***), Douglas fir, red cedar (** *Juniperus virginiana***), Scotch pine**; Zones 7 and 8–**Arizona cypress (** *Cupressus arizonica* **subsp.** *arizonica***), deodar cedar (** *Cedrus deodara***), red cedar, Virginia pine,** and **Leyland cypress.** Zone 9–**Arizona cypress, deodar cedar, Leyland cypress,** and **southern red cedar (** *Juniperus virginiana* **var.** *silicicola***).** Follow these steps to choose the right live tree this holiday season:

1 Choose a balled-and-burlapped tree with a firm rootball. Grab the trunk and push it back and forth once or twice. If the root system is healthy and unbroken, the tree will bend along its length. It's damaged if it rocks at its base before it bends.

2 Store the tree in a protected location before bringing it inside. Put it in a place where it won't freeze such as an unheated garage, porch, or cool basement.

3 Once you bring the tree indoors, keep it inside for as short a time as possible: no more than ten days, but five to seven days would be better. Keep the tree away from heating vents, fireplaces, and other heat sources.

4 Place the rootball in a large tub and water from the top. **Check** the rootball daily and water often enough to keep the soil moist.

5 After the holiday, plant your tree immediately. The rootball will be very heavy, so enlist the help of any holiday guests to help you carry it outside.

6 Plant the tree in a sunny well-drained location with plenty of room to spread out. We hope you heeded our advice and scouted the perfect spot before you purchased the tree!

7 **Dig** the hole at least twice the diameter of the rootball and as deep. Place the tree in the hole, stand it straight, and fill in with soil. **Water** thoroughly and mulch with 2 to 4 inches of compost, shredded bark, or pine straw. Keep the tree well watered during the winter months to help it become established.

Planning

The first Friday in December is Arbor Day in South Carolina. Only South Carolinians in the warmer areas of zone 8 can expect **cabbage palmetto** to survive the winter, but other adapted trees can be planted this month as long as the weather is mild and the soil does not freeze and thaw during the winter months. Try something new. Just as you may feel comfortable with a particular entrée at a restaurant but sometimes want something different, get adventurous—*Carpe diem*—and try something new.

Planting

For good establishment, transplant at least 4 weeks before the soil temperature goes below 40 degrees Fahrenheit. Newly planted trees should be watered in immediately after planting. Continue to water them during the winter months if the soil isn't frozen. Don't keep them waterlogged, however.

Root hardwood stem cuttings of coniferous evergreens such as **juniper, cypress (*Cupressus*), false-cypress (*Chamaecyparis*),** and **cryptomeria.** Some broadleaf evergreens that can be propagated now are **holly, arborvitae,** and **hemlock.**

Care for Your Trees

Check on the water in your **Christmas tree** stand on a daily basis and replenish it so the stand won't go dry.

Pruning

Wait until after the coldest of winter has passed before doing any major structural pruning that would remove large limbs. It may encourage new growth or make the tree susceptible to winter injury.

Watering

Water newly planted trees. Drain the hoses and store them where you can get to them in midwinter if you need to water.

Never allow the reservoir of your **Christmas tree** holder to go dry, as an air lock can form in the trunk that can keep the tree from absorbing water again. Researchers have shown that plain water is best.

Pest Control

Insects and mites: If scale insects and mites have been a problem this past season, apply a dormant horticultural oil when the plants go dormant. Be sure to spray the trunk, branches, and stems and both sides of the leaves thoroughly. Read the label for precautions regarding the high and low temperature limits at the time of application.

Check your plants for the spindle-shaped bags of bagworms which contain 500 to 1,000 eggs that will hatch next spring.

Animals: Take precautions against deer and rodents. Protect trees from deer with fencing or repellents. Rabbits can be deterred by installing wire or plastic guards around the trunks of young shade trees and fruit trees. To discourage voles, pull the mulch away from the trunk about a foot. Refer to Pest Appendix, p. 365, for more information about controlling voles.

Helpful Hint

When choosing a **Christmas tree,** be sure it is not too large for the room. Take a tape measure or folding ruler with you so you'll have less trimming to do once you get the tree home.

Vines and Ground Covers

Some gardeners have shied away from vines and ground covers because of what they've seen running amok in the countryside: **oriental bittersweet (***Celastrus orbiculatus***)** swallowing up trees in the Mountains and **kudzu (***Pueraria lobata***)**—"the vine that ate the South"—engulfing trees, utility poles, abandoned houses, and everything else in its path. But these invasive bullies have well-mannered cousins that can be introduced into their landscapes.

Vines and ground covers are more than just drab living screens or blankets. Vines can be bold and colorful. They can be used as accent plants or attention-grabbers with bold and decorative leaves, beautiful fragrant flowers, and decorative fruits and seedheads. Many offer brilliant fall color and provide shelter for wildlife. Flowering annual vines, many of which are native to tropical regions, hold up well in our hot and humid summers, blooming well until the first frost.

Ground covers can be functional as well as ornamental. Ranging in height from as little as 2 inches to 2 feet, ground covers can be low-growing and spreading evergreen or deciduous shrubs, perennials, or even vines. Some have colorful flowers, while others have showy leaves splashed with pink, silver, white, or yellow. When they're used to fill in gaps around shrubs and trees they create interesting patterns and textures that unite the individual plantings into a single, solid-looking planting.

When vines and ground covers are used together they offer your landscape the dimensions of height and breadth, uniting function with beauty.

Planning

Before selecting vines and ground covers for your landscape, become familiar with the environmental conditions of the site: light exposure (full sun, partial shade, or dense shade), soil moisture, and drainage. Most flowering vines perform best in full sunlight to partial shade. Coastal gardeners need to select vines that tolerate salt spray. Always match the plant to the site rather then attempting to change the environment to accommodate the plant.

Before purchasing vines for your landscape, become familiar with the way they climb so you'll know the kind of support to select for them and how to maintain them. If you already have a support, select a vine that will be able to climb it with ease.

Twining vines twist their stems around supports. With a little coaxing. **mandevilla (***Mandevilla splendens***)**, **confederate jasmine (***Trachelosperum jasminoides***)**, and **swamp jessamine (***Gelsemium rankinii***)** happily wrap themselves around mailbox posts, lampposts, and railings.

Some vines use tendrils to cling to objects. **Morning glory (***Ipomoea***)**, **passionflower (***Passiflora***)**, and **sweet pea (***Lathyrus odoratus***)** need thin supports or wires for the tendrils to grasp.

Finally, some vines use specialized structures to give them a foothold. **Climbing fig (***Ficus pumila***)**, **climbing hydrangea, English ivy, Japanese hydrangea-vine (***Schizophragma hydrangeoides***)**, and **Virginia creeper (***Parthenocissus quinquefolia***)** produce rootlets along their stems that have adhesive, suction cup–like disks at their tips for attaching to surfaces.

Vines and Ground Covers

Keep vines off wooden walls—they trap moisture and slow the drying of wood, which can encourage decay. When shading brick or masonry walls with clinging vines that have aerial rootlets or adhesive disks (like **English** and **Boston ivies** and **climbing hydrangea**), think twice before allowing them to cling to the walls. Once you allow them to climb on the walls, they're very difficult to remove. After you tear down the vine you're left with rootlets and disks that can only be removed with a stiff scrub brush.

If you're planning on using ground covers on steep slopes, select evergreen ground covers, especially those that form a dense blanket of leaves and branches to shade the soil and suppress weeds year-round.

If you have large areas that allow plants to roam freely, select aggressive ground covers that spread above- and below-ground. A handful of **blue periwinkle** (*Vinca minor*) or **creeping liriope** (*Liriope spicata*) can be used to fill an area in short time. Vines such as **Asiatic jasmine** (*Trachelospermum asiaticum*), **ivy,** or **Carolina jessamine** will run along the top, sometimes rooting as they go to form a dense impenetrable mat.

For smaller areas with mixed planting use clumping plants such as **bordergrass lilyturf** (*Liriope muscari*), **hosta,** or **Lenten rose** (*Helleborus orientalis*). These plants need to be planted close together to create a ground cover. Although it means buying more plants, you won't have to struggle to keep them in bounds.

Planting

A few weeks before planting, select the area to receive the vines or ground covers and till it to a depth of 8 to 12 inches. Spread a 2- to 4-inch layer of organic matter such as compost or composted pine bark mulch over the bed, and work it to a depth of 4 to 6 inches. Test the soil for pH and fertility levels. Add any lime or sulfur and any nutrients as recommended by soil-test results.

When planting ground covers on slopes, dig individual planting holes since cultivating the area could increase the chances for soil erosion.

1 Dig a wide, shallow hole, one that is at least two to three times the diameter of the rootball but no deeper than the height of the rootball. Roots will grow quickly into the loosened soil and will speed up the plant's establishment into its new home.

In heavy clay soils, dig the hole so the rootball will be 1 to 2 inches higher than the surrounding soil. It's always better to err on the side of planting higher than the surrounding soil. Never place the plant so the top of the rootball is below the soil surface. When planting high, cover the exposed rootball with mulch.

2 Slip the plant out of the pot and examine the rootball. Vines or ground covers growing in plastic or other hard-sided containers may have roots circling around the outside of the rootball. Encourage roots to grow along the entire length of the rootball by lightly scoring the rootball in three or four places with a knife, pruning shears, or the end of a sharp spade. Make shallow cuts from the top to the bottom of the rootball. Gently tease the sides apart. Now this "doctored" plant will produce new roots from the cuts all around the rootball.

3 Plant even with or slightly above the surrounding soil. Place the vine or ground cover into the hole and measure the height of the rootball against the surrounding soil. Lay your shovel across the hole to see that the rootball is even or slightly above the handle. If the hole is too deep, put some soil on the bottom of the hole, tamp it down with your feet to give the plant some solid footing, and put the plant back in the hole.

Vines and Ground Covers

4 Loosen and break up any clods of soil before backfilling half the hole. Never add any organic matter or sand into the backfill soil when digging individual planting holes—doing so will create problems with water movement and root growth between the rootball and soil.

5 Lightly tamp down the soil with your feet or hands, not so heavily that you compact the soil. *Water* when half the rootball is covered, to settle out any air pockets and to remoisten the soil in the rootball. Finish backfilling and water again.

6 *Mulch.* Apply a 2- to 3-inch layer of organic mulch such as compost, leaf litter, shredded wood, or pine straw.

Watering

Water newly planted vines and ground covers frequently until they become established. Water—not fertilizer—is the most important ingredient for helping them get established in the landscape. Keep the soil moist, but not sopping wet.

Refer to Trees, October Watering on p. 304 to learn how to water on an "as-needed" basis by testing the soil and rootball for moisture.

Fertilizing

Once newly planted vines and ground covers become established in the landscape, they can benefit from fertilizer applications from late spring to early fall which will stimulate growth and help them fill in their allotted space in the landscape.

To take the guesswork out of fertilizing your vines and ground covers, rely on a soil test. In the absence of a soil test, use a complete fertilizer with a ratio of 3:1:2 or 3:1:3 (for example, 16-4-8). The rule of thumb is to apply 1 pound of nitrogen per 1,000 square feet of bed area. Follow these steps to determine how much fertilizer to apply over a ground cover bed.

1 Assume the bed is 20 feet long and 10 feet wide. The bed area = length × width; 20 ft × 10 ft = 200 sq. ft.

2 Because fertilizer recommendations are given on a 1,000-sq.-ft. basis, divide the area of the bed by 1,000. So $\frac{200 \text{ sq. ft.}}{1,000 \text{ sq. ft.}} = 0.2$

3 Determine the amount of 16-4-8 fertilizer needed to apply 1 lb. of nitrogen per 1,000 sq. ft.

$\frac{100}{16} = 6.25$ lb. of 16-4-8 per 1000 sq. ft.

4 To determine the amount of fertilizer required in the 200-sq.-ft. bed, make this calculation: 0.2 × 6.25 lb. = 1.25 lb. of 16-4-8. Therefore, $1\frac{1}{4}$ lb.* of 16-4-8 spread evenly over the bed will supply the appropriate amount.

*2 cups of a synthetic inorganic fertilizer is equivalent to 1 lb. of fertilizer.

Pruning

Vines and ground covers require little pruning except to keep them confined to their allotted space and to keep vines on their supports. Woody vines that produce flowers on last-year's growth should be pruned after they flower. Some ground covers should be pruned annually in the spring before new growth emerges, removing winterkilled shoots and tattered leaves.

Pest Control

Select vines and ground covers that have few, if any, pest problems. Meeting their growing conditions and keeping them healthy should help them avoid confrontations with insects and diseases.

Carolina Vines

Annual Vines

Common Name (Botanical Name)	Light Exposure	Height (feet)	Flower Color	Climbing Method	Comments
Black-eyed Susan vine (*Thunbergia alata*)	Morning sun and afternoon shade	6 to 8	Yellow, white, orange	Twining stems	Tender perennial has dark-eyed flowers in gold, orange, and creamy white.
Canary creeper; Canary bird flower (*Tropaeolum peregrinum*)	Sun to partial shade	8 to 10	Yellow	Twining stems	Blooms from summer to frost.
Butterfly pea (*Clitoria ternatea*)	Sun	10	Purple, pealike flowers	Twining stems	Old-fashioned vine that flowers from midsummer to frost.
Firecracker vine (*Ipomoea lobata*)	Sun	10 to 20	Reddish-orange, fading to orange, yellow, and then white	Twining stems	Multicolored display of flowers from late summer to fall.
Cypress vine (*Ipomoea quamoclit*)	Sun to shade	10 to 20	Red	Twining stems	Lacy, fernlike leaves.
Hyacinth bean (*Lablab purpureus*)	Sun	15 to 25	Pink-purple, white, lilac	Twining stems	Cultivated in gardens since the 1800s, this heat-loving rapid grower is a vegetable that doubles as an ornamental. The 6- to 8-in.-long spikes of fragrant pinkish-purple flowers give rise to edible purple beans throughout the summer.
Mandevilla (*Mandevilla × amabalis*)	Sun; will tolerate afternoon shade	8 to 10	Pink	Twining stems	Tender vine can be brought indoors for the winter and then replanted the following spring.
Morning glory (*Ipomoea* spp.)	Sun	10	Blue, pink, lavender, white	Twining stems	Tried-and-true annual vine that grows quickly and blooms with abandon. A night-blooming member of the morning glory clan, moonvine (*I. alba*) bears fragrant white flowers that unfurl in late afternoon and close at dawn. All morning glory seeds have a hard seed coat; to help germination, nick the seed with a file and then soak overnight.
Sweet pea (*Lathyrus odoratus*)	Sun to partial shade	6+	Blue, lavender, pink, purple, salmon, red, white	Clinging tendrils that coil	Cool-loving vine, although heat-resistant cultivars are available; look for scented varieties.

Carolina Vines

Perennial Vines

Common Name (Botanical Name)	Group	Hardiness Zone	Light Exposure	Height (feet)	Climbing Method	Comments
Carolina jessamine (*Gelseminum sempervirens*)	Evergreen	6 to 9	Sun to partial shade	10 to 20	Twining	State flower of South Carolina. Bright yellow fragrant flowers in spring. 'Pride of Augusta' and *G. rankinii* also flower in autumn.
Chinese trumpetcreeper (*Campsis grandiflora*)	Deciduous	6 to 9	Sun	15 to 20	Clinging by aerial rootlets	Trumpet-shaped, salmon-orange flowers on new growth.
Clematis (*Clematis* spp. and hybrids)	Evergreen to deciduous	3 to 9	Sun—shade for roots	5 to 20	Twisting petioles	Most widely recognized and used climbing plants for flowers in spring, summer, or fall.
Confederate jasmine (*Trachelospermum jasminoides*)	Evergreen	7b to 10	Sun to partial shade	10 to 15	Twining vine	Fragrant, star-shaped creamy-white flowers in late spring.
Cross vine (*Bignonia capreolata*)	Deciduous to evergreen	6 to 9	Sun to shade	30 to 50	Clinging tendrils with disk-like adhesive tips	Trumpet-shaped flowers, yellow with red throats. Choice cultivars include 'Atrosanguinea', 'Tangerine Beauty' and 'Jekyll'.
Japanese hydrangea vine (*Schizophragma hydrangeioides*)	Deciduous	5 to 7(8)	Sun to partial shade	20 to 30	Clinging tendrils with disk-like adhesive tips	Large flattened flowerheads in summer. 'Moonlight' has leaves frosted with silver. 'Brookside Miniature' is a dwarf form that produces similar flowers.
Virginia creeper (*Parthenocissus quinquefolia*)	Deciduous	3	Sun to partial shade	30+	Clinging tendrils with disk-like adhesive tips	Adapted to poor soils and tough urban conditions, puts on a brilliant autumn display when the glossy dark-green leaves turn brilliant red and purple.
Wisteria (*Wisteria* spp.)	Deciduous	5 to 8	Sun	25 to 30+	Twining	Chinese (*W. sinensis*) and Japanese wisteria (*W. floribunda*) are vigorous rampant vines valued for their 1- to 2-ft.-long hanging clusters of fragrant pealike flowers. American wisteria (*W. frutescens*) is less vigorous, blooming in summer on new growth bearing showy 4- to 6-inch-long fragrant lavender blossoms. 'Amethyst Falls' has blue flowers; it reblooms sporadically in the summer; 20 to 30 feet.

Carolina Groundcovers

Evergreen Perennial Groundcovers

Common Name (Botanical Name)	Hardiness Zone	Group	Light Exposure	Comments
Ajuga or Carpet bugleweed (*Ajuga reptans*)	6 to 8	Herbaceous	Partial shade to shade	Growing 6 to 9 in. high, cultivars offer a variety of leaf colors including shades of bronze, maroon, and purple. A few choice cultivars include 'Bronze Beauty', 'Burgundy Glow', and 'Rubra'. Crown rot can be a problem.
Green-and-gold (*Chrysogonum virginianum*)	5 to 8	Herbaceous	Partial shade to shade	Forms a low-growing and spreading dense ground cover from 6 to 9 in. high. Small yellow flowers are produced over a period of several weeks from spring to early summer. Grows best in moist soils and under light shade.
Ice plant (*Delosperma cooperi*)	7 to 9	Herbaceous	Sun	Low-growing, 3- to 6-in.-high trailing ground cover with succulent, cylindrical pencil-thick leaves and fluorescent pink flowers in summer and fall.
Juniper, creeping (*Juniperus horizontalis*), Shore juniper (*J. conferta*), and Japanese garden juniper (*J. procumbens* 'Nana')	6 to 8	Woody	Sun	Standard widely-used ground covers noted for their tolerance of a wide range of soils from heavy clay to dry sand, and ability to thrive in tough, urban environments. Many choice cultivars, particularly 'Blue Rug' (4 to 6 in. tall with a 6-ft. spread), which is the lowest and possibly the slowest-growing juniper. 'Blue Pacific' and 'Emerald Sea' shore junipers are two widely grown cultivars growing 6 to 12 in. high with a 6-ft. spread. Japanese garden juniper grows up to 2 ft. tall with an 8-ft. spread.
English ivy (*Hedera helix*)	4 to 9	Woody	Sun or shade	Low, aggressive ground cover from 6 to 8 in. high, it can also be grown as a vine, climbing with root holdfasts. Many cultivars are available. Algerian ivy (**H. canariensis**) can be grown in coastal areas (zones 9 to 10) because of its salt tolerance. Colchis ivy (**H. colchica**) is hardy in zones (6)7 to 9 and has larger, coarser leaves than English ivy.
Japanese spurge (*Pachysandra terminalis*)	4 to 8	Herbaceous	Partial shade to shade	Well suited for light to deep shade where other ground covers fear to tread. It grows 9 to 12 in. high. Allegheny spurge (**P. procumbens**) is a semi-evergreen native pachysandra with leaves mottled with gray and white. Not troubled by any of the problems facing Japanese pachysandra (such as dieback, scale, and leaf spot).

Carolina Groundcovers

Evergreen Perennial Groundcovers

Common Name (Botanical Name)	Hardiness Zone	Group	Light Exposure	Comments
Liriope, Creeping lilyturf (*Liriope spicata*) and bordergrass (*L. muscari*)	6 to 9	Herbaceous	Sun to shade	Creeping lilyturf reaches 8 to 12 in. tall and spreads to form a dense impenetrable cover. Bordergrass grows up to 18 in. tall and forms a clump making it suitable for edgeing Both produce white, blue, or purple flower spikes in late summer.
Dwarf mondograss or monkeygrass (*Ophiopogon japonicus*)	6 to 9	Herbaceous	Sun to shade	Dwarf mondograss forms a thick dense mat of grasslike leaves 6 to 8 in. high. Lower-growing (less than 4 in. high) cultivars include 'Nana' and 'Gyoko-ryu'. Black mondograss (**O. planiscapus 'Nigrescens'**) grows 6 in. high with dark-purple, nearly black leaves that give rise to light lilac to pink flowers.
Periwinkle (*Vinca minor*) Large periwinkle (*Vinca major*)	6 to 8(9)	Woody	Partial shade to shade	Periwinkle forms a carpet of glossy dark-green leaves. Both have purple flowers in spring; periwinkle grows up to 8 in. high and large periwinkle can reach up to 18 in.
Wintercreeper euonymus (*Euonymus fortunei*)	5 to 8	Woody	Sun to shade	Numerous cultivars offer a wide variety of leaf shapes and colors. As a ground cover grows from 1 to 2 ft. high; can also be grown as a vine reaching a height of 15 to 20 ft. Susceptible to euonymus scale.
Yellow archangel (*Lamium galeobdolon*)	4 to 8	Herbaceous	Partial to full shade	Forms a low-spreading mat of heart-shaped leaves between 9 and 15 in. high; tolrates dry shade and flowers in late spring. Herman's Pride is a choice cultivar whose green leaves are streaked with siliver markings.

Planning

As the gardening catalogs arrive this month, plan to scan them for unique and interesting vines and ground covers that will complement your landscape. Think about some troublesome areas that would benefit from a colorful vine or ground cover. Look for multiseason ornamental characteristics in the plants. The leaves of evergreens offer year-round interest. Deciduous plants can offer attractive leaves and fall color that can enhance the architectural features of a trellis or latticework. Don't forget about fragrant flowers, colorful fruit, and unique seedpods.

As you compile your list of favorites, remember the importance of matching the vine or ground cover to the site. Avoid the disappointment you will have if you try to force a vine or ground cover to grow where it just doesn't belong.

Planting

In the warmer parts of the Carolinas, plant vines and ground covers now when the soil can be worked. Before you dig, test the soil for moisture by squeezing a handful. A soil that can be dug is lightly moist and will loosely hold its shape after you squeeze it. If the soil forms a sticky ball in your hand, it's too wet to work. If you dig a wet soil, you can ruin its structure, creating large clods that will dry out to become rock-hard with few pore spaces for air and water. At the other extreme is very dry soil, which also should not be worked. If a handful of soil when squeezed turns to dust, wait for a rain shower a day or two before digging to prevent the topsoil from eroding away.

Care for Your Plants

Check the condition of the vines growing on trellises or supports and see that they're still attached.

Watering

Water fall-planted vines and ground covers, especially evergreen types, if the soil is dry.

Pruning

Wait until next month (or even March in the Mountains) after the coldest part of winter is over before pruning ground covers and vines.

Fertilizing

Do not fertilize at this time.

Pest Control

Insects and Mites: To control overwintering insects and spider mite eggs, apply a dormant oil spray before new growth emerges. Read the label for cautions regarding the limits of high and low temperatures at the time of application.

Weeds: As ground covers are settling in, fill the open areas with mulch. An alternative to mulching is interplanting with annuals. Use transplants for small areas and direct-sow large areas. A couple of points to consider when interplanting with annuals:

1 When using a pre-emergent herbicide, you cannot seed with annuals—they will be controlled by the herbicide.

2 Select well-behaved varieties of annuals, and don't plant them so densely that they'll shade or crowd out ground covers or compete for light or nutrients. As the ground cover plants spread, fewer annuals can safely be planted without encroaching on the permanent plantings.

Helpful Hint

Mailboxes and fence posts make good supports for certain vines that don't get very heavy and can be easily pruned if they get too long. A few good choices of annual vines that can be grown from seed: **cypress vine (*Ipomoea quamoclit*), morning-glory (*Ipomoea hederacea*),** and **scarlet runner bean (*Phaseolus coccineus*).**

Showy tropical vines include **allamanda (*Allamanda cathartica*)** and **mandevilla (*Mandevilla splendens*).**

Perennial deciduous vines include **goldflame honeysuckle (*Lonicera × heckrottii*)** and **clematis,** notably **scarlet clematis (*Clematis texensis* 'Gravetye Beauty', 'Duchess of Albany',** and **'Etoile Rose'** are good cultivars**). Madison confederate jasmine (*Trachelospermum jasminoides* 'Madison')** is a fragrant twining evergreen vine.

Planning

There are some vines that are just plain frightening. When **kudzu** made its American debut at the United States Centennial Exposition's Japanese Pavilion in Philadelphia in 1876, little did the organizers and visitors know that this lovely "porch vine" would eventually be billed as the world's fastest vine, growing a foot a day and up to 100 feet in a single season. The rest is history.

Vines like **Japanese wisteria** can become botanical pythons, strangling trees and pergolas with their sheer weight. Some vines raise concern because of their rampant free-wheeling nature, not only in the landscape but also in nature where they've escaped. These include **English ivy** (*Hedera helix*), **Hall's Japanese honeysuckle** (*Lonicera japonica* 'Halliana'), **Oriental bittersweet** (*Celastrus orbiculatus*), and **porcelainberry** (*Ampelopsis brevipedunculata*).

Do some research at your local library. Read local gardening columns in newspapers and gardening magazine articles, and visit private and public gardens to see these vines in action in the landscape. Speak to the gardeners and get their opinions. These background checks will alert you to any landscape surprises.

Planting

For those heavily shaded areas where grass won't grow, try ground covers. **English ivy** and **periwinkle** are excellent choices for shaded areas.

If you didn't plant **sweet peas** last October or November, plant them outdoors this month. You can even start the seed indoors in peat pots four to five weeks before setting them out, giving them a head start before the temperatures get too hot. Refer to the October Planting section, p. 334, to learn how.

Dig up, divide, and replant overgrown clumps of **liriope.** Mountain gardeners can postpone this chore until late March or April. Replant the liriope divisions about a foot apart.

Care for Your Plants

In cold Mountain areas, some shallow-rooted ground covers may have been heaved out of the ground by freezing and thawing soil. Once the soil is not frozen and is fairly dry, gently press the plants back into the ground to prevent them from drying out.

Watering

Keep newly planted ground covers and vines well watered to help them establish quickly.

Fertilizing

Fertilize ground covers and vines based on need. It's best to rely on soil-test results when you are going to replace any nutrients that are deficient in the soil. Don't be too hasty to fertilize your vines and ground covers. Fertilize when new growth begins.

Pruning

Overgrown vines that have outgrown their spaces can be cut back now. Prune other vines that bloom on current-season's growth now. Avoid pruning vines that will be blooming in the spring on last year's growth. After the coldest part of winter has passed, prune summer-flowering vines such as **Confederate jasmine** (*Trachelospermum jasminoides*), **Mme. Galen trumpetcreeper** (*Campis × tagliabuana*), and **Japanese hydrangea vine** (*Schizophragma hydrangeoides*).

Cut **liriope** back to within 3 to 4 inches of the ground using clippers, a string trimmer, or a mower set at its highest setting. If you wait, you'll have to do it carefully by hand to avoid nipping the new growth which will be left with brown edges on the leaves throughout the season.

Dwarf mondo grass (*Ophiopogon japonicus* 'Nana') grows more slowly than liriope and usually requires cutting back every two or three years. If the leaves look unsightly, trim it lightly to encourage the production of new leaves.

Pest Control

Insects and mites: See January.

Weeds: Some weed control will be required early in the establishment of ground covers. *Handpull* young weeds or suppress their growth with mulch. When a good ground cover eventually becomes established and spreads, it should be able to outcompete marauding weeds and stay relatively weed-free.

Helpful Hints

The key to determining when to prune your **clematis** is knowing whether it flowers on last year's wood, this year's wood, or both. Experts divide the genus into three groups: Group I contains all the early-spring-flowering evergreen clematis and early- and mid-flowering species. This group includes *Clematis alpina*, **Armand's clematis (*C. armandii*), downy clematis (*C. macropetala*),** and **anemone clematis (*C. montana*).** These clematis flower on last year's wood and should be pruned after the flowers fade but no later than July. The only pruning really needed is to remove weak or dead stems and to confine the plant to its allotted space.

Group II consists of clematis that also flower on last year's growth but will produce a second flush of bloom on new growth. Included mid-season large-flowered cultivars such as **'Bees Jubilee,' *C.* 'Henry', 'Nelly Moser',** and **'Vyvyan Pennell'.** Remove all dead and weak stems in late winter or early spring, and cut the remaining stems back to a pair of strong buds which will produce the first blooms. Occasional pinching after flowering will stimulate branching.

Group III consists of late-flowering cultivars and species that flower on this season's growth such as **golden clematis (*C. flammula*), solitary clematis (*C. integrifolia*),** *C.* × *jackmanii*, **Italian clematis (*C. viticella*), golden clematis (*C. tangutica*), scarlet clematis (*C. texensis*),** and the herbaceous species. These can also be pruned in late winter or early spring. For the first two or three years they may be cut back to a foot from the ground. Later, cut them back to 2 feet. If not cut regularly, this group can become very leggy and overgrown.

The boundaries between these three groups are not absolute. Certain Group III clematis, for example, can be treated as Group II to produce early blooms on previous year's wood. The groups serve as a rough guide to keeping your clematis vines within bounds.

Planning

Strawberries can make an uncommon ground cover for edging the walkway or flower beds in full sun or part shade. **Alpine strawberries (*Fragaria vesca*)** are attractive ground-hugging choices, particularly **'Improved Rugen'** and **'Semperflorens'.** But when you want big, luscious strawberries on your cereal in the morning, you need to grow the **cultivated strawberry (*F. × ananassa*).** Although not as compact or as contained as **alpines,** each plant can be expected to bear a quart of home-grown berries.

Select strawberry varieties that are June-bearers or "single-croppers." These short-day plants develop flower buds in the short days of the fall and produce one heavy crop in April in the Coastal Plain and May in the Piedmont and Mountains ("June-bearer" is a bit of a misnomer). During the long days of summer they produce above-ground runners called stolons.

Coastal Plain gardeners can plant June-bearers from November to March and Piedmont and Mountain gardeners can plant during March or April. Plan to purchase June-bearing varieties for early, mid-, and late-season harvests. Contact your county cooperative extension service office for the recommended varieties for your area. **Strawberries** are not permanent ground covers because they have to be replaced every two or three years, but they do add a whole new edible dimension to ground cover plantings.

Planting

Piedmont and Coastal Plains gardeners can plant container-grown ground covers and vines this month. Refer to p. 310 in the introduction to this chapter for the step-by-step instructions. Plant them as early in the season as possible to help them get established before the heat of summer.

Care for Your Plants

If you've overwintered your **mandevilla** indoors, wait until late winter or early spring before growth begins to *prune out* old, crowded stems and to shorten others.

Watering

Spring is rarely dry, so newly established plants may not require frequent irrigation. Check the soil, however, to make sure the roots are moist during their first few weeks.

Check mulched areas and replenish where needed. Organic mulches such as compost, pine needles ("straw"), and shredded leaves or wood conserve moisture, reduce weed growth, prevent soil compaction, and supply nutrients as they decompose.

Pruning

Mow your **liriope** beds before the new growth emerges in the spring. Browned or unsightly leaves of **mondo grass** can also be cut back at this time.

Cut back the winterscorched or winterkilled leaves and shoots of **St. John's-wort** before new growth begins, using a pair of pruning shears or a nylon string trimmer.

Spring-flowering vines such as **Carolina jessamine, Armand clematis,** and **cross vine** should be pruned as necessary after flowering. *Remove* any dead or damaged shoots and cut back others to keep the vine in bounds.

Thin out the congested shoots of fall-flowering vines such as **sweet-autumn clematis (*C. terniflora*)** before growth begins since it flowers on current-season's shoots.

Helpful Hint

To determine how many ground cover plants you'll need, refer to the following table: Plant Spacing ("on center" spacing-plants are spaced from the center of one plant to the center of the next one)

Square Spacing*

Area (sq. feet)	4 in.	6 in.	8 in.	10 in.	12 in.	15 in.	18 in.	24 in.
25	225	100	56	36	25	16	11	6
50	450	200	113	72	50	32	22	12
100	900	400	225	144	100	64	44	25
200	1,800	800	450	288	200	128	89	50
300	2,700	1,200	675	432	300	192	133	75
1,000	9,000	4,000	2,250	1,440	1,000	641	444	250
Spacing Multiplier	9	4	2.25	1.44	1	0.64	0.44	0.25

*"on center" spacing (plants are spaced from the center of one plant to the center of the next one)

For an area not found in the chart, use the following formula:

Area in square feet × Spacing Multiplier = Number of plants needed

OR use this simple formula: $N = \dfrac{A}{D^2}$

Where N = the number of plants in a given bed;
A = the area of the bed in square inches, and
D = the distance in inches between plants in the row and between rows.

Fertilizing

Ground covers can be fertilized when new growth begins. Sweep any fertilizer from the leaves to avoid burning them.

Pest Control

Insects and mites: Mountain gardeners can apply a dormant oil spray before new growth emerges as described in January.

Diseases: Sanitation is a cost-effective way to reduce disease problems. *Rake out* dead leaves from ground covers and *prune out* any dead, diseased, or broken limbs from vines. Before treating with a fungicide, identify the disease and determine if chemical control is warranted.

Weeds: Ground cover beds should be relatively free of weeds until they are dense enough to crowd them out. Instead of handpulling or mulching, you can control weeds with a pre-emergent herbicide, which kills germinating weeds before they appear. See p. 35 for pointers on selecting a pre-emergent herbicide.

Early this month, Coastal Plain gardeners can apply a pre-emergent herbicide to control summer annuals such as crabgrass and goosegrass (the application is made when they germinate but before they emerge). Wait until later this month to do this in the Piedmont, and do it early next month in the Mountains.

Planning

Plan to take your camera with you outside during the next few months so you can take photographs of your landscape as a way of taking notes of your garden. Take pictures of various views to see where vines and ground covers can be used to bring color to otherwise nondescript areas. Use variegated plants to add the illusion of light to a dark area. Shade-loving ground covers such as **hosta, ivies,** variegated **liriope,** and **wintercreeper euonymous** can be suitable choices. Take a look at the color of your home, fences, and paving to see if any ground covers can be used to unite and harmonize these features with the landscape.

Planting

Sow seeds of tender summer-flowering annual vines in pots this month in the Mountains so they'll be large enough to move outdoors after the last freeze. Gardeners in the milder parts of the Carolinas can direct-sow the seeds to the garden after the last expected freeze, and they will have flowering in midsummer to fall. For more information about sowing annuals, refer to the Annuals chapter, p. 33. Some choice summer-flowering annual vines can be found in the Planting Chart on p. 312.

Some seeds require special treatment prior to sowing to encourage germination. The seeds of **morning-glory** and **moonflower** (*Ipomoea*) should be nicked with a knife or file and then soaked overnight to allow water to be absorbed by the seed for germination to occur.

Care for Your Plants

If **sweet peas** are heavily mulched, their roots will be kept cooler and their season prolonged. Use rough plant litter or grass clippings for mulch. A little shade at midday will also help maintain the quality of the flowers and prolong the blooming season. *Remove* the pods, which inhibit flowering (unless you want to save the seed).

A few weeks after the last freeze in your area, bring your **mandevilla** outdoors. Before planting it in its permanent location, acclimatize the vine to the outdoors. First set it in a shaded location for about a week or two; move it to a partially shaded location the following week. Finally, plant it in its permanent location, which should be partially shaded with protection from the hot afternoon sun. *Fertilize* every other month from spring through fall with a soluble houseplant fertilizer such as 20-20-20.

Watering

Water any newly planted vines or ground covers. *Check* the soil in the rootball regularly and water it when necessary.

Fertilizing

Fertilize ground covers and vines based on need. Vines may not need fertilizer if they look robust and are vigorously growing. Any excessive amount of fertilizer may encourage a lot of leafy growth at the expense of flowers, and vigorous vines may become unmanageable and will require excessive pruning.

Pruning

Prune **wisterias, Carolina jessamine,** and other spring-flowering vines after last flowers have faded.

Pest Control

Insects and mites: Watch out for aphids, whiteflies, spider mites, and euonymus scale. Evaluate the injury and decide if pest control measures are warranted.

Helpful Hints

- If you want to cut **sweet pea** flowers, collect them when at least one flower in a cluster has fully opened and the others are just beginning to unfurl. They can last up to ten days in a vase.

- A common question asked by exasperated gardeners is: "Why doesn't my **wisteria** bloom?" First of all, bear in mind that wisterias in general may require five or six years before flowering. If your plant was seed-propagated or is an unnamed cultivar, you may have to keep waiting—perhaps for several more years—before you see it bloom.

Wisteria can be encouraged to bloom by meeting certain cultural requirements. It should be planted in full sun and in a fertile, well-drained site. Fertilize only when necessary. Excessive fertilization, especially with nitrogen, triggers leafy shoot growth at the expense of flowers.

Superphosphate is often touted as an elixir for flowering. If adequate levels of phosphorus are already present in the soil as determined by the results of a soil test, additional amounts are wasteful.

Prune properly. Avoid indiscriminate hacking, which inspires vigorous vegetative growth and further delays flowering. Instead, aim to restrict growth to spurlike shoots that produce the flowers. Flower buds form on previous-year's wood. In midsummer, cut the lateral shoots in half or just beyond the sixth or seventh leaf. New shoots may break from buds behind the cut; wait until they have developed one or two leaves, then cut them back beyond this point as well. In late winter before budbreak, shorten the side shoots coming off the main framework branches to three or four buds. Over time, these shoots will be converted to short, flowering spurs. Head back the main branches to three or four buds.

In addition to this careful pruning, remove dead, dying, or diseased branches as soon as you notice them. Thin out branches which are not growing in the direction you want them to. In addition to pruning the top, pruning the roots in the fall may further coerce your wisteria to bloom. Root-prune as if you were going to transplant the vine. Divide the root zone area into four quadrants. Select two quadrants on opposite sides of the rootball and excavate a trench 8 to 12 inches deep. Slice the roots cleanly with a sharp spade (pruning shears may be necessary for thick roots), and then backfill.

Water your wisteria during dry periods if the foliage begins to wilt. Once it finally flowers, expect it to bloom in subsequent years.

Diseases: Large-flowered **clematis** are highly susceptible to a notorious fungal disease called clematis wilt. See May Diseases, p. 325, for description and controls.

Weeds: *Handpull* bittercress, chickweed, henbit, and other winter annuals before they go to seed. Weeds can be hoed out, but lightly, so as not to disturb the ground covers. Grassy weeds can be controlled with a selective post-emergent grass herbicide.

Planning

This month, keep an eye out for troubling spots in the landscape. If you've been struggling to grow turfgrass in an area that receives less than four hours of sunlight and you choose not to thin out the tree canopy to admit more sunlight, consider evergreen shade-loving ground covers. Some shade-loving ground covers that can be used in place of turf are **carpet bugleweed** (*Ajuga*), **English ivy**, **liriope, pachysandra, periwinkle** (*Vinca minor*), and **wintercreeper euonymus.**

Planting

It's a good time to dig and divide those crowded **liriope** borders. You may be able to find enough neighbors to share the bounty. *Plant* container-grown vines and ground covers, but be careful—they'll need attention after planting until they get established. Make sure you're familiar with the plant's site preferences prior to planting. *Plant* seeds or seedlings of annual vines like **morning-glory, moonflower,** and **scarlet runner bean.** *Plant* the summer annuals you sowed indoors into the garden after the last freeze in your area.

Care for Your Plants

Mulch vines and ground covers to suppress weeds and to conserve moisture. Organic mulches will break down and enrich the soil with nutrients. Create supports for annual vines before they become a tangled mess. Use strings, trellises, or other supports, making sure that they'll be strong enough to support the weight of the vines. Train newly planted vines onto their vertical supports by securing one end of the string to the support and the other end to a stick driven next to the vine or a rock. As the vine grows, use soft twine or nylon to tie the vine to the support until it begins to twine or cling.

Pruning

Limit pruning to plants that have already finished flowering.

Watering

May can be a dry month. *Water* newly planted vines and ground covers.

Fertilizing

Ground cover plants can be fertilized to encourage their spread. If vines need to be fertilized, avoid adding too much, which can make them produce a lot of leaves at the expense of flowers.

Pest Control

Insects and mites: Aphids, Japanese beetles, and spider mites can be a problem. Look for spider mites on **junipers, pachysandra,** and other ground covers (see Shrubs, p. 272).

Other pests: Watch out for snails and slugs on your ground covers. See p. 366 for descriptions and controls.

Diseases: Several fungi cause leaf spots on **English, Algerian,** and other **ivies.** A bacterial disease called bacterial spot and canker is more serious because it attacks the leaves and produces cankers—discolored areas of dead tissue—on the stems, which result in dieback. *Clip off* infected leaves. *Prune out and discard* dead or dying plants. Identify the particular disease before seeking control with a fungicide.

Leaf and stem blight is a serious pest of **pachysandra**—brown blotches appear on the leaves and spread to the stems. *Remove and discard* infected plants. To avoid this blight, rake up and compost any leaves in the fall. Fallen leaves create moist conditions that favor the growth and spread of disease.

Scale insects are often associated with leaf and stem blight. Control them with a horticultural oil or other insecticide.

Large-flowered **clematis** are highly susceptible to a notorious fungal disease called clematis wilt. The disease strikes in early summer, often when plants are on the verge of flowering. Although wilted leaves and stems that droop and turn black are the first signs, the fungus initially attacks the stem close to the soil line, invading cracked, damaged, or weak tissue. Lesions or discolored areas associated with the fungus girdling the stem can usually be seen below the first pair of wilted leaves.

Despite its devastating appearance, clematis wilt is rarely fatal. Even when all topgrowth is killed, new healthy shoots can emerge from basal buds below the soil surface. This is the reason for the recommendation that **clematis** be planted with the crown at a depth of $2^{1}/_{2}$ inches below soil level.

Prune back infected stems to healthy tissue and discard the trimmings. *Fertilize and water* to encourage regrowth. To encourage the production of woody tissue on the lower stem, pinch out the tips of new shoots when they reach 2 to 3 inches in length. Carefully tie the shoots that emerge from below the pinch to avoid damage from wind and rain.

At present there is no registered fungicide for controlling clematis wilt. You may want to plant some of the smaller-flowered **clematis** such as *C. alpina, C. macropetala, C. viticella,* and their hybrids, which are less susceptible to clematis wilt.

Juniper tip blight, caused by a fungus called *Phomopsis,* attacks the tips of **shore** and **creeping junipers** and others in the spring. The dead branches gradually turn gray. Tiny black dots on recently killed needles are the fruiting bodies of the fungus. *Prune out* infected plant parts and discard them, since this fungus survives in dead and decaying plant material.

Weeds: *Handpull* weeds when they're young. Try not to put off this chore until next weekend. Hoeing and maintaining a shallow mulch layer will also help. If you use a nonselective herbicide containing glyphosate (Roundup®), glufosinate (Finale®), or one containing potassium salts of fatty acids (Sharpshooter®), use a piece of cardboard to shield your desirable plants from any accidental contact with the herbicide. Apply the herbicide according to label directions in the early morning or late evening when the air is still (to reduce the chances of drift).

Planning

Take notes on your vines and ground covers this month and over the next few months, and record your observations in your gardening journal. Take notes on bloom times, ornamental features, growth rates, and pest problems. Use this information to begin making plans to correct any problems or to make arrangements to replace some of the poorly performing plants.

Planting

You can still plant container-grown vines and ground covers from nurseries and garden centers. Get them into the ground as soon as possible so they can get established before the heat of summer bears down on them.

Care for Your Plants

Train the new growth of **clematis, Confederate jasmine, swamp jessamine, trumpet honeysuckle,** and other twining vines to guide them onto the trellis. Use soft twine to give the new shoots a start. Keep the "feet" of your clematis cool by creating shade with shrubs or planting a ground cover or perennial that will not be invasive. Some good clematis companions are **candytuft, coralbells, creeping phlox, hardy geraniums** (*Geranium*), **Silver Mound artemisia,** and most **veronicas.**

Watering

Apply water as needed to keep newly planted ground covers and vines from wilting. Use soaker hoses to water ground covers on slopes; this will reduce water runoff and soil erosion. If you have an automated irrigation system, water for short periods rather than all at once, reducing the chance of runoff. Keep ground covers and vines mulched with compost, pine straw, or shredded wood.

Fertilizing

Follow soil-test results when fertilizing your vines and ground covers. Supplement mulch with well-rotted horse or cow manure to add nutrients.

Pruning

Limit your pruning to vines that have already flowered on last year's growth. Shear off the flower buds of silver-leaved **lavender-cotton** (*Santolina chamacyparissus*). These ground-hugging plants tend to decline after flowering, so diverting the plant's energy to the leaves will prevent them from deteriorating.

Pest Control

Insects and mites: Look for the telltale signs of these pests: Japanese beetles skeletonize leaves and feed on flower buds and flowers; aphids occur in clusters near the tips of shoots and their feeding causes leaves to become wrinkled, sticky, and sometimes coated with a black sooty mold; spider mites cause yellow or bronze stippling on the leaf surface; thrips damage flower buds, creating streaks or spots on the open blooms and brown edges on flower buds that fail to bloom.

Diseases: Avoid overhead watering and remove spent flowers and dead or dying leaves. *Keeping plants clean will reduce the chances of infection.* Crown rot is the only serious pest of **ajuga** or **carpet bugleweed** (*Ajuga reptans*). Look for a roughly circular patch of dead or dying plants with blackened leaves. A "cottony" fungus may be visible in damp, shady areas. The roots of affected plants are often discolored and rotted and can be easily lifted from the ground. *Remove* dead and dying plants. In the future, provide good, well-drained conditions and avoid excess watering. Infested areas can be treated with a fungicide prior to replanting.

Weeds: *Handpull* or hoe out any weeds to prevent them from stealing water and nutrients from your annuals. Suppress their emergence with a layer of mulch—cover any bare ground with mulch. Sheets of newspaper camouflaged with grass clippings or other organic matter will suppress subsequent growth.

Helpful Hint

A simple way to propagate vines is by layering. Here's how to layer a **clematis** vine:

1 In the spring select one or two dormant shoots of last year's wood.

2 With a sharp knife, start about $1/2$ inch away from a node (the point of attachment of the leaves and buds) and make an angled cut halfway into the underside of the stem toward the node.

3 To encourage rooting, **dust** the wound with a rooting hormone and bury that portion of the stem 2 inches deep. A stiff U-shaped wire can be used to peg the stem into the ground so that it doesn't pop up.

4 Secure the growing tip to a cane or pole so it can grow upward.

5 Lightly **mulch** the layered stem and keep the soil moist.

6 Every month or two, check the stem for any roots. Give the stem a tug, and if it feels well rooted, sever it from the parent plant.

Vigorous vines may form roots in a few weeks, while others may be rooted by the end of the growing season.

Planning

If you're going to go on vacation during this month, plan on finding someone to take care of your plants while you're gone. Not only does this keep up the appearance of the plants, it also makes it look as if someone is home. If you'll be gone for an extended time, these tasks will need attention:

• Water newly planted vines and ground covers.

• Edge the ground cover beds

• *Trim* vines that are escaping from their allotted space.

Planting

Has the lawn beneath your trees disappeared? Extend the mulch area up to or beyond the drip line of your trees, or try planting **ajuga, ivy, liriope, vinca,** or other shade-tolerant ground covers beneath the trees (this chore can wait until fall).

Clematis can be propagated by seed, but the seedlings will not be identical to the parent; therefore, this method is usually reserved for the species and not cultivars. Here's how to start **clematis** from seed:

1 When the seedheads have turned brown, you can shake out the seeds. Select the swollen ones.

2 In general, clematis seeds require cold stratification at 40 degrees F. To stratify the seeds, fill a plastic bag with equal parts damp peat moss and perlite. *Remove* the feathery styles before mixing the seeds with the medium.

3 Place the bag in the refrigerator for three months.

4 Sow the seeds in a flat filled with the same mix, covering them lightly. Move the flat to a location in bright, indirect sunlight and water as needed.

5 Seeds can take from three weeks to several months or longer to sprout. When the seedlings have developed at least one pair of true leaves, transplant them into 3-inch pots filled with standard potting mix.

Care for Your Plants

Use compost, shredded bark or wood, or pine straw to mulch around ground covers and vines.

Watering

See June.

Fertilizing

Don't fertilize your vines and ground covers unless you are willing to provide adequate moisture for roots to grow and absorb the applied minerals. Water is necessary to make the fertilizer available to the plant roots, and it's also important to keep that new growth healthy and alive.

Pruning

Ground covers that have become overgrown need to be pruned back into shape. Make thinning cuts inside the plant so the cuts will be hidden. Use sharp pruning shears to make clean cuts that will heal rapidly. Dead, broken, or diseased limbs and shoots should be removed any time during the growing season.

Your **wisteria** may need to be pruned to encourage the production of spurs, which will provide next year's floral display. Cut the lateral shoots in half or just beyond the sixth or seventh leaf. New shoots may break from buds behind the cut; wait until they have developed one or two leaves, then cut them back beyond this point as well.

Pest Control

Insects and mites: Pests to watch for include aphids, spider mites, and Japanese beetles. Aphids and spider mites can be washed from plants with a strong stream of water. Use insecticidal soap and insecticides for aphids and miticides to keep mites in check.

Watch out for Japanese beetles this month. These big slow-flying bugs, metallic green with bronze wing covers, skeletonize leaves, leaving only a lacy network of leaf veins after their feeding. They also feed on flowers. Pick them off and *discard* them into a jar of soapy water. Neem can be applied to the leaves to reduce feeding by the adults. Other insecticides can be used for heavy infestations. If you choose to use Japanese beetle traps, place them far away from your susceptible shrubs. Thankfully, there's only one generation a year.

Diseases: Kabatina blight is a disease that attacks the tips of **shore** and **creeping junipers** and others in the summer. *Prune out* infected plant parts and discard them, since this fungus survives in dead and decaying plant material.

Weeds: Start pulling weeds out of ground cover beds. Maintain a shallow layer of mulch to suppress them. The weeds are competing with the ground covers for light, water, and nutrients. Eventually the ground covers should shade the soil surface when they fill in to naturally prevent their emergence.

Planning

Summer takes its toll on plants. High nighttime heat and humidity, pests, and storms with high winds are a few natural problems faced by Carolina gardeners. Since the cool temperatures of fall are ideal for planting new vines and ground covers or transplanting established plants, spend some time in the early morning or late afternoon evaluating your landscape. Make plans to replace your annual flowering vines with something more vigorous or tolerant of the summertime conditions. If you've tired of pruning a highly vigorous specimen, make plans to transplant it this fall, giving it to a friend who's willing to take it on. For ground cover plantings that haven't filled out very much, determine why they didn't and make plans to fertilize them this fall to when they're dormant and to keep them well watered and mulched during their establishment period. *Take along your gardening journal and jot down notes for things to do next month.*

Planting

You can still plant container-grown vines and ground covers. This is a very stressful time, however, and unless there is sufficient water available you may want to wait until September or October when the temperatures are more favorable for planting.

Care for Your Plants

Collect seeds from annual vines and store them for planting next year. Actively growing vines may need to be secured to their moorings. Vines that do not have tendrils will have to be secured to their moorings with soft twine. Check on the fastening of other shoots to see that the stems aren't being girdled.

Watering

Apply water as needed to vines and ground covers to prevent them from wilting. Check the soil before watering and look at the plant to see if water is necessary. When you water, water deeply, and thoroughly wet the soil.

Fertilizing

If you want to fertilize your vines and ground covers now, use a slow-release fertilizer to avoid encouraging the rapid, succulent growth which can be killed by early fall freezes. Otherwise, wait until next spring when new growth begins.

Pruning

Remove dead, damaged, or pest-ridden shoots or limbs. *Trim* renegade shoots from tangled vines.

Pest Control

Insects and mites: Inspect your vines and ground covers for aphids and spider mites. Evaluate the extent of injury and take action if the health of the vine or ground cover is in jeopardy.

Nematodes: Nematodes are microscopic organisms that live in the soil and attack the roots of plants. They are more commonly found in coarse-textured sandy soils than in fine-textured clay soils. See Roses, July Pest Control on p. 240 for more information.

Diseases: Watch out for leaf spot diseases. Infected leaves can be trimmed out and discarded. Severe infections can be treated with a fungicide. If fungicides are required on a regular basis, plan on replacing the vine.

Weeds: See July.

Helpful Hints

- If the flowers in your perennial garden are quickly fading in the hot summer sun, think about creating a trellis and covering it with vines. This will protect the flowers from the hot afternoon sun and will make them last a little longer.

- To cover large areas inexpensively with a ground cover such as **lily turf (*Liriope muscari*)** or **mondo grass (*Ophiopogon japonicus*),** purchase large pots and tease apart the clumps. Plant individuals plants at the appropriate spacing.

- Erect a trellis on the south-facing side of your house a few feet away to shade the house from the sun. If you have an attractive trellis, you can even use deciduous or annual vines that will allow sunlight to warm your home during the winter months. Keeping the vine away from the house will keep it away from siding or shingles.

Planning

For something completely different, plan to grow some well-behaved vines on some of the shrubs and trees in your landscape. Draping vines on other plants allows you to create some eye-catching combinations. Think about using flowers and leaves to create contrasting colors and textures, extending the flowering display of tree with flowering vines, and dressing up otherwise boring plants with a feather boa of vines. Annual vines good for this purpose include **air potato** (*Dioscorea bulbifera*), **black-eyed-susan vine**, **love-in-a-puff** (*Cardiospermum halicacabum*), and **moonvine**. Some choice perennials are **clematis, Tangerine Beauty cross vine, potato vine** (*Solanum jasminoides*), and **hairy Virginia creeper** (*Parthenocissus quinquefolia* var. *hirsuta*). To select the right vine-shrub/tree associations, keep these points in mind:

1 The vine should not be too small compared to the shrub; at the same time it shouldn't be so vigorous that it completely engulfs the shrub.

2 Both vine and shrub or tree should share the same preferences for soil and light.

3 Dabble with mixing and matching flower colors, leaf textures, and bloom times.

To help vines that need a little structural help in starting their ascent, use fishing line, twigs, or the black plastic bird netting used for protecting fruit trees.

Planting

Fall is the prime-time planting season. Select healthy container-grown or balled-and burlapped shrubs and plant them properly in the right location in your landscape. Container-grown vines and ground covers can be planted this month in the Mountains. *Water* the plants well following planting and until they become established. It's a good time to transplant ground covers to fill in bare areas. Some ground covers such as **euonymus** and **English ivy** already have visible roots. Prune a stem and bury the shoots with soil. Root will form and you can start another ground cover bed.

Care for Your Plants

Mandevilla is a common "mailbox vine" that blooms all summer long. This native to the tropical parts of South America should not be exposed to freezing temperatures in regions colder than zone 9 in Charleston and southward along the coast. If you want to overwinter your **mandevilla** indoors and replant it outside next spring, you have two ways of doing this. The first approach is to root stem cuttings before the first expected freeze:

1 Take 4- to 6-inch-long cuttings that include a "heel" or portion of the bark and stem.

2 Dip the bottom of each stem in a rooting hormone and insert the stems in a sterile well-drained medium such as equal parts of peat and perlite.

3 Water them in and enclose the pot inside a clear plastic bag. Move the pot to a warm spot receiving bright, indirect light.

4 After the cuttings have sufficiently rooted—usually in about eight to twelve weeks—take the pot out of the bag and repot the cuttings into larger pots, using your favorite houseplant potting mix. Gradually expose the rooted **mandevillas** to brighter light. Eventually move them to a window that receives bright light. A spot on your fluorescent light table where the **mandevillas** can receive light fourteen to sixteen hours a day would be ideal.

The second approach is to rescue the entire plant and bring it indoors:

1 *Prune back* the plant to a manageable height of about 2 feet, then lift it out of the ground with as much of the intact root system as possible. Shake off some of the soil and pot it up. Any houseplant potting soil may be used, as long as it allows good drainage and is heavy enough to support the plant.

2 *Quarantine* the plant for several days before moving it indoors. If you see any insects that may have hitched a free ride inside, take action and control them immediately to prevent them from attacking other plants. When you're confident that your **mandevilla** is pest-free, move it to a window that receives bright, direct sunlight.

3 *Water* the **mandevilla** often enough to keep the soil from drying out. In the fall and winter, locate the plant in a cool room with a night temperature of 60 to 65 degrees Fahrenheit (although temperatures as low as 45 to 50 degrees can be tolerated). Water sparingly and cease fertilizing altogether.

4 In late winter or early spring before growth begins, *prune out* old, crowded stems and shorten others. Flowers are produced on the current season's growth. Next year, a few weeks after the last freeze in your area, bring your **mandevilla** outdoors.

5 Before planting it in its permanent location, acclimatize the vine to the outdoors. First set it in a shaded location for about a week; move it to a partially shaded location the following week. Finally, plant it in its permanent location in full sun.

Pruning

Any major pruning should be saved until late winter or early spring. *Remove* dead, damaged, insect-infested, or diseased shoots now and any stray shoots.

Watering

Water all newly planted vines and ground covers thoroughly until they become established.

Fertilizing

If your vines and ground covers have produced sufficient growth this year, fertilizing may not be necessary. If you choose to fertilize, rely on soil test results to apply the nutrients required by your plants. See p. 330. If they're showing their fall colors, wait until next year.

Pest Control

Insects and mites: Aphids and spider mites may still be active. Evaluate the extent of injury and decide if pest control measures are warranted.

Diseases: Clean up fallen leaves. They can harbor disease and insect pests over the winter if allowed to remain on the ground.

Weeds: Watch out for germinating winter annuals such as annual bluegrass, chickweed, and henbit. *Remove* them now while they're young and easy to remove. Don't wait until spring when they'll be well established and poised to go to seed.

OCTOBER

Planning

If you have a slope whose steepness makes mowing a dangerous gardening activity, plan a few low-maintenance solutions:

1 Plant ground covers on the existing slope. Some good slope-stabilizers include **Asian star jasmine, daylily, English ivy, Juniper, liriope, periwinkle** (*Vinca minor*), **willowleaf cotoneaster** (*Cotoneaster salicifolius*), **wintercreeper euonymus,** and **winter jasmine** (*Jasminum nudiflorum*). Be sure to choose hardy ground covers adapted to your region and match their preferences for sunlight or shade with the site.

2 On very steep slopes, build a retaining wall to reduce the height of the slope above and below the wall to create usable gardening space. If the wall is less than a $1^{1}/_{2}$ feet in height, it could be a do-it-yourself project.

3 Long and steep slopes can be terraced with a series of walls to create several layers of gardening space.

Planting

Interplant spring-flowering bulbs with your ground covers for splashes of color next year. Mountain gardeners need to get their vines and ground covers planted this month so they will become established before winter arrives. Snow cover in the higher elevations will insulate them from severe winter cold. In the milder parts of the Carolinas, planting can continue into December. The keys to growing **sweet peas** are cool weather, full sun, and fertile soil. Here's how to plant them:

1 Select a well-drained site in full sun. Prepare the bed by adding generous amounts of organic matter such as compost. Add ground limestone if the soil is acid; **sweet peas** prefer a nearly neutral soil pH.

2 Sow seed now or next month, or wait until very early spring of next year in the Mountains as early as the soil can be worked. Consider cultivating **sweet peas** that combine colorful flowers with a heady aroma—included in this group are **'Firecrest', 'Maggie May',** and **'White Supreme'.** Improve germination by soaking the seeds in warm water for a couple of days. Alternatively, you can sandpaper the seeds just enough to make a hole in the seed coat.

3 Space the seeds 4 to 6 inches apart and plant them 2 inches deep. Expect the seeds to germinate in two to three weeks.

4 When the seedlings reach 4 inches in height, sidedress with a complete fertilizer such as 10-10-10 at a rate of 3 tablespoons per 10 feet of row.

5 *Mulch* the seedlings with a 2-inch layer of mulch to conserve moisture.

6 Support the climbing types with wire fencing or string supports. When the plants flower, remove the faded flower stalks to encourage repeat flowering and provide plenty of moisture during the growing season.

Care for Your Plants

Dig up **sweet potato** roots of **'Blackie', 'Marguerite', 'Pink Frost',** and others, and store them in a cool, dry location for replanting next year. An eye will sprout on the root.

In the Mountains, *mulch* newly planted vines and ground covers after the ground freezes. (After the ground freezes the pests should have found other winter quarters, reducing the chances of their bedding down next to your new plantings.) Annual vines that have been killed with the first freeze should be cut back from their supports and composted or buried in the vegetable garden.

Watering

See September.

Fertilizing

Do not fertilize vines and ground covers when they or other plants are displaying their fall colors—wait until next year.

Pruning

Limit pruning to the removal of dead, damaged, or diseased branches and any wayward shoots.

Pest Control

Mites: Sorry, but spider mites can still be active in the warmer parts of the Carolinas. Controlling the overwintering eggs with a dormant horticultural oil this fall when the plants go dormant may be all that's needed to kill the eggs and any active mites that may be present.

Diseases: Clean up the plantings to get rid of diseased leaves.

Weeds: Weeds continue to germinate and emerge. *Handpull* them while they're young and suppress their growth with mulch.

Planning

Throughout history gardeners have showcased their vines on structures that ranged from the simple to the elegant. You can buy ready-made fan-shaped or rectangular trellises at garden centers. If you're a do-it-yourselfer, you can plan to build your own this month after you decide on the kinds of vines you're going to support. Twining vines with long flexible stems—**hyacinth bean, moonvine, morning-glory,** and **trumpet honeysuckle**—need to wrap themselves around something like a string, wire, or trellis. They climb best on narrow, vertically-oriented trellises.

Climbing vines that use tendrils need a support that's small enough for their threadlike "fingers" to grasp. Fine lattice work or a structure that includes wire, string, or plastic mesh is suitable for **morning-glory (*Ipomoea*), passionflower (*Passiflora*),** and **sweet pea (*Lathyrus odoratus*).** Chicken wire can be wrapped around a freestanding pole or pillar to give the vines something to hold onto. A tripod is a simple way of mixing these climbers into borders of annual and perennials.

Use your gardening journal to record any observations about the expected vigor and eventual weight of these vines. If you're going to be growing a heavyweight like **Japanese (*Wisteria floribunda*)** or **Chinese wisteria (*W. sinensis*),** be prepared to build a sturdy structure and foundation. Arbors need to have 6x6 posts set in concrete with 4x4 cross members. **American wisteria** isn't as heavy and doesn't require an arbor of this magnitude.

Planting

Plant container-grown vines and ground covers. In the colder areas of the Carolinas, *mulch* with oak leaves, wood chips, shredded bark, pine needles, or shredded leaves to keep the soil from freezing too rapidly and to moderate temperature shifts.

Care for Your Plants

Don't hesitate to tie uncooperative vines in place with twine or twist ties. This will help your **clematis, climbing hydrangeas,** and Confederate jasmine find their way across arbors.

Fertilizing

Do not fertilize vines and ground covers at this time. Wait until next year. Keep in mind that if they have already filled in their allotted space and have grown vigorously this past year, fertilizing may not be necessary. In fact, it can result in a lot of excess, junglelike growth that would have to be removed with a machete.

Watering

Fall is unusually dry in the Carolinas, so don't rely on Mother Nature to water newly planted vines and ground covers. A few weeks after planting, start cutting back on watering to every few days or longer, especially with cloudy, rainy, or cool weather. Eventually you can water on a weekly or "as-needed" basis, testing the soil and rootball for moisture. Established plants, especially evergreens, should be watered during the winter months so they won't go into the winter on the dry side.

Pruning

Limit any removal to dead, damaged, or overly long branches.

Pest Control

Insects and mites: If there is any evidence of scale on vines and ground covers, *spray* with dormant oil in late fall and again in early spring when the plants are dormant.

Diseases: Rake up fallen leaves from your ground covers and compost them or bury them in the vegetable garden. See the Helpful Hint on this page.

Weeds: Geotextile or landscape fabrics are synthetic mulch underliners that are used to suppress weeds on a long-term basis. When placed on the soil surface and covered with mulch, they enhance the ability of the mulch to suppress weeds. Geotextiles are woven and nonwoven fabrics of polypropylene or polyester that have been developed to replace black plastic. Black plastic, a solid polyethylene material, has been used underneath mulches to provide excellent control of annual weeds and suppress perennial weeds; black plastic isn't porous, however, and doesn't allow for air and water movement. Geotextiles overcome this disadvantage by admitting air and water. They should not be used in plantings where the fabric would inhibit rooting and spreading of the ground cover.

Helpful Hints

When growing ground covers beneath trees such as **maples** and **oaks,** it's a chore to remove fallen leaves from the ground cover beds. (The leaves should be removed because they can smother the ground cover plants.) There are several ways of managing these leaves:

• Blow off the leaves into windrows and shred them with a lawn mower. Then return them to the bed as an attractive mulch. Shredding the leaves beforehand reduces their volume, increases surface area to speed-up decomposition, and keeps them secured to the soil surface.

• Use netting to capture the leaves. Buy large plastic bird netting sold for protecting fruit trees and stretch it over the ground cover in the fall. It won't be noticeable from a distance and it won't crush the ground cover. After the leaves have collected on the net, drag it off or roll it up and move the leaves to an area where they can be shredded with the lawn mower and composted or used as mulch and sifted back into the ground cover.

• If harvesting and shredding the leaves proves to be a daunting chore, transplant the ground covers and allow the leaves to fall naturally in place. If you want to convince your neighbors that not raking your leaves is a conscientious decision, border this area with timbers, stones, or turf to impart a natural, forested design to your landscape.

Planning

Update your gardening journal this month and make plans for improvements next year. See if you've cured any of your troubled spots with vines and ground covers. Are there any other areas in the landscape that need to be fixed with a ground cover? Perhaps you'll have to replace the annual vines with perennial woody types to give you year-round privacy. Were pests a problem this season? Make plans to learn more about how to control the most troublesome insects and diseases by refining your pest control techniques or simply replacing the pest-prone plants with more resistant ones.

During the year you may have saved newspaper and magazine clippings of articles from local garden writers who touted certain ground covers and vines. Perhaps you wrote down comments from friends and others regarding some aspect of their gardening or the names of a few plants. Compile these notes and plan on acting on them next growing season.

Planting

Container-grown plants can still be planted in the warmer parts of the Carolinas.

Care for Your Plants

Keep vines off wooden walls—the vines trap moisture and slow the drying of wood, which can encourage decay. When shading brick or masonry walls with clinging vines that have aerial rootlets or adhesive disks such as **English** and **Boston ivies** and **climbing hydrangea,** think twice before allowing them to cling to the walls. Once you allow them to climb on the walls, they're very difficult to remove. After you tear down the vine you're left with rootlets and disks that can only be removed with a stiff scrub brush.

Give **English ivy** a trim and pull it off house walls or trees. Ivy which grows up into a tree may eventually cover too much of the crown and cause the tree to die. Heavy infestations have been known to break tree limbs.

Watering

Pay special attention to watering newly planted vines and ground covers.

Fertilizing

Wait until spring when new growth begins before fertilizing vines and ground covers.

Pruning

Remove damaged branches and those overly long shoots that are being whipped around by the wind.

Pest Control

Insects and mites: Apply a dormant oil spray early in the month before new growth emerges to control overwintering insect and spider mite eggs. Read the label for cautions regarding the limits of high and low temperatures at the time of application.

Diseases: *Rake out* the leaves and dispose of them in the compost pile, or bury them in the vegetable garden to reduce the amount of fungal spores next year.

Weeds: *Handpull* any young winter annuals or cover them with a shallow layer of compost. Weeding is never fun, but the cooler temperatures can make it more bearable.

Water Gardening

Compared to "terrestrial" gardening, water and bog gardening offers a different set of challenges and experiences. You'll be introduced to a whole new range of unique plants that don't mind "wet feet" or poorly drained soils. You can also introduce fish into your garden. Eventually you'll find that your simple water garden has become a complex ecosystem with dragonflies, tadpoles, frogs, toads, turtles, and birds. With luck, the residents of your water garden will consume the pests in your vegetable garden and landscape.

Planning

Before you start digging, you should plan. While a tub or half-whiskey-barrel can be moved from one end of the patio to the other, an underground water feature cannot be moved so easily. Choose the right location.

1 The plants need at least six hours of sun a day.

2 A spot near your home makes a good place to enjoy your water garden—and it will be easy to keep an eye on your children.

3 Putting a water garden beneath trees can result in maintenance problems—there are falling leaves and the potential for tree roots cracking the walls of hard pools. Besides, excavating around tree roots can harm the tree. If this happens to be the best place, consider an above-ground water garden.

If you're going to create a below-ground water garden, it can be made of a variety of materials:

- Natural mud-bottom ponds have clay bottoms that create a rubberlike waterproof seal.

- Flexible liners can be used to create any shape or size pool.

- Polyethylene is the least expensive and least durable liner. Use the best grade and purchase enough so you can double it over itself to increase its thickness.

- Polyvinyl chloride (PVC) liners are more durable and flexible and longer-lasting than poly-ethylene. Depending on the gauge, they may last from five to twenty years before breaking down.

- Rubber or synthetic rubber liners are even more durable and flexible than PVC. Two common materials are butyl rubber and EPDM (ethylene propylene diene monomer) rubber. They can last up to fifty years.

- Rigid preformed liners are made of fiberglass or plastic. Fiberglass liners are more durable and more expensive than plastic. If you want fish in your water garden, make sure the preformed pool is at least 24 inches deep.

- Concrete pools are well suited for the warmer regions of the Carolinas; in colder areas, freezing temperatures can cause cracking unless the concrete is properly reinforced. Don't be timid about relying on an experienced professional to construct a concrete pool for you.

Once you've determined the location, size, and shape of your pond, install it. See February for step-by-step instructions on installing your water garden.

Water Gardening

Planting

Water garden plants can be separated into four general groups:

1. **Floating-leaved plants,** such as **lotus, water lilies,** and **water snowflakes,** are rooted on the bottom and produce leaves and flowers on the surface.

2. **Marginal or bog plants** such as **cannas, pickerel rush,** and **water irises** grow in shallow water along the edges of ponds and generally have very showy flowers. Some marginals can handle either shallow or deep water levels, even dry areas, while others need a certain depth of water above their crowns. A vast majority of them appreciate shallow water over their crowns that's 2 to 6 inches deep. Bog or marginal plants differ from moisture-loving plants, which will languish if their roots are waterlogged for any length of time.

3. **Free-floating plants** float on the surface with their roots suspended in the water. They are capable of spreading rapidly, so use free-floating plants with caution.

4. **Submerged or oxygen-producing plants** maintain the health of the water garden. These underwater "oxygenating" plants release oxygen into the water and absorb nutrients and carbon dioxide produced by animal wastes and decaying plants. They also provide food and shelter for fish.

Refer to the Planting Chart on p. 341–42 for a list of aquatic plants suitable for your water garden. Suppress the urge to completely fill your water garden with plants. Only one-half to three-quarters of the surface of the pond should be covered with leaves. Refer to March Planting for "how to plant" information.

Care for Your Water and Bog Plants

Like garden plants, aquatic plants need some attention during the season to keep them healthy and attractive. Prune and trim away dying or dead leaves on a regular basis. Any fallen leaves should be removed from the water.

Some plants will have to be removed when they become too numerous. **Canadian elodea (*Elodea canadensis*)** and **cabomba (*Cabomba caroliniana*)** can cover the entire water surface and will have to be periodically "pruned" to expose the surface of the water to light.

Tropical water lilies and other tender plants will have to be lifted and overwintered indoors for the winter.

Fertilizing

Use slow-release fertilizers in pellet form that are especially made for water plants. Other experts recommend making a sachet of fertilizer by wrapping a granular garden-type fertilizer in a paper towel; excessive amounts, however, can "burn" the plant. It may be best to simply follow the manufacturer's instructions and use a fertilizer especially created for aquatic plants.

Bog plants do not feed as heavily as **water lilies** and **lotuses.** When fertilizing them, let their growth rate, flowering, and leaf color guide you.

Watering

Maintain water levels throughout the season. To help the fish survive during hot weather, it may be necessary to aerate the water to boost oxygen levels in the pond.

Pest Control

Most pests are controlled by scavengers and by carefully maintaining the environment. Pesticides are difficult to use around pools that contain fish. Avoid using any insecticides or herbicides around the pond which may kill your fish and beneficial insects such as dragonflies.

Carolina Aquatic Plants

Submerged Aquatic Plants

("oxygenators" or oxygen-producing plants)

Common Name (Botanical Name)	Comments
Coontail (*Ceratophyllum demersum*)	Threadlike whorls of dark-green bristly leaves. Zones 4 to 10. Tiny flowers are hidden in the axils of leaves.
Gray fanwort (*Cabomba caroliniana*)	Lacy bright-green to reddish-brown leaves that whorl into small fans; tiny white flowers in summer. Zones 6 to 10.
Tape grass or eel grass (*Vallisneria americana*)	Pale-green translucent ribbons of leaves offer fine cover for fish. Dormant in the winter, produces tiny nonshowy flowers in early summer. Zones 4 to 10.

Floating Aquatic Plants

(deep-rooted aquatic plants with surface-floating leaves)

Common Name (Botanical Name)	Light Exposure	Comments
Lotus, Asian or sacred lotus (*Nelumbo nucifera*) and American lotus (*Nelumbo lutea*)	Full sun	Need at least 6 or more hours of sunlight for the best flowering. Asian lotus has pink or white flowers; American lotus has yellow flowers. Zones 4 to 11.
White snowflake (*Nymphoides cristata*)	Full or partial sun	A tiny white-flowered water lily–lookalike that is well suited for very small ponds and tubs. The green leaves are mottled with burgundy. Zones 7 to 11.
Yellow floating heart (*Nymphoides peltata*)	Full or partial sun	Looks like a water lily with cup-shaped yellow flowers. Zones 6 to 11.
Water lilies, Hardy (*Nymphaea* species and cultivars)	Full sun	For the best flowering, hardy water lilies need at least 4 hours of full sun a day. Flower colors come in pink, white, yellow, changeable (flowers change color shades as the bloom ages), peach, salmon, and red. Flowers occur throughout the summer, opening in the morning and closing in the afternoon. Zones 3 to 10.
Water lilies, Tropical (*Nymphaea* species and cultivars)	Full sun to partial shade	Need at least 5 to 6 hours of sunlight with some exceptions. Day- and night-blooming species and cultivars are available in white, yellow, apricot, pink, blue, violet, and red. Zones 10 to 11.

Carolina Aquatic Plants

Marginal and Bog Plants

(waterlogged or submerged soils generally up to 2 to 6 inches deep)

Common Name (Botanical Name)	Growth Habit	Light Exposure	Comments
Canna (*Canna* spp.)	6 ft. or more	Full sun	Often viewed as a terrestrial plant, cannas can be adapted to growing in up to 6 in. of water. Large boat-shaped leaves and vividly colored red, pink, or yellow flowers held in clusters at the top of upright stalks. Zones 7 to 10.
Corkscrew rush (*Juncus effusus* 'Spiralis')	2 to 2½ ft.	Full sun	Eye-catching, twisted, electrified-looking stems. Zones 5 to 9.
Golden club (*Orontium aquaticum*)	18 in.	Full sun to shade	Oval dark-green leaves can be a foot long. Thin white flower spikes tipped in yellow appear in spring and early summer. Zones 6 to 10.
Iris (*Iris* spp. and hybrids)	Up to 3 ft.	Sun to partial shade	Many beautiful species and hybrids with a wide range of colors. Japanese iris (*I. ensata*) flowers mostly whites, blues, and reddish-purples. Numerous cultivars. Yellow flag (*I. pseudoacorus*), yellow flowers up to 5 ft. high. Water iris (*I. laevigata*) has blue-purple to white flowers. Erect to 2 ft. Many cultivars. Southern blue flag (*I. virginica*) has blue flowers and grows up to 3 ft. or more tall. Louisiana iris (*Iris* hybrids), a group of multicolored iris that are upright and erect, 2 to 5 ft. Numerous cultivars in nearly all colors. Zones 6 to 11.
Lizard's tail (*Saururus cernuus*)	Up to 2 ft.	Full to partial sun	Heart-shaped leaves and in the summer white, citrus-smelling flower spikes. Zones 4 to 9
Parrot's feather (*Myriophyllum aquaticum*)	8 in. above water surface, 3 to 12 in. deep	Full or partial sun	Pink-colored stems with feathery leaves that look like asparagus fern. Summer-blooming flowers are not very showy. Zones 6 to 10.
Pickerel weed (*Pontederia cordata*)	Up to 4 ft.	Full sun	Produces upright spikes of blue-violet from late spring to autumn. Flowers are a nectar source for butterflies and hummingbirds. Zones 5 to 9.
Sweet flag (*Acorus calamus*)	Upright, 2 to 4 ft. tall	Full sun or shade	Aromatic swordlike leaves with a citruslike fragrance. Zones 4 to 10.
Water arum (*Peltandra virginica*)	1 to 2 ft.	Sun or shade	Handsome arrow-shaped leaves, produces calla-like flowers on a tall spike in late spring. Blooms are followed by berry clusters which lean down to the water at the end of the season. Zones 5 to 9.
Umbrella palm (*Cyperus alternifolius*)	Up to 5 ft.	Full sun to shade	Bright-green whorls of grasslike leaves arranged like bicycle spokes. Topped by brown flower heads in summer. A dwarf form grows to 3 ft. Zones 7 to 11.

Planning

Whether you have a small container or a large pond, sit down and select the right plants for your water garden. As you swoon over the colorful catalogs, compile a list of plants that you'd like to add to your water garden. Study the ornamental features of each plant and their optimum water depth, but most important, know the plant's mature spread. Avoid focusing on the intense 6- to 7-inch-wide flower of the **hardy water lily 'Escarboucle'** without knowing that it will spread up to 7 feet. **'Pink Shadow'**, with $3^1/2$-inch-wide off-white flowers, spreads half as much and would be a better choice for smaller pools and containers. *If size is a limitation, consider dwarf cultivars, purchase fewer plants, or build a larger garden.*

Planting

Planting will occur later in spring when you'll also have to divide and repot plants. If you haven't got containers, aquatic plant fertilizer tablets, and pea gravel, order them now. Aquatic plants are commonly planted in pots for a number of reasons: 1) It keeps them from getting out of hand, which is very important when growing aquatic plants that can spread aggressively, such as **lotus** and **watershield** (*Brasenia schreberi*). 2) You can lift them for trimming, dividing, or storing for the winter without having to contend with a mass of roots. 3) You can easily set them at the appropriate depth and make regular adjustments. 4) It's very easy to remove them when it's time to clean the pool, which is best done in the spring before plant growth begins.

Helpful Hints

Some helpful formulas for water gardeners to determine how many plants and fish your pool can support:

- To determine the amount of water in your pool, use this simple formula: Length × width × depth × 7.5 gallons/cubic foot = Total gallons in the pond

- To determine the surface area for a square or rectangular pool, use this formula: Length × width = Surface area

- To calculate the volume of a rectangular pond, multiply the surface area by the depth: (Length × width) × depth = Volume

- To calculate the volume of a circular pool, use the formula: πr^2 or 3.14 × (¹/₂ the diameter × ¹/₂ the diameter) × depth = Volume

- If you plan to dig a pond rather than construct an above-ground pool, find out where your underground utilities and pipes are located. Most gas, electric, water, and telephone companies will locate and mark their lines on your property. Either contact the company directly or call a toll-free "Call before you dig" number to have your utility cables located and marked. In North Carolina call 1-800-632-4949; in South Carolina call 1-800-922-0983.

Be aware of any local building codes that may affect the placement of your water garden, its size, and depth. Anything that's deeper than a couple of feet could be classified as a pool, and pools often require fencing.

Care for Your Water and Bog Plants

Examine the **tropical water lilies** you overwintered indoors. Any tubers showing signs of rot should be discarded. Check to see that the sand is damp and hasn't dried out.

Planning

There are a number of plants that are the "kudzus" of the aquatic world. When they escape into streams, lakes, and estuaries, they form dense colonies which interfere with boating, fishing, and other recreational activities. They degrade water quality by reducing oxygen levels in the water and displace desirable plants. Millions of dollars are spent annually to control these thugs.

The State of North Carolina Department of Environment and Natural Resources Division of Water Resources and the South Carolina Department of Natural Resources Aquatic Plant Management Program educate the public and the plant nursery industry about these noxious exotic aquatic weeds. A few of them that are on the Federal and State "most wanted" lists in the Carolinas are:

- **African elodea** (*Lagarosiphon major*)
- **Alligatorweed** (*Alternanthra philoxeroides*)
- **Ambulia** (*Limnophila sessiliflora*)
- **Arrowhead** (*Sagittaria sagittifolia*)
- **Arrow-leaved monochoria** (*Monochoria hastata*)
- **Brazilian elodea** (*Egeria densa*)
- **Brittleleaf naiad** (*Najas minor*)

- **Common reed** (*Phragmites communis*)
- **Eurasian watermilfoil** (*Myriophyllum spicatum*)
- **Exotic burreed** (*Sparganium erectum*)
- **Giant salvinia** (*Salvinia auriculata, S. biloba, S. herzogii, S. molesta*)
- **Hydrilla** (*Hydrilla verticallata*)
- **Melaleuca** (*Malaleuca quinquenervia*)
- **Miramar weed** (*Hygrophila polysperma*)
- **Monochoria** (*Monochoria vaginalis*)
- **Mosquito fern** (*Azolla pinnata*)
- **Rooted water hyacinth** (*Eichhornia azurea*)
- **Water aloe** (*Stratiotes aloides*)
- **Water chestnut** (*Trapa natans*)
- **Water hyacinth** (*Eichhornia crassipes*)
- **Water primrose** (*Ludwigia uruguayensis*)
- **Water spinach** (*Ipomoea aquatica*)

For a complete list of the Federal Noxious Weeds in North and South Carolina, contact the following agencies for more information.

In North Carolina:

Division of Water Resources
Department of Environment and Natural Resources
1611 Mail Service Center
Raleigh, NC 27699-1611

In South Carolina:

Aquatic Plant Management Program
Water Resources Division
South Carolina Department of Natural Resources
1201 Main Street, Suite 1100, Columbia, SC 29201

A good time to install a small water garden is in the spring when the ground can be worked. Here's how:

1 Outline the shape of a flexible liner with a rope or garden hose. Mark the border with spray paint, builder's chalk, lime, or sand. If you have a preformed pond, set it on the ground and mark its outline with the same marking materials.

2 Start digging from the edges to create a permanent outline, and excavate toward the center. Make the sides steeply sloped (about a 20-degree angle from the vertical) to achieve good volume relative to surface area—an important factor in avoiding algae problems.

3 Check the edge of the pond frequently as you dig to make sure it's level. The edge should be even all around to prevent water from overflowing before it's completely full. Place a carpenter's level on top of a long straight piece of lumber laid across the hole.

4 Create an underwater shelf along the inside wall to hold potted marginal or bog plants and rocks. The shelves are typically 10 inches long and about 18 inches wide (if raccoons are in your area, these shelves will be used as fishing platforms!). You can still grow marginals in shallow water by placing them on clean bricks or upside-down flower pots.

5 Dig the hole at least 2 feet deep, allowing for a 1- to 2-inch layer of sand. With a preformed liner, dig the hole about 2 inches deeper and 3 to 5 inches wider on the sides.

6 For flexible liners, apply a 1- to 2-inch layer of damp river sand, old indoor-outdoor carpeting, or any other soft materials to protect the liner from sharp rocks.

To calculate the size of the pond liner you need to outline the area and decide on a depth.

1 Measure the length and width of the pool. If it's a circle or irregularly shaped, draw a square or rectangle around it and use the length and width of the square or rectangle.

2 Use this equation to calculate the length and width of your pond liner:

Helpful Hints

Submerged "oxygenating" plants that grow completely or mostly underwater produce oxygen as they photosynthesize. This dissolved oxygen is important for supporting fish and other aquatic life. The plants also provide food and cover for fish and other aquatic organisms. However, some of these oxygenators can become invasive and have been labeled aquatic nuisance weeds. Some are sold by the common name of **Anacharis,** which can be one of three possible species: **Canadian elodea (*Elodea canadensis*), Brazilian elodea (*Egeria densa*),** or **hydrilla (*Hydrilla verticillata*).** Of these three, only **Canadian elodea** can be legally sold in the Carolinas. When you purchase submerged plants, ask the proprietor for the scientific name of the plant. Here's where knowing its Latin botanical name will help you make the right purchase. If you're buying "Anacharis," make sure it's the right one.

Length = Maximum length of pond + (2 × maximum depth) + (2 × edging allowance)

Width = Maximum width of pond + (2 × maximum depth) + (2 × edging allowance)

3 Center the liner over the hole and weigh down its edges with smooth stones or bricks. Slowly fill the pond with water. As the pond fills, gradually take the weights off the edges so the water will fill into the crevices. When the water comes within 1 inch of the top, shut it off and cut any excess material, leaving about a foot beyond the rim. Line the edge of the pond with stones, pavers, bricks, or other suitable materials.

4 For preformed pools, spread an inch or two of damp sand on the bottom. Set the form in the hole so the rim is just above ground level. Take it out and make any adjustments. When it's level, firmly pack soil around its edges. Fill the pool with water. Hide the rim with rocks or use a spreading ground cover.

Care for Your Water and Bog Plants

Check the tender aquatic plants you overwintered indoors. Make sure they're covered with water and don't allow them to dry out. Clean the pond of any debris.

Planning

If you're planning on introducing fish to your water garden, spend some time this month learning more about them. Visit your public library, visit water specialty centers, read mail-order catalogs, and talk to other water gardeners. Not only do fish add ornamental interest and movement, but they'll improve water quality as they feast on mosquitoes and their larvae, algae, and plant debris. The plants will be fertilized by the waste created by the fish, and the submerged plants will use the carbon dioxide they exhale to produce oxygen.

Many different kinds of fish are available, such as the typical goldfish-in-a-bowl variety (which can grow up to a foot in length in ponds), long-lived colorful koi, speedy golden orfes, and mosquito fish. If you lack experience and confidence with fish, start small with a few inexpensive goldfish. As you sharpen your water gardening skills, you can add more fish later.

Planting

Plant aquatics in nursery pots, laundry baskets, shallow pans, and large tubs. Use a heavy clay-based garden soil. Avoid amending it with peat moss, vermiculite, or perlite, which tend to float away. Submerged plants can be planted in containers filled with sand or tied to a stone where they're kept just below the water surface.

After you pot up your plant, add a 1-inch layer of pea or aquarium gravel on the surface to prevent the soil from muddying up the water. Before submersing the container, water it thoroughly and then place it in the pool.

In the warmer parts of the Carolinas, **hardy water lilies** may need to be divided every year or two. They can be divided at any time during the growing season, **starting** six weeks before the last expected freeze. Here's how:

1 Lift the pot out of the pool and take the clump out of the pot.

2 Look along the length of the rhizome for buds or growing points called "eyes." Tiny lime-green or bronze leaves may be emerging from the growing point.

3 With a sharp knife or pruning shears, cut sections of the rhizome into 3- to 4-inch long pieces or divisions that have eyes and accompanying roots.

4 Repot the division, making sure that the growing point is above the soil level.

Divide both **Asian** (*Nelumbo nucifera*) and **American lotus** (*N. lutea*) the same time you divide **hardy water lilies.**

About a month before the last expected freeze, check to see if the **tropical water lilies** have sprouted. If they haven't, put the tubers in water near a sunny windowsill to coerce them into growth. Once they've sprouted, pot them up in temporary pots:

1 Fill a 5-inch pot with soil and plant the tuber about $1/4$ inch deep. Add a layer of pebbles or gravel to the top and label it.

2 Move the pots to an aquarium or a large bucket. Add enough water so the tops of the pots are covered by 3 inches of water. The water should be 70 to 80 degrees Fahrenheit, so an aquarium heater may be necessary.

3 In two to six weeks when new leaves have formed, move the plants into bright light.

4 Transplant the tubers into permanent containers (see May Planting, p. 350). Wait until the water warms up to 70 degrees before placing them in your water garden. Very cold water can shock the plant, slowing down the growth of leaves and flowers for many weeks.

Care for Your Water and Bog Plants

Inspect the tender aquatic plants you kept indoors over the winter, making sure that they're healthy and haven't dried out. Keep the containers filled with water. If the area is too warm, move them to cooler temperatures of 40 to 50 degrees F.

Prune away any winterkilled leaves from the plants around your water garden before or when the new growth emerges. Compost these trimmings or bury them in the vegetable garden.

Remove any floating debris from the surface of the pool. If you have to empty and clean the pool, it's best to begin this job before plant growth begins in the spring.

Draining and cleaning the pool is a drastic measure that may be unnecessary if you regularly remove floating debris and groom the plants. You can even occasionally siphon out sludge from the bottom. When you do empty and clean your pool, don't scrub it free of algae. A small amount of algae is an essential part of a healthy pool.

Helpful Hints

Wait two to four weeks before introducing fish into your newly created water garden. During that time you can finish planting, install any equipment, and keep an eye on the water temperature and pH. A pH less than 6.8 or more than 8 can be harmful to your fish.

Planning

Know someone who's apprehensive about digging up a part of the backyard and is afraid they'll tire of their in-ground water garden and will end up with a mess? Consider water gardening in a container. Because of the small size, there's less room for error than with larger pools. Anything that holds water and does not have a toxic lining can be used. Containers can vary from plastic to concrete to ceramic to wooden barrels lined with plastic liners. Any of the plants used in water gardening in pools or ponds can be grown in a container. Keep in mind, however, that the mature size of the plant deserves special consideration. The plants can be grown in individual pots and the pots staged atop bricks or other supports so that their rims are at the appropriate level. You have a wide variety of plants to choose from. Here are some of my favorites:

1 The first group of plants are those that are happy with wet feet but whose crowns can stick above the surface of the water. **Striped giant reed** (*Arundo donax* 'Variegata'), **elephant ear** (*Colcasia* 'Black Magic'), and **giant taro** (*Alocasia macrorrhiza*) fall into this category.

2 The next group of plants are those that like their crowns to be level with the water surface. These include **dwarf papyrus** (*Cyperus papyrus* 'Nanus'), **yellow-flowered water canna** (*Canna glauca* 'Ra'), and *Hibiscus moscheutos* 'Blue River II'.

3 Third, there are plants whose crowns should always be covered by several inches of water. Cultivars of **lotus** (*Nelumbo* 'Angel Wings' and *N.* 'Baby Doll' are both suited for pot culture) and **parrot's feather** (*Myriophyllum aquaticum*) are examples.

Pot the plant in a clay-based soil and topped with a layer of gravel to prevent the soil from washing into the water. Plan to put the container on rollers so you can move it around easily.

Planting

Hardy water lilies and **lotuses** that have spent the winter in the deeper parts of your pool to protect their roots from freezing need to be returned to shallower depths when the ice has melted completely.

Hardy water lilies are sold dormant/bare-root or nondormant with a few leaves, roots, and perhaps buds. It's important that you prevent the rhizome from drying out. Put the lily in a bowl of water before planting. Here's how to plant a **hardy water lily:**

1 Select a roomy container with a drainage hole. **Hardy water lilies** grow horizontally, so select a container that is wider than tall. A pot that is 7 to 9 inches deep and 15 to 17 inches wide is fine for most hardy water lilies; the most vigorous need a container a few inches wider. Fill the container one-third full with slightly damp, heavy, clay-based garden soil. Insert a water lily fertilizing tablet. Depending on the manufacturer, one fertilizer tablet may be required per 5 quarts of soil.

2 Fill the container to the top with soil and then add water until it seeps out of the drainage hole.

3 Dig out a depression in the medium for the rhizome. Set it near the side of the container at a 45-degree angle with the cut end at the side and the crown pointing up and oriented across the container. The rhizome should be deep enough to be covered with an inch of soil.

4 Fill the pot to within an inch or two of the rim. Let the growing tip protrude through the surface. Press the soil in and be careful around the crown.

5 Water the pot again. Top off the pot with pea gravel, leaving the growing point visible to prevent soil from washing away or muddying up the water.

6 Place the pot in the water. Lower the pot slowly at an angle to allow any air bubbles to escape, preventing the water from becoming clouded with mud.

7 The crowns of most **hardy water lilies** can be located 6 to 18 inches below the water surface. To keep them at this depth, place them on bricks or an empty overturned pot. To speed up their growth, place them on a pot 6 inches below the surface. As more leaves grow, move the plant gradually to deeper depths.

Divide your bog plants just before or when the new growth is just emerging. Rhizomes such as those of **striped rush** can be divided into sections with shoots and roots. Fibrous-rooted plants such as **pickerel rush** can be teased apart into separate plants. Keep these marginal plants confined to containers like a nursery pot, which makes fertilizing and future dividing easier. Use the same heavy clay soil used for planting **water lilies** and other floating-leaved plants.

Place them on the shelf inside the pond or set them on bricks, weathered cinder blocks, or upside down pots so they're at the appropriate shallow depth.

Any submerged plants that have become overgrown need to be thinned out. Compost the trimmings or incorporate them into the vegetable garden. You can propagate the trimmings by anchoring them in pots filled with sand.

Care for Your Water and Bog Plants

If you hadn't cut back the dead leaves from your marginal plants in the fall, now is a good time to remove them before or as the new growth emerges. Compost the trimmings or recycle them in the vegetable garden where they can be mixed into the soil.

Continue to remove fallen leaves and any floating organic debris from the surface of the pond.

Fertilizing

Fertilize bog plants with aquatic-plant-fertilizer tablets when new growth emerges. Instead of the tablets, you can use a slow-release nitrogen granular fertilizer following manufacturers' instructions. Avoid spilling any fertilizer into the pool.

Feed **hardy water lilies** once a month with the aquatic fertilizer tablets pushed into the soil when the water temperature goes above 70 degrees. Keep the tablet about 2 inches away from the rhizome or tuber.

Pest Control

Diseases: Any diseased leaves should be removed and discarded promptly.

Planning

Consider expanding your pool to include a bog garden. Creating a bog will be easy if you have a naturally low, poorly drained area that collects water.

If you're going to install a bog garden, you can dig a shallow depression outside of the water garden that can catch any overflow. Extend the flexible liner over this basin and fill it with soil.

To create a bog:

1 Dig a hole 2 to 2¹/₂ feet and as wide as you like. Twelve to 15 square feet would be the minimum size.

2 Lay a thin liner over the hole and press it in. Weigh the ends down with bricks or stones to keep it in place.

3 Fill in the hole with soil to within 3 or 4 inches of the top.

4 Trim the edges of the liner and fold them back into the hole. Add the remaining soil to hide the edges.

5 Wet the soil heavily and then let it settle for a day or two before planting it.

6 Water your bog garden whenever the surface feels dry. Stop watering when water starts to come up to the surface.

Visit The Bog Garden in Greensboro and the University of North Carolina at Charlotte Botanical Gardens to see the beauty and diversity of bog plants.

Planting

Time the planting of your **tropical water lilies** with the planting of your planting of your tender vegetables and warm season annuals after the last expected freeze. They can be planted in your water garden when the water temperature stays above 70 degrees.

Tropical water lilies are sold dormant and bare root or nondormant with a few leaves, roots, and perhaps buds. It's important that you prevent the tuber from drying out. Put it in a bowl of water before planting. Here's how to plant a **tropical water lily:**

1 Select a roomy container with a drainage hole. **Tropical water lilies** grow from a tuber so a deep 5 gallon pot that allows for more vertical growth than horizontal growth would be fine. Fill the container one-third full with slightly damp heavy, clay-based garden soil. Insert a water lily fertilizing tablet. Depending on the manufacturer, one fertilizer tablet may be required per 5 quarts of soil.

2 Fill the container to the top with soil and then add water until it seeps out of the drainage hole.

3 Plant the tuber in the center of the pot. Look for a white line on the tuber. This is where the soil level should be once you refill the pot.

4 Fill the pot to within an inch or two of the rim. Let the growing tip protrude through the surface. Press the soil in and be careful around the crown.

5 Water the pot again. Top off the pot with pea gravel, leaving the growing point visible to prevent soil from washing away. Experts feel that pea gravel is unsightly and is not necessary if you lower the pot slowly into the water.

6 Place the pot in the water. Lower it slowly and at a slight angle allowing any air bubbles to escape. This will prevent you from muddying up the water.

7 The depth for **tropical water lilies** should be between 6 and 12 inches from the crown to the water surface.

Care for Your Water and Bog Plants

Remove faded, dying, or dead leaves from water lilies, lotus, and bog plants.

Fertilizing

When the water temperature stays above 70 degrees F., fertilize all **water lilies** at least once a month (or follow label instructions) with a tablet-form of fertilizer especially formulated for aquatics. It should contain both slow- and fast-release nitrogen. Follow the manufacturer's instructions regarding the amounts and frequency of application.

Pest Control

Diseases: *Trim off* any diseased leaves from your **water lilies** and marginal plants and discard them.

Helpful Hints

- To adequately maintain fish and plants in above-ground pools, choose a deep container that holds between 50 to 100 gallons of water. Position this container in an area that receives morning sun and afternoon shade to benefit the aquatic plants and the fish. Be careful if you're going to place this container on the deck, because water is very heavy and extra support may be needed.

  Fish such as Koi carp and goldfish can be grown successfully in garden ponds or pools. An unaerated pond can carry one to six inches of fish (measured from tip to tail) per five square feet of surface area. Aerated ponds can carry 12 inches of fish per five square feet of surface area.

  Make sure you're using dechlorinated water before introducing any fish to the pond. To dechlorinate treated water, allow the water to stand for at least one week before introducing any fish. Aerated water will dechlorinate in 24 hours. You can also use a dechlorinating agent available from water gardening suppliers.

- Fish are a lot like houseplants that have been indoors all winter. Both need to be acclimatized to allow them to get used to their new environment. When you've taken your fish home, leave them in their plastic bag in a shady spot in the pool until the water in the bag reaches the same temperature as the pond water. This may take about 20 minutes. Then open the bag and release the fish.

- Bring your **hardy water lily** flowers to enjoy indoors. Cut them on their first day of bloom—they'll last for three or four days in a vase or bowl as if they were still in the garden.

Planning

If you've seen everyone around you enjoying water lilies in containers, you can do the same. This is especially useful if you can't accommodate an in-ground water garden. **Water lilies (*Nymphaea* spp.)** need at least six hours of direct sun. Choose a watertight container that's at least 18 inches in diameter and a foot deep. Fill the container with water and let it sit for about twenty-four hours to allow any chlorine to evaporate and for the water to come to air temperature. Some **hardy water lilies** that do well in above-ground containers that stay above freezing in winter are yellow-flowering 'Chromatella' and 'Helvola'; white 'Hermine'; deep-red 'Froebeli'; and orange-red 'Graziella.'

Planting

Plant bog plants such as **umbrella palm, water canna,** and **Japanese iris.** Grow them in containers of ordinary garden soil and either place them on ledges in the pool or set them on an inverted pot at their required depth. Marginal plants provide shelter for wildlife and offer shade and protection for fish. Some marginals can handle either shallow or deep water levels, even dry areas, while others need a certain depth of water above their crowns. If your pool doesn't have shelves, raise or lower the plant by using inverted pots, bricks, or weathered cinder blocks.

Don't forget the importance of submerged plants—these are essential underwater plants that release oxygen into the water and compete with algae for nutrients to keep the water clear. Some of the most popular submerged plants are **Cabomba (*Cabomba caroliniana*), Canadian elodea (*Elodea canadensis*), Coontail (*Ceratophyllum demersum*),** and **tape grass (*Vallisneria americana*).**

You can plant **hardy water lilies** now. Mountain gardeners should be able to plant **tropical water lilies** safely when the water temperature has reached 70 degrees F. and is not expected to go lower.

Care for Your Water and Bog Plants

Deadhead **water lilies** to encourage more flowers. Notice that it's easy to tell the **hardy water lilies** apart form the tropicals: most **tropical water lilies** hold their flowers above the water. Leave the spent flowers on **lotus** because the ornamental pods that develop will look terrific in flower arrangements.

Remove any yellow leaves or any damaged by insects or diseases. Continue to remove organic debris—grass clippings, fallen leaves, needles, etc.—from the pond.

Keep an eye on invasive plants and trim them or remove them so they won't crowd out more restrained growers. Some of the plants that float free on the surface may grow with abandon. One of these, the **pond lily (*Nuphar* spp.),** can become a pest if left to grow unchecked and will crowd out slower-growing plants. You may want to experiment with tropical floating aquatics such as the lacy delicate **mosaic plant (*Ludwigia sedioides*)** or, for gardens in partial shade, the chartreuse-green **water lettuce (*Pistia stratiotes*).**

Keep track of water pH, ammonia, and nitrate levels, especially if you have fish. If you don't stock your above-ground half-barrel or other water container with fish to consume mosquito eggs and larvae, mosquitoes will breed and can become a problem. Buy a few briquettes of mosquito larvae killer sold as Mosquito Dunks® (it contains a bacterial insecticide called ***Bacillus thuringiensis* var. *israelensis*).** One briquette can treat 100 square feet of water regardless of its depth. Break them up into four pieces and put them out at the start of each month to float on the surface of the water.

Watering

Add water to your container or pool to maintain it at the appropriate level. Add the water slowly.

Fertilizing

Fertilize water lilies with aquatic fertilizer tablets, using the amount prescribed by the manufacturer. Bog plants can be fertilized based on their growth rate and appearance. To play it safe, fertilize them at half the rate of your **water lilies.**

Pest Control

Insects and mites: Black water lily aphids can disfigure leaves and flowers. *Remove* them with a strong spray of water or submerge them and give them a shake. Spider mites can appear on the undersides of raised **water lily** leaves and **lotus.** Clip off heavily infested leaves and dislodge the mites with a strong spray of water from the hose.

Other pests: *Handpick* brown snails from **iris** leaves.

Diseases: Continue to *trim away* any dead, damaged, or diseased leaves.

Helpful Hint

A healthy pond has a small amount of algae. After all, it's not a chlorinated swimming pool. A water garden is a thriving community of algae, bacteria, organic matter, plants, fish, and scavengers.

Brief explosions of algal growth called "blooms" commonly occur in ponds, especially during the first few weeks in newly constructed ponds or in early spring. This algal growth spurt occurs because there's no competition: the plants are just beginning to come out of dormancy and grow and the fish and scavengers haven't yet awakened. With plenty of sunlight and dissolved nutrients, the algae grows with abandon. Once the surface of the pool becomes shaded, the plants compete with the algae for nutrients, and the fish and scavengers start feeding on the algae, the water should clear up by itself—if the water garden is in balance.

An out-of-balance pool can look like month-old pea soup in short time. There are a couple of solutions to this problem:

1   Feed your fish only what they'll eat in 3 to 5 minutes. Any uneaten food will decompose and encourage algae. Many water gardeners have found that when they stop feeding their fish and the fish are restricted to eating algae, plants, and insects, their water becomes clearer.

2   Add more plants. Remember that between one-half and three-quarters of the surface area of a mature pool should be covered with leaves.

If all else fails, consider installing a pump and mechanical or biological filter. In addition to having cleaner water, you can appreciate the sound of moving water.

Again, aquatic plants are active biological filters, and if you get the right balance between the number of plants, the number of fish, and the amount of nutrients the pool receives, no other filtration may be necessary. You'll discover that water gardening involves both art and science.

Planning

This is a good month to update your gardening journal and make plans for improvements to your water garden next year. Did the **tropical water lilies** look at good as the pictures in the catalog? Have some of the aquatic plants turned out to be thugs in disguise by taking more space than you allotted to them?

Record your observations in your journal; include newspaper and magazine clippings of articles by local garden writers who touted certain aquatic plants.

Perhaps you heard some recommendations from friends and other water gardening enthusiasts regarding some aspect of pond care. Compile these notes and plan on acting on them next season.

Planting

If less than half your pond is covered with plants, consider adding more **water lilies.**

If you find choice marginal plants that will complement the planting you already have, go ahead and purchase them and plant them in your water garden.

Divide your irises—**Japanese iris (*Iris kaempferi*), variegated rabbit ear iris (*Iris laevigata* 'Variegata'), yellow flag (*I. pseudacorus*),** and **Louisiana hybrid irises**—in late summer and repot them.

Care for Your Water and Bog Plants

Remove spent flowers to encourage the production of more blooms. You may want to allow some flowers to remain so you can harvest the fruits and sow the seed to produce some home-grown plants. Yellow leaves should be trimmed off and discarded.

Remove any debris from the surface of the pond and add it to your compost pile.

Watering

Check the level of your pool to see if the level has dropped. Tap water shouldn't be added directly to a water garden containing fish because the chlorine is toxic to them. If you add less than an inch of tap water to your pool, a dechlorinating agent won't be necessary. For larger amounts, a dechlorinating chemical will have to be added.

Chloramine is another water treatment agent that's used to treat tap water. Unlike chlorine, it doesn't escape naturally from the water, and a special water conditioner needs to be added to remove it. Contact your local public water department to find out which chlorinating product is used in your water supply, and use a dechlorinating agent designed for that product.

Helpful Hints

- The two most serious threats to pond fish are a lack of oxygen and high ammonia levels in the water. The warmer the water, the less oxygen there is. At the same time, high temperatures speed up fish metabolism, increasing their need for oxygen. Aerate the water with a pump, keep a good supply of submerged plants, and monitor water quality to keep oxygen available to the fish. Keep fish populations low. Ammonia is produced by fish waste and decaying plant debris and other gases are produced as it breaks down. High levels of ammonia are toxic to fish and lead to their quick death.

- Gardeners who cannot enjoy the blooms of their **tropical water lilies** during the day can enjoy them in the twilight hours. Tropicals may bloom either during the day or at night. **Hardy water lilies** bloom only during the day. Night-blooming **water lilies** bloom at dusk and their flowers usually remain open until late the next morning—even longer if the day is cloudy. They also permeate the air with a musky fragrance that's alluring to pollinators and gardeners alike. Tropical night-blooming **water lilies** are very vigorous and need plenty of room—at least a bathtub-sized pool. Here are a few nocturnal **water lilies** recommended by Joe Granato, owner of Star Ridge Aquatics in Carthage, North Carolina.

  White: 'Missouri' and 'Woods White Knight'

  Pink: 'Texas Shell Pink' and 'Emily Grant Hutchings'

  Red: 'Red Flare' and 'Jennifer Rebecca'

Fertilizing

Fertilize floating-leaved plants with slow-release aquatic plant tablets available from water garden suppliers. Bury the tablets in the soil so the fertilizer will be available to the roots and not leach out into the water (which can stimulate the growth of algae).

Insects: Water lilies and some marginal plants may be attacked by aphids. which can be found clustered at the tips of new shoots. Dislodge them, and knock them into the water where they can be eaten by fish. Holes in water lily leaves may be caused by water lily beetles or midges. Simply *pick off* the infested leaves to destroy the insect eggs or larvae.

Diseases: Several diseases may occur while hot and humid conditions prevail. *Trim off* any diseased leaves and discard them.

Planning

In the hotter areas of the Carolinas, shade is a welcome respite from the blazing sun. And there are some **water lilies** that will perform well with as little as three hours of sunlight. To decorate your shady water garden you can use traditional shade-loving plants like **hostas, astilbes,** and **ferns,** which will also benefit from the moist soil at the garden's edge. The following plants perform best with six hours of sun, but they will flower and grow with as little as three or four hours of sun each day:

Hardy Water Lilies
  Charlene Strawn
  James Brydon
  Virginia

Tropical Water Lilies
  Albert Greenberg
  Director George T. Moore
  Panama Pacific

Marginal Plants
  Elephant's Ear (*Alocasia* **spp.**)
  Cord grass (*Spartina* **spp.**)
  Papyrus (*Cyperus* **spp.**)
  Taro (*Xanthosoma* **spp.**)

Planting

American lotus (*Nelumbo lutea*), commonly known as **water chinquapin,** is native to the eastern half of the United States. It is closely related to the **water lily** and produces a large, round arrangement of floating leaves joined by stalks to a thick, below-ground stem or rhizome.

As new growth emerges over the course of a season, aerial leaves shaped like shallow bowls are produced on stems that rise high above the pad, sometimes 5 feet or more. Magnificent flowers are borne high over the water on a thick stalk above the aerial leaves. The flowers may be white, pale yellow, pink, or deep rose, depending on the species, and range from 4 to 12 inches across. In the center of each flower is a yellow receptacle with tiny holes that looks like a shower head. This "seedpod" enlarges as it matures, changing to green and then to brown. By that point the individual seeds are held loosely in depressions on the pod's face. Because of their decorative value, these seedpods are often dried, bronzed, or silvered and used in floral arrangements.

To root a seed, scarify or abrade the impervious seed coat with sandpaper or a file prior to sowing. Sow the seed in a mix of two parts heavy garden soil and one part coarse sand, in a non-draining container. Plant the seed at a depth twice its diameter and fill the container with water so that the mix is submerged by 2 inches.

Set the container in a window with a southern exposure where the air temperature is above 75 degrees F. and the water temperature above 65 degrees. The seed should germinate in two to three weeks. When three leaves have appeared, the seedlings can be transplanted to larger pots filled with heavy garden soil. These pots can then be set in a larger container of water.

Transplant again whenever a seedling has filled its pot. Be sure to allow the delicate root tips to protrude from the soil and that there is enough water to support the developing leaf pad.

When water temperatures outside have reached at least 70 degrees F., young **lotuses** can be moved outdoors. Each plant should then be given a container at least 9 to 10 inches deep and 16 to 20 inches in diameter.

Use 1/2 pound commercial aquatic plant fertilizer per bushel of soil. Add a 1-inch layer of pea gravel on the surface. Before submersing the container, water it thoroughly; then place it in the pool. The gravel layer should be 3 or 4 inches below the water surface. As growth continues, the lotus plants can be moved to deeper water, 6 to 12 inches in depth.

But choose the site carefully: Lotus is a very invasive plant. In a few growing seasons it can spread rapidly and overtake a shallow pond. Keep the surface of the pond covered so that one-half to three-quarters of its surface is covered with leaves.

Care for Your Water and Bog Plants

Inspect the submerged plants in your pool and thin them out if necessary. Compost them or recycle them in the vegetable garden as mulch.

Trim off spent flowers and clip away any leaves that may be in the water. The leaves and other organic matter can break down in the water, especially in hot weather, and can harm plants and fish. *Clean the surface of the pond of debris to prevent it from sinking to the bottom and fouling the water.*

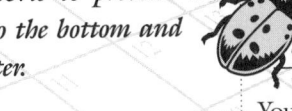

Watering

Check the level of your pool to see if the level has dropped. Tap water shouldn't be added directly to a water garden containing fish because the chlorine is toxic to them. If you add less than an inch of tap water to your pool, a dechlorinating agent won't be necessary. For larger amounts, a dechlorinating chemical will have to be added.

Fertilizing

Fertilize floating-leaved plants with slow-release aquatic plant tablets available from water garden suppliers. Bury the tablets in the soil so the fertilizer will be available to the roots and not leach out into the water, which can stimulate the growth of algae. Bog plants can be fertilized based on their growth rate and appearance. To play it safe, fertilize them at half the rate of your **water lilies.**

Pest Control

Your aquatic plants may be attacked by insects. Cut off any infested plant parts. You can also remove the offenders by submerging them in the water and giving them a shake. *Handpick* brown snails from iris leaves. *Trim away* any dead, damaged, or diseased leaves.

Planning

Although your water garden may be a focal point in your landscape, it should blend harmoniously with the rest of your terrestrial plantings of trees, shrubs, perennials, annuals, ground covers, and bulbs. Plan to grow some woody or perennial ground covers about 3 to 4 feet from the edge of the water garden. As they grow and fill in, they'll create a natural look to the edge of the pool. Think about picking up some of the variegated colors of the aquatic plants and repeating the colors in a nearby flower bed.

To get some design ideas, study water gardens in person and those featured in magazines and books. If you do visit, take along your gardening journal and a camera.

Helpful Hints

- Fallen leaves in water will decompose, releasing minerals and gases that are toxic to fish—and the decaying organic matter will encourage algae. To prevent leaves from nearby trees and shrubs from falling into your pond, use netting to capture the leaves. Buy large plastic bird netting sold for protecting fruit trees and stretch it over the pond; it won't be noticeable from distance. After the leaves have collected on the net, drag it off or roll it up and move the leaves to an area where they can be shredded with the lawn mower and composted or used as mulch.

- Terrestrial plants that need to be fertilized should be located far enough away from the edge of your water garden to prevent fertilizer from washing into and polluting the water. Consider using hardscape instead of plants for the edge: paving stones, gravel, or mulch.

 ## Watering

Fall is a dry season in the Carolinas. Maintain the water level in the pond.

 ## Pest Control

Trim away any damaged, dead, diseased, or pest-ridden leaves. Compost them or bring them into the garden to be buried to enrich the soil.

Care for Your Water and Bog Plants

Before freezing weather arrives, bring tender marginals and others indoors, where you will store them. Continue to trim spent flowers and foliage that has matured on your marginals. Clean up any leaves that may have sloughed off into the pond, and compost them.

 ## Fertilizing

As the water temperature cools, the plants will cease growth and will be going dormant. They do not have to be fertilized.

Planning

Make plans this month to evaluate the plants in your water garden and decide whether you're going to save questionable plants: those that have become too invasive for your garden, some that looked shabby all season long, and tender plants that will have to be overwintered indoors. Some gardeners treat tender floating-leaved and marginal plants like annuals and replace them like annuals. But if you want to save your **tropical water lilies,** plan to find some room indoors.

Care for Your Water and Bog Plants

Oxygenating plants should be cut back hard in the fall. *Remove* dead leaves from marginals. Move any cold-hardy aquatic plants to the lowest part of the pond or water garden. After the first killing frost, *trim away* the dead leaves of your **hardy water lilies.** In the Mountains where ice will form on the ponds, move the pots to the deepest part of your pond (at least 2 feet or more in depth). Rest assured that hardy water lilies will overwinter in the Carolinas (they're hardy to zone 3) as long as their roots are protected from freezing. To store a **tropical water lily,** follow these steps:

1 When they stop blooming in the fall and are going dormant with the cooler fall temperatures, take them out of the pool. Gently remove the plant from the pot and wash away the soil.

2 Look for a smooth black walnut-sized tuber (many form when the parent is potbound) beneath the crown. Separate the tuber and put in water. If the tuber sinks, it's alive and can be stored over the winter. If the tuber floats, discard it.

3 Store the tubers over the winter in a plastic bag filled with cool damp sand. Put the tuber inside the bag and top it off with more sand. Seal and label the bag with the name of the variety. Store the bag in a cool 55- to 60-degree F. location.

If you want to overwinter your tropical marginal plants, move them indoors and treat them like houseplants. Set them on a water-filled saucer in a bright, south-facing window. They need ten to twelve hours of light to remain healthy throughout the winter months, so consider supplementing natural sunlight with fluorescent light (see the Houseplants chapter, Planning, p. 116, for more information). Prevent the pond from freezing—any organic matter trapped at the bottom of the pond may decay, producing toxic levels of methane gases that can be toxic to fish. Install a pump or a heater designed for water garden pools. *Remove* any fallen debris, dead plants in the water.

Watering

Maintain the water level in your pond. The plants and fish that overwinter outdoors in the pond can use the depth.

Pruning

After the first hard frost, *trim away* any dead leaves from marginals and compost them.

Pest Control

Trim away any damaged, dead, diseased, or pest-ridden leaves. Compost them or bring them into the garden to be buried to enrich the soil.

Planning

It is hoped that you've had an enjoyable water gardening experience that inspired you to learn more about this exciting field. The South Carolina Water Gardening Society, founded by Cherrie and Don McKinney "as a nonprofit organization to promote the greater appreciation and understanding of aquatic plants and fish through water gardening," is always looking for new enthusiastic members. Remember that many water gardeners are happy to share their experiences (and their plants and fish) with you. To learn about a water gardening society in your area, speak to an aquatic nursery staff or water garden suppliers. Surf the Internet for water gardening information to learn about different approaches and techniques. You can also subscribe to a water gardening magazine.

Care for Your Water and Bog Plants

If your pond is too shallow or you have tender plants that won't survive the winter, you need to overwinter them indoors. Lift hardy water lilies out of the pond, cut away the leaves, and move them to a cool location (40 to 50 degrees F. is ideal). Keep the soil moist. (This also works for most hardy marginal plants.)

Tropical floating plants are inexpensive to replace, so they can be discarded after the first frost. Allowing them to remain in the pond can cause them to rot and foul the water.

Above-ground water containers such as tub gardens can freeze during extended cold periods, so move them into a greenhouse or indoors in the colder parts of the state.

To prevent ice from forming on the surface of your pond—trapping carbon dioxide and other noxious gases that can kill fish—keep the water pump running. This will create water movement, preventing at least a small area from freezing so the top of the pond won't be completely sealed.

If the water does ice up, avoid the urge to smash a hole in the ice; this could damage plants and injure the fish. Set a kettle or pan of hot water on the surface of the ice to melt an opening.

To prevent ice from cracking the walls of the pool, float a tennis ball, soccer ball, or other air-filled or rubber object before a hard freezing weather. The ball will absorb the expanding pressure from the ice and will relieve pressure from the pool walls.

Pest Control

Trim away any damaged, dead, diseased, or pest-ridden leaves. Compost them or bring them into the garden to be buried to enrich the soil.

Planning

There's not much to be done with the water garden this month except to plan for next season. Review your journal and draw some conclusions about this past year's water garden. If there were problems with algae or if the fish weren't thriving, you need to look back at your journal to see if your observations will lead you to a solution. As with most garden maintenance, monitoring the garden on a regular basis will prevent many serious problems from occurring.

Make plans to spruce up your water garden next year with some exciting plants. The nursery industry is responding to the popularity of water gardening with new colors and forms of **water lilies** and marginal and edge-of-the-pond plants that have variegated stems and leaves. And "smaller is in," with a greater selection of smaller **water lilies** and compact marginal plants.

Just when you thought you were going to enhance your border with more perennials, you may be forced to choose between your perennials or your aquatics. Why not just splurge and give both gardens a makeover with some new plants?

Care for Your Water and Bog Plants

In the milder Coastal Plain, gardeners need to thin out the submerged plants if that wasn't done last month.

Remove the dead leaves from your marginal plants.

Trim dead leaves from **hardy water lilies** and cold-hardy aquatic plants and discard them. If there's a threat of ice forming on your pool, move the plants to the lowest part of the pond or pool.

Above-ground water containers such as tub gardens can freeze during extended cold periods, so it's best to locate them in a southern exposure for most of the winter. Cover them during the cold nights to trap stored heat and to offer some protection from freezing. Prevent the pond from freezing because any organic matter frozen at the bottom of the pond may eventually decay, producing levels of methane gases that can be toxic to fish. Install a pump or a heater designed for water garden pools.

Remove dead leaves and other debris that may gather around the pond or on the surface of the water.

Helpful Hints

Check out some books that will help you become a water gardening expert:

Water Gardens (from the editors of **Horticulture Magazine**). Primedia Special Interest Publications, Boston, MA, 1998.

Aulbach-Smith, C. A. and S. J. deKozlowski, **Aquatic and Wetland Plants of South Carolina.** South Carolina Dept. of Natural Resources, 1996.

Slocum, P. D., P. Robinson, and F. Perry, **Water Gardening.** Timber Press, 1996.

Tomocik, J., **Water Gardening.** Pantheon Books, Knopf Publishing Group, New York, 1996.

Watering

Maintain the water level in your pond for the plants and fish who spend the winter outdoors.

Appendix—Pest Control

Due to space constraints, the following pests could not be addressed in the monthly chapters. Take some time to learn how to identify and manage these and other pests that afflict our plants—both indoors and out—in the Carolinas. As they say, "Never stop learning."

Common Houseplant Pests and Their Control

Aphids or "plant lice": These soft-bodied insects suck plant sap, causing new growth to turn yellow, curl, and distort. They are usually green but may be pink, brown, black, or yellow. Look for them clustered at the tips of new shoots. Even if you can't see them, look for telltale signs: skins cast off as they molt and a sticky "honeydew" coating they exude on leaves and stems.

Scale insects: They attach themselves to stems and leaves, feed on sap, and exude sticky "honeydew" on leaves and furniture. Look for round or pear-shaped disks, or scales, often protected by a waxy covering. When young, the "crawlers" or young scales scurry about like tiny flat pancakes, looking for a suitable spot to settle down. Once they secure themselves to a leaf or twig, they produce a shieldlike outer shell and never move again. Female scales lay eggs underneath their shells, which hatch to produce another generation of marauding crawlers.

Mealybugs: Oval-shaped and covered with a white, woolly coat, they feed on plant sap and exude honeydew. Look for them in the stem crevice and leaf joints.

Fungus gnats: They are rarely harmful, but the tiny black adults are annoying as they hover over the potting mix. The larvae hatch in the mix and are relatively harmless. They may feed on roots of seedlings; usually, however, they feed on decaying roots and organic matter. Look for them in moist mixes that contain a lot of peat moss. You can repot your plant using pasteurized growing media. When storing potting medium, keep it sealed. Cultural methods for controlling fungus gnats include changing your watering habits. Allow the surface of the potting mix to dry out between waterings. Whenever you water, empty the plate or dish so the pot won't be resting in water; otherwise, elevate the pot on a shallow layer of pebbles. Remove any fallen leaves or other debris from the surface of the pot.

Spider mites: Inspect the undersides of leaves with a magnifying glass to see these tiny sap suckers—they look like red or gray eight-legged specks. Or try shaking a leaf over a white paper and looking for moving specks. Heavily infected plants are covered with fine webs that hold eggs and molting adults. Since spider mites are hard to see, their damage is often the first sign of their presence. It begins with light-colored speckling on the upper surface of the leaf. If the mites are unchecked, leaves become bronzed or yellowed and the plant dies. Spider mites like dry conditions.

Houseplant Pest Controls: Banish mites by bathing plants in warm water followed by a spray of insecticidal soap. Be sure to hit the underside of each leaf. Mist plants daily and repeat the soap spray after two weeks if mites are still seen. Dislodge both aphids and spider mites with a forceful spray from a hose. Prune out and discard heavily infested shoots, if possible. Daub light infestations of aphids or mealybugs with a swab dipped in isopropyl (rubbing) alcohol. Try not to overapply; alcohol can damage leaves. Fight scale insects with systemic insecticides. These are taken up by the plant and make its sap toxic to certain pests. Follow label directions. Make sure that the pesticide is suitable for your plants and that the pest that you want to control is listed on the label. Good ventilation is important when treating plants. A good way is to pick a warm day to bring the plant outside—a balcony or the garden will do—for treatment. Quarantine the plant until you've controlled the problem.

Diseases: Diseases are rarely a problem indoors because of the low humidity levels. A few diseases may appear as a result of unfavorable growing conditions. For example, root and stem rots are usually caused by overwatering or by bacteria in the potting medium. Sometimes when plants are crowded or if their leaves are wet, fungal leaf spots develop. *Control: Remove the diseased portions of the leaves and discard them.*

Rose Pests

The following are the most important rose pests in the Carolinas.

Aphids: Pink, purplish, or green, these sap suckers colonize new shoots and rose flowerbuds. Leaves and stems are stunted and deformed. The sticky substance they excrete is often colonized by a black, sooty mold fungus. *Control: Wash off the adults with a strong spray of water. Spot-treat with insecticidal soap or neem. Summer oils can also help during the growing season if your plants are not drought-stressed. Water your roses beforehand and spray in early morning or on cloudy days to reduce the risk of injury. Your cooperative extension service can recommend other appropriate pesticides.*

Flower thrips: These tiny yellowish-brown to amber-colored insects damage rose flowers by rasping the tissues and sucking up the sap that oozes out. Rosebuds become streaked and discolored and often fail to open. Flowers are distorted. Thrips are especially attracted to white or light-colored flowers. To check for them, open up a suspected flower over a sheet of white paper and watch for tiny scurrying slivers. *Control: Difficult. Fortunately, they're preyed upon by minute pirate bugs, ladybugs, lacewings, and big-eyed bugs. Remove and discard any infested flowers. Apply recommended insecticides.*

Japanese beetles: Metallic green with copper-brown wings, these pests feed on rosebuds, flowers, and leaves. They leave ragged edges in buds and flowers and skeletonize the leaves. *Control: Handpick and drop them in a jar of soapy water. Apply neem and other insecticides as a control. Set out traps, keeping them far away from your roses and other plants attractive to Japanese beetles.*

Spider mites: These pests suck plant sap from the undersides of rose leaves, causing the upper surfaces to turn bronze or yellow. Eventually the leaves may turn brown and fall off. Heavily infested leaves can be covered with webs. Two kinds attack roses in the Carolinas: southern red (or "cool-weather") mites, which reproduce rapidly in spring and fall, and two-spotted spider mites (pale yellow, green, brown or red), which become active during the heat of summer. Identify them by tapping an affected leaf over a piece of white paper and looking for tiny moving specks. *Control: Spray a dormant oil in late winter or early spring before growth starts. During the growing season a strong spray of water from the hose, applied to the undersides of the leaves, will dislodge the adults. An insecticidal soap, neem, or a miticide will also be effective, although repeated applications may be necessary.*

Appendix–Pest Control

Diseases: Black spot is probably the most infamous and most serious rose disease in the Carolinas. Look for round or irregular black splotches with fringed margins, mostly on the upper leaf surfaces. Eventually a yellow halo develops around the spots, and heavily infected leaves turn yellow and drop off. Heavily infected plants will weaken and produce few flowers. Sometimes they die. Infections can occur anytime during the growing season, but the spots are most likely to show up during periods of high humidity or persistent rainfall. Some roses are "black spot magnets"; others exhibit resistance. The fungus overwinters on fallen leaves and diseased canes. The spores are splashed onto newly emerging leaves and stems by spring rains. *Control: There are several ways to control this disease: (1) Plant roses in a sunny location with good air movement to speed drying after rains. (2) Prune to open up the roses for better air circulation. (3) Avoid wetting the leaves, especially late in the day. (4) Collect and remove spotted and fallen leaves during the season and prune out dead, damaged, and diseased canes. (5) Take preventive measures. Apply fungicides on highly susceptible roses before the spots appear. This protective barrier should go on right before the leaves emerge and kept on throughout the growing season.*

Powdery mildew: This fungus is present when you see a grayish-white powder on the young leaves, shoots, and flower buds. It typically occurs in spring and fall when days are warm and humid and nights are cool. It thrives on plants that are shaded or crowded. Its spores are spread by the wind. *To reduce the risk of infection: (1) select resistant varieties and (2) improve air movement within the plant by siting it in an open location and by pruning out interior stems to open it up.*

Crown gall: Suspect this soilborne bacterial disease when you see stunted, weak plants that lack normal green color. It infects stems and roots through wounds. The plant forms galls, or swellings, usually around the crown at or just below the soil surface, as well as higher on the stems. Younger galls are nearly white. As they grow, sometimes reaching 2 inches in diameter, and age, they darken, become woody, and take on a cauliflower-like appearance. Galls constrict the plant tissues, disrupting the flow of water and nutrients to the canes, weakening and often killing them. *Control: Prune out the swellings when first noticed. Sterilize your pruner between cuts on the same plant with Lysol® or a 20 percent solution of household chlorine bleach to avoid spreading this disease to other canes. When using bleach, rinse your shears in water and then oil them before storing them to prevent metal corrosion. Remove and discard heavily infected plants. Remove the related soil, too, before planting healthy roses in the site, unless the soil has been replaced. Purchase healthy, disease-free plants and plant them in an area that has been free of crown gall–infected plants for at least two years. To avoid infections, avoid wounding the roots or crown.*

Gray mold or Botrytis blight: This spring fungus infects flower buds and flowers, covering them with grayish-brown fuzz. Often they droop and fail to open. It also attacks new shoots damaged by early-fall and late-spring freezes, producing cankers that extend down the stem, sometimes killing the entire shoot. It's most active when weather is cool and wet. *Controls: (1) Collect and discard the infected flowers and promptly prune discolored canes back to*

Appendix—Pest Control

healthy tissue. Disinfect pruning shears (see above) between plants to avoid spreading this disease to healthy plants. (2) After pruning, treat plants with a recommended fungicide to protect the wounds.

Pests of Trees, Shrubs, Vines and Ground Covers

Voles, meadow and field mice: These rodents damage ornamental and fruit trees by gnawing the bark and roots. Some tunnel through lawns and gardens. *Controls: (1) Barriers—use hardware cloth cylinders around trunks to keep them away. Bury the bottom edge at least 6 inches below the surface. To avoid injuring roots, remove it after one or two years or re-install it further away from the trunk. (2) Population control of voles—reduce the numbers of these efficient reproducers by trapping or by using rodenticides. Snap traps are especially effective in fall and late winter. Rodenticides or toxicants work best in warmer months. (3) Trapping—locate vole tunnels by probing with a stick. Open them at 10-foot intervals, removing enough soil to allow a mousetrap to sit crosswise on the bottom. Bait the trap with peanut butter. Light must not reach the trap sight, so cover it*

with an inverted flowerpot. Check traps daily until no rodents are caught for a week. In multiple planting beds, treat one bed at a time. (4) Rodenticides—use with care. They are potentially lethal to children, pets, and other nontarget mammals, including birds and fish. Place the bait in runways next to tunnels or in burrow entrances, or broadcast it evenly over the entire infested area. Usually baiting every other day for five days will take care of the problem. Anticoagulant baits are slow-acting and must be consumed over a period of five days or more to be effective. The bait must be available until the pest population is controlled.

Whiteflies: These are common pests of gardenias. They suck plant juices from the undersides of the leaves and excrete a sticky "honeydew" that is often colonized by a sooty mold. The leaves develop a sooty-looking appearance. Lightly infested leaves develop a mottled look. Higher populations cause leaves to yellow, shrivel, and die prematurely. These tiny mothlike

pests are barely visible until you shake the plant and they fly away in a white cloud. *Controls: Spray with an insecticide or use one of the following non-chemical approaches. (1) Encourage natural enemies such as on minute pirate bugs, lacewings, lady beetles, and big-eyed bugs. Trim away only portions of heavily infested young shoots. Mature foliage provides predators a refuge from which they will attack the whiteflies remaining on the new growth. (2) Use traps. Whiteflies are attracted to bright yellow surfaces. You can trap them with commercially available yellow sticky traps. Wash off the bothersome honeydew first with a strong stream from your garden hose. You can create your own traps by coating bright-yellow cards with mineral oil. Empty yellow antifreeze or oil jugs can be recycled to make whitefly traps, too. Cover the jug with clear plastic wrap and coat lightly with mineral oil. Set traps out when you first observe whiteflies on your plants. Place them at intervals very close to the plants as the insects must see them to be attracted. (3) Spray with horticultural oils, neem, and insecticidal soaps to suppress whitefly populations. Take care to cover the undersides of leaves thoroughly with the solution.*

Appendix—Pest Control

Bagworms: The larvae of this pest live in cocoon-like bags that hang from branches of the host and eat its leaves. The bag is covered with bits of leaves from the host plant and therefore looks quite different from plant to plant. Needle-type evergreens like blue spruce and hemlock, as well as arborvitae, juniper, and Leyland cypress, are favorite targets. They also attack the leaves of many broadleaf shrubs and trees including rose, sycamore, maple, elm, and black locust. Excessive defoliation may kill conifers within one or two seasons. The spindle-shaped bag is carried around as the larva feeds, enlarging the bag as it grows. Eggs hatch inside the bag in early spring. When the larva matures, it stops feeding and firmly attaches the bag to a twig. In late summer, winged males emerge and mate with the wingless females in the bags. The female moths lay 500 to 1,000 eggs and die. The eggs overwinter inside the bag and hatch the following spring. *Control: Handpick and dispose of the bags in a jar of soapy water or in deep containers that allow any parasites to escape but keep the larvae in.* Bacillus thuringiensis (BT) *is effective when the bagworms are small, during May or early June. Other insecticides are available.*

Pests of Annuals and Perennials

Snails and slugs: The most characteristic signs of their presence are the damage they do and the trails of mucus they leave wherever they crawl. They feed on both decaying and living leaves, stems, and below-ground plant parts. They produce large, ragged holes in leaves of a wide variety of plants and can completely consume young seedlings. You don't see them at work. They feed at night and on cloudy days; during the day they hide in damp places such as thick mulches and groundcovers. These soft-bodied, wormlike animals are similar to each other except snails have hard shells and slugs do not. Their activity begins in the spring and continues until the first frost. They are particularly fond of wet, damp areas, since moisture is required for their survival. They become less active during periods of drought. *Controls: (1) Sanitation—discourage slugs and snails by removing mulch and leaf litter near plants. (2) Handpicking (when you find them). (3) Trapping—set simple, effective traps. They are attracted to and will drown in a shallow pan of stale beer sunken so that the container lip is level with the soil surface. Or place a board on the ground, raised about an inch above the surface. It provides a daytime hiding place for these pests. Lift the board and dispose of the pests. (4) Barriers—protect seedlings by sprinkling diatomaceous earth around them. It is sharp enough to scratch the skin of soft-bodied critters, resulting in dehydration and death. It must be reapplied after a rain or watering. Slug baits are also available to poison them.*

Bulb Pests

Aphids and spider mites: Inspect the leaves of your bulbs for them. For controls, see p. 363.

Appendix—Pest Control

Vegetable Pests

Aphids and mites: Aphids are soft-bodied insects that range in color from green, yellow, red, and gray to black. They suck the juices from leaves and stems, causing stunted or deformed buds and flowers and sometimes curled or puckered leaves. Expect many generations per year. *Controls: Encourage beneficial insects such as lady beetles and syrphid flies. Aphids can sometimes be washed from plants with a strong stream of water. Insecticidal soaps are effective. Many other insecticides are available.*

Whiteflies are tiny insects that attack tomato, pepper, bean, cucumber, squash, melon, and okra. Their name is derived from the white waxy covering on the adult's wings and body. If you happen to disturb a plant infested by whiteflies, look for the adults rising upwards in a white cloud. The tiny mothlike adults (about $1/12$ inch long) usually lay eggs on the undersides of the leaves. Upon hatching, the nymphs or crawlers feed, like the adults, by sucking plant sap from the leaves. Lightly infested leaves develop a mottled appearance while higher populations cause leaves to yellow, shrivel, and die prematurely. Heavy infestations result in sticky leaves covered with a thin black film of sooty mold, a fungus that feeds on the honeydew excreted by the whiteflies. They produce many generations per year. *Controls: Yellow cards coated with mineral oil will trap adults. Insecticidal soaps are effective. Other insecticides are available.*

Slugs and snails are soft-bodied and wormlike. Snails have coiled shells and slugs have no shells. They feed at night, producing large holes in the leaves, stems, and below-ground parts of plants. Slugs and snails leave characteristic trails of mucus wherever they crawl. *Controls: (1) Protect plants by wrapping copper strips around the bases of stems. (2) Attract the pests with pieces of potato or cabbage underneath a board; collect and destroy them during the day. (3) Trap the pests in shallow pans of stale beer sunken deep enough so the container lip is even with the soil surface. (4) Protect young seedlings by sprinkling bands of wood ashes or diatomaceous earth. (5) Chemical baits are available.*

Public Gardens

Along the Carolina Coast

Airlie Gardens
Wilmington, NC
(910) 763-4646

Boone Hall Plantation
Mt. Pleasant, SC
(843) 884-4371

Brookgreen Gardens
Pawleys Island, SC
(800) 849-1931

Cypress Gardens
Moncks Corner, SC
(843) 553-0515

Elizabethan Gardens
Manteo, NC
(919) 473-3234

Greenfleld Gardens
Wilmington, NC
(910) 341-7855

Magnolia Plantation and Gardens
Charleston, SC
(843) 571-1266

Middleton Place
Charleston, SC
(800) 782-3608

Nancy Bryan Luce Garden
Moncks Corner, SC
(843) 761-8509

New Hanover County
    Extension Service Arboretum
Wilmington, NC
(910) 452-6393

Orton Plantation Gardens
Wilmington, NC
(910) 371-6851

Roycroft Daylily Nursery
Georgetown, SC
(800) 950-5459

Tryon Palace and Gardens
New Bern, NC
(800) 767-1560

Of the Carolina Piedmont and Coastal Plain

Cape Fear Botanical Garden
Fayetteville, NC
(910) 486-0221

Chinqua-Penn Plantation
Reidsville, NC
(336) 349-4576

Clemson University
Sandhill Research and Education
    Center
Columbia, SC
(803) 788-5700

Daniel Stowe Botanical Garden
Belmont, NC
(704) 825-4492

Davidson College Arboretum
Davidson, NC
(704) 892-2596

De Hart Botanical Gardens
Louisburg, NC
(919) 496-4771

Edisto Memorial Gardens
Orangeburg, SC
(803) 533-6020

Fearrington Village
Pittsboro, NC
(919) 542-1145

Flora Macdonald Gardens
Red Springs, NC
(910) 843-5000

Francis Beidler Forest
Harleyville, SC
(843) 462-2150

Gardens of Greensboro
Greensboro, NC
(336) 373-2199

Hamlin Sensory Garden
Salisbury, NC
(704) 637-1881

Hatcher Gardens
Spartanburg, SC
(864) 574-7724

Hemlock Bluffs Nature Preserve
Cary, NC
(919) 387-5980

Hezeldan Alexander Homesite
Charlotte, NC
(704) 568-1774

Historic Bethabara Park
    Community/Medical Gardens
Winston-Salem, NC
(336) 924-8191

Historic Mill Hill Plantation
Concord, NC
(704) 786-3990

Hopeland Gardens and Rye Patch
Aiken, SC
(803) 642-7630

Hurley Park
Salisbury, NC
(704) 638-5260

Iron Gate Gardens
Kings Mountain, NC
(704) 435-6178

JC Raulston Arboretum*
Raleigh, NC
(919) 515-3132

Kalmia Gardens of Coker College
Hartsville, SC
(843) 383-8145

*All-America Selections Display Gardens

Public Gardens

Of the Carolina Piedmont and Coastal Plain

Memorial Garden
Concord, NC
(704) 786-8009

Mordecai Historic Park
Raleigh, NC
(919) 834-4844

Municipal Rose Garden
Raleigh, NC
(919) 821-4579

NC Botanical Garden
Chapel Hill, NC
(919) 962-0522

NC Wesleyan College
Rocky Mount, NC
(252) 985-5100

NC Zoological Park
Asheboro, NC
(800) 488-0444

Old Salem
Winston-Salem, NC
(800) 441-5305

Park Seed Co. Trial and
    Display Gardens*
Greenwood, SC
(803) 223-7333

Reynolda Gardens of Wake Forest
    University*
Winston-Salem, NC
(336) 758-5593

Ribbon Walk
Charlotte, NC
(704) 365-9080

Riverbanks Zoological Park and
    Botanical Garden
Columbia, SC
(803) 779-8717

Robert Mills Historic House
    and Garden
Columbia, SC
(803) 252-1770

Rose Hill Plantation State Park
Union, SC
(803) 427-5966

Sarah P. Duke Memorial Gardens
Durham, NC
(919) 684-3698

Sandhills Horticultural Gardens
Pinehurst, NC
(910) 695-3882

SC Botanical Garden*
Clemson, SC
(864) 656-3405

Swan Lake Iris Gardens
Sumter, SC
(803) 773-3371

Tanglewood Park
Clemmons, NC
(910) 766-0591

UNC-Charlotte Botanical Gardens
Charlotte, NC
(704) 547-2555

White Pines Natural Area
Raleigh, NC
(919) 833-3662

Wing Haven Gardens and Bird
    Sanctuary
Charlotte, NC
(704) 334-0664

WRAL Gardens*
Raleigh, NC
(919) 821-8555

Of the Carolina Mountains

Biltmore House and Gardens
Asheville, NC
(800) 543-2961

Blue Ridge Community College*
Flat Rock, NC
(828) 692-3572

Botanical Gardens of Asheville
Asheville, NC
(828) 252-5190

Campus Arboretum of Haywood
    Community College
Clyde, NC
(828) 627-4640

Cherokee Botanical Garden
Cherokee, NC
(704) 497-2111

Chimney Rock Park
Chimney Rock, NC
(800) 277-9611

Daniel Boone Native Gardens
Boone, NC
(828) 264-2120

Grandfather Mountain
Linville, NC
(828) 733-2013

N.C. Arboretum
Asheville, NC
(828) 665-2492

Pearson's Falls
Tryon, NC
(828) 749-3031

Wilkes Community College
    Gardens*
Wilkesboro, NC
(336) 838-6100

*All-America Selections Display Gardens

Selected Bibliography

Aquatic Plants and their Cultivation, Helen Nash with Steve Stroupe, Sterling Publishing Co., Inc., NY, 1998.

Bulletproof Flowers for the South, Jim Wilson, Taylor Publishing Co., Dallas, TX, 1999.

Commonsense Vegetable Gardening for the South, William D. Adams and Thomas LeRoy, Taylor Publishing Co., Dallas, TX, 1995.

Daffodils for American Gardens, Brent and Becky Heath, Elliott & Clark Publishing, Washington, DC, 1995.

Easy Roses for North American Gardens, Tom Christopher, The Reader's Digest Association, Inc., Pleasantville, NY, 1999.

The Encyclopedia of Ornamental Grasses, John Greenlee, Michael Friedman Publishing Group, Inc., NY, 1992.

The Encyclopedia of Roses, Judith C. McKeon, Rodale Press, Inc., Emmaus, PA, 1995.

Garden Bulbs for the South, Scott Ogden, Taylor Publishing Co., Dallas, TX, 1994.

Garden Guide to the Lower South, Trustees' Garden Club (P. O. Box 24215, Savannah, GA 31403-4215), 1991.

Growing and Propagating Showy Native Woody Plants, Richard E. Bir, The University of North Carolina Press, Chapel Hill, NC, 1992.

Herbaceous Perennial Plants, 2nd Edition, Allan M. Armitage, Stipes Publishing L. L. C., Champaign, IL, 1997.

House Plants, John Brookes, ed., The Reader's Digest Association, Inc., Pleasantville, NY, 1990.

Landscaping with Natives, Guy Sternberg and Jim Wilson, Chapters Publishing Ltd., Vermont, 1995.

Manual of Woody Landscape Plants, 5th Edition, Michael A. Dirr, Stipes Publishing L. L. C., Champaign, IL, 1998.

The National Arboretum Book of Outstanding Garden Plants, Jacqueline Heriteau with Dr. H. Marc Cathey, Simon and Schuster, NY, 1990.

North Carolina Gardener's Guide, Toby Bost, Cool Springs Press, Franklin, TN, 1997.

Ortho®'s All About Roses, Tommy Cairns, Meredith(r) Books, Des Moines, Iowa, 1999.

The Palm Reader: A Manual for Growing Palms Outdoors in the Southeast, compiled by members of The Southeastern Palm and Exotic Plant Society, 1994.

Perennials: How to Select, Grow and Enjoy, Pamela Harper and Frederick McGourty, HP Books, Tucson, AZ, 1985.

Plants that Merit Attention, Vol. 1, Trees, Janet Meakin Poor, ed., Timber Press, Inc., Portland, OR, 1984.

Plants that Merit Attention, Vol. 2, Shrubs, Janet Meakin Poor and Nancy Peterson Brewster, Timber Press, Inc., Portland, OR, 1996.

Selected Bibliography

The Practical Gardener: A Guide to Breaking New Ground, Roger B. Swain, Little, Brown and Co., 1989.

Reader's Digest Success with House Plants, Anthony Huxley, The Reader's Digest Association, Inc., Pleasantville, NY, 1979.

Rodale's Successful Organic Gardening: Trees, Shrubs, and Vines, Bonnie Lee Appleton and A. F. Scheider, Rodale Press, Emmaus, PA, 1993.

The Rose Book, Maggie Oster, Rodale Press, Emmaus, PA, 1994.

Rose Gardening in the Carolinas: Culture and Care. C. Douglas Baker, Thomas W. Estridge, and Roderick J. Humphreys, The Greater Columbia Rose Society, Columbia, SC, 1997.

Roses for Dummies, Lance Walheim and the editors of the National Gardening Association, IDG Books Worldwide, Inc., Foster City, CA, 1997.

South Carolina Gardener's Guide, Jim Wilson, Cool Springs Press, Franklin, TN, 1997.

Southern Living® Garden Problem Solver, Steve Bender, ed., Oxmoor House, Inc., Birmingham, AL, 1999.

Southern Seasons: Month-by-Month Gardening in the Piedmont Plateau, Frances Worthington, Shurcliff Press, Greenville, SC, 1993.

Sunset Annuals and Perennials, Sunset Publishing Corp., Menlo Park, CA, 1993.

Treasury of Gardening, C. Colston Burrell et al. Publications International, Ltd. Lincolnwood, IL, 1998.

Trees for Urban and Suburban Landscapes, Edward F. Gilman, Delmar Publishers, Albany, NY, 1997.

Water Gardening, Joseph Tomocik, Pantheon Books, Knopf Publishing Group, NY, 1996.

Water Gardening: Water Lilies and Lotuses, Perry D. Slocum and Peter Robinson with Frances Perry, Timber Press, Inc., Portland, OR, 1996.

Water Gardens, Thomas C. Cooper, Ed., Primedia, Inc., Peoria, IL, 1998.

Well-clad Windowsills: Houseplants for Four Exposures, Tovah Martin, Macmillan, NY, 1994.

The Well-Tended Perennial Garden: Planting and Pruning Techniques, Tracy DiSabato-Aust, Timber Press, OR, 1998.

The Year in Trees: Superb Woody Plants for Four-season Gardens, Kim E. Tripp and J. C. Raulston, Timber Press, Portland, OR, 1995.

* * *

Magazines: *Carolina Gardener,* (P.O. Box 4504, Greensboro, NC 27404), *Horticulture* (98 North Washington Street, Boston, MA 02114), and *Neil Sperry's Gardens* (P.O. Box 864, McKinney, TX 75070-0864)

Assorted publications from the NC Cooperative Extension Service (http://www.ces.ncsu.edu/) and Clemson University Cooperative Extension Service (http://virtual.clemson.edu/groups/public/nsweb/nsindex.htm)

Index

Index

Index

Index

Index

Index

Index

Index

Index

Index

Index

Index

About the Author

ob Polomski is widely known and respected for his down-to-earth gardening expertise as he interprets the latest technical information for the gardener to put to use. His numerous publications range from scientific papers to magazine and newspaper articles. He has written over 250 Clemson Extension *Buds 'n Blooms* press releases distributed to newspapers statewide. He has also published articles in *Carolina Gardener, Fine Gardening,* and *Horticulture,* where he has written a monthly "Questions and Answers" column since 1994.

He appears on television programs devoted to gardening and can be heard on "Just Ask Us," a Clemson University–sponsored program broadcast statewide on South Carolina Educational Radio with listeners in portions of North Carolina and Georgia. He has also conducted garden study tours in England and France.

Bob Polomski

Attesting to his expertise and communication skills, the author has accumulated many honors, among them First Place National awards from the National Association of County Agricultural Agents (NACAA) for his *Anderson Independent-Mail* newspaper column (1998) and radio program (1996), Garden Writers Association of America Quill & Trowel Award for his "Listen to Your Lawn: Recycle Your Grass Clippings" public service announcement videotape (1977), and the National Extension Educational Aids Award from the American Society of Horticultural Science (1995). He received a Distinguished Service Award from the NACAA in 2000. *Month-by-Month Gardening in the Carolinas,* his first book for Cool Springs Press, is an extension of his daily responsibilities as Clemson Extension Horticulturist at Clemson University and State Coordinator of the SC Master Gardener Program.

The author and his wife Susan live in Easley, South Carolina, with their children—three aspiring gardeners—Tyler, Cameron, and Justine.